ANDRESSA ZOI NATHANAILIDIS

SONG OF THE DISPLACED:
RAP AND MIGRATION IN GLOBALIZED TIMES

2017

GlobalSouth
P R E S S

For more information, please contact info@globalsouthpress.com or
go to http://www.globalsouthpress.com/

Song of the Displaced

By NATHANAILIDIS, Andressa Zoi—1st ed. — 2017

Includes bibliographical references and index

ISBN:978-1-943350-45-2

1. Social Sciences — Migration

2. Music— Social Studies

3. International Studies — Social Phenomenons

GlobalSouth
P R E S S

Bulent Acma, Ph.D.
Anadolu University, Eskişehir, Turkey.

Flavio Saraiva, Ph.D.
Universidade de Brasília, Brasilia, Brazil.

Helmunt Schlenter, Ph.D.
Institute for Global Dialogue, Pretoria, South Africa.

Tullo Vigevani, Ph.D.
Sao Paulo State University, Sao Paulo, Brazil.

Monica Arruda Almeida, Ph. D.
Georgetown University, Washington, D.C., United States of America.

Yong J. Wang, Ph.D.
Ohio University, Columbus, United States of America.

Chih-yu Shih, Ph.D.
National Taiwan University (ROC), Taipei, Taiwan.

Irene Klumbies, Ph.D.
Jacobs University Bremen, Bremen, Germany.

Sai Felicia Krishna-Hensel, Ph.D.
Center Business and Econ. Develop., Auburn University, Montgomery, United States of America.

José Álvaro Moisés, Ph.D.
Universidade de São Paulo (USP), São Paulo, Brazil.

Martina Kaller, Ph.D.
Standford University, California, United States of America

"To the biggest encourager of all (my) progress: Dona Carmen G. Nathanailidis, my mother!

"The revolution first of all, will conquer for each individual, through tough fights, the right to poetry, not only to bread."

(Leon Trotsky)

Summary

Preface

The discussion of conviviality, diaspora, a territorial aesthetic and cosmopolitan multicultural work over against poverty, struggle, resistance and power – the context in which a discussion of rap and rap video as immigrant art politics is translated here to help us understand a wider predicament. Words as weapons of a war fought on a mobile terrain – it might be the idiomatic expression that stops you and requires attention, thought demands reconsideration to assess what is going on here. If this study offers anything to take away, it is an exploration of possibilities – the Japan-Brazil-Greece-Chile-France nexus of creative resistance. The translation of experience making partners of elemental forces, snatched images, hidden meanings. Music video with opaque melodies that would bug most people just might be the message you need to work to hear. Elements cascade dialogically across borders and eardrums, beating out patterns discerned or abstract – political art relies so much on interpretation, any setting of the record on the track towards agreement should be considered with care. Not every interpretation is true, not every truth is a metaphor, rap is not always the times, but layered significance, accrued audio encounters build tempo and tension, demanding recognition. Overlapping sound, technology, identity, political circumstance and transformative change, this book sings the songs in print to the music read as social refusal – the rap-ideological act is a key concept, more alive than much existing, prevailing, safe musicology. Here we have experiments in comprehension that circle around a realisation – Honneth, Glissant, Gilroy and Taylor offer starting codes, surprising innovations add Rorty and pragmatism, history and Baumgarten, the poets and playwrights of the German – Herder, Schiller, Holderin – and the romantic age, glossed through Ranciére. William James among many others, and the pragmatist massive versus John Dewey and the gang. Later there will be Che Guevara, but first philosophy finds its grove, also anti-foundational.

What a vitally impressive opening for an elaborate way of saying we wanna get paid.

The hybdridity discussion was getting old but it is renewed here, with much for us to learn – transported to new and old contexts by movements, also old and new. Performance and narrative – not just the storytelling griot art recuperated – gives another dimension. You will read here of Ana Tijoux as a kind of post-surrealist, Manolis Afolanio's combative migrant militancy, *Samurai Malandro*, *Pássaro Imigrante* and others well worth catching up with, familiarising, experiencing – being tricked again, in translation, always betwixt and between the idiomatic. Something can be heard here, listen to these words, even as words are not always there in the refuge of mobilisation. Also coin tricks.

Again, so much more to learn here. I am lost in these worlds, wonderfully lost, wandering and wondering how this can be such a rich and remarkably verdant collection. Detailed and impressive scholarship, this is also a work of care and love, that ranges from slavery to immigration to travel. As such, it deserves a place in the reading lists and compendiums of all those who would refine the ear and the mind. It is an archive of liberated treasures, displayed with concern and context, making it both pedagogic and curationally, correctional, indeed revolutionary. Let there be more books like this. We may learn to listen anew.

I am so happy to recommend this volume for readers, for the press, for the record. It is an enormous contribution of significance and effort. I commend it to the tables that turn, for your own recoding.

- John Hutnyk, author of Critique of Exotica (2000), and Pantomime Terror: Music and Politics (2014).

Prologue

About possible dialogues

The foreigner's friends, aside from bleeding hearts who feel obliged to do good, could only be those who feel foreign to themselves. (Julia Kristeva)

The book presented here is, by itself, a small picture, a discursive frame of the contemporary world, this world of constant movement in which the territoriality is fluid and elusive, one world whose mainspring is immateriality. On the other hand, if the territories are related to the rule of the land, of space, migratory processes are bringing the displacement as a way of subverting the order of masters possessing the wealthy parts of the world. Here, then, formulations are presented on production of performative narratives, as noted by Homi Bhabha, which are the reverse of pedagogical narratives that constitute the expressivity of Nations. If the closing of the fluid orders is the capital base of power, it is against such hegemonic forces that invests the material presented here. The study promotes itself as a dialogue that could be thought of as impossible. By crossing the speech narratives of wandering subjects, the analytical capabilities of a phenomenon that accompanies humanity from long time ago emerge, but that took a specific catastrophic course on the twenty-first century: the migrations. I believe that the greatest merit of this work is from the generality of the concepts and phenomena to achieve the cultural critique of mass products, available in a network of virtual landscapes. Here contemporary human flows are thought and discussed from poetic subjects, issuers of their versions of the world. Going through the global macrocosm to the particularities that permeate the performative and poetic production of beings that experience and translate these experiences into words in languages that denounce, through the poetic content and their own bodies enrolled in urbanities, the world today.

As a legacy of so-called postcolonial studies, here we have proven the thesis that the multiplicity of voices that populate the paths of these current cyberspace announce new bio-politics formulations, disciplined bodies that wish to raise flight to release themselves from parents, countries of nations, and bosses. But make no mistake, the process of "become a foreigner" is a painful process, the loss of ancestral ties redefines the subject in its relationship with the Others and with himself. Having the body and its vital essences fragmented in the space of not belonging is a learning process, of forced self-recognition. And how do such crises have repercussions on the individual, on his way to understand and tell the world? It is here that the analytical part of the research focuses on how now it has taken its final version. And that's where the arguments and the perception join the poetic sensibility of the author, which is a creative and productive comparatist.

Dealing with different performing poetic formulations of different issuers subjects is a job that requires high levels of perception that such content - in several languages - are formulated. If hybridity is by itself a translation process, the translation of poetic texts in various languages is how to bring the hybrid, the torn, to the dialogic terrain that ultimately seeks to understand and play the voice of alterity. With Spivak, we know that to take possession of the voice, the subaltern ceases to be. By extending and extending through the translation and analytical process, the voices of these poets scattered in the cities of the world, this research finds one more way as dialogical possibility of producing other senses. In her theoretical path from varied references and through a disciplinary process, it is also stitched the frameworks of a critical analysis that discusses the society focused on dispersion processes arising from migration. It is addressed the discussions between Yoka (Brazil/World); MC Yinka (Africa/Greece); Ana Tijoux (Chile/France) and Tensais MCS Group (Brazil/Japan). That is, these scattered voices coalescing, pass through the questioner look of a Brazilian (the author) descendant of Greeks and translated. The support of the neopragmatist philosophy, mainly through Richard Rorty and John Dewey, points to the decentralization of analysis of the issues and consequences of migration processes. Using the rap as poetic *corpus,* arguing that the contemporary multicultural models are developed and reinforced, but as an active multiculturalism, critical, which recognizes the participation of capital and consumerism, which realizes the wealth of centralization as a fundamental part of the equation that is established. If the transnational capital creates insurmountable differences, they are the physical and symbolic fences and boundaries that work for the permanence of some and to the exclusion of many others, fueling and perpetuating differences. Hence that the migrant rap, a category brought and thought with wit and shrewdness, comes to represent the plurality of voices that inhabit the field of individual and collective battles presented here poetically. From individual psychologies to the treatment of more general issues, the raps here presented and studied are samples of the voices that are imposed on the world, jumping barriers and fences with confidence that they have a lot to say: about being a woman, being black, being another person, about owning on itself, in their bodies and their souls, the stigma that brand and excludes. So relations between Ethics and Aesthetics are discussed, this means, that a discussion on politics is promoted. But the *polis* mentioned in this book is no longer the classical *polis,* but the mutant and hybrid cities that our fragmented contemporaneity also dilutes the individuals and their expressive potential. The grandeur of the research undertaken is demonstrated, among many other things, by the definition of the parameters that guide the choice of the *corpus,* the seriousness and competence of the analysis, the incessant discussion of macroeconomic and macro policy issues that permeate the reporting relationships that impact the processes of forced migration. Being a form of hybrid approach also for its trans- disciplinary character in several areas of knowledge mentioned, the text that is presented here, on the other hand, is not satisfied with these characteristics. It goes beyond, seeking to promote a critique in which the issuers subject of poetic speeches are also placed as analytical possibilities. We could even say that rappers are brought from their poetic speeches to transform into true organic intellectuals, dispelling the difference between deprived and intellectuals. The artists - and their art - are used as a poetic reference, as an analytical *corpus,* but also they enter on the discussion dialoguing without hierarchies with the academic knowledge: great merit. Such dialogue, to undo the privilege of academic theorists, search, if we think about it, in putting into practice a utopian equality, again linking ethical and aesthetic criteria, or making policy within the space of academic speculation.

The work here is given to be read. It is the result of research conducted at the Federal University of Espirito Santo, Brazil. In other words, it is a discourse that parts from here, from this far south of the Greater Caribbean perceived by Paul Gilroy in his "Black Atlantic". Coming from a heiress voice of migrations produced in a location that is joining European, African and Indigenous, I firmly believe that this book is a significant contribution to the study of the subaltern cultures and their expressive and communicative possibilities.

Jorge Nascimento
(Vitoria, Brazil, Winter 2016.)

Introduction: rap, globe and migration - decentralization of ghettos and the transnational discourse of the new political song

In the middle of the fifteenth and sixteenth centuries, an extensive process involving world trade would cause the beginning of profound changes in human history. Changes in the economic sphere, culminating in the current global economy today.

Guided by the logic of productivity and cultural consumption, globalization is a complex reality, which begins to be found approximately in the late 80's and that today appears as a subject of study in several areas of knowledge. It is basically an irreversible reality, which both excludes and integrates the individual to the universe that surrounds it, operating exclusively in terms of its origins and financial capabilities. This scenario, present in intensified forms to the present day, reflects far - reaching consequences in the social body.

For the sociologist Zygmunt Bauman (1999), "globalization" is established, effectively, as a result of changes in the political world system, whose control remained long divided between the blocks of "socialists" and "capitalists". After the fall of the "socialist block" and the end of this hegemonic division, the world would then have an indefinite character. Accordingly, the author states:

> Everything in the world had a meaning and that meaning emanated from a divided but unified core, two huge blocks of power, tied and glued together in full combat. With the Great Schism out of the way, the world no longer seems a totality, but a field of scattered and disparate forces united at some hard to predict points and gaining momentum without anyone knowing how to stop them. (BAUMAN, 1999, p. 66).

The missing notion of a government axis would not be, however, something unreasonable. Rather, it would have been meticulously engineered, from the consensual settlement between the hegemonic elites of the capitalist block. In an agreement called "neoliberal consensus" or "Washington Consensus" in the mid-eighties, the United States barred the future of the world economy.

On the grounds of termination of the imperialist rivalries between the hegemonic countries and the beginning of a reality focused on the interdependence of powers, cooperation and regional integration, assumptions were created, involving policy development and, above all, the role of the state in the economy.

Although not all the dimensions of globalization were inscribed in the same way in that consensus, all were affected by its impact (SANTOS, 2005).

After this capitalist reconfiguration, the world begins to experience a different reality, permeated by progressive transnational interactions, gaps between borders, homogenization of production systems, financial transfers, cultural interference and serial human deslocation.

Through actions aimed at the expanding trade, lowering taxes related to industrial machine series, privatizating and reducing interference of National States in the economy to the maximum, the world seemed to be able to live a prosperous and balanced reality, in regards to social contexts. Everything was permanently new, in which flows of information and various technological devices circulated.

However, a closer look at this globalized reality shows, currently, greatly intensified effects - revealing an illusory context, with respect to aspects a "homogenised social life". In fact, if on one hand the neoliberal practices provided and spread this idea, on the other, they were also responsible for the intensification of global poverty rates and the consequent proliferation of separated universes inhabited by practices and people often excluded from the overall process.

Since it was established, the neoliberal logic went on to reveal, little by little, its effects, the extent of which, though large, was not essentially "global", "homogeneous" and either "beneficial" to the macropopulation. This is the conclusion of Davis (2006, p. 166), in the the work *Planet Favela:*

> Throughout the Third World, a new wave of SAPs and voluntary neoliberal programs, accelerated the demolition of state employment, local industry and agriculture for the domestic market. The large industrial cities of Latin America - Mexico City, São Paulo, Belo Horizonte and Buenos Aires - have suffered massive loss of jobs in the industry.In São Paulo, the industry's participation in the supply of jobs fell from 40% in 1980 to 15% in 2004. The cost of debt service (which in a country like Jamaica accounted for 60% of the budget in the late 1990s) absorbed resources of social programs and housing assistance.

According to Davis (2006), some parts of the world felt the negative effects of neoliberalism more acutely, like the Middle East and Muslim South Asia. Among the practices that corroborated the intensification of inequality in these countries, the privatization of state enterprises and the incessant corruption of the governing regimes is emphasized.

> (...)The global turmoil at the end of the decade could be mapped with uncanny accuracy in cities and regions that suffered the greatest inequality increases. Throughout the Middle East and Muslim South Asia, the deepening gap between the rich and the urban poor corroborated the arguments of the Islamists and even the more radical Salafists regarding the incorrigible corruption of the ruling regimes. The final attack on the remaining "socialist" state of the National Liberation Front in Algeria began in 1995 with the privatization of 230 companies and the firing of 130,000 state employees. Poverty soared from 15% in 1988 to 23% in 1995. Also in Tehran, when the Islamic Revolution retreated from its original policy favorable to the poor, poverty has skyrocketed from 26% to 31% between 1993 and 1995.(DAVIS, 2006, p. 167).

In these regions, after the global reconfiguration provided by neoliberal practices, even countries that might across some economic growth suffered impacts of financial and social order. The competitiveness imposed by large markets and the difficulty in reducing urban poverty rates were constant, as Davis explained (2006, p. 167-168.):

> In Egypt, despite five years of economic growth, World Bank data from 1999 showed no decline in family poverty (defined as income of US $610 or less per year), but recorded a drop in per capita consumption. Pakistan also faced a double crisis, due to the fall in industrial competitiveness with its textile exports threatened by China and with declining agricultural productivity due to chronic underinvestment in irrigation. Therefore, the wages of the casual and informal workforce fell, poverty soared at a pace that the National Human Development Report characterized as "unprecedented in the history of Pakistan," and inequality of urban income, as measured by the Gini coefficient, rose from 31.7% in 1992 to 36% in 1998.

Besides the regions mentioned, Davis (2006) also points out that the nations of the former "Second World" - European and Asian countries governed by socialist systems - went through a sort of economic conversion, after the advent of the neoliberal system. "Those considered in extreme poverty within the 'former transition countries' (...) soared from 14 million to 168 million people: one almost instantaneous and unprecedented in history mass pauperization." (DAVIS, 2006, p. 168)

The data shows, however, the existence of a metaphoric and chimerical "globalization", to the extent that not all who were (and are) part of this context can live it in its prosperous fullness. In this regard, a more careful study of the flow of transnational immigrants can clarify the existence of a dichotomous reality in which the clash between the fanciful idea of globalization and the concrete existence of economically distinct strata that compose it, becomes evident.

Regarding this latter category, Haesbaert (2009) explains that it is a very complex group and at the same time, vast, "There are the so-called 'economic' migration, mobility linked to the work; migration caused by political issues and other cultural or environmental issues." (HAESBAERT, 2009, p. 246)

Regarding contemporary migrations, it is also possible to associate it with the displacement caused by the consumism inherent in the context of "globalization" and the attractive function performed by the large urban centers - "potential employers"- before historically poor nations and, generally, subject to colonial pasts. There are specific movements coming from the poorest sectors towards the gravitational centers of urban consumption. (HALL, 2007, p. 81) There are many reasons that drive the "conscious diaspora dream" and awaken within groups of immigrants, the common sense of courage, fundamental to those who assume the condition of foreigners.

Instigated for various reasons (and sometimes even unknown), individuals that lend themselves to migrate, present border and also contradictory psychological mindsets. The absence of some factors not supplied by the mother country - usually fairly estimated by those who migrate - generates the search for a "dream-country". An invisible but promising territory of benefits and, above all, some kind of security.

By leaving their countries seeking for better conditions for survival, migrants intend to face the mishaps of a path outlined by insults and humiliations of various kinds. They lose amid unknown realities, they become foreigners: different in language and body in relation to those with whom they share the conviviality.

Foreigners in general, are known to be reserved to a life of solitude and intense work. Discoursing on the condition of the "foreign", Kristeva (1994, p. 25) states:

> The foreigner is the one who works. While the natives of the civilized world, of the developed countries, find the common labor and take the aristocratic airs of resourcefulness and whim (when they can ...) you will recognize the stranger by the fact that he still considers the work as a value. It certainly is a vital necessity, the only means of survival, that does not

necessarily crown him of glory, but which he simply claims as a basic right, fundament of dignity. Although some, once satisfied the minimum also feel an acute happiness in asserting themselves at work and for the work: as if it was a chosen land, the only possible source of success and, above all, the personal quality unalterable, non-transferable, but transportable across borders and properties (...).

By taking the foreign condition upon himself, the immigrant renounces to their rights of choice. Above personal preferences, remains the duty to fight for the daily sustenance, to endure sacrifices and to act according to the rules filed by the "game of the day". In his argument, Kristeva (1994, p. 26) goes on to say that:

> (...) The immigrant, he is not there to waste his time. Battler, daring or smartass, according to his abilities and circumstances, he reaps all the jobs that no one wants, but also those about whom no one thought. Employee and maid, but also a pioneer of cutting-edge disciplines, improvised expert of unusual or advanced professions, the foreign invests and expandes himself. If it is true that by doing it he intends, like everyone else, profit and future savings for his people, his economy passes (to achieve this goal, more than in others) through a prodigality of energy and resources. Since he has nothing and is nothing, he can sacrifice everything. And the sacrifice begins through work: the only good exportable without customs. Value, universal refuge within a wandering condition.

The maximum dedication to work usually keeps in itself a greater purpose: to achieve financial conditions to enable the return to the country of origin. Sayad (1998), recalls the fact that, for the migrant, there is always the certainty of the return. It is around virtually, as a part of the very act of emigrating. This return, however, is almost always a utopia.

Unfortunately, talking of migration is also to speak about peculiar experiences regarding the relationship between space and time experienced by the displaced.

The decision of those who lend themselves to migrate incurs often in state-controlled counterparts, culminating in reallocations and exclusionary process of ghettoization, related to these groups.

> In many cases, by becoming scapegoats for the governability crisis, migrants end up having a more fragile condition, especially when faced with laws that harden territorial restrictions of entry, movement and residence. The recent upsurge of the terrorist movement has further aggravated the problem, building up general and hasty linkages between migration and international terrorism. There is no doubt, however, that regarding the control of the flow of people, the clear trend of territorialization, in a functional sense, is the reinvigoration of attempts to control through zone-territories, areas with well-defined borders (...)(Haesbaert, 2009, p. 248).

The delimitations faced by the immigrant, on the evidence of the existence of a "global" illusory scenario, are reflected in the lack of places within the labor market, permanence in well defined geographical areas, and especially in the absence of decent survival and human fundamental rights.

However, it is within this very "metaphoric-global-scenario" that these immigrants find inspiration and reason to boost their aesthetic creations, bearers of incontestable ideological loads and dialogical educational nature. Such aesthetics, are generally based on performances and narratives emerging from the new territorial concepts developed by the intensification of the use of technological means and closer interpersonal relationships, characteristic factors of contemporaneity. These practices are, in fact, simulations, able to surmount to the virtual reality, the experiences of the real world; and, in addition, to persuade and generate identifications.

It is, according to the author, a reality that must be analyzed by a new notion of multiculturalism; not the old and ethnocentric notion of the nation state (white, European and guided by culture-practices), but a new understanding that must account for the presence of poor immigrants in contemporary megalopolises and rescue minority ethnic and cultural groups, historically disadvantaged and silenced.

Regarding immigrants - who by virtue of their economic and social situations end up taking such a cosmopolitan condition - it is necessary to assume that they speak to us, aesthetically, through a kind of "in-between". This "in-between", although fundamental to the systemic-capitalist operation, present in contemporary times, is undeniably disadvantaged and immersed in intense economic and social difficulties.

By realizing that the world's territory is a space where freedom of physical displacement is not the same for all, and human incorporations to different national settings also are not homogenized, the immigrant develops the perception of time and, aware of all the real possibilities offered by the global structure. He appropriates of the technological tools that are available and finds the complexity needed to provide his aesthetic. Hybrid speeches are therefore broadcasted by new forms of territory that ratifies a kind of time overlap upon space, enhancing the network of identity relations.

About the latter, Haesbaert (2009) argues, the existence of a concomitant process of destruction and reconstruction of territories in the contemporaneity, through which the territorial joints occur through new forms, combining, for example, what the author calls "zone territories" and "network territories".

By defining the current processes of displacement, Haesbaert (2009, p. 344) proposes the concept of multiterritoriality, consisting of:

> (...) Multiterritoriality (or multiterritorialization if we want to emphasize it as an action or a process) thus implies the ability to Accessed or connect several territories, which can occur either through a "concrete mobility" in the sense of a physical shift, as "virtual", through triggering different territorialities even without physical displacement, as in the new space-temporal experiences provided through the cyberspace

(...) today we have a much greater (and multiple) diversity of Accessed and traffic through these territoriality - being themselves more unstable and mobile - and, depending on our social condition, also more options to constantly undo and redo this multiterritoriality (...).

The relatively "free flow" to which Haesbaert (2009) also calls "multiterritoriality" allows immigrants the construction and placement of aesthetic products in which they externalize voices, identities and hybrid cultures. Perhaps it allows more than that: the conduction of immigrants voices beyond the state confinement, allowing, through these aesthetic changes, a sharing of information and experiences, which attracts the attention of contemporary society, to the seriousness of a problem and that is witnessed and present throughout the world: social inequality.

In this regard, it is relevant to recall the theoretical position of the geographer Milton Santos (2011), when he considers that, alongside the massive practices required by the globalizing process - stationary in its symbols of power and often restricting various aspects of regional culture - There is a popular resistance that intelligently appropriates of the technological and mass tools to survive and assume a political organization in society.

The author argues that such resistance aesthetically reveals the existential truth and actual movements that occur in a schizophrenic world space. In the work *"Por uma outra globalização: do pensamento único à consciência universal"*, Santos (2011, p. 144) explains how this process takes place:

(...) There is also - and fortunately - the possibility, increasingly frequent, of a rematch of popular culture on mass culture, when, for example, it diffuses through the use of instruments that are, in origin, particular to the mass culture. In this case, popular culture exerts the quality discourse of the "poor", emphasizing the daily lives of the poor, the minorities, the excluded, through the exaltation of every day life. Such expressions of popular culture are much stronger and able to spread as revealing what we might call universalist regionalisms, form of expression that associates the very spontaneity of popular ingenuity to search for a universal discourse, which turns out to be a supply for politics.

The author reports the existence of a *structural poverty*, characteristic of our time. Constructed from an administrative apparatus, that poverty is imposed in a Cartesian way, by an ideological system that appropriates the misery and proceeds to sell it as something definite and inevitable. Santos (2011), however, sees among the marginalized layers, the possibility of aesthetic-clashes that would expose common dissonances arising from various locations, proving the segregating consequences of the neoliberal system and its globalized practices.

> (...) Generated from within, this endogenous culture imposes itself as a supply for the politics of poverty, which takes place independently and above parties and organizations. Such a culture is carried out using lower technical, capital and organizational levels, hence its typical forms of creation. This was apparently a weakness, but in reality is a streng, as it generates an organic integration with the territory of the poor and their human content. Hence the expressiveness of its symbols, as manifested in speech, music and in the richness of its forms of connectivity and solidarity between people. (SANTOS, 2011, p. 145).

In the light of theories here exposed, and the proposal to defend the existence of a migration and ideological dimension within the rapper art[1], this study is dedicated to the interpretation and comparative analysis of artistic productions, whose composition and propagation happens through immigrants and their descendants.

To the interested reader, only a few hours "traveling" through cyberspace are neccesary to become aware of immigrants' testimonials, available in the "virtual multiterritory", such as rap-

---

1   The vocative immigrant *rap* is a creation of the author of this work

pers songs or videoclips, in which those appear represented also by imagistic performance.

Endowed with a peculiar feature - the fact that they do not contain attachments related to the written record of its lyrics, which requires from viewers and listeners the ability to seize them through the auditory and visual memory - such songs, as well as representing the political positioning of foreign minorities in relation to the contemporary transnational environment, acting as "revolutionary aesthetic weapons" fired before the "war" to social injustic, also externalize the negotiations and identity exchanges set amid different cultures and people, persuading its listeners through the performance, seeking to clarify them in order to consolidate, next to them, a gregarious environment in which vigorates the ideology of resistance and the will of "contributing" to societal transformation.

Trying to understand, in depth, how is this process, it was decided to research the cultural translation and intersemiotic concerning immigrants rappers productions. Thus, scattered songs and videoclips were selected, linked to the following works and artists: 1) *Mestisoul* - CD produced in 2008 by Tensais MCS group. Said group, initially created by Japanese-Brazilian descendants who migrated to Japan, now has, also, the participation of Japanese members; 2) *Pássaro Imigrante (Inmigrant Bird)* - Vinyl, produced and released into circulation of only 300 copies in 2011 by DJ and producer in Brazil Caio Abumanssur Beraldo (Yoka), which was settled at the time in Barcelona and decided to produce a record for the musical translation of the migrant's experience, similarly to a journal. The work, carried out in partnership, brings together groups from Brazil and Europe; 3) *Αλάνα* - CD produced in 2009 in Greece by the rapper Manolis Afolanios (MC Yinka), son of Nigerian parents, born in Greece and not recognized as a citizen by the State; 4) *La Bala (The bullet)* - CD produced in France in 2011 by rapper Ana Maria Merino (Ana Tijoux), born in the city of Lille, daughter of Chilean exiles in France and not recognized as a French citizen.

It is important to explain that not all songs studied in this work have been recorded in video format. Most productions, instead, are only presented in audio. However, it is still important, in parallel to the interpretation and comparative analysis of transcribed and translated lyrics to establish, among the material available, a study regarding the audiovisual representation.

Thus, within the chapter that contains transcriptions, translations and interpretive analyzes of selected songs, a specific chapter for the interpretative analysis of videoclips has been developed. Guided by the theory of *intersemiotic translation* of Plaza (2003), this section analyzes the following works: *Sacar la voz* (2012), *Shock* (2011); *Pássaro Imigrante* (2011); *To Κέρμα* (2010).

Regarding music videos, it is believed that, by the intersection of meanings offered by the musical basis through words, gestures and scenarios; for editing and inserting special effects - And other elements that may establish the composition of these products - it is possible to complement the study of sound material, which will provide a deeper understanding of the immigrational rapper dimension, the object of study of this research.

The association between the verbal content of the songs and videoclips, such self-representative productions offers accessed to the identification of a politicized art, free from the hegemony of Eurocentric stereotypes and, above all, provides a broad discussion about the foreign reality in the present, whose production and distribution became easier in the last twenty years -whether due to the intensification of media processes aimed at mass culture or even through the popularization and creation of alternative channels on the internet, such as Youtube.

Over the years, marginalized groups remained deprived of control of their own representation, subject to conceptual distortions about themselves. However, the current technological tools led to the emergence of alternative aesthetics, enthralled by the identity of self-representation policies that purport to make public different versions of the Official History, whose domination was made over many years by the American narrative.

According to Shohat and Stam (2006) in the work *"Critique of Eurocentric image"*, a variety of alternative aesthetic questions the hegemonic model of audiovisual. Such variety, "includes films and videos that challenge the formal conventions of dramatic realism in favor of approaches and strategies such as the carnival, cannibalism, magical realism, reflective modernism and postmodern resistance."(SHOHAT; STAM, 2006, p. 445).

It is due to this latter approach, especially, that this research is directed. This study covers the border breach established by the space-temporal reality of the twenty-first century and returns to research rapper art as a form of political action and communication, linked to issues of foreignness.

It is understood that there is, within this ideological and foreign rapper dimension, a virtual sharing of identities that reveals and denounces realities nationally experience, while it takes the serious challenge of touching base on a global problem: the exclusionary poverty, woven in wires inherited from the colonial practices.

The emerging discourse of immigrants is shown as one of the most current attempts of postcolonial expression. Despite the non-consensual theoretical foundations that underlie the term "postcolonial", we will focus in Hall's proposition (2007, p. 109.), Which tells us the following:

> The term "postcolonial" is not restricted to describe a particular society or epoch. He rereads the "colonization" as part of an essentially transnational and transcultural global process - and produces a decentered, diasporic or "global" of rewriting of the great imperial narratives of the past, focused on the nation. Its theoretical value, therefore, rests precisely on its refusal of a perspective of the "here and there" a "then" and "now", a "home" and "abroad".

In order to understand these discourses a broad comparative approach of the language used in these *raps* is necessary in order to consider issues involving the historicity and the testimonial character transmitted to the voices subject of such songs and videos.

Based in Bakhtin's theory (1992), it is believed to be possible to consider such products as dialogical events, or artistic expressions that keep in itself echoes fragments and images related to the social universe in which they are immersed. Bakhtin (1992) establishes a reflection on the origin of enunciations. For the philosopher, the authorship of a text always presupposes the consciousness of the subject. But this, in turn, is generated from the contextually established dialogues.

According to Bakhtin (1992), the individual concepts never appear as impermeable or unchanging. They are composed, on the contrary, by the view and the words of the "other". In these terms, the author says:

> Everything that concerns me, starting with my name, and that penetrates into my consciousness, comes to me from the outside world, from the mouth of the other (the mother, etc.), and is given to me with the tone, the emotive tone of their values. I become aware of me, originally, through others: from them I get the word, the form and the tone that will serve to the original representation I have of myself (BAKHTIN, 1992, p. 378).

Through Bakhtinian conceptions, one might infer, then, that from a societal speech, creator of various stereotypes arise, inevitably, other discourses, and they can be of acceptance or repudiation of the dominant ideological purposes. Regarding the social strata put into marginality what we have are propositions classified in the latter category. The "other" - passed over physically, verbally and humanely by the systemic order - finds in the "power of speech" an alternative to self-representation and repudiation of "foreign identities" imposed on himself.

Williams (1979) has a similar position to Bakhtin (1992). In the essay *"Signs and Notations"* the author is categorical when discussing the issues of language. For Williams (1979), language is not only a mean, as it is a constitutive element of social-material practice; something complex, which contains human activities;

perhaps of less material nature, such as information, imagination, abstract thinking and immediate emotion. Thus, Williams (1979) understands that applied language must not be reduced to categorical factors, nor to signs; but assimilated through a contextual frame that permeates directly or indirectly its use and takes into account specific situations, which affect various relationships between subjects. About the experimental work, he states:

> The "Experimental" work depends largely on a shared awareness of already available meanings. These are the defining characteristics, and then,the real. determination process of language In other words, no expression - no reports, discretion, picture, portrait - is "natural" or "direct". These terms are, at most, socially relative terms. Language is not a pure mean by which the reality of a full life can "flow". It is a socially shared and with reciprocal reality, already incorporated in the active relationships within which all movement is an activation of what is, or may become, shared and reciprocal. (WILLIAMS, 1979, p. 166)

Uttered by subjects historically passed over by judgments and practices that support the neo-liberal system, rappers songs are examples of what Williams (1979) calls "experimental work", since they require the task to be elucidated as hybrid productions that directly echo from existing policies and structural transactions, existing globally in the present.

In order to understand them, we start from the assumption that these are politicized and dynamic aesthetics, fruits of experiences in the real world, by the marginalized layers. Such groups, before the feeling of not being recognized in several instances of societal context - political, legislative, labor, medical, etc. - often appropriate of different languages fragments to prepare a different song, in which the verb is the largest recovery tool, designed to self-representation and clarification of the listener so that it develops "other" view of himself and of the society in which he lives.

In addition to breaking with possible stereotypical conceptions, providing, through aesthetics, information about their own history and the objectives existing in it, such manifestos also suggests the setting of a critic that transcends territorial and governmental boundaries of where it was made, once it addresses typical problems of globalization, which arepresent throughout the world.

It starts from the principle that, once launched in the virtual spaces and therefore susceptible to the "encounter" whether with other manifestos of the same order or with other enunciators set in different areas of the world - such productions do transpire that criticism, suggesting an aesthetic counter-ideology of transnational order, since its contents reveal many similarities.

Currently, various currents within the academic field have resumed discussions about social recognition. In the case of Humanities, authors such as Taylor (2011) and Honneth (2003) have assumed prominence. Both inspired in assumptions inherent in Hegelian philosophy, they discuss the importance of subjective inter-recognition for self-fulfillment of individuals and the consequent construction of social justice.

For Honneth (2003), for example, social contexts operate by means of meaning frames, kinds of mirrors that are subjected (or not) to the possibility of identification, or recognition. If any, recognition guarantees to the subject the full realization of their capabilities, as well as a kind of self-relation focused on integrity. When it is inexistent, however - either in the field of affective relationships, rights and or moral values - it creates disrespects of different orders, creating in modern societies the threat of identities and the possibility of permanent emergence of conflicts of symbolic force, focused on the review of these frameworks and redemption of relations of social esteem.

According to Honneth (2003, p. 224)

> Every negative emotional reaction that goes hand in hand with the experience of a disrespect of claims of recognition, contains within it the possibility that the injustice inflicted

on the subject will be revealed to him in cognitive terms and become the subject of political resistance.

Taylor (2011), in turn, argues that the self-realization of individuals is necessarily linked to the intersubjective recognition processes. According to the author, after a decline of hierarchically stablished modern societies, there was a change of estamental honor towards a feeling focused on widespread dignity. In these terms, it would have incurred today the configurtion of the *"self"*, individual, category, established from the notions of rationality, autonomy, inwardness and authenticity.

Driven by the idea that "everyone deserves respect", the subjects would have the association of singular identities, modeled on the ideals of authenticity, to get their recognition.

The recognition for Taylor (2011), therefore, involves the fusion of universal policies and policies of the difference. When inexistent, it represents a possibility of damage to the social structure. This happens because negative meanings attributed to certain groups can be reversed in identity negotiations, held through the symbolic struggle: namely, the struggle in pursuit of social recognition.

> In social terms, the understanding that identities are formed in open dialogue, not shaped by a predefined social script, made the politics of equal recognition more central and stressed. In fact, it is not only thee appropriate way for a healthy democratic society. Its refusal can inflict damage to those for which it is denied, according to a widespread modern view. The projection of a lower or degrading image over someone else can actually distort and overwhelm, as it is internalized. Not only contemporary feminism, but also race relations and multiculturalism discussions are underpinned by the assumption that denies recognition as a form of oppression.(TAYLOR, 2011, p. 56-57).

Like feminism, mentioned by Taylor (2011), *Hip-Hop* is a movement that arises from the lack of social recognition. Joining identities and common stigmas, Jamaican immigrants and veterans of the Vietnam War gave life to such a movement, which today produces politicized aesthetical practices, aimed not only at entertainment, but at the ideological attempt to advance the social spaces, leaving the ghettos and inserting fully marginalized layers in social and global context. Among these aesthetic practices, the rapper song is undoubtedly present, as the foundation-stone of the whole movement.

Born in the ghettos of major American metropoli, rap acts as the main voice for the *Hip-Hop* movement and contains in itself two of the four elements that compose it: the Master of Ceremonies (MC) and the *Disk Jockey* (DJ).

While in the contemporary aesthetic form, rap challenges conceptions and establishes debates through the intelectuality that aims to understand it, associating it as an innovative part (or not) linked to to "the ways" of making music or literature.

It is neccessary to note the existence of these opinionated records, sometimes heated and divergent. In Brazil, for example, the composer Francisco Buarque de Hollanda (born in 1944) triggered a series of discussions after considering the existence of a possible "death of music" in favor of the "new rap genre". Researchers from the popular music field have expressed themselves in this regard. For Bosco (2007), we find today a new way to do songs in the Brazilian context, "a denial of the song as we know it, within the historical-cultural and historical-formal plans".

Valverde (2008) believes that rap should be considered as a result of a historical crossing performed by the song, a practice that has suffered a series of transformations over the years. Valverde sees this process as a phenomenon of the very "music history" that gave the song the possibility of a "creative openness", with rap being the very reflection of this opening.

Demonstrating a similar position, also manifest Tatit (Accessed on July 30th 2013) and Wisnik (Accessed in Sep 15th, 2015). Both recognize the changes in the ways of making music. For Tatit, for example, rap is a radical form in which the song is constituted. In this regard, it states:

One of the misconceptions of today is precisely saying that the song tends to end because it is losing ground to rap! It is like saying that it loses ground to itself, because nothing is more radical as a song than a explicitt speech that neutralizes the "romantic" oscillations of melody and conserves raw intonation, its raw material. The existence of rap and other genres today only confirms the vitality of the song. That is, the song is not a gender, but a language class that coexists with music, literature, visual arts, comics, dance, etc. It is everything that sings with melodic inflection and letter. No matter the configuration that trends give to it over time. (TATIT, Accessed on July 30th, 2013)

Wisnik also corroborates the view that rap is the result of a song that changes every day, built by hitherto unknown forms, which come together to advance the story and the emergence of a different "musical experience".

In an interview with professor and filmmaker Lisandro Nogueira, Wisnik (Accessed on Sep 15th, 2013) spoke on the topic:

- The effects that songs provoke in people today are given in the same way as before? We live in a much more frantic world, with less time for reflection, and less will to stop and listen to music. Do you think this has changed in that sense?
- I think so. You said that since 2008 we live, as sung by Ernesto Nazareth, crisis in bunches (laughs). But I think that life is crisis. Life is much more a crisis than pacification and resolution. We are always in crisis. Now, in fact, I think we live in a situation where there is some kind of crises crossing at various levels. This critical basis of life, perhaps, has become more evident. I also think that we live a time that this place of musicality, listening, free association, these affections undergoes major changes. I agree with this. And I think the song itself mutates. There are forms of song, like rap, which is rhythm and poetry. It is much closer to the spoken discourse and draws many melodic aspects of the song that we were talking about. It is a cruder thing. This has to do with these contem-

porary possibilities that you were talking about. This also goes for electronic music, with another form of exploitation of sonorities (...) They create sound lagoons starting in one place, but you do not know exactly where they go. And they are mass songs and hits at the same time. I think this is not linked only to the frantic time, to the speed. I think that this mutation is also linked to songs that cover other type of sensitivity.

In the academic discussion of song's transformations, rap also find personalities that are resistant to it. Tinhorão is one of them.

For Tinhorão the occurrence of "cancioneira death" is an undeniable fact, having this scholar attested to by giving rap characteristics linked to "collectivism", the "poverty of melodies and harmonies" and at the same time, the dependence on electroacoustic resources (VALVERDE, 2008).

Among the most radical opponents of rap presence in Brazilian society is also the conductor and former director of the Theatro Municipal, Júlio Medaglia, who believes that this musical genre is an aesthetic devoid of originality and richness. Referring to the rapper practice, the conductor said: "(...) is a very limited, musically impoverished thing" (MEDAGLIA, cited SHETARA, 2005, p. 158).

In this work, the reflections around rap occur from the theoretical bases that consider it as a phenomenon, as the result of changes and historical "crises" that interceded and focus also on the music making proccess. We live in the time of globalization guided by language and their respective effects.

There is, within the great world metropoli, problematic coincidences that make us realize similar existential scenarios, characterized by the practice of urban violence, the population swelling resulting from incessant migration flows, the economic and social segregation, prejudice, and labor exploitation. Considering the presence of such transformations worldwide, coexisting with the spread of the rapper ideological aspect, spread around the world from the 80's, with the popularity of rap genre; this research seeks to address a contemporary way to make songs that, while held in different territorial bases, guard discursive similarities in relation to the transnational character, which can be assessed through the diffusing possibility exerted by digital channels today.

The rapper song in this work, as noted, is taken up by a central issue, which refers to the origins of rap and, consequently, the *Hip-Hop* movement itself: immigration. This reality experienced by Jamaicans in the movement's origin, is reflected in the contemporary world, through profitable production of immigrants of different nationalities.

Such production signals the existence of groups that favor the "singing" of socio-cultural segregation experienced by immigrants, a theme extracted from experience. Subverting the logic of global consumption, "immigrant rap" is spreading in contemporary times, whether from the tools provided by mass culture or digital channels, dealing with foreign issues through an urban and performative poetics[2] , that "calls" amid the virtual space, the renovation of a real space, fragmented and experienced by foreign minority layers on issues that are similar.

Impregnated of minimalistic designs, rap had its broadcasting which concomitantly started with the beginning of global processes. It has been hybridized, has gained new dimensions and to date, it follows the changes across space. However, despite the changes, it still retains the blunt side of art-activists, by which it assumes, in its ideological aspect, an essential role in the formation of opinionated listeners and their artistic appreciation modes.

Many rappers through rough words and performances sing everyday and capture numerous attentive receivers capable of reproducing their ideals and taking them as a form of knowledge and identity sharing.

Thus, overlapping the sound layers - built by the technological apparatus, they extol their voices and show their profiles,

---

2   We consider the rapper production as urban poetry, coming from the life experience of those who survive at the outskirts of the big and enabled by the translation and influence of everyday imagery, as well as the natural human capacity of imitation. See Aristoteles (1990), Paz (1996) and Frye (1973).

giving form to repetitive choruses, which suggests a pragmatic ped-agogy of reality to those who cross it without having theoretically greater awareness of it.

The possibility of the rap-ideological act is undeniable, there-fore, as sociologically active and an important form of art, able to overcome the boundaries of contemplation and generate questions and reflections about the moments lived in society.

Glissant (2005), in the work *"Introduction to a poetics of diversity"*, suggests the need for poetic presence during the process of teaching as fundamental to cope with the world's conflicts. In these terms, the author states:

> I think these cultural and political battles that everyone has waged and continue to wage fall within a global context in which it is necessary, while we fight this fight, to pour the poetic value, contribute to changing the mentality of human-ities (...) In my understanding, this is another form of combat, unlike the daily fighting, and the artist, I think, seems to be one of the most suitable for this form of combat. Because the artist is one who approaches the imaginary world; the world's ideologies, worldviews, the forecasts, the sand castles begin to fail; we must therefore begin to emerge from this imaginary. And then it is no longer to dream the world, but to penetrate it. (GLISSANT, 2005, p. 69).

It is true that, more than anything related to artistic fruition, such *raps* gather the fusion of aesthetic standards and ethical pre-suppositions that guarantee the implementation of the "symbol-ic confrontation" and "struggle for social recognition", which we mention above.

In thirty years the rap genre has became global and ex-panded not only on types, but also in relation to the identities with which it correlates. If initially, its ideological strand was focused on the performance of the black stigma, today it also covers other stories, other contexts, other offsets.

Ideological rap followed the course of social history and remains with it in constant dialogue, providing expressiveness and union of social layers who experience the world's territorialized segregation, but not confined to ghettos of political space control.

In the book *The Black Atlantic*, Gilroy (2001) draws attention to the size assumed by the field of the arts in daily lives of slaves. Banned from the right to exercise citizenship, silenced politically, slaves spoke through art, making orality a knowledge:

> (...) Art has become the backbone of the political cultures of the slaves and their cultural history. It continues to be the means by which cultural activists today are "engaged in rescuing criticism" of this, not only through the mobilization of memories of the past, but also by the intervention of an imaginary past that can feed their utopian hopes. (GILROY, 2001, p. 129).

In this research, therefore, it has been proposed as an update of this statement, aimed at the diasporic reality. Today we can talk about a "post-diaspora" speech, hybrid and visual, which tells not only about the effects of colonization; but also shows the results of a neoliberal policy that regardless of "pure" ethnic amid the discourse of the capitalist spectacle, seeks to generate the silence of displaced persons. People who occupy different parts of the global territory and break the system logic, using art as an ethical haven instrument and flight line. Rap, then, in its oral forms thus becomes a means to take counter-hegemonic positions, being awareness to potential supporters through aesthetic combat, and seeking some recognition in society .

Thus, the attempt of gathering is established, understanding and translating some of the current rapper-ideological culture, sung by foreign individuals into their reality. It starts from the principle that the immigrant stigma delivered from available aesthetic manifestations and captured through the internet reflects the world felt by foreign, but also the world's functionality.

For organizational purposes, this work was divided into chapters, and entitled: 1. (Neo) pragmatism and Rapper Ideological Aesthetics: Foundations for Understanding a Phenomenon; 2. Dissolving Borders Translating the Present: Rap as Identitarian Hybridism, Social difference and Transnationality; 3. Considerations about Performance; 4. Transcribe, Translate and Compare: The Lyrics 5. An Intersemiotic Proposal: Interpretation of music videos; 6. Final considerations

Chapter 1, arranged in the following section, promotes a theoretical approach about the similarities between the ideologial rap and neopragmatist philosophy, represented in this work mainly by the strands of Richard Rorty (2005, 2007) and Richard Schustermann (1998) .

(Neo) Pragmatism and the rapper ideological aesthetics: grounds for understanding a contemporary phenomenon

To begin the exposure of this research, it is necessary to state some theoretical formulations concerning (neo)pragmatist aesthetics and philosophy. This demand is due to our main purpose: at the end of this thesis, we are to be able to present immigrant rap to readers as a relevant contemporary aesthetic manifestations.

Initial considerations for understanding the contemporary rapper aesthetic

Since the dawn of human history, artistic expressions can be found. Through the creative proccess, men expose their interpretations of nature and at the same time, they performan a kind of self-knowledge. There is no civilization in history that has not produced art. (BUORO, 2000)

However, although art has always accompanied the development of human history, it was not until the eighteenth century that the term "aesthetic" begin to be used by Baumgarten (1714-1762), as a designation of science dedicated to the investigations of art and of beauty (TOMAS, 2004).

There was, at that historic moment, a series of disagreements about the subject of "art". These disagreements culminated in various efforts to determine the nature of aesthetics. At that time, philosophers and poets - among them Herder, Schiller, Rousseau, Schelling, Holderlin, etc. - by resisting the dominant rationalist parameters in the period, made contributions to the breakdown of barriers regarding the sensitive experience. Aesthetics began, from that point on, being associated with subjective taste components which, in turn, allowed the understanding of the art as a single element, independent in relation to external objects.

According to Tomas (2004), philosopher Baumgarten (1714-1762) was the first to offer a modern definition of aesthetics as a science, attributing emotional and cognitive characteristics to it. Hermann (2005) draws attention to the fact in the work *"Ethics and aesthetics : the almost forgotten relationship"* :

> The first definition of aesthetics, in the modern sense, was made by Alexander Baumgarten (1714-1762) as "science of sensitive knowledge, inferior gnoseology". This definition appears in 1750, in the work "Aesthetica", and marks its emergence as a philosophical discipline, alongside logic, metaphysics and ethics, initially concerned with the definition of beauty, with an intellectualistic character. (HERMANN, 2005, p. 33)

Despite the undeniable importance of the concept of Baumgarten (1714-1762), however, it is necessary to note that throughout the history of mankind there are records and different positions about the nature of art making; therefore understanding this has always set a great challenge for scholars of various periods (TOMAS, 2004).

In this work, we sought to evaluate migrant lyrics and to place them as representative art object of ideologies and timestamps derived from ignored historical segregations - especially by those who experience, in fact, the pleasant side of the possibilities offered by the globalization process. Therefore, we understand the need to promote research aimed at understanding the social place inherent to contemporary rapper-ideological aesthetics.

It is interesting in this regard, to remember the thought proposed by Rancière (2009) in the work *"Sharing of the Sensible"*. The author identifies a kind of "Aesthetic Revolution" inaugurated in the Romantic Age, from which a politicized way of making art emerges, in which the boundaries between fictional rationality and historical-social reality start to blur. In this regard, Rancière says (2009, p. 54):

> The aesthetic revolution redistributes the game associating two things: the blurring of boundaries between the reason of the facts and fictions of reason and the new model of rationality and historical science. Stating that the principle of poetry is not fiction, but a certain arrangement of signs and language, the romantic age blurrred the line that isolated art from the jurisdiction of statements or images, as well as that which separated the reason of the facts and the ratio of stories. (...) Romantic age in fact forced language to penetrate the materiality of the traits by which the historical and social world becomes visible to itself, albeit in the form of the mute language of things and coded language of images. It is the movement in this landscape of signs that defines the new fictionality: a new way of telling stories that is, first and foremost, a way to make sense of the "empirical" universe of dark deeds and banal objects.

Contrary to important aesthetic conceptions, Ranciére (2009) believes that romanticism introduces an art capable of changing the sensory experience, establishing new spatiotemporal relationships that enable for other subjects to emerge on the scene: artists, from the subjective symbolism of their productions, raise important public issues, hitherto invisible to the eyes of society. According to the author:

> The real must be fictionalized in order to be thought. This is not to say that everything is fiction. It is noted that the fiction of the aesthetic era has defined connection models between the presentation of the facts and forms of intelligibility that makes indefinite the border between reason of facts and reason of fiction, and that these connection modes were taken over by historians and analysts of social reality. Writing history and writing stories that belong to the same

regime of truth. (...) Politics and art, as well as the knowledge, build "fictions", in other words, material rearrangements of signs and images, of the relationship between what is seen and what is said, between what is done and what is possible to be done (RANCIÈRE, 2009, p. 54).

In order to assume a position before the function occupied by the immigrant rapper aesthetic today, we will resume the fundaments related to art concepts established by the contemporary pragmatist philosophical thought, also known as "neo-pragmatism"; a vertient that rescues and reformulates the principles of philosophical pragmatism. In order to allow for adequate contextualization, we will discuss in the following sections, the pragmatist philosophical thought and (neo) pragmatist philosophical thought respectively.

Brief considerations about pragmatism: dialogue between thought and its practical effects

Born in the United States, the pragmatist philosophical current appears at the end of the nineteenth century, in the post-civil war period, in which the North American society went through reconfigurations of various orders. At the time, a series of debates favored the emergence of this philosophical current, as explained in Sofia Vanni Rovighi's work *"History of Contemporary Philosophy: from the nineteenth century to neoescolástica"*:

> The discussions on the theoretic limits of science, the renewed interest in logic, the dissatisfaction of many scholars with the metaphysical theses of reborn idealism (neo-Hegelian), the attempt by some to recover religious faith in not intellectualist terms, and the usage of psichology's results-trending science at that period- favored the emergence of pragmatism.(ROVIGHI, 2004, p. 459)

The debates about this philosophical aspect had as "cornerstone" a kind of "brotherhood" composed of young intellectuals and friends, who gathered to discuss philosophical issues. Named the "Metaphysical Club", this group aggregated thinkers who advocated the implementation of a pragmatic metaphysics, instead of classical metaphysics, as explained by Cornelis de Waal (2007), in the work "*On Pragmatism*" :

> Pragmatism emerged in the early 1870s, when a group of young men from Cambridge, Massachusetts, met regularly to discuss philosophy. The group included, among others, William James, Charles Sanders Peirce, Oliver Wendell Holms Jr. and Nicholas St. John Green. These men called themselves half defiantly, half ironically, "The Metaphysical Club" once in the early 1870s, metaphysics was considered unfashionable. Alexander Bain's definition of belief, according to which a belief is "that basis on which a man is prepared to act" was central to their discussions. (WAAL, 2007, p. 17)

Thus, members of the "Metaphysical Club" argued a close link between the existence of meanings and their practical effects. The term "pragmatism" - which comes from the Greek term "*pragma*" that means action, practice - was first used by Charles Sanders Peirce (1839-1914), during the discussions of the Metaphysical Club, as explained by Thamy Pogrebinschi:

> It was in one of the meetings of the Metaphysical Club, around 1872, that one of its most active members, Charles Peirce, exposed to the others a draft with some notes resulting from their collective discussions, which intended to possibly add to a book on logic, he planned to one day write. The ideas and opinions contained within this draft that were presented to his colleagues, Peirce called pragmatism. It was initially a "method of determining the meanings of difficult words and abstract concepts," said its creator. His colleagues suggested he called it a practicism theory (practicism) or practicalism (practicalism), but Peirce, who knew the distinction between

the Kantian terms praktisch and pragmatisch, knew what he was doing and did not change his mind.(POGREBINSCHI, 2005, p. 12)

Peirce spread the idea of pragmatism by publishing the articles *"The fixation of belief"* and *"How to Make our Ideas Clear"* - the latter considered a sort of manifesto of the doctrine in question. Both, based at the thought of Alexander Bain (1818-1913) - to which beliefs are a kind of support to human action, started from the idea that the meaning of the theories and concepts should be linked to the knowledge of the effects for themselves posed and levied on the practical experience of human life.

Peirce, was among the largest of pragmatist thought diffusers, becoming known worldwide for his "theory of meaning" or "semiotic". Sofia Vanni Rovighi explains said theory:

(...) The concept of an object is the concept of all its possible effects; while an object is not subjected to the test for human experimental action through operations that man realizes with it, we can even say that such an object has properties that then will later be atributed to it (since they are real only when they correspond to tests that man carries on them). Peirce said, by the way, that two different perspectives in their theoretical abstracity produce the same practical consequences, actually not differing at all. The idea, for example, that a chemical element (Peirce spoke of Lithium) is the representation of its effects and, at the same time, of the operations carried out to discover it. (...) (ROVIGHI, 2004, p. 461)

Rovighi (2004) warns that the ideas defended by Peirce are not mere theories to be proposed in an speculative way, but due to the capacity it holds in practically organizing the conduct, by allowing the verification and control by the members of a given society.

Although Peirce was the first ones to use the term "pragmatism" and to spread the ideals of the above club of young thinkers, it was another intellectual, William James (1842-1910), who was responsible for inserting the North American philosophical school in academia and society. In 1898, within the conference *"Philosophical Conceptions and Practical Results"*, James introduced the term to the general and academic community, recognizing the authorship due to Charles Peirce. From this conference, the pragmatist philosophy breaks borders with its ideals disseminated by other North American states and also through the world. (POGREBINSCHI, 2005)

In 1907, William James publishes the work *"Pragmatism"*. The popularity of the book resulted in other major conferences and the consequent expansion of pragmatic ideals. Durkheim, in the lessons published by the title *"Sociology, Philosophy and Pragmatism"*, even states that (...) "William James is the real father of pragmatism" (...) (S.D. p. 14)

The bulky expansion of pragmatist philosophy has gained adepts in various locations. Besides North-American philosophers, emerged others such as: FSS Schiller (England); Henri Bergson, Maurice Blondel, Émile Boutroux, Pierre Duhem, Henri Poincaré (France); Giovanni Papini and Giuseppe Prezzolini (Italy) and Anísio Spíndola (Brazil). (SHOOK, 2002)

Despite assuming different interpretations inherent to multiple theories dedicated to "pragmatist" approach and their academic interests (SHOOK, 2002), the American philosophy had a common core, established under the notion of "real plastic" and the idea that a given phenomenon is proportional to the knowledge of its effects and the verification of its contributions to practical experience of life.

Shook (2002) points out some common traits of this philosophical aspect, such as the review of the empiricism; the overcoming of the contemplative philosophy by scientific rationality; the objection to skepticism and the formulation of a new conception of truth.

Thamy Pogrebinschi (2005), on the other hand, mentions three common attributes arranged in the midst of such a current. They are: anti-foundationalism - permanent rejection of any kind of metaphysical entities, abstract concepts, perpetual principles, last instance, dogmas, among other possible foundations to thinking; namely a negation of the thoughts founded in a static context - Consequentialism or instrumentalism - the belief that every thought should address the issues of the future: the experience, the future consequences must be anticipated so that it is possible to know which is the one that best suits and benefits, as well as to know those that generate bad effects - and Contextualism - keeping a careful look at the flow and context of the dynamics in which they are inserted to, considering factors such as political, religious and scientific beliefs, which are part of the societal environment and/or their respective cultural practices.

Pragmatism has remained as the main philosophical current up to half of the twentieth century. Only in the mid-1950s, this aspect began to decline, brought about by the "analytic turn". With the presence of European immigrants in the United States, philosophers running away from the Nazi persecution during World War II, members of the Vienna Circle, most teachers within university departments began to be composed of intellectuals dedicated to the analytical philosophical line.

Pragmatic ideas are resumed only in the 1970's; when Richard Rorty proposes to rescue the principles of John Dewey (1859-1952), one of the most prominent pragmatic American philosophers, alongside Peirce and James during the golden age of the vertient of throughts in question. Aiming to better develop the work in the next section, we will weave brief notes about the actions and thoughts developed by Dewey, a North American philosopher, educator and psychologist.

John Dewey: fundamentals for understanding Dewey's thought

Born on October 20, 1859, in the town of Vermont, United States, John Dewey was recognized alongside Peirce and William James as one of the three greatest exponents of pragmatist studies. Although not integrating the Metaphysical Club of Cambridge, Dewey, before learning about the pragmatist line guided his studies from concepts related to the themes of experience, action, learning and democracy; influences arising from his own training, as explained by Cunha:

> Dewey certainly integrated to his personality and his intellectual conceptions the lessons of democratic community life he learnt in childhood and youth, articulating philosophical and educational ideas that precisely reflect confidence in the individual and the human capacity to seek and exercise freedom without the rigidity imposed by dogmas and hierarchies (CUNHA, 2011, p. 9).

Author of works such as *"The School and the Society"* (1899), *"The Child and the Curriculum"* (1902), *"How we think"* (1910), *"Democracy and education"* (1916), *"The Public and its Problems"* (1917) and *"Experience and Education"* (1938), John Dewey learnt about the pragmatist philosophical line through the famous lectures given by William James (POGREBINSCHI, 2005). At the time, he was head of the Department of Psychology, Pedagogy and Philosophy at the University of Chicago and was involved with a number of activities provided with social-political engagement, as shown by Cornelius de Waal:

> In Chicago, Dewey was actively involved with the Hull House- a social setting to improve the social conditions of the impoverished working class. Hull House was a higher education institution which initially had a curriculum of hu-

manities and general culture and was later adapted to meet the needs of the industrial society, in 1895, Dewey helped to found the Laboratory School of the University of Chicago. A school designed to test his pedagogical and psychological theories and in 1937 he chaired the commission to investigate the charges of conspiracy made by the Soviet government against Leon Trotsky, and other political and social causes in the scenario of American life. (WAAL, 2007, p. 154)

Like other pragmatists, Dewey believed in action related to knowledge and consequent reorganization of experience, so that every idea or belief should be subjected to tests, so that it could be verified as valid or not. (Apple, Teitelbaum. Accessed on February 4th 2014)

Under the influence of Hegel, he launches a more "organic" interpretation of the term "pragmatism", that comprehended it - not only as a philosophical method, but also as an open tool which helps men to adapt to their natural environment, enabling and generating a democratic and humanitarian environment. According to Leonardo Sartori Porto:

> Dewey opposed Hegelian idealism to Rousseau's naturalism: the intellectual abilities of the individual does not develop spontaneously from nature, being society an impediment to the proper development of such capabilities, as argued by Rousseau; on the contrary, we must learn from Hegel that our intellectual abilities are formed from the social interaction that generates the language, culture, government, art and religion. The origin of cognitive abilities may be natural, but its development occurs in the interaction of the individual with social institutions. Since society is nothing more than a gathering of individuals, developing them culturally is the way to keep the culture of society, and even improve it. (PORTO, 2006, p. 42-43)

Dewey associates the philosophical reflection to research and experiences that are developed within the educational field. Thus, the educational context plays a critical role, as Dewey sees in the school, a kind of cell, miniature of the societal body, where it is possible to work for the construction of moral and democratic environment.

Regarding the latter, it is important to clarify that the idea of "democracy", based on Deweyian studies, consists not only in the operation of a government system, but the equal and routine participation of citizens, within the dynamic of the social body referring not only to political bodies, but also to economic or cultural dimensions. For Dewey, democracy was a way of life correlated to the colectively reported experience. (Apple, Teitelbaum. Accessed on February 4th 2014)

When thinking of the consolidation of an innovative education, Dewey experiments with the creation of a "new scholasticism", with the proposal to "create in schools a projection of the kind of society we desire, so that people would be trained there to transform the existing society" (PIMENTA, 2010, p. 67)

This proposal is based on stimulating the critical capacity of students and in the practice of learning, originating from the interaction between subject and within their awakenings, regarding to being integral members of a particular social context, immersed and committed therefore with the issues that concern the reality of such a context.

In this regard, the thought is valued as one of the vital processes that make up the human being; an effort that the body performs to keep its organization, its life. Porto (2006) explains that there is a certain continuity between biological processes and intellectual processes, with possible incentives and transmission of social behavior through education, through the generations, which would also imply a certain evolution.

From this awakening - regarding their own actions and its effects towards the experienced reality, new experiences are enabled to the subject. The "plunge" in the days' experience, combined with action and knowledge imply, according to Dewey, incessant discoveries that interconnect the realities of the past and present and produce, inevitably, new experiences. There is within the life experience, a succession of acts, phenomena that occur through the interaction between the living-subjects, constituting units full of meanings.

In these terms, Dewey tells us about a principle of continuity, he says: "The principle of continuity of experience means that all experiences take something away from those that happened before and modify the quality of those who come after somehow."(DEWEY, 1958, p. 35).

Contrary to the absolutist and aristocratic cultural practices, the traditional, static teaching based on dualisms- "theory and practice", "individual or group", "public or private", etc. - Dewey retains the vision of building a progressive society based on integrating discussions and the experience of curricular plafinication; interdisciplinary practice, based on current interests pursued by students. (Apple, Teitelbaum. Accessed February 4th 2014)

In the work *"Experience and Education"*, Dewey compares the traditional school to what should be the "new school". According to the philosopher, for the school to be available to the new practices of progressive thought, "encyclopedists" tendencies should be eliminated, so as to avoid the proliferation of mechanical and static reflections and taking upon itself the task of moral education, solidified in continuous pair of action-information. In Dewey's words:

> The matter or content of education consists on sets of information and skills that have been developed in the past; the main task of the school is therefore to transmit them to the next generation. In the past, also standards and rules of conduct have been established; therefore, moral education consists in acquiring habits of action in accordance with such rules and standards. This makes the school a radically different institution from other social institutions (DEWEY, 1974, p. 4)

The school is, in the conception of John Dewey, a tool to minimize social differences. In this context, the role played by those dedicated to teaching would be of paramount importance. In an article entitled *"My Pedagogic Creed"* (1897), Dewey provides his opinion about the role played by the teacher; it should not be anyone to impose ideas but a professional to select the influences inflicted on their students, assessing how the discipline of life must get to them. Thus, Dewey says:

> I believe every teacher should realize the dignity of his calling; he is a different social servant because of the maintenance of proper social order and the assurance of the right social growth. (DEWEY, Accessed Feb 4th 2014)

Although he had his name consagrated in history, as one of the greatest North American theorists dedicated to social transformation, especially in the areas of Education, Philosophy, Politics and Psychology, John Dewey was sometimes challenged and questioned by scholars from other philosophical-educational dimensions. In this sense, Apple and Teitelbaum explain:

> His antipathy to the teaching of socially fixed beliefs contrasted approaches of many social-reconstrucionist educators who believed that such political advocacy was an inevitable aspect in education. Unlike Dewey, they thought the students should identify and examine specific problems of American capitalism to encourage not only an understanding, but also an alliance with more cooperative social and economic relations. The socialist educators hesitated even less to teach the values of collectivism and class struggle to [the] students, justifying this position as a necessity to counter-react to the pernicious influence of capitalist culture in the lives of children and of the working class. The maximum allowed by Dewey was the application of a creative and scientific research to social problems (...) it is questionable whether a certain type of common social purpose and active citizenship advocated by Dewey is possible

in a capitalist society with such great and sharp inequalities of power and wealth and dominated by consumerism. Some also presented Dewey's belief in science as a mistake. As C. Wright Mills pointed out, scientific intelligence could be used as easily as much to serve democratic purposes and to increase domination. (Apple, Teitel baum. Accessed Feb 4th 2014)

In Brazil, as well, when Deweyian concepts were inserted in the educational field, mainly by Teixeira, in the early twentieth century, there was resistance from many teachers, as Ana Mae Barbosa explains, in the title *"John Dewey and the Art of Teaching in Brazil"*:

> In Brazil, with the anti "new school," policy, John Dewey, due to inspiring what has been pejoratively called "novismo school" was banned from educational studies. He was seen for a long time as a defender of an elitist education by those who considered themselves reformers, and by conservatists, as an American leftist who had to be erased. There were even those who considered themselves as leftist and nationalists by refusing any American influence and sought to demonstrate their leftism through joining European thought and pedagogy, despising everything that came from the United States. As if, from the cultural identity point of view, there was some progress in lowering a colonizing flag only to raise another equally colonizing. (BARBOSA, 2002, p. 15)

Despite the controversies found in relation to the philosophical and educational theory spread by John Dewey, the influence of this scholar is undeniable, amid the aforementioned fields. We recall, thus the need to establish a separation between what his political beliefs were and the economic reality experienced at the period. We emphasize the words of Leonardo Sartori Porto, with which we agree:

> It is necessary, however, to resolve a possible misunderstanding regarding Dewey's political convictions: the fact he was a defender of liberalism, does not mean he defended the

contemporary version of economic liberalism that exempts the great capital from its social responsibilities; on the contrary, the philosopher defended what was later called social liberalism; in other words, a democratic system where there is a social control to prevent the emergence of inequalities between individuals. This social control would not occur through direct governmental intervention, but through education, once a more democratic education enables "a more equitable and informed social order". (PORTO, 2006, p. 43-44)

We had, in this subsection, the intent of tracing the general aspects of the pragmatist thought developed by John Dewey. Next, we have as the foundations of the neopragmatist philosophy, proposed by Richard Rorty; which take up and reconfigure Dewey's ideal and under which there are peculiar explanations of rappers discourses and productions, as we will present in this paper.

Richard Rorty's neopragmatic thought and the importance of art as a social tool

Born in 1931 in New York City, Richard Rorty was a philosopher who held a fruitful work in the fields of philosophy, politics and literary theory, having been consolidated as one of the leading thinkers of contemporaneity.

Influenced by the socialist and democratic ideas of his parents, who were political activists and writers - but also by the works of different philosophers such as Hegel, Heidegger, James, Wittgenstein, Quinte, Gadamer, Derrida, Nietzsche and Dewey (DAZZANI, 2010), Rorty is considered the founder of the neopragmatist philosophical current.

The neopragmatism comes at the end of the 1970's, when Richard Rorty publishes the work *"Philosophy and the Mirror of Nature"*. Through this work, he established the critical theories that conceive knowledge and truth as correspondence between our minds and external reality, sustaining metaphysical dualisms of mind-body type, such as universalism-relativism, rationalism-irrationalism, science-art. (DAZZANI, 2010)

Anti-foundationalist, like John Dewey, Rorty believes in the absence of a fixed concept of truth, such as the one that has governed the traditional philosophy of the West, from ancient Greece. For Rorty, the truth is found in the cultural sphere, through the experience, the societal and interactive practice of the subject, that is, something that should be put apart from the idealism or abstract constructions arising from philosophy. Also, he thought there was, within the traditional philosophy, an erroneous use of language as representation, which should be, rather, a kind of tool facilitating the interaction between subjects that make up a particular group or community.

For Rorty, what linguists understand by "language", an ontologically fixated concept, simply does not exist. The phenomenon that occurs in society's environment, and that Rorty understands as language, presupposes communication, the construction of common elements in social exchanges and interactions that take place among the experiences.(GHIRALDELLI, 2005).

Unlike Dewey - who believed in experience and moral education, of scientistic basis to transform realities - Rorty works with the importance of the effect of language arrengements through the practical life of the communities in which different traditions, vocabulary and ways of thinking and acting coexist.

In his proposal, therefore, he replaces the idea of objectivity of scientistic-transformative experience with the notion of intersubjectivity (or solidarity), which takes into account the interactions and cultural exchanges effected through communication. Explaining how this new social situation would take place, Rorty tells us:

> Our certainty will be related to dialogues between people, more than a matter of interaction with a non-human reality. We will not see, therefore, a gender difference between "nec-

essary" and "contingent" truths. At most, we will see differences in degree of difficulty in objection to our convictions. (RORTY, 1988, p. 128)

In the course of his work, Rorty points out the necessary expansion of vocabulary, even on the part of philosophy; and the importance of the role of so-called "edifying philosophers", whose role would be to spare society of already rooted metaphors and vocabularies, stemming from the foundational school, always remaining open to dialogue and exchange between subjects. According to the neopragmatist, the "edifying philosophers" are in favor of an infinite trend of "tending towards the truth"; and against the "whole truth" configuration seen as absurd. (RORTY cited REALE, 2011, p. 204)

The broad exercise of language between speakers of the constituent social groups of contemporary reality would be, for Rorty, a way to freedom. In the article *"Truth and Freedom"*, there is the following placement, uttered by the philosopher:

> My guess, or at least my hope, is that our culture is gradually becoming structured around the idea of freedom - to let people , dream and think and live for themselves, as they wish, provided they do not infringe pain to other people - and that this idea gives such a viscous glue as that of unconditional validity. (RORTY, Accessed March 14th 2014).

Rorty (2007), in the book *"Contingency, Irony and Solidarity"* - considered one of his most important works - confirms the abandonment of any metaphysical and ontological dimensions and proposes the rescue of a peaceful contingency, based on social cooperative and supportive practices. These practices would be a remnant positive substrate of the ideals of enlightenment, but not yet taken up by men. Such absorption, according to Rorty (2007), would take place only from the establishment of a "new liberal society", consisting of unique subjects, self-sufficient in the use of language and able to rewrite themselves at all times.

In this imaginary society, philosophy and art take on the important function of acting as mediators to linguistic practices, aimed at cultural innovation and improvement of ethical decisions. To philosophers and artists - especially poets and novelists - Rorty gives prime importance because they create new metaphors and new languages on the subject, thus, widening its spectrum of ethical decisions (HERMANN, 2005).

According to Rorty (2007), the group of revolutionaries of the eighteenth century and Romantic poets left us as an inheritance, an important tool for redescription: the imaginary, fundamental regarding the implementation of cultural innovations, necessary for the institution of the new liberal society proposed by him.

> I can sum up with a new description of what revolutionaries and poets of two centuries ago intended to say, in my view. What we saw in the late eighteenth century was that anything could be made to look good or bad, important or unimportant, useful or useless, when redescribed. What Hegel described as the process by which the spirit is gradually aware of its intrinsic nature is best described as the process of European linguistic practices, changing at increasingly rapid pace (...) What romantic expressed as the assertion that the imagination is the central human faculty- and not reason - was the recognition that the talent to speak differently, not aiming at having a good argument, was the main instrument of cultural change (RORTY, 2007, p. 32-33).

Throughout his work, Rorty (2005) reflects on moral attitudes as aestheticized facts. According to Rorty, the contemporary subject is faced with a wide range of possibilities, so that the simple choice of a "style" of life or social "posture", also imply an "aesthetic action", hence the importance of artists and philosophers while supporters that through language, deconstructing stablished socially-intellectual paradigms and proposing new thoughts, new interactions.

Rorty (2007), who advocated the paths of ethics and aesthetics, side by side, open to reinterpretation of language, also attributes fundamental importance to so-called "liberal ironists": renewed human beings, to which all violence is rejected and all truth, questioned. Fearful of old vocabularies, the ironists develop a kind of poetic language and transcend common sense: they are actually intellectually aimed at exercising dialectics and able to develop self-description at any time.

The definition of this group is given as follows, by Rorty (2007, p. 134):

> I will define the "ironist" as someone who meets three conditions: (1) has radical and continuing doubts about the final vocabulary he currently uses, fearing it has been marked by other vocabularies, vocabularies taken as final by people or books faced by it; (2) realizes that the arguments set out in his current vocabulary can not confirm or discard these doubts; (3) to the extent that he reflects about his situation, that person does not think his vocabulary is closer to reality than others, which is in contact with a force other than himself. The ironists are inclined to philosophize, seeing the choice between vocabularies as a choice that is not made within a neutral and universal metavocabulary, nor by an attempt to fight to overcome appearances and get to the reality, more simply as a play of new against the old.

The ironist is thus someone who retains the intention of becoming a better person. Hopeful, he values the literary character of books and works through continuous descriptions and revaluations of his moral identity: the ironist revises himself, others and the culture (HERMANN, 2005).

This idea, based on the criticism of the tradition - by which they inherit vocabularies, values and specific limits - is guided, therefore, in constant metaphorization of the individual. What Rorty (2007) proposes is the abandonment of the requirements for subscribing to the fixed identity of the "self", since they are not timeless nor depart from any foundations.

In the essay *"A world without substance or essence"*, he even refutes the Greek notions dating back to a nature intrinsic to mankind. Rorty says (2005, p 64): *"Pragmatism dispenses this assumption and insists that humanity is an open concept, that the word "human" names not an essence, but a messy, while promising project"*.

Rorty (2007) believes that by transfering to the future of human life the feelings of "respect" and "mystery" attributed by the Greeks to the metaphysical plane, pragmatism may offer the subject the opportunity to make their own ethical choices and to consequently achieve a routine of greater well-being and happiness.

In order to clarify which aesthetic and social place the aesthetic rapper can assume, if seen through the neopragmatist philosophical look, we also present reflections established by another author: Richard Schustermann whose notes about art are presented in the next section.

Richard Schustermann's neopragmatist thought : A look at the rapper art

The reflective attitude adopted by Rorty (2007) admits exceptions under the thought of another neopragmatist theorist, Richard Schusterman (1998) which, while recognizing the promising content brought by rotyana philosophy, does not agree with the constant use of metaphors set to the "self".

Despite also considering the contemporary as a period absolutely devoid of essentialisms - in which morality becomes insufficient to determine the multiple ethical roles assumed by postmodern men and women - Shustermann (1998) presents disagreements to the thought of Rorty (2007), regarding the need to have a coherence regarding the narratives produced by the subject.

For the author, Rorty (2007) proposes a very limited picture of what constitutes life and the aesthetically satisfactory self-creation. Schusterman (1998) believes that this constant recycling of the individual proposed by Rorty (2007) has reached excessive levels related to the private, diverging from public morality, with no such need.

In the work *"Living art: the pragmatist thought and popular aesthetics"* the author explains that:

> This life of an essentially romantic and burlesque style is an insatiable Faustian search of excitement and curiosity for novelty, a search as broad as dysfunctional by the lack of center that it celebrates (...) Unlimited generation of alternative vocabularies and narratives (often inconsistent) of the "self" - that aim to dismantle all stable "self", making it a shifting and growing multiplicity of egos, or descriptions of themselves - making the design of a integral and du rable self look empty and suspect (...) Without such "self", who mantains an identity in through change or changing description, there can not be a "self" able to enrich or expand, and this would nullify Rorty's design of an aesthetic life , making it meaningless (SCHUSTERMAN, 1998, p. 210).

Also starting from the pragmatist reflections proposed by Dewey, Schusterman (1998) suggests similarities between philosophy, and the aesthetic making of experience of life inherent in the subject.

Assessing the contemporary condition, characterized by the force of the mass media and establishment of a consumer society, Schusterman (1998) identifies the recurring presence of a "aestheticization of ethics" as able to escape the hegemony of a corporate morality.

Through the multiple roles and small individual ethics, made by postmodern individuals, Schustermann (1998) notes in today's society that the simple choice of a *modus vivendi* is also a formal selection, an aesthetic action. However, he believes that analyzing contemporary aesthetics is also turning to concepts historically rooted by analytical and continental traditions stemming from the modern ideals, which they attributed an elitist and hermetic positioning to the art, restricted to the contemplation of uncritical receptors.

Schustermann (1998), then, suggests a confrontation to such traditions, heirs of the romantic assumptions of the eighteenth and nineteenth centuries and responsible for "(...) 'museological conceptions' and 'esoteric' of the fine arts" (id., 249).

When discussing the transcending of the concept of art along the traditions and strong distancing consequences and ideological domination entailed through this process, Schusterman (1998) proposes a progressive action of reintegration of making art to everyday life. Such reintegration to be carried out by the popular arts, would gradually deconstruct the legacy of traditions and work also as a critical and libertarian base in relation to the social understanding of art. In this sense, it is justified:

> The popular Art could offer this base, presenting itself as a promising force to guide our concept of art and its institutions towards greater freedom and integration in the praxis of life. The popular arts of media culture (movies, comedies and soap operas, pop music, videos, etc.) are appreciated by all classes of our society; recognizing its aesthetic legitimacy as cultural products would help reduce the oppressive identification of art and aesthetic taste with the socio-cultural elite of high art. Moreover, as even hits critics say, the aesthetic direction of popular art walks towards art reintegration in life. (SCHUSTERMANN, 1998, p. 66)

The author acknowledges that the postmodern aesthetic practices are complex, and course resistent to any clear and agreed definitions. However, he admits that it is also possible to identify some stylistic and thematic traits that are inherent, such as the trend more directed towards recycled appropriation than for a single original creation, the eclectic mix of styles, the enthusiastic adherence to the technology and mass culture, the challenge of "modernist notions" of aesthetical autonomy and artistic purity, the emphasis on the spatial and temporal location than on the universal or eternal. (Schustermann, 1998, p. 145).

As an example, Schusterman (1998) cites the rap music *genre*. According to the author, rap is a current aesthetic reinterpretation that goes back to the tradition of African *griots* and a challenge to traditional conceptions of art as it consists of a complex and polysemic text production.

> An attentive and unimpeded reading reveals within many lyrics spirituous expressions, acute insighst, as well as forms of linguistic subtlety and different levels of meaning, whose polysemic complexity, ambiguity and intertextuality can often oppose to qualities of the alledgedly greatest works. (SCHUSTERMAN, 1998, p. 147)

So it was a genre that - with its verbal power and sound appropriations (collages) - is able to demonstrate that a new textual unit is nothing more than a tissue of echoes of previous texts and fragments. Thus he says:

> I think rap is a postmodern popular art that challenges some of the aesthetic conventions more inculcated, which belong not only to modernism as a style and as an ideology, but to the philosophical doctrine of modernity and sharp differentiation between the cultural spheres. However, while challenging such conventions, rap still satisfies, in my opinion, the standards set more decisive in terms of aesthetic legitimacy, usually denied to popular art. It thus defies any rigid distinction between high art and popular art founded on purely aesthetic criteria, and calls into question the very notion of such criteria. (SCHUSTERMAN, 1998, p. 144)

For Schustermann (1998), rap goes against the consequences of the rationalization project initiated by modernity, whose conception of the world (compartmentalized into three spheres: science, art and morality), kept the art in certain isolation, separated from any and all sensory character with regard to the nature of man.

Based on Jameson, the author argues that the Hip-Hop (movement which includes among its members the rap music genre) - away from the isolation typically related to "high art" - Born in a capitalist context of consumption and dissemination through the mass media, maintaining, at the same time, the lucrative character and critical-instructive posture before his hearers (SCHUSTERMAN, 1998).

> The hip-hop is not outside of what Jameson (a questionable assertion organismic) sees as the "global space totalizer of a new world system" of multinational capitalism - as if the contingent events and the chaotic processes of our world could be aggregated in one space or system! But assuming such a system exists, why lucrative rap implications with some aspects of this system should annul its power of social criticism? We must be completely outside in order to criticize it in fact? Decentralized criticism that postmodernism and post-structuralism are against the final borders, founded ontologically, does not necessarily put into question the very notion of being "totally out"? (SCHUSTERMAN, 1998, p. 162).

Subversive, rap uses the media to spread historically muted cultures and experiences and forgotten by capitalists alienating rostification[3]. Junction of artistic languages, proposed through a new form established in hybridity, rap is now a much debated aesthetic, about which there are still many doubts, questions and assessments.

Trying to qualify it as a "new" aesthetic form, popularized in its ideological aspect also implies the next attempt to rescue theories or proposed to understand such a manifestation; task we seek to fulfill in this chapter - to capture the inspiring wire of its collages, efforts and goals in order to denounce injustices and transgress hedonists institutions, based on the logic of pleasure and immediate consumption.

After this dissertation, through the second chapter, we will continue the presentation of this research. The next section approaches mainly aspects related to identity issues, hybridity and cultural translation.

---

3   For the concept of rostification, see: DELEUZE, G.; GUATTARI, F. **Mil platôs**: capitalismo e esquizofrenia. Rio de Janeiro: Editora 34, 1996. v. 3.

Dissolving borders and translating the present: rap as identity hybridity, social difference and transnationality

We experience a contemporaneity in which there are complex and varied studies regarding identity issues. From the point of view of cultural theory, there are several concepts attributed to identity. The concepts related to social class, ethnicity, sexuality and nationality have proved to be unstable over time, as they did not refer to unified understandings. The old references that applied to modern society have become insufficient in the face of contemporary practices, with all the multiple interactions established and experienced in space-time.

Hall (2007) attributes the decentralization of social identities to the globalization process, which exposes financial antagonisms and establishes the possibility of different life experiences, in which individuals also assume different roles in society. Highlighting the provisions proposed by McGrew (1992), Hall (2007, p. 68) argues:

> (...) "Globalization" refers to those processes, acting on a global scale, that cross national borders, integrating and connecting communities and organizations in new combinations of space and time, making the world more interconnected, in reality and experience. Globalization implies a distantiation of the classical idea of "society" as a well - defined system and its replacement by a perspective that focuses on how social life is ordered over time and space. These new temporal and spatial characteristics that result in the compression of distances and timescales, are among the most important aspects of globalization to have an effect on cultural identities.

The characteristics described by Hall (2006) attest to the fact that with the expansion of interactional possibilities among humans, technological advances and intensifying political and economic forces in the world, the identity certainties have become non-existent.

In this way, thinking globally of "identity" also involves breaking border's stereotypes and recognizing that in the midst of dichotomies hidden by the homogeneity of the term "globalization", there are subjects conditioned to perform different social roles, acting as protagonists of widely divergent life stories with each other.

Silva (2012), on the essay *"The social production of identity and difference"* draws attention to the fact that the terms "identity" and "difference" assume, among each other, dependency links.

> (...) Identity and difference are in a close relationship of dependency. The Affirmative way in which we express identity tends to hide this relationship. When I say "I am Brazilian", it seems that I am referring to an identity that depletes itself. "I am brazilian"- period. However, I just need to make that statement because there are other people who are not Brazilian. In a totally homogeneous imaginary world in which all people would share the same identity, the identity claims would not make sense. In a way, this is exactly what happens with our "human" identity. It is only in very special circumstances that we need to say "we are human". The statement "I am Brazilian", in fact, is part of an extensive chain of "denial" of negative identity expressions, of differences. Behind the statement "I am Brazilian" we should read: "I am not Argentine", "I am not Chinese," 'I am not Japanese' and so on. (SILVA, 2012, p. 74-75).

Silva (2012) explains that these terms are actually cultural creations of language and that, precisely because of this factor, they become unstable and undeterminable. However, those terms are configured as elements of social dispute between men, as they serve for the definition of the individual and can extend (or not) accessed to material and moral possibilities of social welfare.

> In the dispute over identity it is involved a wider dispute by other symbolic and material resources of society. The affirmation of identity and the enunciation of the difference reflected the desire of different social groups, asymmetrically located,

to ensure privileged accessed to social goods. The identity and difference are therefore closely connected with the relations of power. The power to define identity and make a difference can not be separated from wider power relations. The identity and difference are never innocent. (SILVA, 2012, p. 81).

The often subjective, multiple and indeterminate character of identity in contemporary times arises from the complex relationships between social individuals and political-economic system that surrounds them.

On the one hand, there are individuals that devote themselves to the ongoing attempt to define who they actually are and what (or which) segment (s) they may occupy in society; on the other hand, there are systemic delegations and their effects, that at all times, designate social roles to these individuals.

This is a controversial cycle that opposes the exercise of power to the yearnings of 'want to be'.

About this uncertain process of 'search' for a place in society, Bauman (1999) also manifests. In the work *"Identity"*, the author confirms the fact that this 'search' something permanent, a path whose ending culminates in frustration, as the social individual, while experiencing the present, aims always at the uncertain future. Bauman (1999) compares the contemporary identity with a kind of endless mosaic, to which he says:

> Yes, it is necessary to compose your personal identity (or their personal identities?) the way we compose an image with the pieces of a puzzle, but one can compare the biography with an incomplete puzzle, with many missing parts (and never know how many) (...), there is a lot of little pieces on the table, that you expect to join in order to form a meaningful whole - but the image that should appear at the end of this work is not given in advance, so you can not be sure you have all the parts needed to mount it , to have selected the right pieces among those who are on the table, to have them placed in the proper place or that they really fit together to form the final figure at all (Bauman, 2009, p. 54-55).

In this search process for personal essences, mechanisms related to representation become important because they are the tools able to derive some meaning about the social and psychological conditions of their own enunciators. Regarding representations, Silva (2012, p. 91) considers:

> (...)The representation is connected to identity and difference. Identity and difference are closely dependent on the representation. It is through this representation thus understood that the identity and the difference acquire sense. It is through the representation that the identity and the difference now exist. Representing means in this case to say "this is the identity", "identity is that." It is also through the representation that the identity and the difference connect to power systems. Who has the power to represent, has the power of defining and determining identity.

Easy Accessed to technological tools, a common characteristic of our time, however, allows us to find something not seen before: a virtual disclosure of arising representations of minority classes who spread the witness of a life usually immersed in difficulties and denounce the administrative and legal wrong-doing to which they are submitted to.

Driven by the need to belong or for social recognition, individuals propose the holding of enunciations that keep in itself related purposes: on the one hand, they seek to join others virtually who they have cultural similarities with (sharing, for example, habits, memories, traditions and existential difficulties); on the other, they aim at the symbolic confrontation of the system, claiming the acceptance of identity they believe to be due to them and the group to which they belong.

Among the identity manifestations available on the internet, draw attention those that incorporate aesthetic purposes. Unlinked binarisms of the modern traditions, such aesthetic historically transposing earlier limits, describe and dialogue with the social context in a rather politicized way. They are generally characterized by having a hybrid constitution, which incorporates recycled aspects form both elements of tradition and typical factors of the contemporary universe, such as images, people, capital, goods, ideas, etc.

Because of the plurality of sources, hybrid raw material of these productions, the recollection of important studies developed around the encounters between cultures and identities that culminate later in what we call "cultural hybridity" is necessary at this time, a theoretical foundation so important for effectively understanding global movements and their relations with the population groups socially and humanely excluded.

In this sense, researchers Haesbart and Mondardo (2010), in the Article *"Transterritoriality and Antropofagia: Traffic Territorialities from a Brazilian-Latin American Perspective"* highlight two important authors who have offered valuable contributions, precursors of the theories related to cultural hybridity: Fernando Ortiz (1999) and Angel Rama (2007).

According to Haesbart and Mondardo (2010), the first notions that pervade this theme emerge in the 40s, when the Cuban Ortiz (1999), in his work *"Contrapunteo del azúcar y del tobacco"*, proposes the concept of transculturation. Trying to overcome the "European" concept of acculturation and structural miscegenation, he has highlighted the movement of cultures and the creation of new cultural phenomena.

Justified by the absence of a word that could describe the encounter between different subjects and cultures, Ortiz (1999), based on Malinowski, said that the word transculturation:

> (...) Better expresses stages of the process of transition from one culture to another , as this is not only to acquire a different culture, such as rigor suggests the Anglo-Saxon word, "acculturation", but also necessarily implies the loss or uprooting of a previous culture, which could be called a partial deculturation and furthermore means the creation of new cultural

phenomena that might be called neoculturação ("neo-accul-turation") (...) Overall, the process is a transculturalization and this term includes all stages of the trajectory (ORTIZ, 1999 apud HAESBART; MONDARDO, 2010, p. 24).

The Uruguayan Angel Rama (2007), also cited by the re-searchers, was responsible for the appropriation of the concept of "narrative transculturation" and also by applying it in the field of literary studies, in the 1970s.When performing approaches involv-ing the regionalist literary and the arrival of modernity, he diag-nosed the emergence of a new "plastic" literature to which he gave the name of "transcultural literature". Haesbaert and Modardo (2010) cite Rama (2007) to highlight the importance of this no-tion of the mixture of cultures of modern and regional orders "in-cluding what may have incorrect interpretation by considering the passive or inferior part of the contact of cultures, aimed at higher losses, without any creative response".

Issues related to multiculturalism and cultural hybridity take effect in Latin America, by Canclini (2008, p. 29), which de-fines the cultural hybridity as the establishment of (...) sociocultural processes in which discrete structures or practices, that exist sepa-rately, combine to generate new structures, objects and practices".

When considering interactions and settings established in the Latin American scenario, Canclini (2008) comes to the conclu-sion that it is impossible, after the advent of modernity, to speak about essentialism and pure cultures. In the current period, which many call postmodern, objects, ideas, groups are inevitably mixed up. There is no need to talk about archaic, modern, traditional or massive anymore. But rather on cultural identity and plurality.

At the end of his work *"Cultures Hibrids: Strategies for get-ting in and out of modernity"*, Canclini (2008) tells us about *in-ter-gender,* a nomenclature that refers to new forms of expression, born of the interaction of various speeches, like the imagistic, tex-tual and musical discourses. According to him, the subjects in their various performances simulate and reflect daily life and, moreover, always remain open to the possibility of transformative reinterpretation. The author states:

> All cultures are border. All the arts are developed in relation to other arts: crafts migrate from the countryside to the city. Films, videos and songs that narrate events of a people are interchanged with others. Thus, cultures lose their exclusive relationship with its territory, but gain in communication and knowledge. (CANCLINI, 2008, p. 348).

Historian Peter Burke (2006, 2009) is also an important reference in the treatment of issues related to cultural hybridity. In dealing with the presence of this factor in contemporary forms, we believe that we are living in a kind of cultural-global reconfiguration. In this process, practices and products resulting from the massive cultural industry become intertwined with local traditions, generating the emergence of new and resistant strains, therefore constant cultural exchanges arise.

The approaches mentioned here seem perfect to act as guiding factors of this work, due to the origins of rap itself and the societal position in which the migrant groups operate. Both fundamental aspects to this study.

Quite academically explored today - as an aesthetic-urban phenomenon parallel to social segregation and accumulation of regions of poverty around the world - rap is seen as a demonstration that the "emerging" in every big city, is already considered hybrid in its own genesis, since its existence depends on a process of unifying different forms of expression.

Born of a succession of diasporic processes, rap consolidates itself as an aesthetic of permanent novelty, in which the elements of oral traditions that precede it, like *griot* African narrative and *toaster* poetics, assert themselves as pillars subject to continuous recycling and reinterpretation of content and addressed ways.

When talking about the origins of rapper aesthetics, researcher Amarino Queiroz (2005, p. 11-12) demonstrates how this process started:

In the mid-60's of last century, feeding on the spoken songs of Africa, the discourse on electronic musical bases emerged in dances on the outskirts of Kingston, Jamaica, and was amplified, reissuing the traditional counter/singer in another version: the toaster. This, in its turn, would eventually unfold in the DJ and rapper poet within the Hip Hop culture to come. Early in the next decade, what we now identify as rap would give another jump: the economic crisis in the Caribbean, triggering new diasporic process that would make the rhythm & poetry of toasters come to the urban environment of USA post-industrial metropolis, there infiltrating and from there spreading all over the world (...).

While it spreads across the globe, rap absorbs elements of each location it enters, features that will therefore manifest themselves in their own aesthetics-constitution, whether in regard to the verbally content sung, or even in relation to electronic databases that accompany it.

Regarding the narrative rapper, for example, there are evident urban social issues relating to different spaces; issues often controversial that ultimately constitute the driving force of the poetic-narrative established by the song. It is from the daily life that the rapper compositor- takes the experience, feeling and appropriating the raw material that will establish the core of his aesthetic discourse.

In the article *"Culture and Consciousness: the "function" of Rational MCS"*, researcher Jorge Nascimento (Accessed on Sep 10, 2014), returning to the precepts of Benjamin (1994), explains how this process takes place:

> (...) Focusing on what is said in the rap, we can then approach this popular poetic expression that has ancient ancestors in men's expressive formulations. The benjaminian narrators come here disguised as life experiences in the urban struggle and even say: *I was hunted yesterday and today, man!I am the predator" (Otus 500)*. Then, his speech is full of authority. Here, it will be privileged the spoken word, trans-

formed into a sign so that we can, somehow grasp it, even with all the above caveats. But oralized word, technologically enhanced, here has a "social impact" and even deprived of its other performatic attributes , still has, in our view, a communicative strength in unveiling inte esting reviews of reality. (NASCIMENTO, Accessed on September 10th 2014)

With regard to electronic databases, there are also rhythmic and melodic innovations, mixing the primary elements of rapper practice *to* their own *cultural traditions* to the nations in which they come into existence. It is common in that sense, to find, for example, rappers productions composed by Brazilians - as some of you will see later in this research - which simulate in their accompaning bases sounds, rhythms and those similar melodies practiced in traditional aspects of Brazilian music, like samba and MPB[4].

Rap is,therefore, an element in constant transformation, given from the meeting between its originating aspects and traditions and the socio-cultural dynamics present in each new location where it is acting. Thus, initially, we could consider it as what Canclini (1995), in the work *"Consumers and citizens: multicultural conflicts of globalization"*, calls of *glocal* manifestation*:* something which constitutes a demonstration at the same time, global - disseminated through massive technological apparatus - and local - due to its peculiar forms, regionalized and distinct from each other.

Nevertheless, when it comes to considering the presence of multiterritories, made possible because of technological and digital advances, rap still lacks nomenclatures and philosophical and cultural theories that adequately reflect it as an aesthetic manifestation associated with popular culture. Already in the early stages of this research, we dare to propose then a little questioning in relation to the characteristic elements of rap, appointed by Schustermann (1998)[5]. It is not about considering rap as an aesthetic whose em-

---

4   Available at <http://www.pacc.ufrj.br/z/ano5/3/index.php>. Acessed on: set 10th . 2014.

5   See page 35

phasis is more regarding its location than its universality. Rather, as contemporary aesthetics, rap also takes advantage of features of the multiterritory and virtually acts politically reverberating local voices, direct towards the issues inherent in the present historical context.

Among the rappers productions that call our attention in this sense are those produced by diaspora groups and their direct descendants.

Such aesthetics are notable in the virtual space and visibly act as identity negotiations, addressing immigrants and their absorption by the systematicaly structured poverty.

It is understood that the border position of immigrants evidentiates even more the unstable situation of their identities. The foreigner, generally helpless by the laws, becomes an individual suffering the moral and cultural effects of this condition.

Socially seen in the image of a "marginal man", he absorbs the cultural rules of the new country, being conditioned to often undesirable and instigated hybridizations of the symbolic negotiation of identity. This negotiation finds an important ally in cyberspace, since it has the opportunity to expand the intellectual interactions between subjects.

Although cyberspace is not the main objective of this research, it is necessary to conceptually consider it, since it propagates immigrants productions, analyzed at a later time.

Castells (2008) defines cyberspace as a network society, a global village, a dynamic scenario based on the flow and exchange of information, capital and culture. Cyberspace and internet are for Castells (2008), in fact, synonyms. The author understands the space as a featured network due to the multiplicity of services and products it offers, including being able to make changes in the routines of various segments (social, cultural, economic, political, educational, etc.).

Recuero (2009) reminds us that after the decade of 1990, the virtual space had an even greater interaction of people. This was due to the emergence of a number of tools aimed at socialization: such as the creation of websites related to information sharing and content production *(weblogs, Slideshare, Youtube,* among others). In accordance with Castells (2008), Recuero (2009) also said that we live in times of "networks". On the term, the researcher says:

> Social networking is people, is interaction is social exchange. It is a group of people, understood through a metaphoric structure; the network structure. Network nodes represent each individual and their connections, the social bonds that make up the groups. These ties are magnified, complexificated and modified through every new person we meet and interact. (RECUERO, 2009, p. 29).

True "arenas" capable of embracing people or different interest groups, social networks include the organization of individuals and groups, mediated by their computers, dealing with various issues, ranging from personal interests, to issues related to the economy, political and corporate reality.

Santaella (2003) in the work *"posthuman cultures and arts: From the media culture to cyberculture"* also discusses the advantages and possibilities offered by the virtual environment. Santaella Says (2003, p. 103):

> When connected to digital networks, the computer lets people exchange all kinds of messages between individuals or within groups, participating in electronic conferences on thousands of different topics, having Accessed to public information in the computers participating in the network, being able to calculate machines located thousands of kilometers, building together purely ludic virtual worlds - or more serious - constituting one another an immense living encyclopedia, developing political projects, friendships, cooperation.

Regarding the nature of this space, it is important to apply the provisions of Trivinho (2007). In this sense, the author uses the term "glocal" to refer to the environment created by the internet. According to him, it is an environment that is neither exclusively global or exclusively local. In this environment, a specific logic exists (to which the author calls "dromocracy"), in which the traditional concepts related to territory and social organization of ideas are diluted. What we have, in fact, is a new way of living, a new culture based on speed media and technological devices.

> The cyberculture, digital construction in and of history, when sewing indissolubly dromocratic sophistication and media saturation, presents itself as an advanced glocal civilization. Under the base of computerization, virtualization and ciberespacialization of social life in cities, towns and other urban affluent perimeters (...), most of the social and cultural values are significantly modified, some entirely unrecognizable as they are expressed in relation to time and space, with the urban and social, with local and transnational cultures, with the body, with the identity and otherness (...). (TRIVINHO, 2007, p. 25)

The intention of working with songs of the ideological-rap produced by immigrants, assumes that these songs, although spread through a "glocal" environment, address issues of transnational order, architected throughout history.

Quite recurring on the internet, the immigrant songs are undoubtedly products that reflect the environment itself - territories connected to the global ideology and its consequences, such as the "structural poverty" seen in all parts of the world.

Their issuers, voices of foreign classes, perform in hybrid languages, the reality of a period which reflects the effects of world history itself - architected in exploitative practices, based on the violent logic of oppression and profit.

To aesthetically represent this period, said immigrant song confronts the recipient with the image represented as a often overlooked "real world". Full of descriptions that sound "uncomfortable" and "violent" to those who are unaware of this context, foreign rappers' songs keep the complaint tone and consciousness, being composed from the inspiration provided by the very act of living. Considering them implies, therefore, to admit that they "honor" hard purposes of the ideological rapper strand and are conscious compositions; in which the pedagogical aspect assumed by the song, in relation to minorities, is paralelly developed to the quest for recognition in society - both of the composers voices, and of the "other voices", represented by them.

The immigrants rappers songs carry, thus, all the impetus proposed by the present ideologically rapper that, historically disconnected from classifications and practices considered as part of the "high culture" and the "great knowledge", are devoted to didacticism and suggestions, necessary for the overhaul of the regulatory mechanisms of social functioning.

In the article "*Titanic sank: poetry, culture, rap and society*", Nascimento (2011) highlights the functioning of the ideological rapper strand. The researcher explains that this is a strand devoted to the establishment of communications, and whose performance is given differently to what is generally termed as "poetry". Thus, he argues:

> As the "ideological" rap is a means of transmission of messages considered important for their "authors", it is obvious that such a poetic representation moves, often in a different direction to what is commonly termed as "poetry". The search for 'knowledge', one of the precepts of the Hip Hop movement - of which rap is an integral part - should also be made for seeking recognition of the value of these voices, and that value would be measured by the level of effectiveness of such poetic educational discourse (NASCIMENTO, 2011, p. 218).

The study of these immigrants songs, whose ideological content in our view manifests itself incontrovertibly, allows once again that we should turn to Bakhtin's theory (1992) which was one of the first theorists to link the issue of language to power relations.

In the book "*Marxism and Philosophy of Language*", Bakhtin (1979) sets out the word as an instrument related to the consciousness of men.

Regardless of the quality of absorption of linguistic signs by the subject (material knowledge); the external word expresses ideologies and inserts itself in all social relations. According to Bakhtin:

> (...) The word is not only the purest, more indicative sign; it is also a neutral sign. Each of the other systems of signs is specific to a particular field of ideological creation. Each domain has its own ideological material and formulates signs and symbols that are specific and are not applicable to other areas. The sign, then, is created by a precise ideological function and remains inseparable from it. The word, in contrast, is neutral with respect to any specific ideological function. It can fill any kind of ideological function: aesthetic, scientific, moral, religious. (BAKHTIN, 1979, p. 37).

Bakhtin (1979), therefore, understands the word as part of a historical and ideological system; something social, that manifests the interaction between people and allows them the realization of both agreements and direct confrontation, something that occurs through the application of speeches of different natures. "We know that every word appears as a miniature arena where social values of contradictory guidance intertwine and fight. The word is revealed at the time of its expression, as a product of interaction of social forces". (BAKTIIIN, 1979, p. 67).

The bakthinian positioning about the possibilities of ideological appropriation regarding the linguistic signs, is associated with the reactionary and hybrid nature of the constituent speech of the songs analyzed in this study and also refers to the theoretical provisions of another author: Roland Barthes (2004).

Just as Bakhtin (1979), Barthes (2004) also sees language as a phenomenon resulting from social reality. The author defends the fact that every spoken word is part of a kind of network called "sociolect".

For Barthes (2004), the use of language monitors the stratification so as to be an idiomatic instrument in varying ways, in accordance to the group that applies it.

According to Barthes (2004) there were two types of sociolects: one linked to the hegemonic discourse relations (so-called "discourses of power" or "encratic", from the state apparatus and its agents), the other of counter-hegemonic and revolutionary nature (so-called "acratic" discourses, which constitute at the same time, questions and attempts to "take power"). In these terms, the author defines:

> Thus, as Aristotle in the work "Rhetoric", distinguished two types of evidence: the *internal* evidence to tékhne (*éntekhnoi*) and the *external* evidence to tékhne (*átekhnoi*), I suggest to distinguish themselves from the original two groups of sociolects: speeches *in power* (to the shadow of power) and the speeches *out of power* (or powerless, or even in the light of the non-power); using pedantic neologisms (but how do otherwise?), let's call the first *encratic* speeches and second, the *acratic* speeches (BARTHES, 2004, p. 127, emphasis added).

Surely the immigrants songs discussed in this work are of "acratic" nature. By sharing a "greater characteristic" inherent to rap genre - the verbal momentum overwrites the sound accompaniment - such objects of study externalize a counter hegemonic look, consisting of multicultural experiences and of a capitalist exploratory reality (both characteristics of the "global" context), which abroad is generally subjected.

With the protagonism of plural subjects in their own identities and subjectivities, immigrant rap reveals the existence of an "in-between" place aesthetically occupied by the foreign individual. This individual, integrating different languages and cultures, devotes himself to the creation of identity ties with foreigners from other parts of the world. By launching his voice amid the cyberspace, he also throws the attempt to in fact "socially exist" finding others in the same conditions and, join forces with them to try to achieve the recognition of this group and reverse the condition of neglect to which the immigrants are subjected.

Speaking of immigrant rap is considering the presence of speakers who see in aesthetization a way to stop the muting to which they have been or are submitted, the song is, in that sense, a tool used for a need: the need for expression. Thus, the rap expands senses and enables individual experiences or small groups' experiences to echo in other communities, allowing the emergence of identifications resulting from experience that "describes" "poeticizes" and "performs".

This is a musical type that tells the loneliness and abandonment of the immigrant and exposes to those who never went through such a reality, the truth of an "other" universe, doomed to exclusion. In the dark uncertainty of cyberspace, we find in the form of rap numerous voices of immigrants, loose and determined to raise gather other voices, intending to create a speech that destabilize or even deconstructs the official hegemonic discourse.

Let us remember Bhabha (2007) and Hall (2007), thinking the cultural aspects through postcolonial criticism, drawing special attention to relations between the colonizers and the less favored societies, proposing interesting considerations, linked to the process of cultural translation.

Both work with the issue of discursive polyphony of cultures, the result of the identity formation in history of cultural clash, whose work seeks affirmative responses or negotiations for their permanence, in oppressive territories.

Bhabha (2007), for example, believes that beyond the tensions and paradoxes established from these relations between the oppressors (settlers) and the oppressed (colonized), there are individuals whose identity formation takes place amid this scenario of exploitation. In it, these individuals then begin to make connections between facts and often question the established history, launching a new look at it. In the work "*The local of culture*", Bhabha (2007, p. 228) proposes the following reflection:

> Cultural difference is not simply a dispute between oppositional content or antagonistic traditions of cultural value. Cultural difference introduces within the process of cultural judgment and interpretation, that sudden shock of the succes-

sive moment of meaning, not synchronic. The very possibility of cultural contestation, the ability to change the knowledge base, or to engage in the "war of position", marks the establishment of new forms of meaning and identification strategies. Designations of cultural difference interpellate forms of identity that, due to its continue implication in other symbolic systems, are always "incomplete" or open to cultural translation.

In his approach, Bhabha (2007) emphasizes the importance of cultural expressions spoken by minorities, believing that these are always subject to cultural translation processes. According to the author, the fact that they promote new meanings around the story itself would generate too, within these enunciating groups, the ability to produce aesthetic products and independent moral views of any cultural inflexibility, that are hybrid constitutions themselves, disassociated from any cultures or fixed identities.

Such manifestations - in fact, identity negotiations established at an individual or collective level - would bring with them the responsibility to reveal the existing spatio-temporal disjunctions in modern society, claiming the right to meanings, appropriated under the sign of violence, by colonizing classes.

> The community ("comunidade") is the antagonistic supplement of modernity: within the metropolitan area, it is the territory of the minority, endangering the requirements of civility. within the Transnational world it becomes the boundary problem of diasporic, migrants, of refugees. The binary divisions of social space have neglected the deep temporal disjunction - the time and space of translation - By which the minority communities negotiate their collective identifications (BHABHA, 2007, p. 317).

Using the benjaminian conceptions exposed in *"the task of the translator"*, Bhabha (2007) seeks to suggest a less totalitarian approach to translations. In the author's opinion, they should encourage decentralization, considering exactly the *untranslatable* and *foreignity of language* as central themes throughout the translation process. In Bhabha (2007), intercultural communication functions as a kind of revenge possible to migrants, while translations would be a way to understand them. For the author, the cultural translation is actually an interdisciplinary and constant reinterpretation moment. The path leading to the understanding of the other, never admits, the application of theories and conceptual bases taken as absolute. Faced with the "translation of foreign" any essentialism starts to become an arbitrariness.

Regarding intercultural translation

Considering a possible translation process, Bhabha (2007) refers to theorists like Paul Mann and Derrida, declaring himself then as a little worried about the possible metonymic loss of an original text. According to the author:

> Translation is the performative nature of cultural communication. language is more an actu (enunciation, positionality) than a in situ language (énoncé or propositionality). And the sign of translation shows, or sings, continuously, the different times and spaces between cultural authority and its performative practices. The time of translation represents that movement of meaning, the principle and practice of communication that, in Paul de Man's words, "puts the original in place to destigmatize it, giving it the fragmentation of movement, a wandering of wanderings a kind of permanent exile" (...) The cultural translation desacralizes transparent assumptions of cultural supremacy, and this act requires a contextual specificity, a historical differentiation within the minoritary positions.(BHABHA, 2007, p. 313-314).

Following arguments similar to those proposed by Bhabha (2007), Hall (2007) in his work *"Cultural identity in postmodernity"*, analyzes the identity changes crossed by the modern subject that culminated with the advent of globalization, in a time of crisis and dilution of great centers of power and identity formations.

By analyzing the experience of diaspora to which the Caribbean underwent in Britain, Hall (2007) points to the existence of hybridity as a violent form of adaptation to which the subjugated peoples are subjected to. He states:

> The hybridization does not refer to hybrid individuals who may be contrasted with the "traditional" and "modern" as fully formed subjects. It is a process of agonistic cultural translation, since it isn never completed, but remains unfinished. (HALL, 2007, p. 74).

From this perspective, Hall (2007) considers the concept of cultural translation, as absolutely necessary to ensure the survival of the identity groups located in the context of "border", originated from the postcolonial reality. Translation allows visibility to these groups, acting as an instrument to reveal hybridity and question formations, guaranteeing their permanency to such groups. Hall says (2007, p 88-89):

> This concept (translation) describes those identity formations that cross and intersect natural boundaries, composed of people who were scattered forever from their homeland. These people retain strong ties to their places of origin and their traditions, but without the illusion of a return to the past. They are required to negotiate with the new cultures in which they live, without simply being assimilated by them and without completely losing their identities. They carry traces of cultures, traditions, languages and particular stories by which they were marked. The difference is that they are not and will never be unified in the old sense, because they are irrevocably the product of several interconnected stories and cultures, belonging to several "houses" at the same time (and not to a private house).

Thus, unable to rediscover any kind of pure identity, such identity formations affirm and reaffirm themselves constantly from their hybrid cultural practices, which are nothing more than a sublimating process[6], which demonstrates that the present of these groups is actually the result of a centralized and tyrannical past.

> Persons belonging to these *hybrid cultures* have been forced to give up the dream or ambition to rediscover any kind of lost "cultural purity" or ethnic absolutism. They are irrevocably *translated*. The word translation, as noted by Salman Rushdie, comes etimologic ously, from the Latin, meaning "transfer"; "carry across borders". Migrant writers, like him, who belong to two worlds at once, "having been transported across the world (...) are translated men". They are the product of the *new diasporas* created by postcolonial migration. They must learn to live at least two identities, speak two cultural languages, translate and negotiate between them. Hybrid cultures are one of several types of new distinctive identity produced in modernity. (HALL, 2007, p. 89).

In this work, we are addressing these new diasporas, which reverberate not only the violent sign of ancient settlements, but next

---

6   Sublimation - Defense mechanism by which the psychic energy of trends and primitive unacceptable impulses, turns and heads towards socially acceptable goals, that is, the unconscious shifts power of certain reprehensible and unacceptable trends, achievements considered "superior". Thus, the instinctual needs and unacceptable impulses find, in sublimation, an "exit" a way for "normal" expression. Those trends and unacceptable primitive impulses - with goals by personal example, selfish, prohibited "irregular" - are transformed and their energy is directed to activities say scientific, altruistic, political, artistic, etc., by the sublimation mechanism. so we see that the individual at the same time eliminates or reduces possibilities of perversion, neuroses, psychic abnormalities, through sublimation forwards its attention and its potential for positive achievements and creations. Thus we have developed great social and cultural promotions based on the work of a person, and also many great achievements in science, literature, religion, etc. Therefore, the sublimation is seen as the most important unconscious mechanism for normal functioning. PORTAL DA PSIQUE, acessed on jun. 13th 2014

to it, witness the stigmata filed by a new form of, more current and perhaps more violent colonization: capitalism.

Capitalism is an economic system that generates more harm than virtues, especially in socio-spatial context. There is, every day, the incidence of its detrimental effects - either through damage to the environment (such as the constant pollution and disorderly geographic growth of large cities), or the permanent amplification in unemployment and violence; aspects that culminate and externalize the world's great misery.

Amid the harmful consequences caused by this system are also national and international migration, - carried out by groups marked by colonial history and driven by promising systemic speeches leading up to the image of a benevolent hegemony, wishing well and offering better conditions of survival.

By addressing, in this work, the aestheticized reflection given by some of the protagonists of the so called "international migration", we believe we can also speak of performative testimonies of the "new diaspora". The intention is, therefore, to propose an "other applicability" to the statements established by Canclini (2005; 2008), Bhabha (2007) and Hall (2003; 2007), transferring their findings to lead an attempt of interpretation of this reality.

Therefore, we attempted, through this research, the challenge of recognizing and interpreting these "songs of the becoming", manifestations of the present that strive to poetically narrate the gaps caused by the expatriation, and consequences of denial and dispossession of citizenship-related rights. Also at the end of this study , we seek to attest to the classification of these events as something that, at the same time, can be considered as the result of the clash (BHABHA 2007; HALL, 2003; 2007) and cultural wealth (CANCLINI, 2005; 2008).

Although largely present in the cyberspace, immigrants songs and performances remain targets of estrangement and ignorance of those who do not live, in fact, the place of enunciation. Essentially oral and devoid of any written records, such forms remain as hermetic texts of the virtual space, arousing curiosity and the need for an urgent translational-interpretative study.

Aiming at the task of understanding and revealing the reflective *ethos* that makes up such aesthetic manifestations, we devote ouserlves to this complex cultural translation task. In order to untie the possible linguistic and cultural bonds - while knowing the impossibility of achieving synonyms and perfect reinterpretation - a comparative analysis of songs and videos treated in this work, focusing on similarities between socio-cultural and ideological conjunctures distanced the course of Western hegemonic history .

We seek to understand what is this place of enunciation, inhabited by rhizomatic groups, who at the same time have in common the fact that they have transposed the geographical boundaries of the globe and the constant effort of ideological transposition: through the art of the word they find the right measure to assert themselves as worthy of social recognition, denouncing injustice and a series of rejections to which they are submitted to on a daily basis.

Deslocating themselves virtually, deepening the look on another, whose reality is physically distant, but virtually near through the screens of computers and televisions in alternative channels, open to various aesthetic expressions and new possibilities.

Translating what is still little known, entering the unseen in the academic field, transiting through languages and cultures, discussing them... There are, in fact, many objectives of this work and to the tasks assigned to the cultural translation.

Researchers Ana Isabel Borges and José Marildo Nercolini (2003) remind us that to translate someonelse's culture, it is necessary to allow the same achievement without perpetrating rules, imposing systems. Translating the culture of someone, as stated by Borges and Nercolini (2003), is actually allowing themselves to be transformed by the other. In these terms, the researchers say:

> If I do not allow the Other to penetrate me and do its "damage", questioning what is my own, I will not allow the cultural translation to be carried out in a consistent way, as the attempt to reduce another culture to existing standards in my imposition. I am exercising the power of command.

The cultural translation calls for an erotic relationship (understanding the Other not as a threat to their own existence, but as a challenge and promise) in which the subject certainly comes out different and transformed at the end of the process,. They are still themselves, but penetrated by the Other (BORGES; NERCOLINI, 2003, p. 74).

Other authors also address the issue of cultural translation. Burke (2006, p. 55), for example, states that the concept of cultural translation is used to "(...) describe the mechanism through which cultural encounters produce new and hybrid forms." The author also points out that the term translation "(...) has the great advantage of emphasizing the work that has to be done by individuals or groups to domesticate what is foreign, in other words, the strategies and tactics employed". (BURKE, 2006, p. 58)

In the work *Cultural translation in early modern Europe*, Burke (2009) stresses the importance of translation as a discipline capable of generating studies, particularly of historical character. Based on the anthropological research of Evans and Pritchard, Burke (2009) fundaments his concept of cultural translation, understanding this process as a kind of specific study, based on intercultural communication, established either in a specific social context, or even a textual unit.

For Burke (2009), cultural translation is a kind of negotiation that can be understood as a double process of decontextualization and recontextualisation, that first seeks to appropriate something strange and then domesticates it. As the author points out, this is a process that involves, always, losses and gains.

Translation between languages can be seen not only as an example of this process, but also as a kind of sunflower role, which makes it unusually visible or audible. For the receiver, it is a medium gain, enriching the host culture, as a result of skilful adaptation. From The donor's point of view, on the other hand, the translation is one form of loss, leading to misunderstandings and violating the original (BURKE, 2009, p. 16).

In order to enable the cultural translation task - disregarding any intentions related to "domesticating" proposed above, but aiming only at cultural contact and the understanding of these "other" migrants in new diasporas exercised in multi-territories - we have selected specific products, to be interpreted through this research.

It was necessary, therefore, to also adopt as a guiding framework, the concepts of another category of traductory studies: intersemiotic translation. Through this, it was possible to transcend the verbal sign, seizing the gregarious sense of poetic orality amid other artistic manifestations.

In order to understand the foundations that underlie the theory of intersemiotic translation, we turn to the work of Plaza (2003), homonymous.

According Plaza (2003), the theory to first define the concept of inter-semiotic translation was by Roman Jakobson (2007) [7]. To quote him, Plaza (2003, p. 11) offers the following explanation for the term:

> The Intersemiotic translation or "transmutation" was for him defined as the kind of translation, which consists in the interpretation of verbal signs by means of non-verbal signs or from one sign system to another, for example, the verbal art for music, dance, cinema or painting.

In his opening arguments about the translation exercise properties - based on the monadic concept of History, proposed in the *"History of Philosophy Thesis"*, Walter Benjamin (1994) - Plaza (2003) atributtes to translation the property of recovering history. According to the author, an effective recovery of the history would be given by means of three ways, namely:

---

7   He proposes the following classification in categories that refer to translations of verbal language: 1) Intralanguage translation: is the interpretation of verbal signs by means of other signs of the same language; 2) interlanguage translation: is the interpretation of verbal signs by means of another language; 3) inter-semiotics translation: it consists in the interpretation of verbal signs by means of non-verbal signs.

1) "As poetic-political or artistic strategy towards a construction project of the present": in this case, are offered, through a critical artistic - perspective, other versions of history; with translation acting as an invitation to counterhegemonic reflections;

2) "As a capitalist practice of accumulation": this, as an appeal to the old, incites consumption like a fetish. Incurs in this category, an appeal to constancy, the recovery of the traditional establishment of that as novelty; a factor that reverses the translation product, making it an instrument of capitalism;

3) "As an elective-affinity": in which there is an insertion of the history of sensitivity not only in a poetic but also political project. Such a project would act as an reorganizing factor of the perception of the system of relations and sensitivity in dialogue with the "new"; ambiguous and also dialectic category.

Plaza (2003) points out that the last of the categories listed, is the more "tuned" to the translation process, and dialogues towards the "new" are something that can be studied from Charles Peirce's theory "(...) as being that production feature of the artwork, in other words, the 'idea' as an icon, not as updated possibility" (PLAZA, 2003, p. 8).

Based on overlaps and the recycling processes, the rapper aesthetics, even when isolated from its imagery performances, consists of a series of simulated narratives. Voices, melodies and sounds come together constituting a single and hybrid matrix, where at the same time dialogue externalizes how relations are given nowadays.

In the Article *"Mó mamão, só catá, demorô, ó só: traduzindo o rap dos Racionais MC'"*, Nascimento (2006) argues about the rapper composition. For the researcher, such aesthetics enable the emergency of new poetic possibilities - in which multiple sounds and verses that are also reflections of real life affect – event acting as mediators of discourse. The "technologically mediated" talk, proposed by rap, suggests a smorgasbord of sounds and verses that aim to act uniquely and performatively, establishing itself as a palimpsest filled with complex meanings.

Following thus the line established by the studies of Plaza (2003), we understand that a contemporary phenomena like rap - often associated with technological apparatus - are actually flows that externalize and establish a kind of sensory and not categorized culture, parallel to the official and hegemonic culture. Within these flows, senders and receivers of art set countercultural communications, recover oppressive pasts, promoting aesthetic that propose the critical reinterpretations of reality and its official historical narratives. Through these flows a conceptual challenge of art in history is released, by which the construction of the "new" in reality, unknown but desired in justices and reformulations is encouraged.

The art, now far from contemplation and purisms related to authorship, is invited to join the problems and virtues of the historical present, to launch in contributions and changes to a complex social present and stratified inequalities. About the dimensions assumed by contemporary art, Plaza says (2003, p. 12):

> Contemporary art is, therefore, not more than an immense and formidable bricolage of history in synchronic interaction, where the "new" appears rarely, but has the ability to appear just from this interaction. The current period is characterized by the coexistence of previous periods that, isolated, provide us with the infrastructural conditions for material development of art as a sphere of the superstructure. Hence the arts of primary activities, craft, industrial, secondary tertiary and quaternary activities. The current period has reached the stage of the electronics revolution, that offers an universe of information and knowledge through technologies that operate in a similar way to the human brain, at high speeds. This stage of civilization and its system of production tend to replace the industrial assembly line as the most complete expression of modernity, and therefore the tendency to descentrallization and simultaneous information exchange. A linear historical and hierarchical view is not possible anymore, as each people,

country or place provide us with the information from which you can draw a story. One can even retrieve history, as long as it is stored by a computer.

Thus, given the need to establish a translation process that would capture beyond the literal aesthetic expressions, making it possible to contextualize art before the sociocultural reality in which it is produced, intersemiotic translation has also been used in this research. About the importance of this, Campos states ([20--] p. 283):

> The intersemiotic translation, in my view, extends the horizon of artistic enjoyment and at the same time, according to the very poundian concepts, may constitute a form of criticism, especially when it is a translation not merely literal, constituting a proposal that requires from the translator one molecular "approach" covering the form without losing the emotional tension of the original poem, which still requires a knowledge of artistic repertoire and even biographic facts of its original author.

In the case of immigrant rap, specifically, we acknowledge the emergence of possible difficulties during said translation process. The fast-talking exercised in foreign languages or divided into two or more signs, the visual and verbal aggression, the intent of the enunciator to devote songs to listeners seen as "ideal", in other words, equal in precarious experiences and life stories, make this decoding of aesthetic elements available in digital media a little more complex and restricted.

However, it must be admitted that this fact only magnifies the role of such a task. Decoding these signs and transporting them to "open coding", ready to be widely understood by the various cultures that make up the Western culture, it is also a cross-cultural act that can contribute to the disruption of conservative and intolerant ideas that hover on the subject. Assisting in the acceptance of what is different, not giving it a specific identity or behavioral classification (this would be an arbitrary conduct), but simply seeing them respectfully... The translation process we set out to accomplish was guided in that way.

As highlighted by Jorge Luis Pardo, respect is a fundamental part of the attempt to understand "the other".

> Respecting differences can not mean "allowing the other to be as I am" or "allowing the other to be different from me" just like I'm different (from the other), but allowing the other to be as I am not, allowing the other to be this one that can not be me, that I cannot be, that can not be a (another) me; means letting the other be different, let it be a difference that is not an absolute difference between two identities, but difference of identity, letting it be an alterity that is not different related to me "or related to the similar" but that is absolutely different, unrelated to identity or sameness (PARDO, apud SILVA, 2012, p. 101).

Unraveling the large existing palimpsest existing within these songs was an attempt to hear what the groups of immigrants who make up the analytical body of this work have to say and, more than that, to understand the movements of the world, turning the light on historical arbitrariness, if not unknown, at least little discussed as of yet, in the academic and social field. Art is one of the practices that reflects the time and brings together the story as Plaza (2003) points out.

> I mean, in short, that the past-present-future, or original-translation-reception, are necessarily crossed by social and artistic means of production, as is the translation of the moments of history to the present appearing as the dominant form "not the truth of the past, but the intelligible construction of our time"(PLAZA, 2003, p. 13).

Thus, despite the widely recurrent "losses" to most jobs related to transcriptions and translations, we believe that this research, above all, is an attempt to see an important part with regards to the history of the contemporary world: the displacements caused by its own global dynamics and social relations arising from them - a result also of previous issues related to the settlement and exploitation of territories.

Such shifts, translated into rapper art, launch inquiries into the present, a foreseeable future in relation to imposed pasts. But more than that, once devoted to decoding, they can also contribute to our own conception of the different motivations that trigger the movement of our global present and can also compose not-so-distant futures.

Once the proposals and considerations for this section are finished, we initiate the next chapter, which discusses the fundamentals of performance and applicability of these grounds towards rapper art.

Brief observations on rap and performance

"Rhythm and Poetry" expression carries in itself clues about the aesthetic to which it refers. Contrary to the reception of some musical genres, good apprehension of a rap song dispenses naive interpretations, gathering sound overlaps and verses that have the ability to communicate, first of all.

In these terms, it is possible to associate rap to the concept of performance that, although it is an open concept, applied to various activities and, in general, difficult to define, it refers to the artistic processes of exchange between the sender and receiver, to the idea of art in movement.

Pavis (2010) in *"Contemporary Storyboard"*, comprises contemporary performance as something closely linked to action. The author states:

> In the field of art, the term "performance" (in French "performance", or in English "performance art") also designates a genre that has developed considerably in the 1970s in the United States. In both senses of the term, the performance indicates that an action is performed by the artists, which is also a result of this execution. (PAVIS, 2010, p. 44).

Zumthor (1997), on the other hand, establishes the performance as a form of representation; something which presupposes the existence of an audience, being directly prepared for it. Through the application of visual and verbal resources, the performance makes the song an immediate tool of identitary recognition, able to "transport" the listener to the emotional sensations of experiences lived in daily life.

In the work *"Performance , Reception and Reading"* (2007), the author explains the origin of the term "performance". According Zumthor (2007), the word has European roots, and between the 1930's and 1940's, it was widely used by US researchers - like Abrams, Ben Amos, Dundee, Lomax and others - that took it as a constitutive concept inherent to recreational cultural expressions (singing, song, ritual, dance).

Such a view, however, given the transmission performance as a scientific object - Conducted through impressions or conferences - was gradually being deconstructed.

Zumthor (2007) states that, starting at 1950, the performance begins to be seen as a central aspect of communication held in orality, the subject of studies in Linguistics and fundamental to pragmatic and generative issues. On the term, the author says:

> Anthropological and non-historical term, relative, on one hand, to the conditions of expression and to the perception, on the other, that the performance represents an act of communication as such. It refers to a time seen as the present. The word represents the actual number of participants currently involved in such act. In this sense, it is not wrong to say that performance exists outside of duration. It updates more or less numerous virtualities, felt more and less clearly. It makes them turn into realizty, without any consideration of time. Therefore, the performance is the one that accomplishes what the German authors, with the purpose of reception, call concretion. (ZUMTHOR, 2007, p. 50).

Cohen (2002) suggests the applicability of the term *"live art"*. Such an expression would aim to reference contemporary performances that transcend the artistic concepts assigned by modernity. Explaining the expression, the author says:

> The performance is ontologically connected to a larger movement, a way of looking art. The live art is only live, but it is also the living art. It is a way to see art which seeks a

direct approach with life, in which it encourages the sponta-
neous, natural, instead of the elaborate, of the rehearsed (...)
The live art is a breakthrough that aims to desacralize art, taking it from a purely aesthetic and stylist function. The idea is
to rescue the ritualistic feature of art, taking it from the "dead
spaces" such as museums, galleries, theaters, and putting it in
a "live", modifying position. (COHEN, 2002, p. 38).

To Cohen (2002), performance is "border art", in which collages of interdisciplinary axes and hybrid languages are mixed. For
being a point of borderly artistic expression, Cohen believes that
the performance ends up embarking in ways not previously considered as art. In this sense, the performance is a breaking tool, open
work that deviates from the principle of enjoyment and which can
shock viewers by tracing a new esthetic for existential questions.

The work of artistic performance is basically a humanist
work, aiming to free the man from his conditioning moor-
ings, and art, from the common places imposed by the system. Practitioners of performance in a direct line with the
practitioners of the counterculture, are part of the last re-
doubt (...) people who do not submit to the system of cyni-
cism and practice it at the expense of their personal lives, an
art of transcendence. (COHEN, 2002, p. 38)

Analyzing the rap performances inherent to the ideological genre,
what is happening is just an aesthetic in pastiche, which may shock
possible recipients in dealing with everyday, but unknown, issues.

An aesthetic is intended for those who do not have access to
concert halls and art galleries, criticizing pre-established social values and often also subject to rejection.

Popularized from the 1980s, the rapper aesthetic is, according
to Carlson (2010), one of the possibilities in existing performance
nowadays. In the work *"Performance: A Critical Introduction"*, the
author tells us about the contemporary trend of a performance
based on the body and the word. A performance with consolidated
artistic and political purposes is often autobiographical material.

Carlson (2010), for instance, cites a publication made in 1995 by The New Yorker. On the occasion, a new performative trend was presented to the world entitled *"raps meet poetry"*.

> Henri Louis Junior, in a number of 1995 of The New Yorker, says that the recent emergence of a new "scene" or "movement" in the language performance titled "raps meet poetry" in two performance spaces in the center of New York (the Fez and the Nuryorican Coffee) (...) Gates' description of the performance space of this work shows that it is very similar to the liminoide performance space of Victor Turner, "a hybrid space" where cultural styles push up and collide; where the wars of culture spread no new resentments, but new cultures. (CARLSON, 2010, p. 134).

Essentially political, we believe a rapper's performance to be not a situation that is restricted to specific times of performances, but rather something that is perpetuated in different products and instruments; diverse material that allows the receiver to experience the performed song at the same time they identify with it and triggers the memory of their own experience.

In this sense, we resorted to Finnegan (2008). The researcher reminds us that the performance is not limited to instant and specific manifestations in which sounds, movements and lyrics work together. Rather, going beyond the moment in which presentations are held, performance usually constitutes more or less subjective forms that communicate at the same time urging the mnemonic capacities of their listeners. Consider the following passage:

> (...) A song can be experienced - can exist- within a live performance, a printed page, a cassette tape, an LP in a video, on a CD, in radio or television broadcasts }and can be "downloaded from the internet", discussed in an email, sent by a cellphone; or it may be recited from memory, recreated aloud or silently, into pieces or fragmented (...) And all these ways are viable embodiments with regard to the agents involved. (FINNEGAN, 2008, p. 37).

For this path, taking into account all the performative potential presented in the content of the recordings taken as objects of study in this research, we continue the analysis proposed in this paper. It is assumed that the "rapper performance" eternalized - whether in virtual spaces or even CDs and vinyl records (we note, at present, a gradual return of this tool by the phonographic industrial space) - awakens in your receiver not only the image of a moving body or listening to the familiar sounds that allude to the urban routine found in large contemporary metropoli. More than that, such performances also eternalize testimonial poetic narratives that generate, in most of its listeners, the feeling of "aesthetic appreciation in direct agreement". This fact is because these listeners not only appreciate the performance that represents them, but share with it all the experiential content narrated.

Thus, when analyzing the selected foreign songs for this study, the goal of feeling the degree of representation of these performances was maintained, including the real intention of them and what, in fact, they deny and intend to entice in the listeners - whether direct recipients of the song, or single recipients thereof.

So, having established these brief notes about the song as an act of performance, we move forward to the presentation of artists, composers, whose works are part of the analysis of this research.

Who performs? - notes on the artists in this research

Tensais MCS

Created in 2000, the Tensais MCS group was born in the Kanagawa Province (Japan), as a result of the partnership between Brazilian immigrants and locals.

The group consists of seven components: the Japanese-Brazilian brothers MC Beto, Roza and Rose; the Brazilian MC Q;

the japanese Sat-Skill (rapper), Pay-ment (musician) and Hiroto da Muscle (musician).

In an interview with the author of this work[8], the leader of the group, Roberto Araujo Ishikawa (MC Bob) explained that even before immigrating he was already a connoisseur of rapper art and the idea of creating the Tensais MCS group came when he was working in a Japanese factory and met the Brazilian immigrant Fábio Mesquita.

> I liked to dance Hip-Hop and a DJ friend gave me a tape of Racionais MCS. As their reality was not very different from what I had experienced in my life, I decided to write my own lyrics. This began in Brazil and took a turn when I started Tensais MCS in Japan. I met Fábio Mesquita who was nicknamed Kyu (or Q in English) and we had our first presentation in a house called Fuzzy Hon Atsugi. I had invited some Japanese, one of whom worked with me, and they had a band called Hotch Potch Workshop which later would join us to do a collaboration. The chemistry was so good that we came together as Tensais MCS and, from there, we won a hearing produced by Sony Music Entarteinment, Embassy of Brazil in Tokyo and the Club of Brazil. This was the beginning of everything.

MC Beto, who left Brazil at 17, reported it had never been possible to live only of music. For him, Japan is not a country open to cultural differences.

Immigrants who get there are exposed to many factors that impose difficulties: illiteracy before the Japanese (katakana, hiragana and kanji), discrimination, ignorance, cultural and legislative aspects. The rapper says[9]:

> Here in Japan, the opening to multicultural artists are very rare and the music market is somewhat monopolized. Surviving of rap here is dificult. I, myself, work as an electrician or any other job that is available to support my family.

---

8   Interview to the author. See appendix B.
9   Interview to the author. See appendix B.

MC Beto also informed that currently (and temporarily), the group is inactive due to the necessary removal of one of the members. Tensais MCS has recorded two CDs, "Do the Right Thing" (2002) and "Mestisoul" (2007), productions that have bilingual tracks and generally address the issue of immigration. These tracks are often merged into rap and other rhythms such as bossa nova.

Yoka and the immigrants birds

On the record "*Pássaro Imigrante*" (Inmigrant Bird) performances of five different rap groups are included, namely: Partnership of Sound (London), Elo da Corrente (SP), Indigesto (Rio/Barcelona), Mamelo Sound System (SP) and Pulcro (Barcelona).

In an interview with the author of this research[10], the disc's producer, Caio Abumanssur Beraldo (known as Yoka) explained that this is a different initiative, which originated from their own history.

> When I lived in London between 2001-2006, we had a group called Illegal project, I produced and the MC was an immigrant from Bahia, he was graduated in literature and knew many books and writers of our literature. Cias was older than me, I was 18 at the time, and he influenced me to open up my head to the social bias that we were experiencing there too, I mean, when you leave your country because its social conditions are shit, and over time you start to notice that your refuge also provides you a shit condition. Good. We bought a lot of records, especially Brazilian music, I met a lot of Brazilian music while I lived in London. One day we found a vinyl of a Brazilian artist, Claudia, the album name was "*Pássaro Emigrante*" 1978 (inversely proportional to my bird, haha) and of course, the name really caught our attention, we enjoyed this record for a long time, until today I am a fan of this work. When I was living in Spain, doing my

---

10 Interview to the author. See appendix A.

course in Audio Engineering, I felt the need to assert myself as a producer because I had released stuff on the internet, but did not see much value in a job that was not physical, tangible, because we are always tucked in bookstores, buying and rediscovering old and forgotten music, I've always wanted to also make a vinyl record that one day was rediscovered too, anyway... At this point, I had already lived in four other countries, knew enough people in the middle and also had a very mature opinion on the subject and decided to dedicate the album to this path, that's when I decided to gather people I met on this journey and honor Claudia's disc .

Desiring to create a kind of travel journal built under the LP format, Yoka invited some MCS and DJS, who he befriended over his eleven years of self-exile from Brazil to produce *"Pássaro Imigrante"*. It is a work that is dedicated, in each of its tracks, to reveal the fractions of experiences enthralled by foreigners. While not all groups were composed of people with immigrant experience, according to Caio[11] everyone was influenced by his idea and sought to perform realities that did not require specific territorial references, to reveal verbally and strikingly what is like to be an immigrant in global circumstances.

> (...) There is, in a certain way, in much of the performance the sense of walking in the counter direction of the majority, this is what we do, when you rap, you ask things that people are too lazy to speak or do not even realize that this is part of their daily lives. I think that's the common factor, so if y ou are outside the majority, you feel exiled from their way of living, ideas, general customs and question that, you do not cease to be an immigrant bird, or "foreign", as defined by Albert Camus.

The professionals that make up the disk were gathered in Barcelona, Spain, at the time of the production of the vinyl.

---

11 Interview to the author. See appendix A.

Ana Tijoux

Born in the French town of Lille in 1977, the rapper Anamaria Merino Tijoux is the daughter of Chilean immigrants who left the country due to the severe dictatorship led by Augusto Pinochet.

At six, Ana Tijoux moved to Paris with her family. While living in the Parisian capital, Ana began her career as a break dancer. She returned to Chile in 1993 after the reestablishment of democracy in the country.

In Chile, she helped in the foundation of several rap genre groups, including the Makiza band with which she recorded three albums, becoming nationally known. In 2006, Tijoux began a solo career with the single *Ya no fue*. Soon after, in 2007, she launched the album Kaos

Since starting her solo career, Ana Tijoux has become an artist of remarkable ascension. She obtained, in 2011 and 2012, with the album *1977* and *La Bala*, consecutive nominations for the Grammy Awards, the highest award of the international music industry.

On the work *Song and Social Change in Latin America*, contains the transcript of an interview given by Tijoux to the journalist and researcher Lauren Shaw (2013). In this interview, there are important statements about the intersections between the history of Tijoux's family, music and political participation through aesthetics. Some relevant passages will be analyzed below so as to help understand the rapper trajectory of the MC in question.

In the first, Ana Tijoux explained how the Chilean scene was when her parents left the country[12].

> You know we had the coup on September 11th 1973, and my family, like so many people, was involved in the political movement. At that time, they participated in the ELN: National Liberation Army and then in the MIR: Movimiento de Izquierda Revolucionaria. And of course, like so many young

---

12 Our translation.

people at that time, my mother was a student of philosophy, and my father was studying to be a lawyer. They were involved in the political movement, and paid the price. They were imprisoned for many years, and 75 was a very bloody year in Chile. A lot of people were disappearing, so my parents left the country. My mother went to France and my father to Germany. And that's why I was born in France in 1977. She went into exile in 1976. She was a political refugee. We lived together in France. Now my mother is a sociologist, and my father is a professor of Political Science and Human Rights in Chile. We all returned together in 1993.

Admirer of the artistic avant-garde movements, Ana Tijoux found in rapper activities a form of protest against the injustices of the world. Throughout the interview, a second moment must be highlighted: when asked about the reason of her choice for rap and not for other musical genres, the singer cites admiration for Surrealism and Dadaism, also revealing a non-belief in her own musical talent[13].

When I was in school, I was always in a cloud, dreaming. And the only thing that captured my attention were the lessons of Surrealism and Dadaism. And this was the only topic that really caught all my attention. I'm crazy for Antonin Artaud and Robert Desmos. For me, the surrealists were the perfect door between politics, poetry and music. I always said that if I could have decided in which era to live, it would have been the time of this movement. At that time in my life, I did not feel I had any musical talent. I do not read music. But the words always interest me. And how can you play with the words. How you can change the words and create new meanings for them (...) I met some people in the ghetto, who used to freestyle every day. And for me it was similar to the dadaists and surrealists. The way they worked with the words. I think the Hip-Hop has a perfect build for me because it

---

13 Our translation

combined the world of my parents, the Dadaists, fantasy, music, rhythm, streets, sociology. I was super interested in how Hip-Hop can be almost a new country. It is everywhere, it is the music and the voice of people who do not have voice. That's why I did Hip-Hop at that time. Unaware that I had any drop of talent.

The influence of the artistic avant-garde movements became clear due to the freedom, hybridity and revolutionary intention proposed in the songs of Ana Tijoux. After returning to Chile at sixteen, the artist launched herself as an MC and songwriter. Her productions reveal various sound collages associated with politically motivated verses and, similar to the Surrealist propositions-qualified by the artist as the "perfect door between politics, poetry and music". Also, her work maintains a counter systemic position, whose purpose would be to build an aesthetic awareness on the part of the recipients.

Ana Tijoux, through her productions, reveals the "foreign eyes" through which she sees the world. A look that updates the surrealist intention to reverse the misery in a kind of revolutionary nihilism[14], fighting against the effects of the globalizing process. Such look, once organized on the form of song, allows the French-Chilean rapper to interpretate the events that surround her and, at the same time, establish a politicized aesthetics of her songs.

Although the story of the singer seems to have been key to building her rapper career, when asked by the journalist Lauren Shaw (2013) about a possible influence, Tijoux said, as transcribed below[15]:

---

14 Regarding leftists purposes arising from Surrealism, Walter Benjamin, on the Work "Máfica e Técnica, Arte e Política" states: "Before these seers and signs of interpreters [the surrealists], no one had noticed how the misery, not only social as the architectural, the misery of the interior, things enslaved and enslaving, were transformed into revolutionary nihilism." (BENJAMIN, 2004, p. 25).

15 Our translation

This seems obvious, but I'll ask anyway. It is because of the history of your parents, that you are interested on themes related to social justice?

Yes, but I have met people who do not have my baggage. And these people are more involved with the rapper purpose than I am. So I do not think that's the only reason. Yes, that somehow educated me, but after a while, when you have an idea about how your personality is, your identity, how sensitive you are to the facts, it ends up depending on each one, individually. In my case, I can not deny it. I wanted to study Political Science. It has always interested me. I do not know how I ended up doing music, but I feel that music in the end is a revolution of poetry. Political Science is not so different from music for me.

If the autobiographical references do not get full recognition in the opinion of the author, regarding the influence exerted on her rapper career, the same does not occur in relation to the territory. In the opinion of Tijoux, living in Europe was essential to deepen her work as an MC[16],

Totally. Sometimes what hurts you at the moment is what gives you power. I think growing up with so many immigrants: Algerians, Moroccans caused me to become an African music fan. I like to go there, but not to live there. I'm super-critical to Europe. France is a country whose people are very complicated. Singin there is complicated- for example, in the subway, if you touch someone, it's uncomfortable for them. It is as if they did not want to acknowledge your body. I do not like this.

Currently, Ana Tijoux resides in Chile. When she goes to France - despite having been born in the north of the country and later resided in Paris - she prefers to stay in the south. She does not believe in religious institutions, feels politically orphaned and, for the future, she plans to write a book (SHAW, 2013 p. 233).

---

16 Our translation

Manolis Afolanios (MC Yinka)

Born in Greece in 1981, Manolis Afolanios- known as MC Yinka - is the son of Nigerian immigrants.

He dedicates himself to music since the age of ten. At 17, he became involved with the Hip-Hop movement and began rapping and releasing songs through homemade recordings, available in digital media.

Despite having an extensive musical career - throughout his career, he was next to great names of Greek music, such as Filippe Pliatsikas, Irman Bailde and Dimitra Galani - Manolis Afolanio could only produce his first CD in 2009. Titled *Alana* - the same name given to one of the main leftist magazines in the country - the CD consists of 15 tracks dedicated, in general, to the social problems related to immigration and the country's inequalities.

Afolanios, who was born and raised in a poor neighborhood of immigrants, on the outskirts of Athens (Patissia), was one of the few blacks to attend school in the 80's. Currently, he has excelled in the Greek media, as a personality engaged in issues related to immigration.

In an interview with the leftist newspaper *Εργατική Αλληλεγγυη*[17] (Labor Solidarity), the rapper explains how the children of immigrants, born in Greece, grow[18]:

> Being the son of second-generation immigrants in Greece means having to live for a while in a bubble, thinking that you have equal social and political rights, like the others. And just when you need to make important decisions about your life, defining the path of a professional career, your studies, you suddenly discover that things are not made for you to have the same rights as other "children", who grew up with you .
>
> I was born in Greece in 1981, grew up in Patissia. At the end of the 90's, a period of mass legalization, my parents were

---

17 Available at: <http://ergatiki.gr/index.php?option=com_k2&view=item&id =9096%3Ai1101&Itemid=62>. Accessed: 30 jan. 2014.

18 Our translation.

part of the movement in favor of new legislation of migrants. Growing up, I believed that, by having been born here, I would have no connection with it. I believed and thought I was Greek, with all the rights.

For Afolanios, the immigrant illusion of being recognized as a national citizen is something that breaks at the end of adolescence when, in fact, the individual must take a role in society. The rapper says[19]:

> But then you realize what is evident. After 05 or 06 years, you realize that you have lost time, I could not get into a process to legitimize it. I used to hide, my brother was almost deported. It was very difficult to reach an agreement. It started a whole process, gathering papers everywhere to prove that we are here all these years, to be recognized on the condition of economic immigrants, it was in 2004. And since then, we have always lived renewing the residence permit, certificates, stamps, seals are not enough, the residence permit already won out, it is a stress, an aversion to everything.
>
> In 2009, I entered the long-term resident status, that the law has provided for the children of immigrants a residence permit for five years, then it could be extended for an indefinite period. Then came the Ragous law, that they said was unconstitutional, was removed, and now we are again in the same point, we do not know what will happen with the children of immigrants.

For MC Yinka, the state ignores the more than 300,000 "Greek migrants" born in the country, not recognizing the contribution made by these individuals to the cities, nor their potential in relation to future social developments. Yinka also highlights the poor treatment given by the State to these people, denouncing the formation of sterotypes instituted to "sell" to the great mass, the image of the immigrant as a wrongdoer, murderer or thief.

---

19 Our translation

Yinka is hopeful of the dissemination of reflective processes through the Greek society. According to the rapper, the general perception of the fascist actions have grown, especially after the murder of Pavlos Fyssas (anti-fascist rapper, stabbed to death, in 2013, by a political official of the extreme right). Realizing the growth of conscious actions, he directed to the establishment of a more fair society towards minorities, Yinka explains his contribution[20]:

> With my music. By being an active member of an anti-fascist movement that operates in several areas of policy and fight against the fascist movement, declaring it at events, shows and many antifascist actions. In these conversations, I tell my problems and failures, as the son of immigrants I am. The movement of the fascist governants is an orderly movement. The dog is in front, behind the austerity, layoffs, wages, pensions, that every day devour a little bit more of the worker.

The brief comments above and transcribed statements were aimed to situate the reader of this work in relation to the historical-profile of the artists and authors, whose productions consisted the object of study of our research. The next chapter, entitled *"Transcribe, translate and compare: lyrics"*, presents the results of the translational analysis that was held.

---

20 Our translation

Transcribing and translating: lyrics

"So for us, translating creative texts will always be a re-creation, or creation parallel, autonomous but reciprocal. The more permeated with difficulties the text, the more potential it has for recreation, more seductive as an open possibility of recreating"

(Haroldo de Campos)

This chapter presents the results of the comparative analysis of the verbal content made available by the immigrant rappers songs that support this book. Due to remaining accessesible to listeners only through sound format such songs before being submitted to the review process, went through an intense phase related to transcription.

Despite the fact that it is a complex and inexact process, transcription became an instrument necessary for this research, since it is the only alternative that is able to promote the comparative study proposed.

Assuming that rap "(...) is a form of popular literature aimed directly at transmitting social knowledge related to social practices regarded as significant" (ZUMTHOR, 1997, p. 49), we intend to present the occurrence of this transmission in the immigrant sphere.

Altogether twenty songs were selected which, in our opinion, show the structural poverty translated and faced under the foreign voice.

Much of this material has its composition structured from the use of more than one language. Were present in the translation and transcription process, in all, five languages, namely English, Spanish, Portuguese, Greek and Japanese.

Because of this - and due to not completely dominating all languages, hesitating also in the more accurate translation of recurring terms within the group language/slang - we needed to rely on the help of some people.

For songs that contained excerpts delivered in Japanese, I turned to the translator Larissa Satake Genaro - Member of the Nippon Community of São Paulo; who established contact through social networks (mainly Facebook).

As for the passages in Greek - on which I could not work alone - I had the help of my mother (Carmen Grouios Nathanailidis) and friends Vassula Andrikopulos and Kosmas Poulianitis; all members of the Hellenic Community of the state of Espirito Santo.

Regarding the understanding of some slang terms in English, the help came from friends and English teachers Graziella Baldini and Katherine Schirmer. Finally, in the face of difficulties arising from the translation of some specific expressions of the Spanish language, the assistance of the research advisor Professor Jorge Nascimento, Doctor of Neo-Latin letters was valuable.

The translational and transcription process required a collective effort to thoroughly listen to the selected songs, because, as we said earlier, these products do not have any insert or equivalent official text to the songs performed. The proccess of listening was sometimes difficult, due to the incidence of slang and presence of accents.

With much effort, we transcribed these songs, and after this work, I took the challenge to analyze them individually. The result of this challenge is exposed in this section.

In order to provide some textual clarity to the reader, the letters were divided into subchapters, separated by thematic groups of analysis, namely:

- In the crowd, one more wants to be someone "who am I and who are you" regarding statements and identity perceptions within foreign rapper songs.

Interpreted songs: *Mestisoul* (Tensais MCS), *Samurai Malandro* (Tensais MCS), *Pássaro Imigrante* (Indigesto) *Desclasificado* (Ana Tijoux) and *To Κέρμα* (MC Yinka);

- Amid the capital jungles, acculturation, violence and resistant faith: the system, the origins and the holy sung by the immigrant mass.

Interpreted songs: *Selva do Dinheiro* (Mamelo Sound System) *Exceção à Regra* (Elo da Corrente), *La Bala* (Ana Tijoux), *Si te preguntan* (Ana Tijoux) *Χαιρετισμός* (MC Yinka) *Αφρικά* (MC Yinka) and *Shock* (Ana Tijoux)

- To cross borders, guide or simply survive: the rap word, libertarian aesthetic of conscious and abandoned voices.

Interpreted songs: *Sacar La Voz* (Ana Tijoux); *Αλάνα; Πάνω από το Νέφος* (MC Yinka); *Το επαναστατικό ταξίδι* (MC Yinka); *Unite* (Tensais MCS) and マイクロフォン戦士 *Microphone Soldier* (Tensais MCS); *If you do not believe feat* (Parthership of sound).

- Considerations on a different track and (In) Definitely [Instrumental]

Interpreted Song: Definitivamente [Instrumental] - Yoka

Established the division, we move to the exposure of the results of our analysis, followed by closing remarks.

In the crowd, another one wants to be someone: "who am I and who are you" the identitary representations and perceptions within the foreign rapper song

In this section rappers songs are analyzed whichc keep common content related to similar themes: statements and perceptions of identity, seen from the perspective of foreigners.

The following songs will be analyzed in this order: *Mesti-Soul* (Tensais MCS), *Samurai Malandro* (Tensais MCS), *Pássaro Imigrante* (Indigesto) *Desclasificado* (Ana Tijoux) and *Kepma* (MC

Yinka). These songs reveal the image of the immigrant about themselves, their feelings and ways of conduct before the (new) foreign territory.

Mestisoul: an ode to Brazilian miscegenation

The song "*Mestisoul*" homonym to the CD produced by Tensais MCS group, contains within the formation of its own nomenclature, references to ethnic hybridity. The merging between the "mesti" prefix and the word "sou" ("I'm" in portuguese) creates the neologism "*mestisoul*".

This neologism is phonetically close to the masculine noun 'mestizo' which refers to the individual born of the mixture of two or more ethnic groups.

The sound rapprochement between the terms suggests the opening of an aesthetic-verbal game, which also points to a correlation of meanings, achieved from the poetic structure of the song.

Relatively short, "*Mestisoul*" is a song that tells of the hybridity of the figure of a Brazilian immigrant who, among their various origins, also finds reference in Japanese culture. The song, moreover, is constituted of a hybrid textual body, because it has a narrative in which three languages intertwine: Portuguese, English and Japanese.

Introduced by a continuous electronic base, whose sound seems to simulate the sound of the tambourine (quite traditional in Brazil), the first words of that song sharpen the imaginary receiver from enunciative claims arising from a deterritorialized voice, striving to achieve a kind of collective self-definition. The sound basis establishes a "Brazilian atmosphere" and works as an epigraph for verbalization. In the first few words, the song calls listeners to an affirmative awareness of their hybrid identity. It is noted that the first verse says:

> Mestisoul, pure Brazilian blood
> it is in the face, it is in the color that

Descends the whole world
If you love this country, release your voice *"brow"!*
Brazilian soul, I am Brazilian, I am!

Seeking to define the presence of the "mestisoul" immigrant, the enunciative voice recurs to the antithesis, seen from the expression "pure Brazilian blood", which counteracts the idea of purism to the Brazilian ethnic reality.

This fact becomes easily identifiable, as when thinking about Brazilian - nation as, "(...) human group whose members, fixed in a territory, are linked by historical, cultural, economic and linguistic facts" (MORAES, 2002, p. 213), we must consider the hybridity caused by the exchange between different ethnic groups, among them the White, Black, Indian and Oriental.

A representative mix of "the whole world" assigns the immigrant described features that are different and perhaps little known in foreign territory. Using the English vocative "brow", the enunciator summons the community starting the song with a kind of war cry, "I am Brazilian, I am Brazilian, I am" that established by the verb in the first person ("am") creates an alliteration whose sound approaches the term "soul", also present in the neologism particle in the song's title.

The applicability of the term *soul* can also mean an allusion to *soul music*, popular music style, performed and recorded by North American Blacks from the 60's, which had a strong influence on rap. This style came to Brazil in the next decade, enshrined in the voice of singer Tim Maia and proposed to express the emotions and perceptions more intensely felt by the interpreter, evoking similar feelings in the listener, from the use of passionate expressions, dramatic and excited utterance, as sighs, sobs, falsetto, melismas, declaimed or sung interpolations, issuing cries or harsh sounds. (GROOVE; SADIE, 1994)

Thus, at the beginning of the song we see the presence of a declaimed interpretation, whose height sometimes occurs at exceeding levels, and the lyrics sung in some points very closely to the crying sound - which, perhaps, is a style applicable to the identity reinforcement established by the verses, so that, by inserting the song in an atmosphere of ecstasy that can affect the audience, arousing a gregarious movement generated by the idea of identity.

Starting the second verse, the song establishes a reference to Jean Charles Menezes, a Brazilian immigrant (born in Minas Gerais) that after being mistaken for an Arab terrorist, was killed by London Metropolitan Police. Referring to Jean Charles as a martyr, the letter reports the main motivation of a Brazilian immigrant: work.

> Hail, Hail, Jean Charles our martyr in England
> Brazilian wants to work, so he goes to other lands
> Illegal or not, it is the Brazilian way!
> We export labor to the world
> In all continents, we are present
> With the culture that expands and consequently
> Soccer, our trademark
> Five stars, a very respected brand
> Our sound, our swing and our trickery
> Our food, our girls and all that landscape
> Our modest and quite welcoming ways
> The Brazilian shows their claws in the times of pain
> Our art is present and being preserved
> Capoeira and bossa are very well represented
> Hip-Hop, Funk and Rock
> Gradually become the new MPB
> (Brazilian Popular Music)

Note that the intention to be integrated in the labor market appears in that rapper song as a motivating factor for migration and a characteristic of Brazil. "Brazilian wants to work, so he goes to other lands", says the explanatory verse of the performer.

Another aspect highlighted in this verse is the stereotyping under which the figure of the Brazilian immigrant is inserted, whose presence is evident worldwide.

The "five star" soccer, the music, the beauty of the Brazilian women, cuisine, trickery, the proud, welcoming character and natural landscapes are some of the features mentioned in the song, which allows the imaginary-listener to draw the profile of the Brazilian immigrant and his country. Coincidentally, they are confirmed as significant constitutuents of the prior knowledge based on common sense under which the performer sees himself and shows awareness that he will also be seen in this way.

Regarding stereotypes, Bhabha (2007) considers this to be the main discursive strategy of colonialism. Ambivalent and contradictory mode of representation, the stereotype is born from the feeling of helplessness that arises from the colonizing gaze, from finding and condemning differences (cultural, sexual and ethnic) in society. Acting in a fixed and repetitive way, the stereotype guides the ideological conceptions about the otherness and becomes an antecipated construction of the other, an unrealistic and excessive idea, capable of legitimizing discrimination, to the extent that it is coated by the notion of truth. In this sense, Hommi Bhabha says (2007, p. 117):

> The stereotype, then, as the primary point of subjectification of colonial discourse, both to the colonizer and the colonized, is the scene of similar fantasies and defences - the desire for originality is again threatened by differences of race, color and culture (...) The stereotype is not a simplification because it is a false representation of a given reality. It is a simplification because it is a fixed form of representation that, by denying difference (that denial through the other allows), is a problem for the representation of the subject in the psychic and social relations.

In the song in question, aspects of a positive stereotype, instilled in the psychic reality of the subject-immigrant, institute reasons to justify and ensure its presence within the foreigner. The intended message by the performer is easily identified in the verse *"We come from a place full of natural beauty where the food is tasty.*

Our women are beautiful, our music is attractive ... We can offer a lot to you. If we are illegal, it's just our "way", what we want, in fact, is to work "[21]. Noteworthy is the reference to the Brazilian Popular Music (MPB), an internationally recognized musical style and that through the song becomes also, a reason for the aesthetic persuasion. In this sense the enunciator says: "Hip-Hop, Funk and Rock/ Little by little become the new MPB. "The idea of the verse, given in words, is confirmed by the hybrid sound organization, blending the electronic beat to the sound of the tambourine, which confirms the use of the *samba rap* genre.

In the third verse of the rapper performance, the Japanese language is used, whose translation we list right below the original transcript, in bold.

	Translation:
Mestisoul, pure Brazilian blood It is in the face, it is in the color that Descended the whole world 俺は日本人 but I am also Brazilian! Brazilian Soul, I am Brazilian, I am!	Mestisoul, pure Brazilian blood It is in the face, it is in the color that Descended the whole world I'm Japanese, but I am also Brazilian! Brazilian Soul, I am Brazilian, I am!

The enunciative voice, which began in the third person, shall also express an emotional function (1st person) when referring to their own identity, saying "I am Brazilian". It also highlights the complement to the content narrated in the first strophe that after repeated is increased (and reinforced) by the idea that "a Japanese can also be a Brazilian" and thus "is".

The hybrid song continues. In the fourth strophe, the singing combines again the Japanese and Portuguese languages.

---

21 The parts are on "our highlightment".

Favela 育ち 桜色 Mestisoul ど
こまで揺らす気　お熱いの
は好き 踊り明かす夜 真っ
赤なリオ 伝統の Samba 極
上の音色
Favela 育ち 侍 Mestisoul ど
こまで揺らす 気お熱いの
は好き 踊り明かすYo 毎度
Latin sound 灼熱の めっぽ
うあちぃーの

Translation:

Favela, a samurai warrior who
grows as a Mestisoul
Feel the rhythm of the beat,
the vibe is so good, that Samba
from Rio has become a tradition, everyone likes it.
Favela grows with the color of a
cherry-tree. Mestisoul, feel the
rhythm of the beat, this vibe
is so good ...Yeaah, every time
the Latin makes a hot sound to
delight.

The interpretation shows a expository voice that narrates, in the third person, the reality of a Japanese descent abroad. Latinamerican, this foreigner carries in himself the imaginary subjectivity of territory representative of his origins: Brazil.

In the aestheticized elocution, it must be noted a little of the hybridity established as a cultural negotiation held by the leader-performers of the group in question, Japanese descent Brazilian immigrants that, based in Japan, became individuals located in a transitional cultural context.

Hall (2007) states that such individuals belong to two worlds at the same time, they are "translated men", that dialogue with the new culture without fully integrating to it, in order to retain traces of their original identity. About these people, the author says: "These people retain strong ties to their places of origin and traditions (...) They are obliged to deal with new cultures in which they live, without simply being assimilated by them and without completely losing their identities." (HALL, 200 7, p. 89).

In this sense, the memory of the "favela" by the foreigner demonstrates the stance taken on the grounds of a local transient enunciation, in which elements of old and new traditions coexist. The "favela" is felt and remembered by immigrants and their place of origin and also acts as an essential way to dialogue with the new culture, since it is currently an international tourist destination.

By leaving the "favela" of origin, the sender goes to live abroad in a ghetto, where day after day he experiences the fighting necessary for survival. This fact gives him the conditions to self-affirm himself aesthetically, as a warrior in training, that is, someone who experiences the routinely clashes necessary for survival. The warrior grows with the color of the Sakura (as cherry blossoms are known in Japan), faces the listener with a greeting ("Yo!"/ Or "ae" in Portuguese), with the intention of presenting "samba and their beats", elements that make up the Brazilian cultural wealth and spread feelings of joy, also revealing the hybrid identity, translational aspect of the reality.

In the fifth strophe, the voice of enunciation proposes an evocation that, in a way, references the Brazilian personality. They say:

> Be from the South or North, countryside or capital
> The Hinterland or Cerrado or the coast
> The Amazon forest or the Pantanal
> My soul cries and screams for you, that is eternal
> Tell me if you are a Brazilian?
> Green and yellow engraved in your chest!
> Adding Blue and white, these are the nation's colors
> Of the Flag that I love and respect with all my heart
> And it goes beyond imagination and creation
> Mixing of blood, race, color
> Art, culture, philosophy
> These are us, sufferer!
> Despite the suffering, they are joyful in living
> Overcome the difficulties with a will to win
> The trickery is in the blood and the samba is in the foot
> Conquering their dreams with determination and faith!

Mentioning various regions of the country ("South", "North", "Cerrado", "Pantanal", etc.), the enunciator establishes a call: "My soul cries and screams for you, that is eternal" referring to someone else, an immigrant, also Brazilian who, regardless of time or place of origin, guards family characteristics that make him one of his. In the performance, the hidden caller is described by the enunciator on a condition that it is "eternal" and metaphorically carries the feeling of love for the homeland in the song, from the reference to the colors of the flag. In this sense, it is said "Green and yellow engraved in your chest/adding blue and white, these are the nation's colors/The flag that I love and respect with all my heart. "The Brazilian condition" is a characteristic that is emphasized throughout this verse.

Being Brazilian is to exist beyond the "imagination" and "creation", carrying in the soul a rich cultural background, coming from a country that is hybrid by nature. The enunciator establishes definitions with which he identifies and to which he added: "mixture of blood, race, color/arts, culture, philosophy/These are us, sufferer."

As noted, the vocative "us" is a way in which the enunciator expresses identification before their interlocutors, also Brazilian immigrants, with which he shares experiences, regarding the origin, culture, the aspirations and the difficulties experienced abroad.

When defining the behavior of those who are part of his group (and therefore his own behavior), the enunciator writes verses that address joy and obstinacy: "Despite the suffering is joyful in living/ Exceeds difficulties with a will to win / trickery is in the blood and the samba is in the foot/Achieving his dreams with determination and faith!"

Reading the final verses of this strophe, the image of a Brazilian immigrant who, based on cultural values relating to his country of origin, guides his own actions. Such immigrants have in samba a cultural instrument assigned to the expression of their constant joy; and persist in the midst of obstacles, supported by faith and wiles of trickery[22]. Regarding the latter, consolidated stereotype in Brazil, it is important to point out the historical and cultural significance that it gained in the country. As explained by José Novaes (2001), in the article *"An episode of Subjectivity production*

---

22 Regarding "Trickery", it will be discussed more deeply on the next section.

in the Brazil of 1930: Trickery and the Vargas Era", the trickery is originated in Rio de Janeiro, as an element connected to samba, representing major challenges for the labor ideals of the Vargas Era. Getúlio Vargas fought trickery as this was configured as a popular antagonistist in relation to government purposes. About trickery, Novaes (2001, p. 41) says:

> And it was precisely against this trickster praise that the New State had to fight, to replace this trickster image by that of the worker, essential to its construction project of the Brazilian nation (...) The trickery in the first decades of the twentieth century in Brazil, should be understood as a rejection of the work and as a survival mode. A deeply unjust society in which hundreds of thousands of former slaves were thrown - and this is the correct term, to accentuate the violent and cruel aspect of the fact - to the labor market, without the vast majority having capacity or training to compete with Brazilian white workers and immigrants who came here in large numbers, trickery was one of the strategies that could give minimum guarantees of life. One could not expect work to be considered, by large segments of the population, a worthy activity. It had no moral value, not materially compensating, and only the smallest part of those who sought it as an occupation could reach it.

The allusions to the Brazilian trickery, religion and dance, in a way, make the fifth strophe something that offers the reader-listener, too, a kind of "recipe" - since, through it, you can learn how the experience of actions in exile is.

Abroad, according to the song, perseverance and preservation of cultural values are of paramount attention.

The song continues. In the sixth and seventh verses, there is the repetition of verses previously performed within the third and fourth verses transcribed. So we transcribe them again, as enunciated:

Mestisoul, o puro sangue brasileiro
"Tá" na cara ,tá na cor que
Descende o mundo inteiro
俺は日本人mas sou brasileiro
também

Translation:

Mestisoul, pure Brazilian blood
It is in the face, it is in the color
that Descended the whole
world I'm Japanese, but I am
also Brazilian! Brazilian Soul, I
am Brazilian, I am!

Translation:

Favela 育ち 桜色 Mestisoul ど
こまで揺らす気 お熱いのは
好き 踊り明かす夜 真っ赤
なリオ 伝統の Samba 極上
の音色
Favela 育ち 侍 Mestisoul どこま
で揺らす気お熱いのは好き 踊
り明かすYo 毎度 Latin sound 灼
熱の めっぽうあちぃーの

Favela, a samurai warrior who
grows as a Mestisoul
Feel the rhythm of the beat,
the vibe is so good, that Samba
from Rio has become a tradition, everyone likes it.
Favela grows with the color of a
cherry-tree. Mestisoul, feel the
rhythm of the beat, this vibe
is so good ...Yeaah, every time
the Latin makes a hot sound to
delight.

In the eighth strophe the enunciator deals with the physical distance and the possibility of union between the receptors through
music. It is noticed that even with regards to the constitution of
meaning of the song there is, in the successive applicability of different languages (Portuguese and Japanese Language) a clear attempt to dissolve linguistic boundaries. The identitary negotiation
established by a hybrid translation process, creates an undeniable
cognitive plot which forces a kind of game between signifiers and
meanings produced in both languages and launched to the interpretation of those who are or were in transit - whether they are
between nations or even between performing languages.

日本と地球の真反対だが兄
弟目指すとこ変わんない距
離は遠くない 音楽繋ぐ輪国
境越え広がるひたすら famíl-
ly になってもう 4 年目 Ten-
sais 伝える全身全霊
発信地湘南からホット
なラテンナンバーが登
場だ
Samba, Capoeira, Forró, MPB.
調子よく踊ろうベイベ 君は
素敵な Brazilian 世界一の ま
さに dance cinderella, Cachaça
で乾杯 Made in real Brazil 万歳
"favela" から真実のコール ヤ
ッベーな の Brazilian soul

Translation:

Brazil and Japan may even be in opposite positions on the globe, but the will to be brothers does not change. The distance is not that big for music, it can get easily to the two nations. It's been four years that we are a family and Tensais do not get tired of fighting. They come from South America, these warm traditions, Latin traditions.
Samba, Capoeira, Forro, MPB.
Let's dance Baby, you're a beautiful Brazilian, the princess of dance, may even be a cinderella. Let's toast with a "cachaça", typical of Brazil. From favela it is possible to hear a chorus that says, "Vixe! I am Brazilian, I am! "

The performance unfolds the enunciator, that oscilates from "talking of the other" (third person) and talking of a "collectivized self" that is merged with the very image of the performing group, Tensais MCS, whose trajectory of four years is mentioned in the verse.

The group with origins in the brazilian state of São Paulo, takes, through their performance, the responsibility of disseminating Brazilian regional traditions (samba, capoeira, forró and MPB) and simulates the encounter of a couple of immigrants. The "male self", collectivized, educates "the female other" about her own identity. The "invitation" to dance, introduced by the English vocative "baby" suggests the existence of a Brazilian talent in this area, responsible for the rise of "poor girls" to the condition of "cinderellas".

Dance is a source of pride, which should be celebrated through the traditions referring to the country of origin, Brazil. They call attention to the terms "cachaça", a foreign ghetto also called "favela", besides the use of the interjection "Vixe!", typical of the vocabulary in northeastern Brazil.

The song ends in the ninth strophe, transcribed below. In it are repeated, in chorus, the words already spoken in the song.

Translation:

Mestisoul, o puro sangue brasileiro "Tá" na cara, "tá" na cor que descende o mundo inteiro Se você ama esse país, solta a voz brow! Soul brasileiro, sou brasileiro sou!n Mestisoul, o puro sangue brasileiro "Tá" na cara, "tá" na cor que Descende o mundo inteiro 俺は日本人mas sou brasileiro também! Soul brasileiro, sou brasileiro, sou!

MestiSoul, pure Brazilian blood It is in the face, it is in the color that descended the whole world If you love this country, release your voice brow! Brazilian Soul, I'm Brazilian! Mestisoul, pure Brazilian blood It is in the face, it is in the color that Descended the whole world I'm Japanese, but I am also Brazilian Brazilian Soul, I am Brazilian, I am!

The content verbalized in the *"Mestisoul"* song reflects the identity purpose of music, which seeks to meet, in an aesthetic way, the need for self-recognition of the Japanese-Brazilian community residing in Japan. When responding musically to the question "Who am I?", the rap becomes a kind of ode to the miscegenation and the Brazilian cultural traditions, at the same time in which it operates as a politicized representation and response to a situation in which damning segregations and prejudices to which foreigners are subjected are possibly found.

Samurai Malandro (Samurai Trickster): the immigrant is a warrior and can live well even in the face of oppression

"Samurai Malandro" is a song that already arouses curiosities with its title, in which arranged side by side are terminologies with opposed meanings, usually applied to the fixity of the Japanese and Brazilian stereotypes.

Regarding the first term "samurai", the Aurélio dictionary of the Portuguese language proposes the following entry: "Samurai [jap.Samurai, Emperor's server] Sm Japanese warrior, a member of the family home at the service of a daimyo (emperor)" (FERREIRA, 2010, p. 1884).

Now, about the term "*malandro*", there is the following definition:

> Malandro. [Voc. Deduces. Of malandrim] Sm 1.Individual inclined to abusing the trust of others, or who does not work and lives of expedients; rascal, scoundrel.2. Lazy guy, slacker. 3. Thief 4. Bras. Smart guy, lively, cunning, sly. Adj. trickster. (FERREIRA, 2010, p. 1313)

On the first definition proposed, which refers to the idea of feudal warriors, which in fairness left their homes to serve, fighting for the interests of the emperor (daimyo) - when used in the title of the song in question, it is also a referencing the idea of work, transmitted to the Japanese people throughout history for generations.

According to Kishtara (cited SUDA; SOUZA, 2006), the social organization through which Japan was founded, it gave body to an obedient nation, dedicated to work and studies; as well as conformism and resistance to the application of paradigmatic disruptions. A population that historically transmits to their descendants, characteristics such as shyness, modesty, honesty and effort.

The *malandro* (trickster in English) figure, when associated with a *persona* that has such characteristics related to the work and effort, gives body, to a hybrid personality when it comes to cultural traits.

The subject likely to carry it preserves in itself moral values attached to the praise of the work (heritage of the Japanese warriors, samurai) and the astuteness applicable in their experiences in society (to those resulting of the trickster-Brazilian influence).

The first Brazilian trickster present in a fictional narrative was identified by Cândido (1978), in his text: "*Dialectics of Trickstery: Memoirs of a Milicias Sergeant*". The work is about Leonardo, a character who, through his behavior, also externalizes features present in Brazilian society of the nineteenth century.

To discuss the image of the Brazilian trickster character, Cândido (1978) found them to be able to move freely through the spaces of order and disorder, always hoping to get some advantage, and therefore constantly absorbed by the positive sphere of this relation. For the author, the fiction would externalize a kind of "mediating principle", existing in real life, "(...) the dialectical game of order and disorder, working as a correlative, which was manifested in the society of that time." (CÂNDIDO, 1978, p. 336)

Regarding the trickery, as we said earlier, it has its origins commonly associated with samba musical practice, specifically within the trickster-samba sphere. Corroborating what Novaes (2001) has stated - mentioned earlier - Matos (1982) also points out the existence of trickery, as a feature associated with samba, starting from the 20's. According to Matos (1982), this characteristic emerges simultaneously to the derivation process in a more modern version attributed to this genre, whose development is linked to the compositions in the Estacio de Sá neighborhood, Rio de Janeiro. The characteristic of trickery stems from a state of rejection and discrediting of the working classes, before the labor relations intensified on the national scene. In this sense, he says:

> It is precisely as a criticism of the rules that govern our social life, which results in abundance for the few and scarce for many, that emerges and develops the mythical of trickstery. The rejection of the work takes shape, to the samba and a broad proletarian group whose world view it expresses, in a sense of distrust and disillusionment with the compensation offered by the work as it occurs in our socio-esconomic theme. (...) Such disrepute has a specific motivation, which arises from the place reserved for the proletariat in the capitalist system. (MATOS, 1982, p. 79).

Claiming that there were few compositions that represented trickery as an alternative opposition to work, the researcher Tiago Gomes de Melo (2007), in the article *"Samba People: trickery and national identity at the end of the First Republic"*, he proposes another look on the subject. For the researcher, the opposition to the world of work, usually attributed to the Brazilian proletarianized class, made up of former slaves and their descendants, would be only the reproduction of the arguments proffered by slaveholders, to justify the import of European labor, considered better and more qualified to integrate the paid work mass in the country. Moreover, according to Melo (2007), this point of view - when opposing trickery to the ideology of work - supposes a state imposition of capitalism in the Vargas government, which could also set as a reproduction of the dictating speech.

According to Melo (2007), trickery comes associated with representations of intense identity debates at the beginning of the twentieth century, made through revues, in which the associations established between theatrical performance and music were constant. In this sense, the researcher states:

> Regarding trickery, it is possible to identify a remarkable symmetry between its popularity on stage and its appearance in popular music. The first hit songs based on this theme have appeared in recent years of the 20's.
>
> On stage, on the other hand, though existing for many years, the cunning occupies a more central place from the same period since the 1920s, a "naughty" notion of Brazil assumed great importance in the Rio revues. In this context, trickery came to be seen as representative of a country that was proud of the unique character of their popular classes. (MELO, 2007, p. 8)

Despite its origin, still nonconsensual, the Trickster figure has its origins in the marginalized and usually of African descent classes. This character has the imagery of a person that almost always has white and impeccable clothes on and who lives in a border status between the legal and the illegal, honesty and dishonesty, good and evil. Seeking to describe this ludicrous character, Matos (1982, p.54) states:

> [...] He cannot be classified, not as a well behaved worker nor as a common criminal: he is not honest, but he is not a thief, he is a trickster. His mobility is permanent, he depends on it to escape, even if temporarily, to the system's pressures.

With regards to it, the song title leads us to the idea of a personality "transformed" in its conceptual imaginary, through immigration. The Japanese immigrant in Brazilian soil becomes a subject bearer of hybrid cultural and personal elements. If he was just a warrior, now he also assumes characteristics of the Brazilian trickery. His children, who decide to return to Japan, externalize the "heritage" of the "genetic-cultural" material referring to both identities and traditions they carry, so the two attributes, are constituents of their personalities. In their eyes, they are the "samurais-rascals" stereotype that once again consolidates in a positive way in their psychic realities, thefore, something likely to be represented and distributed through the performance.

Also from a structural point of view, "*Samurai Malandro*" is a hybrid song, in which parts are in Japanese and others in Portuguese.

The beginning of the music appreciation, once again, shows the continuous sound of the tambourine, which extols the Brazilian tradition, perhaps seeking to recreate a climate of familiarity to the listener that has a certain connection or knowledge of the Brazilian culture.

The first strophe begins with an expository voice that oscillates between first and third person of the singular, revealing, in Japanese language, with some difficulty of expression

Translation:

切り捨てごめん　要らぬ世の 中世渡り上手もストリートの マナー コンクリート　サバンナの檻 に解き放たれた侍五人 本当のフィールドで見せるテ クニック　オリジナルスパイ ス　効かすエスニック　剣は抜 かぬが言葉で切る 舌を巻く話術で×かける魔術	Sorry for my way of speaking, it is the fault of this world that deceives us. Five samurais trying to escape a concrete cage. Excerting the technique to show what you really are, the original essence, their ethnicity, what you cannot demonstrate You can even cut the air with the sword, but words cut and hurt more than the blade.

Again, the dislocated identity simulates on the performance which

indeed seems to be the conductor of the subjectivities that surround the routine of five members of the Tensais MCS group; "five
trickster samurais" who through the sung speech, seek to escape the
pressures of an illusory system.

Immersed amidst the oppression of a "misleading world" that
promises freedom and offers confinement, the immigrant finds in
the aestheticized word the opportunity of a powerful verbal mechanism, able to free from the functional words that make up their
routine. For the immigrant, the word is a technique to be exercised, it represents their identities and shows "what they really are".

Aiming through words to offer the listener identity references
that refer to foreign conditions, the lyrics continue to convey the
idea that it is possible to be an immigrant and to live well, provided
that they use a feature to be developed through the social routine:
the trickery.

In the second strophe identified through the process of listening and translating, it has a enunciative voice that seeks to explain
the intentions and aspirations of the immigrant in a foreign land.

> Here is the thing; the brother here also likes refinement
> But living like a trickster is to be in the pinch everyday!
> Trickery means knowing how to live!
> Means dedicating your time to what you like to do
> Dancing, chilling, smiling, kissing, playing!
> But life is not only that, you must know how to do it
> Difficulty... Anywhere in the world has it
> But those who love themselves and others kind of live well
> It is all about knowing how to get there, and how to leave
> Respecting equality means evolving
> I'm not more than anyone else, I just want to conquer.
> What a smile and a hug can provide me
> Happiness, to the trickster, is loving and being loved
> And being with the family and allies
> And as a good trickster, only to remember you
> I work to live, I do not live to work!

The English expression *"pinch"* (which means danger, trouble) is used by the rappers to denote the reality of the immigrant. This is presented as a guy who - although socially positioned as a marginal individual, devoid of consumption conditions and prey to the many existing threats amid a capitalist environment - accepts the challenge of the foreigner difficult social condition, as this condition will bring them an effective access to "refinements", hitherto accessible in their country of origin.

The performed strophe suggests an "ideal" behavior to be adopted by foreigners. Aware that the obstacles are not dependent of the position occupied by the immigrant in the terrestrial globe - *"Difficulty... Anywhere in the world has it"*-, the enunciator alerts to the fact that one must have "street smarts" to live: how to deal with routine problems, balance work, affections and pleasurable activities.

While in *"samurai-malandro"*, the enunciating immigrant externally possesses the awareness of his own desires: optimistically, he shows the will to succeed in life and at the same time than to be next to his family and friends. The positive throughts towards his existencial goals stems, also, from the border and hybrid condition, in which he lives. The *"samurai-malandro"* immigrant is one that will conquer victories of material and social nature through work; but that, through trickery, will also hold the property of "dribbling" a systemic exploitation logic, having time to do whatever he feels like, always close to those to whom he feels affection.

To the attentive listener, this obstinacy is clear at the last strophe performed. In it, the enunciator collectivized in performance simulates to be a trickster immigrant, demonstrating his counter-ideological position, while advising the listener: "I work 'to' live, I do not live 'to' work".

In the third strophe, the expository voice wavers again between the first and the third person of the singular. The simulacrum of the immigrant scene seems to the reality experienced by the enunciator.

What will a lost boy in this big world know?
Know how to arrive and get involved
Immigrates to the other side of the planet
The stars are what guide me
Present, the samurai bombeta!
Hail, Hail, to the warriors that are standing!
The nobility of living, of dodging bad inttentions
I am the Western Samurai, a good trickster

Note that the decision to migrate abroad makes the foreigner assume a warlike posture. The metaphor "*samurai bombeta*" refers to the idea of a contemporary version of these warriors, the samurai rapper, wearing cap (*bombeta*) who has discipline and cunning to survive.

In the fourth strophe, the languages are mixed again, with a predominance in the use of the Japanese language.

The transcript, followed by the translation process, shows the existence of dichotomies in the interpretations made by social agents allocated in different areas of enunciation.

Translation:

マランドロは平成ジ
ゴロクジチュウ転が
す俺のベロとびっき
り良い女もいいもん
な超魅了する調味料は賞味期
限なしの少々危険なsamba の
香がプンプンするぜ可愛いカ
ナリヤかなり鳴いてるそろそ
ろここらで頂き

The trickster is a gigolo of the present times. My tongue calls for a "good woman".
I am fascinated and this fascination is endless. Little by little I feel the samba smell in the air
As if it were a beautiful canary singing

If in the eyes of the elite and of the bourgeois layers, the trickster "is a gigolo", given the understanding of foreign masses, the term refers to a fundamental need for the establishment of a life endowed of minimum quality conditions. The metaphor of "good woman" refers, in fact, to the possibility of living "well" abroad. The "necessary" and "fascinating" trickery turns samba and bossa (Brazilian traditions, references to the country of origin of those who perform the rap in question) into resources able to entertain and at the same time free. The sound base mixes the beat of the tambourine with melodic cuts alluding to another well - known song: *"Mas que nada"* - Jorge Ben Jor (1963).

The sound in which motifs of the two musical genres (Bossa Nova and Samba) are mixed, is mixed to the intonation of the rapper's voice, creating a set of different musical atmospheres. A dialogue is stablished in the fifth strophe:

> Whats up man!
> Whats up Santista, all good?!
> And that Vasco, will win or not?
> It is going well, but nevermind!
> The cod and the fish ...
> We're both from the sea!
> The Sea, the mysterious sea ...
> Man! I know this song!
> Imperio Serrano!
> Tell me, Kta Brazil, what country are you from?
> Japan, but my soul is Brazilian!

Theatricalizing a dialogue between the Brazilian football fans (we note, once again, the presence of tradition concerning the home country), the parties make use of the contraposition related to the mentioned football clubs to discuss the foreignness of their condition. Not a fish, nor a cod, "we're both from the sea", say the performing voices.

Regarding the sea, first space immigrantional transits, it becomes relevant to record its importance to the Japanese culture. Notable in the exercise of economic and social practices - ranging from cuisine to the military training organized by country - the sea is the meeting point between the past and the present: while it is present in the Japanese immigrant's everyday life, it has also a meaning apprehended by the cultural heritage of their ancestors.

The maritime metaphor, parallel to the origins and experiences of the performer, appears in the song as a fertile ground from which transformations associated with existence may emerge.

In the Dictionary of Symbols, written by Jean Chevalier and Alan Gheerbrand (1999), the sea is defined in the following entry:

> Symbol of life's dynamic. Everything comes from the sea, and everything returns to it: place of birth, of transformations and rebirths. moving waters, the sea symbolizes a transitional state between the possibilities yet without shape and configured realities, ambivalence situation, which is the uncertainty, doubt, indecision, and it can be concluded well or badly. From this comes the idea that the sea is at the same time a picture of life and an image of death. The ancient Greeks and Romans offered sacrifices to the sea, among which were horses and bulls, fertility symbols in their culture. From there arose monsters of the deep, also sources of the sea currents, which could be fatal or life - giving (...) (CHEVALIER; GHEERBRANT, 1999, p. 592).

"Sea, mysterious sea," words that attest to the uncertainty of the immigrant regarding the uncertainty of their own destiny, it is also a metalinguistic feature, since it also is part of the opening of the samba *"A lenda das sereias, rainhas do mar"*, with which the samba school G.R.E.S Imperio Serrano got the seventh place of the Special Group during the 1976 carnival championship.

The text in the performance has at this time its meaning corroborated by the sound. The musical texture of samba rap, in which the sound of the tambourine and the joy of the choir performance stand out in harmony, provides the idea that everything will end well, the constitution of a "gregarious environment" established between fraternal "Brazilians" who share difficulties and achievements originated from their foreign reality.

In this sense, it is possible to atribute to the metaphorized-sea of the performance, a messenger function, an element capable of providing the immigrant-hearer identification with other ideals, set apart from those already established in the hegemonic time-space of their experience. The transforming-sea could be understood in this way, as the possibility of communication, which goes against the homogeneous speech filed by the neoliberal system.

The clarification of this notion will find support in the critical post-colonial theory proposed by Bhabha (2007). In dealing with the literature produced by colonizers and colonized, Bhabha (2007) notes the existence of an ambivalent national scene and guides his reflection, focused on the cultural translation of this scenario, from two opposing concepts, also important to the interpretation of contemporary global speeches: "pedagogical time" and "performative time".

To the first the historical-conceptual construction supplied to the idea of nation is atributed. Based on the historicism attributed to nations, this construction proposes a horizontal and fixed gaze towards this practice. The pedagogical temporality, according to Bhabha (2007, p. 209): "(...) Bases its narrative authority in a tradition of the people (...) like a moment of becoming designated by itself, encapsulated in a succession of moments produced by self-generation". Through this concept, under the homogeneous unit of a nationalist narrative attributable to the nation, particular features go unnoticed, muted and doomed to marginal condition.

Considering the existence, in parallel, of various discourses derivative of the margins, Bhabha (2007) proposes the concept of performative time. As opposed to the previous concept, such understanding is configured as a kind of counter-narrative, refusing the notion of a national and unified ethnic reality.

In the performative time, the notion of people is obtained recurrently, from the enunciative present, through which conceptions concerning the national imagination are re-signified. Evidencing the voice of those who are under the condition of "in-betweeners", the performative time is consolidated as the responsible for the instability and disjunction of the centralized perspective, emphasizing the existence of a segmented, multicultural and multi-identitary reality. Regarding this process, Bhabha states (2007, p. 209-210):

Instead of the temporality of a self-generating prefigurative nation "in itself" and other extrinsic nations, the performative introduces the temporality of the in-between. The frontier that marks the individuality of the nation stops the self-generating time of national production and destabilizes the meaning of a nation as homogeneous. The problem is not simply the "individuality" of the nation as opposed to the otherness of other nations. We are facing a divided nation within itself, articulating the diversity of its population. The nation separated from itself, alienated from its eternal self-generation, becomes a liminal space of meaning, which is marked internally by the discourses of minorities, the heterogeneous histories of people in dispute, by antagonistic authorities and tense places of cultural difference.

Based on these two concepts, leading to the recognition of a continuing reality in globalizing and hybrid context in stories and cultural practices, we can infer that there is in the fifth strophe, the performatization of a request, released towards the listener. By promoting the self-assertion "we are both the sea!" and asking the imaginary interlocutor to "abandon" concerns about the results of soccer, the performer seems to actually request a change in behavior, asking the listener to forget one of the most rooted issues - and endowed with cathartic properties - present in the dominant discursive tradition of their country, i.e. soccer, giving reflective space to a counter-discursive and reality-transforming idea - it draws attention to the presence of the word "sea" in its symbolism related to vital transformation.

From this point of our "translational hearing" to the end the song in question, the enunciative voice always goes on alternating Japanese and Portuguese. In the sixth strophe, there is once again the presence of the verb "to be", fundamental to the attempt of foreign self-definition.

Translation:

俺はbrasileiroだしjaponêsだ
ぜ！
描き始めるあふれ出す色

I am Brazilian, but I'm Japanese!
The colors overflow when I
start to draw

The metaphor of drawing, related to self-definition, ratifies the establishment of a multicultural setting where "various colors" live. Different cultures transiting between the new and the old reality, between problems that are at the same time territorial and transnational.

The lyrics go on with a number of loose phrases that refer to the characteristics of Japanese descent abroad, born in Brazil: human warmth, discipline, respect, humility and kindness (seventh, eighth and ninth strophes).

In the tenth strophe, interpellating listeners by applying the first person of the plural, the enunciator proposes an invitation to music, conceived as a powerful instrument in the fight for a change in the social level.

Translation:

奇跡起すぜ、gingaでゆら
すぜ！
O malandro vem sambar a
dança, o nosso samba

Let's make a miracle happen!
With swing we will rock!
The trickster comes to samba
the dance, our samba

The last part of the analyzed song, the eleventh strophe is a refrain. Based on the credibility of the performance, the chorus brings an invitation to the recipient: self-transformation, which can be performed in a pleasant way, in association with the fruition of life itself.

	Translation:
Vem pra beira do mar	Come to the seaside
Vem coração ver	Come heart, come and see the
o 青空	blue sky
Malandragem e saber	Trickery means knowing how to
viver	live
Faço tudo por você	I do everything for you
Vejo o sol amanhecer	I see the dawning sun
間違いないぜ俺に掛けな	It is a sure thing, trust me, I just want to be happy
Faço tudo por você	I do everything for you
Vem coração ver	Come heart, come and see the
o 青空	blue sky

The trickster samurai asks the listener to be seduced by trickery, character flexibility whose adoption and applicability are necessary among the strict procedures governing the Japanese culture.

The music awakens the memory of the traditions of the home country and provides the listener with a sense of hope and peace in the face of difficulties of foreign everyday life. The feeling of serenity, finally, is associated with words that summon to a perky and at the same time harmonious position of being in achieving their own goals, in tune with nature and close to happiness.

Pássaro Imigrante (Inmigrant Bird): awareness of collective non-acceptance and of exploitation at work

Composed and performed by the Brazilian Yoka and MC Indigesto, this song gives its name to the album *Passáro Imigrante* (2011), produced by Caio Abumansur Beraldo.

The first track of the CD, this rap addresses the process of arrival of immigrants to foreign lands, and their identitary self-recognition among the new territory.

This song is introduced by an electronic base that will serve as a follow up along its entire length. After about 0:20 a lonely voice begins its message by using metaphors and rhymes that show awareness on the issues of foreigners.

> I come from the immense blue, this land promises
> Here I am, one more, against the puppets
> Ducks Go to the south, the parrots repeat
> My nest I will build, do not meddle
> My freedom I, myself, will generate
> My passport is a mere detail, zero
> From those I consider sincere, I do not expect
> They cut my wings, I recover

The enunciator, in the first person, reflects the reality of their issuers: Brazilians living in Spain willing to face distance and the dangers of an unknown territory, in which they recognize themselves as resistant differences amid a manipulator system, filled with alienated followers, "puppets".

Like migratory birds abandon their originating niches during the period of wintering, the immigrant leaves his country looking to build better "paths". Unlike those who confirm and reproduce systemic precepts, the "migrant bird" is responsible for the construction of their own destiny ("nest"), while making the song a warning instrument when he says, "Ducks Go to the south, parrots repeat/my nest I will build, do not meddle."

Without intending the aid of anyone - even from those who are worthy of some respect - the foreigner is not intimidated by the occurrence of possible cheating. If "they cut his wings", he "recovers", not allowing it to weaken him.

The song is the simulacrum of an imaginary metropolis, a scene of many dangers: easy women, bad influences, drugs and charlatans.

> I want a wide sight, eyes of eagle
> Having a wise mind, not falling into lies
> Cause dirty beak brought as if it were
> sweet beak, from these refuges I flee

> The bird wanders, through night and morning
> Dodges raptors in every corner
> Corners of all corners, I hear so many tears
> I have dinner once in a while, I send verses to the saints

The third and fourth strophes of the song show, through slang, a pressing posture. The immigrant must have a "wise mind" and a watchful eye ("eagle eye") in order to dodge the dangers and bad influences - there are noted metaphorical expressions such as "dirty beak" (reference to the envious and gossips), "sweet beak" (an allusion to those who have mastered the art of rhetoric or persuasion) and "birds of prey" (term that refers to conniving people).

The foreign territory is a space of many ghettos. The third strophe, built at the intersection of the third and the first verbal person (singular), reflects an enunciating voice that shows their own suffering, interspersed with observation and identification of other sufferings. Thus, while "strolling" through space of the metropolis, the enunciator recounts the experience of need, supported thanks to the faith ("I have dinner once in a while, I send verses to the saints"), while it also notes and witnesses the reality of other immigrants, as well as the hardships that surround them ("corners of all corners, I hear so many tears").

In the fifth transcribed strophe, the chorus comes. Repeated twice, the verses emphasize the sense of uncertainty facing the foreign territory. All around is novelty and challenge, reality to be fought with the obstinacy of those who crave to go "up and above" and have, in the eyes of their families and distant friends, the highlight of a successful life.

> Chorus:
>
> Better on in the hand than two in the bush
> In a distant world
> Nothing is as it was
> Time to break away from the pack
> up and above
> immigrant bird

Continuing the analysis of this song, the text describes the constant daily struggles, immersed in all the obstacles. The sixth strophe has the following content:

> Loneliness strikes
> You search your pack
> Your race ignores you
> Always rebuffing you
> Some kind of captivity

At this point of the transcription, the first verse is of relevance. "Loneliness strikes" appears in the song as a melody opposed to the spoken song, a kind of counterpoint that is the fear of the immigrant, in the face of loneliness and neglect. The verse is also an intertextual reference, allusion to the popular song *"Desde que o samba é samba",* by Caetano Veloso. In this aspect, rap offers the memory of a well-known cultural product in Brazil, country in performance (and in real life), which represents the country of origin of the enunciative voice. The "memory of their own", does not appear here to the immigrant as a driving element of attitudes. Rather, it is an introductory metaphor of a sorrowful longing, that can translate to receptors the image of a foreign and his feeling of helplessness in the face of an unfamiliar context.

The effort described by the enunciator is noteworthy. The textual image is that of an immigrant who tries to mingle, "seeking" assistance in any group or community. Nevertheless, he does not succeed. The verses denouncing the lack of humanity as an integral factor of the human character; to that it states: "You search your pack/Your race ignores you/Always rebuffing you/Some kind of captivity." To reach out for help, the immigrant finds despair and disservice, gestures coming from "trapped" souls on a systemic "captivity".

Interpersonal relationships established by the foreigners are difficult. The "reception" of others are permeated by interests. The seventh strophe transcribed has the following content:

> You're already Captivating
> Beautifull, they arrive with their feathers
> Your crowd
> With those you get used to not having only one
> Tired of grazing revolt tides
> In the wave of soothing, many loose birds
> But if you come now, try to collaborate
> Do not act as the boss, your tricks do not work here
> Best to be with your mouth shut, no wings out
> If you want to sing as a cock, you will sing in a cage

The man who immigrates, cited in rapper poetry, realizes the wide availability of females in modern times. The provocative attitude of the opposite sex is the subject of the strophe. Adorned in "feathers", followed by "crowd", the women described exude an 'easy' behavior, by which it becomes impossible to envision a non-ephemeral relationship. The enunciative voice, in this sense, is tired of repetitive situations whose existence appears as certain. ("Tired of grazing revolt tides/in the soothing wave, many loose birds").

The application of language games carved in rhymes assists in representing the social context. The expertise of the immigrant perception constitutes the expository intention of revealing a behavioral basis to be applied before the "traps" of the diaspora. Again, the interlocutors of the situation are given a warning. "But if you come now, try to collaborate/do not act as the boss, your tricks do not work here." Regarding the possible occurrence of cheating, the immigrant voice declares what will be their position: denouncing any cheating, executed or attempted. Thus, he states: "if you want to sing as a cock, you will sing in the cage." In the face of any exploration, the foreigner is sure their attitudes: is impassive in front of the suffering by the oppressor or his followers. Such an approach arises again, in the eighth strophe.

> I will not feel sorry for anyone who plucks me, Vultures!
> Those who claim to feed you with birdseed, actually feed
> from you.

Blood, sweat and tears are more than oil
They create crows that eat your eyes

Without showing any kind of intimidation, the immigrant voice notes exploitation of the capitalist system, as well as ignorance of their followers: "Those who claim to feed you with birdseed, actually feed from you" he warns.

The "crow", metaphor referring to agents of the system, refers to shareholders, always starved of profits and unbridled consumption, regardless of its consequences. "Blood, sweat and tears" in unknown lands, reflect the rigorous and exploitative working conditions to which immigrants are subject to, in the hope of achieving plans of a better life. The immigrant is far from assuming a naive attitude towards the facts - knowing that his effort is a fundamental systemic mechanism, more valuable than any other currency amid the capitalist machinery.

The intertextuality is also shown in the construction of this verse, since the use of the phrase "blood, sweat and tears" refers to the homonymous title of two other productions: the book written by Richard Donkin (2003) - in which the author exposes the historical trajectory and exploitative reality of labor relations, from prehistoric times to the present - and the rap produced by the Brazilian group Facção Central - in which conscious questions about the importance of the space for rapper shows, work environment and redemption available to the exercise of minority classes are addressed. Obtained from a lot of sacrifice ("blood, sweat and tears") such spaces are described by the Facção Central rap, as places that deserve respect, in which fights should not occur, so that policial censorship and crackdowns are facilitated.

The intertextual approach reflects influences exerted on the performing immigrant pair. Whether through the knowledge acquired through the work "Donkin" (2003), or the significance absorbed by listening to the rapper group Facção Central, Indigesto can demonstrate intellectual mastery over the meaning of labor relations: necessary, but exploitative, to which efforts are dedicated and from which one should not expect recognition

The rapper's song ends with the previously mentioned chorus; verbal portrait of the foreign condition in globalized times:

> Chorus 2x:
>
> Better one in the hand than two in the bush
> In a distant world
> Nothing is as it was
> Time to break away from the pack
> Up and above
> immigrant bird

The closure of the song in question, by the foregoing chorus, emphasizes the thematic purpose voiced in performance: portraying the lonely and impetuous "flight" of the immigrant who abandons his "pack". The metaphor that accompanies the song demonstrates the move of the foreigners from their communities, realizing the impact of differences in an unknown territory and feeling the "weight" offered by the life he chose, apart from his original group.

"Pássaro Imigrante" is, therefore, a song that demonstrates the foreign look on the unpredictable offered by the world, portraying a cautious look towards social obstacles and their own mental-emotional conditions resulting from this immigrant condition (whose image is given by the sense of helplessness conveyed by the performance). The song is established, therefore, as a picture of the troublesome crossing, which is still ongoing due to the impulsion received from the will of recognition and social mobility.

Desclasificado: Sure of being nobody and the hopeful fight for better days

"Desclasificado" is a song with words that are a little "stronger" than those presented in the previously analyzed songs. Although developed from smooth intonations, the voice and instrumental basis integration (which simulates orchestra sounds passages

merged to brief vocals by a male chorus, which makes it possible to identify a melodious atmosphere in the song) clearly shows a foreign sentiment resulting from the violent reality that pervades the capitalist scenario.

The poetic narrative, fully developed in the first person, has a dislocated lyrical voice, which is not limited to soften the image of the space it occupies in society: a marginal and invisible space before the upper classes. The first strophe transcribed is as follows:

Translation:

Soy el último de la eslabón
pirámide
Desclasificado soy el último
eslabón
Que miraron de lado
El corazón anclado
Desparramado porque nunca seré
aceptado
El tiempo, el límite
el... Que nadie mide, el que en-
señaron que nunca será libre
Educarse para mí no sea accesible
Por mas que el commercial diga
que todo es posible
A veces una y a veces nada
En donde quepo en que casilla mi
cara marcada
Perdida la mirada, la distancia, la
Ventana
Que será lo que define ya de mi
cama
Toque todas las puertas
La vida desfilaba en el borde desta
vereda
Me siento silenciado
Yo estoy declasificado

I am the last link of the
pyramid
Disclassified I am the last
link
They looked aside
Heart anchored
Dispersed, because I will never be
accepted
The time, the limit
The one... that none measures, the
one they taught will never be free
Be polite to me, do not be Accessible
As much as the advertisement says
that everything is possible
Sometimes one and sometimes
nothing
Where do I fit in that box, my face
marked
The lost look, the distance, the
window
This will define my bed
Touch every door
Life paraded on the edges of the
sidewalk
I feel muted
I am disclassified

One can note that the enunciating voice attests to the certainty of a time whose mechanisms operate on the basis of exclusion and social prejudice. The enunciation in first person reveals the observation of the social pyramid - "I am the last link of the pyramid" he says - demonstrating a negative view on the (im)possibility of socioeconomic recognition and ascension.

The performed, song describes a scenario of indifference. In it, representing a condemned and stigmatized immigrant, the enunciator is declaring the impossibility of his own inclusion - "They looked sideways/Heart anchored/Dispersed because I will never be accepted" she says.

The gaze resulting from this foreign voice sets up a kind of "window" that allows us to verify the functioning of the contemporary world, in their social strata and dichotomies. Describing the intense crossing, extensive in "time" and "experiences" - a factor that led to her place of enunciation. The enunciator demonstrates his realistic view of the world, emphasizing the limits to which she has been subjected to throughout her existence. "The time limit/Those that no one measures, Those that were thought they will never be free."

In a "time" conditioning only to the tolerance of otherness, the foreigner recognizes, through a construction based on rhymes, the illusion and the ineffectiveness of advertisements, "metaphors" of a better life that one day moved them. Note that they receive a polite treatment, but not inclusive and she recognizes her isolating condition, doomed to an uncertain and little rewarding fate.

Steeped in insights, she assumes her displacement. With a "marked face", element that defines her image in the context, she feels the pain of inhabiting a distant place: "Where do I fit in that box, my marked face/The lost look, the distance, the window/this will define my bed."

The difficulties that crosses her path, forces her to depend on the help of her neighbor. Going from "door to door", she lives in the gutters of a universe that is her, but also of many others. The street is her home, a place of forgetfulness, in which they are ignored and hidden from the attempts of expression "I am muted" says the enunciator, soon after completing with "I'm disclassified".

The idea of being no one remains in the second transcribed strophe, as stated by the enunciator in the chorus:

	Translation:
Oh soy el último eslabón de la pirámide	Oh I am the last link of the pyramid
Pirámide, pirámide, pirámide ...	Pyramid, pyramid, pyramid ...
Subir peldaños toma tiempo toma años	Climbing stairs takes time, it takes years
Los últimos de la fila luego serán los primeros	The last in line will soon be the first

The sequence of the rapper narrative, however, surprises in terms of foreign attitude. Despite awareness with regards to their own marginalization in society, the enunciator does not show any nihilistic behavior. On the contrary, she believes in her rise and long-term effort: "Climbing stairs takes time, it takes years/The last in line will soon be the first," she says.

In the third transcribed strophe, the following content appears:

	Translation:
Desclasificado soy el último peón que cambiaron de lado	Disclassified I am the last pawn that changed sides
El sujeto problema objeto del dilema	The problematic- subject, dilemma object
El que no cabe en este esquema	The one that does not fit in this scheme
Sigo pateando piedras, el que sueña a su manera	I go on kicking stones, a dreamer in his own way
Si me preguntan soy de cemento y tierra	If they ask me, I am made of cement and dust
Cual es mi clase quien dicta las bases	My class is who dictates the rules
Corrido en el disfarce ya que mi envase no clase	Confused, maladjusted, my package has no rating
Todo me delata mi pelo mi facha	Everything betrays me, my hair, my band
Cual es la justicia cuando siempre se te tacha	What is justice when you always need it
Me siento silenciado	I feel muted
Yo soy el desclasificado	I am disclassified

The perception of the place occupied by the foreigner in society is demonstrated in performance by reference to an invisible systemic force to which the enunciator addresses through the use of the third person singular. This force includes property manipulation and displacement of people, and its operation is compared by the enunciator to that performed during a game of chess - "Disclassified I am, the last pawn to change sides"- she says.

Left in the margins, the enunciator is aware of being a problem as well, a social threat to arouse fear and doubt before the other wealthier classes. "Problematic-subject, dilemma object" says the verse in internal rhyme that introduces the existence of a individual displaced in relation to social standards.

To her hard tasks and the property of dreaming are reserved - "I keep kicking stones, a dreamer in his own way", says the self-lyrical, showing awareness of this fact.

Despite being the "last" to whom some importance in the game of life is given to, being inert and vulnerable to visible and invisible allocations existing in the social body, the foreign assumes a posture of bravery. She is someone who faces the hardships of daily life and does not allow the lack of justice to shake her down. - "I'm made of cement and stone", she says.

Guided by their own convictions - "My class is who dictates the rules" - the enunciator aims to fill the gaps in the system, without being devoured. Even with the awareness around the stigma itself - "Everything denounces me, my hair, my band" - she appears strong and exalts his own coping capacity.

The idea of "fortress", however, turns, once again, into the admission of oblivion, when she says, at the end of the strophe: "What is justice when you always need it/I feel muted/I'm disclassified".

In the fourth transcribed strophe, the idea of forgetting is again evident when the enunciator, again repeated:

Translation:

Oh soy el último eslabón de la pirámide	Oh I am the last link of the pyramid
Pirámide, pirámide, pirámide	Pyramid pyramid pyramid
Oh soy el último eslabón de la pirámide	Oh I am the last link of the pyramid
Pirámide, pirámide, pirámide	Pyramid pyramid pyramid

The assessment of the performance of this rap comes to an end at the fifth strophe transcribed, when the following verses arise:

Translation:

Espere, espere, ya necesito ofrecerme al limbo quizás fracase (x3)	Wait, wait, I already need To offer myself to limbo, if I fail (x3)
Pirámide, pirámide, pirámide	Pyramid, pyramid, pyramid
Si soy el último eslabón de la pirámide	If I am the last link of the pyramid

In the second verse of the strophe, the use of the term "limbo" surprises and causes reflections at the translational-interpretive process and may also attribute to the performance metaphysical connotations. According to the Aurélio dictionary of the Portuguese language, the term may take the meanings below:

> Limbo. [Do lat. limbu, edge]. 1. Edge, border, boundary 2. Edge of the disk of a measuring instrument, on which is marked the angular graduation. 3. Anatomy generic term that signifies the edge of certain anatomical formations. 4.Star. Contour of light in a star. [See, this meaning, terminadouro] 5. Bot. enlarged portion of leaf-like organs, such as the leaf itself, petals, sepals, etc. 6. Religion Desus. In the Catholic Church, the place to where, suposedly, goes the soul of a child who died without being baptized 7. Fam. Place where useless things are thrown. 8. Forgetfulness. (FERREIRA, 2010, p. 1266).

When referring only to the mythical-religious significance, attributable to the term, Chevalier and Gheerbrant (1999) state:

Limbo: Imagined apparently by Orphic traditions, Virgil puts it in Hell's entrance (Aeneid, 6, p. 426-429), dwelling place of stillborn children or who lived only a short time, *voice and immense wail, souls of children who cry, these little beings who did not know the sweetness of life and on an unhappy day, were kicked off at the same threshold of existence, from their mother's womb, to dip them in the early evening of the grave.* This idea of limbo was repeated in Christianity to designate the place where down the souls of children who die without baptism, which do not suffer the consequences of the original sin; is also the place that would be reserved for adult souls who have lived in accordance with natural law and for not having the supernatural grace, they would be deprived of eternal beatitude. But this idea, controversial at the very heart of the Catholic Church, does not impose the faith of Christians with perfect clarity. Limbo symbolizes only, in the current sense, the antechamber of paradise, or the preparations of a new era of civilization. (CHEVALIER AND GHEERBRANT, 1999, p . 548).

It is possible to infer from the verse in question that there is an equivalence established by the enunciator: associating the understanding she holds on her own life and the image of a hellish reality, profering in an imperative way - and three times - the idea "wait, wait, now I need/To offer myself to limbo, if I fail (x3)".

Thus, it appears that the expository voice cries out not to be condemned to this perpetual suffering condition. The place from which she speaks is that of oblivion, in which the useless things are thrown into marginality.

In the midst of hardship and violence of all kinds, the enunciator asks the elliptical interlocutor to stop leaving her in this condition, not to abandon him.

At this point the analysis incurs also in a polysemous language game. In the connotation given above - of a more streamlined look, in which the pyramid would be a reference to the "social pyramid" - it appears here that the term may also take meanings related to the metaphysical. To clarify this fact, it is necessary once again, to reference dictionaries. The Aurélio dictionary of the Portuguese language has the following entry for the term pyramid, linked essentially to the formation of this element:

> Pyramid [The Egyptian pi-sea, by gr. pyramis, from the lat. Pyramide] Sf 1.Geom. Polyhedron wherein one face is a polygon, and the others are triangles with a common vertex. 2. Monument in the form of a quadrangular pyramid. 3. Anat. Generic term designating formation. (4) pointy or cone - like.(...) (FERREIRA, 2010, p. 1642).

In Chevalier and Gheerbrant (1999), there are relevant associations to the second significant connotation, proposed here. The authors, when referring to the monumental buildings of Ancient Egypt - necessary for the viability of funeral rites in that society - try to explain the relationship between such constructions and religious beliefs and magical rites practiced at the time by those who lived in such a civilization. On entry, they provide:

> (...) Living growth - perhaps this is the expression that best expresses the global pyramid symbolism. It tends to ensure the pharaoh its apotheosis in the dead man's connection to the sun God, a supreme term of eternal growth.
> A similar idea is attributed to Hermes Trismegisto; the summit of a pyramid symbolizes the demiurgic Word, First Force, not engendered, but emerging from the Father and who governs all things created, totally perfect and fruitful.So at the end of the pyramidal rise, the initiated will achieve union with the verb, as the deceased pharaoh is identified in the hollow of the stone, with the immortal God. (CHEVALIER AND GHEERBRANT, 1999, p. 720-721).

As a building, the pyramid would therefore be a kind of energy transfering place, between the physical world and the spiritual world; link from the dead towards eternity. Through it, therefore, the approach of the dead toward God would be enabled.

The allusion to the term "pyramid", established repeatedly throughout the performance can also represent - amid the polysemic game that is established in the song - a kind of subjective appeal.

He who "is the last link of the social pyramid" living "in limbo", demonstrates his willingness to rise, assuming the social and human scale a prized situationality and wishing to live in a "world" other than that in which he inhabits.

From "cement and dust", the song shows a foreigner who knows the systemic operation inherent in the world he lives in and, bravely, is put in front of it, in shock. Metaphorically, the notions of real world "limbo" and ideal "metaphysical" world are opposed; and aware of his condition, he puts himself at the service of the will of ascension.

An enunciator that demonstrates lucidity and rationality, living his days based on "his own rules"; and knowing how to live like a "pawn" in a chessboard.

Το Κέρμα: *a coin has two sides, the world and the truth, as well*

Tenth track of the album *Αλάνα*, *Το Κέρμα* (Greek, The coin) is an allusion to the game of "Heads or Tails", in which the "heads" are sung and life is seen as a great game of truths. MC Yinka starts the performance of his verses, which contain witness tones. The setting is that of an African born in Greece, strolling the dangerous alleys of the city. The self-awareness arises immediately in the first transcribed strophe, associated with a scathing social criticism. The *flaneur*-rapper going around the lanes of the city, realizes the existence of an indifferent Athens, where the people are cold and silent in the face of social injustice triggered by the system. It states:

Translation:

Στην ζουγκλά του μπέτον ζω	In concrete jungle live
Αφροέλλην ανυπήκοος	Natural African-Greek economic
οικονομίκος μετανάστης	immigrant
Γέννημα θρέμμα Αθήνων	Born and raised in Central Ath-
κεντρικά εκεί που ο κοσμός	ens, there
Ζει πυκνά δεν παρατηρεί,ξέρει	Where people live crowded
καλά ομώς να κοιτά.	Does not notice, but can see.
Καθώς κινούμε στα στένα	While I wander through the
της πόλης μπορεί. να μου την	city's alleys,
πέσουν	Fascists may surround me.
Φασίστες, μπορεί. στο	Can tell me, inside the bus:
λεωφορείο να μου πουν	- Here is Greece, go away and go
– Εδώ είναι Ελλαδα ,γύρνα	back to your country -
πίσω –	And look at me strangely
Η να με κοιτάξουν παράξενα	Especially if I go out with a Greek
Μόλις με ελληνίδα ξεμυτίσω	girl
Η άλλη όψη είναι να μου πουν	On the other side of the coin, they
ΕΪ ΓΙΟ! Μαν εσείς οι μαύροι τα	say:
σπάτε! Έχετε ρυθμό!	- "Oh, son; Oh man, you blacks
Δεν με νοιάζει εάν έχετε νιονιό	rock! You have rhythm!
σας έχω δει στην τι-βι και	I do not care if you stink. I watch
αύτο μου αρκεί μου	you on TV. This is enough for me.

Noteworthy in this strophe is what appears to be a reference to the Greek police, one of the power agents, classified as "fascist" by the enunciator. Impositive, the police represses the marginalized, in the economic and/or ethnic aspect. A foreigner is not welcome, especially if he transcends the "limits of coexistence". In the face of the system, he is a "tolerated" object, by the logic of exploitation. To him, the right to move through the city streets presents, through daily life, in a restrictive manner, as shown by the verse in question. The same is true when it comes to romantic relationships, usually perceived negatively if instituted among individuals belonging to different social classes and ethnic backgrounds.

Noteworthy is the passage in which the enunciator, speaking in the first person singular and assuming the personality of a descendant of black immigrants, chronicles his relationship with a certainly white Greek woman. "Fascists may surround me/They can tell me, inside the bus:/- Here is Greece, go back to your country -/Especially when I go out with a Greek girl".

The establishment of ethnic and social boundaries also assumes visibility in a professional capacity. The performance shows the image of a stigmatized subject, since in marginal condition. This character has before him two professional alternatives: the performance of menial activities considered "minor", or the practice of the arts, for the entertaining of the hegemonic classes. On this point, the end of the strophe, there is the only alternative to "mask" social indifference: the black-foreign performance, pleasent to "the nation's whites".

Performing as a white native, the enunciator apeaks in a way that allows him to forget prejudice or at least minimize it: - "Oh, son; Oh man; you blacks rock! You have rhythm!/I do not care if you stink. I watch you on TV. This is enough for me", he says.

In sequence, the narrative suggests the existence of a rapper - observer through the song, denouncing inequalities, introducing reflections and seeking to awaken consciences. The second transcribred strophe has the following content:

Translation:

Βγάζετε κάτι το θεαμάτικο!βλέπω βίλλες καζίνα τσιφλικάδες να πλουτίζουν	You make beautiful things. I see mansions, casinos, rich farmers
Να πέρνανε φίνα και από την άλλη συνταξιούχοι σε καραντίνα , καμμένα	Living in luxury; and on the other hand, retirees surviving
Δάση μια ντουζίνα . νταβατζιλίκι φόροι. Και η ακρίβεια να σε κάνει να ζεις	burned forests, huge taxes and famine compels you to live
Τσίμα –τσίμα ζούμε ή απλώς υπάρχουμε?	- Do we Live or simply exist?
– Αλήθεια! Σε βρίσκουμε ή σε μαθαίνουμε?	- Truth! Do we find you or know you?
Μίλαμε ή απλως αρθρώνουμε?	Do we articulate or just talk?
Μελετάμε ή απλώς διαβάζουμε?	Do we study or just read?

The complaint inserts luxury as predator of nature: "jungles are cut" and very expensive taxes "force you to live". The performer's look identifies the contrast between rich and poor and do not care about retirees. Rapper questionings call people to get out of alienation ("Do we live or simply exist?"/ "Do we study or just read?"). The interrogative inducements, in part, are answered in an ironic way, by the enunciator; who confirming the second of the listed options ("Truth"), notes the existence of morally precarious and superficial attitudes.

The social dichotomies identified and mocked by verses of the third strophe are followed by a chorus, in the fourth transcribed strophe. This, in turn, also gives a rise to collective reflections, giving the recipient the option of seeing the facts in the manner that suits them.

	Translation:
Espere, espere, ya necesito ofrecerme al limbo quizás fracase (x3)	Wait, wait, I already need To offer myself to limbo, if I fail (x3)
Pirámide, pirámide, pirámide	Pyramid, pyramid, pyramid
Si soy el último eslabón de la pirámide	And I am the last link of the pyramid

	Translation:
Ρεφραίν -2x:	Chorus -2x:
Δες την αλήθεια οπώς θες Το κέρμα είναι στον αέρα. κορώνα ή γράμματα?	See the truth as you wish The coin is in the air, heads or tails?
Δες την αλήθεια οπώς θες Το κέρμα είναι στον αέρα .κορώνα ή γράμματα?	See the truth as you wish The coin is in the air, heads or tails?

The media, instrument and extension of power, is charged as a tool of charm and alienation. The fifth transcribed strophe has the following content:

Τηλεοπτίκες περσόνες
αθλητικά είδωλα, πρότυπα
Γυαλιστέρα πρόσωπα
ρετουσαρισμένα για να
πέφτουν
Πάνω τους λάγνα βλέμματα
του θεάματος τα ψέμματα
Γίναν οι δίκες μας αλήθειες
και όμως μέσα σε βρώμικα δ
ωμάτια
δοθήκανε και επίπεδα
ανεβήκανε.
Αναβολίκα ρουφήξανε
φουσκόσανε
Πουλήσανε την ψύχη τους
στο Διάλο
και όμως ευημερήσανε, πολλά
τα θέλω αναγκές πολλές
Τη σύγχρονη εποχή δουλεύεις
για να θες
Και ας σε κυνηγάνε οι οφείλες
Προτεραιότητα είσαι για
εταιρείες διαφημιστικές
Που μελετάνε την ψυχή σου
και σε κάνουν την κρίση σου
να καις
Τα όμορφα χωριά όμορφα
καίγονται.
Πέφτουν βομβές και μέτα
πεφτούν καρβέλια
Πολιτικοί σε συνόδους
δίνουνε τα χέρια,
Και ο κόσμος γλέντάει μέσα
στα πεδία
Μάχης με κομμένα χέρια.κατώ
από το τράπεζι
Πίσω από την βιτρίνα , τι
ríοκρύβει
Το προσωπείο τι λένε τα ψήλα
τα γράμματα.

Translation:
Screen characters, athletic idols,
examples
Bright faces, retouched after
falling
Under the lustful eyes of the show
of lies
They have become our own
truths, but within dirty rooms
They gave up, climbing social
scales
Stalling, they sucked excuses and
were full
They sold their souls to the devil
And still they thrived, I want a
lot, I need a lot
Today, you work, and by working
generate benefits
And leave the hunters of debt
chasing you
It is the priority, it is advertising
No one looks at the human side,
but build the judgment to burn
you

Small and beautiful villages burn

Bombs fall and then bread falls

Politicians in Congress hold
hands
And the world is partying in the
fields
Battles with cut on the table

Behind the window that hides

The mask, they say, plays high
cards

The poetic narrative at this point, describes in third-person the characters and illusions that are part of the television. According to the passage, the media creates illusory myths that arouse the sexual fantasy of the receiving masses, preventing them from reflecting or questioning reality. The false media spectacle, anchored on advertising strings, "hunts" the intelligence of citizens and enables the capitalist extortion. Thiefs of questioning skills and reflection, media and advertising are operative mechanisms of a larger system that exploits, disintegrates and oppresses. Noteworthy here is the passage in which the enunciator states that "Nobody looks at the human side, but produces the judgment to burn you."

Still in the same strophe, the poetic narrative exemplifies the identity apathy of the Greek people in general. By simulating the image of a small town setting at war, the text suggests that any government counterpart - by "giving some bread" to the people in an emergency or disaster situation - generates contentment within the masses. The little that is done is enough to stagnate the nation.

Politicians are "masked" celebrating fake achievements "hand in hand"; the population is a naive contingent that satisfactorily accepts the crumbs and follows its routine "celebrating" without realizing the stagnation of its own reality.

After the chorus, the sixth strophe suggests the community to choose a side to see the "truth", like a game of "heads or tails". Criticism of the system remains.

In the seventh strophe, the rapper narrative quips the action of power agents and remains simulating, in an aesthetic way, the scenario witnessed by the MC.

Translation:

Ησυχία τάξη και ασφάλεια, πηλίκια νηφάλια	Peace, order and security, military helmets
Οργάνα της τάξης υπηρέτες των πολίτων, μπλε	Maintainers of the blue order, servants of the civils
Σουπερ ήρωες με μπέρτα και ασπίδα	Superheroes with cape and sword
Δίνουν μάχες καθημερίνα για να επικράτησει το δίκαιο	They struggle daily to ensure justice
ΟΥΠΣ τρέλες σφαίρες βλέπω στα εξαρχεία, θέλω να πάνε στον ουράνο μα... βρίσκουν ψάχνο μια 15χρόνη ψυχή	Crazy bullets want to go to heaven But they find a 15 year-old soul that went to heaven
πήγε στο ουράνο	tear gas, panic
Πάνω από τα δακρυγόνα και τον πάνικο	
Ευκολή ζωη γρήγορα όλα τα κομφόρ.	On the other hand, easy life, all the comfort
Όμορφες χρωματιστές τροφές αυτοκίνητα με πολλές στρόφες	Beautiful engines, colorful foods, fast cars
Εργοστάσια πολυεθνικές αχρείαστες συσκευές	Factories, multinationals, beautiful packaging
ΝΑΙ από όλα έχει ο μπαχτσές.	Yes, everything is in the garden
Ο κάρκινος έχει πλέον χίλια πρόσωπα, πιτσίρικια χτυπάνε κάρτα	Cancer has a thousand faces, children hit the card
Και δουλεύουν 15ωρα, η γη ένα θερμοκήπιο μη αναστρέψιμη κατασταση Στενεύουν τα περιθώρια.	And they work 15 hours, the world moves, but nothing changes Spaces shrink

The ironic tone of MC Yinka becomes undeniable when, after describing the activities of the Greek police, he states the following verses: "Crazy bullets want to go to heaven/But they find a 15 year-old soul that went to heaven/tear gas, panic."

The passage possibly refers to an event that occurred in Greece in 2008 (one year before the recording of the *Αλάνα* album, in which this song is included). This is regarding the death of Alexandros Grigoropoulos, an anarchist Greek student, who in the midst of a civil conflict between the national guard and a group of activists, in the neighborhood Exarhia, Athens, was hit in the chest by a bullet fired by police officer Epaminontas Korkoneas. The crime had international repercussions, and in 2010, the police officer was sentenced to life imprisonment (maximum sentence of Greek regime).

The song goes on in its criticism of the system, its habits and indifference. Criticism combined with the description of the difficulties faced by the foreign individual. The verse in question refers to child labor and exploitative reality practiced by the "factories" and "multinationals". The world is the representation of an environment full of historically instituted gaps. The existence portrayed becomes also a dichotomous scenario: on one side, those who suffer in "panic", calling for social change; on the other, the "easy life", alienated in "comfort". Attentive to what happens around him, the enunciator shows that the system always falls above every existential possibility. "The world moves, but nothing changes," he says.

Το Κέρμα, this is a song in which the identity perceptions of the foreign towards the space in which he chose to be are shown. By observing the behavior of individuals that surround him, the foreigner perceives the ratings assigned to his own identity, at the same time he also produces other classifications to the identity of his environment. By perfoming this process, he denounces the perceived injustices, claiming collective actions through a chorus-message:

	Translation:
Ρεφραίν- 2x	Chorus -2x:
Δες την αλήθεια οπώς θες	See the truth as you wish
Το κέρμα είναι στον αέρα.	The coin is in the air, heads or
κορώνα ή γράμματα?	tails?
Δες την αλήθεια οπώς θες	See the truth as you wish
Το κέρμα είναι στον αέρα.	The coin is in the air
κορώνα ή γράμματα?	Heads or tails?

The song, as we see, contains the poetic and descriptive process, performed through the following question proposed in metaphor: "The coin is in the air, heads or tails?" The allusion to the game "heads or tails" - a simple game, which consists in throwing a coin so that, when it falls to the ground, the side pointing up will determine the solution of a conflict between the shareholders or even only the choice of two alternatives proposed - in fact, it is also a warning the listeners-receptors of this aestheticized communication. To them, the existential reality always offers two ways: the neutrality going through life committing injustices or silencing before them; and the possibility of being affected by problems, facing them in order to work for a more egalitarian society.

Amidst the capital jungles, acculturation, violence and faith: the system, the origins and the sacred sung by immigrants

The organization of this subchapter is made from a selection of songs that have the description of the foreign experience among the capitalist metropoli in common, "concrete jungles" full of social obstacles whose nature seems at first insurmountable: it is noted, for example, in those songs, the image of exploitation taken to the last consequences, characteristic of labor markets that lend themselves to absorb foreign labor; urban violence; corruption exercised by political representatives and the call (free of nationalities or specific territories) to all foreigners in marginal situations; therefore a transnational evocation.

The same songs that comprise this section, despite describing the difficulties of the diaspora, they also preach resistance, describing actions and talking to those who primarily retain faith, memory and recognition as references related to protection, driving factors of hope, building futures and fairer days.

Selva do Dinheiro: an alert to the illusions of the system

Performed by the São Paulo group Mamelo Sound System, "*Selva do Dinheiro*" is an aesthetic alert to humanity. This is because, by reporting the exploratory intentions that fundament the neoliberal system and its economic-capitalist model, it tries to awaken the attention of its receptors and reverse the existence of a possible social naivety into attentive gazes and everyday actions guided by utmost caution.

In the strophes that begin the performance of the song, the voice demonstrates awareness of how social relations are operated in the neoliberal framework. Ironically, he begins his speech revealing his own attitude towards the exploratory and stratified scenario in which he lives . Thus, the first and second transcribed strophes have the following content:

> Be a craddle robber, bro, or a undertaker
> Business is business, what matters is how much I earn
> How much dinner I have, ad how much I raise. That is what matters
> Always, everywhere, in every corner,
> Musical, but for real
> Only suckers take me wrong
> When I say, "My sin is not capital"
> Bow Wow Wow, I'm chilling, for real
> And if you insist on telling me that the dollar sign is the new God
> So okay: mine are atheists
> From Osasco to São Mateus, what I really want is to see
> The bros and the girls say goodbye
> To pain of being treated like shit
> While corporations from the US, China, or Japan
> Devastate and plunder the Brazilian soil
> All that remains is to set fire in the hornet's nest

In the early verses, the enunciator recognizes the "logic" of the operation, present "everywhere" even in the intentions of the immigrant performer. Faced with such reasoning, we note that, to succeed, the foreign does not mind taking certain functions through the "diasporic location": he sees everyday as "business" and his aspirations boil down towards "quantitative" growth and the overcoming of a trajectory doomed to a marginalized social framework.

It is important to note, in this sense, the presence of certain expressions used in rap as an illustration of reference: "craddle robber" (one who practices sexual relations with much youger people); "nigger" (allusion to slavery to which black people had been subjected over the colonial processes that crossed the world) or "undertaker" (bookie of funerals) are representative slang of the possible social-places consciously assumed by the foreigner who wants to ascend. Social ascension becomes, according to the enunciator, an issue "lived" and "performed" everywhere, including in the "musical" scene.

Immersing in the system by filling the gaps rejected by other groups is the alternative found by the foreigner for "progress" in society. This strategy, according to the song, is judged in "bad" interpretations [of critical nature], only by the followers of this great "capitalist" system. This can be seen in the verses: "Only suckers take me wrong/When I say, 'My sin is not capital'."

The application of expressions like sucker (referring to the worker who acts "against" the interests of other co-workers or people who flatter someone in order to obtain personal privileges) is noted here.

The second strophe begins with the application of intertextuality. In the verse "Bow Wow Wow, I'm chilling, for real" there is an onomatopoeia that works as an allusion to the song "*Atomic Dog*", from George Clinton's solo album, *Computer Games* (1982). The enunciator behaves as an exception, "chill" towards world's orders and conscious about the role he takes in this space. Thus, if the capital is the "God of the planet", the dollar signs "targeted" by this enunciator are "atheists"; walking "opposite" to the neoliberal logic, subverting it, to the extent that they are used in favor of the rise of the strata in marginal condition. Note the relevance of a voice that speaks ~ not only for himself but for the entire group that constitutes his "enunciating place".

This fact becomes even more apparent from the fourth line in the second strophe, when the enunciator clarifies what he wants, in fact: "From Osasco to São Mateus what I really want is to see/the bros and the girls say goodbye/to the pain of being treated like shit"

The home country memory also appears associated with the exploitation context. In the past, Brazil was a nation subject to Portuguese colonization, today it faces a new colonialism, led by big corporations: US, China or Japan. The dream of the enunciator is composed by the dream of many: the extinction of this scenario, where humans are treated "like shit" in reformulated concepts of slavery, aimed at generating exorbitant profits by such corporations.

By ratifying the existence of this reality, the enunciator finds his power of speech. Given the "devastation", of the "robbery" implemented in Brazilian soil, all that is left is complaint. The song therefore assumes a warlike potential, condensed in its aspect of protest and accusation. It is possible to verify this argument from the interpretative reading of the last line in the second strophe: "All that remains is to set fire to the hornet's nest."

The song continues with the chorus, which consists of the following verses:

Chorus:

Money's Jungle, tell me who is the first
To surrender completely, body and soul
Money's Jungle, tell me who is the first
The surrender completely No guilt or serenity
Money's Jungle, tell me who is the first
The surrender completely, no beef or trauma
Money's Jungle, tell me who is the first
Yeah...

The "jungle" described by the chorus reflects the dynamics of the major centers, "globalized" and governed by the "capital". In these spaces, the inevitable non-absorption of human-force generates sequels: impossible not to feel "trauma" or "guilt". The dangersof the "Jungle" imply in "stratagems", "beefs" that will permeate the survival of those groups who dwell in it. The questioning statement "Jungle money, tell me who is the first (...)", reflects a certainty already rooted: that is virtually impossible to escape the gears and effects of this system.

The music continues and the performative speech is done only by a female voice during the fourth strophe. Once again, the use of intertextuality appears. Note that the song paraphrases the lyrics from "*Ain't got no/I got life*", by the American pianist and composer, Nina Simone. The verses state:

> Ain't got no home
> Ain't got no shoes
> Ain't got no money
> Ain't got no class
> Ain't got no friends
> Ain't got no schooling
> No mother
> No father
> Ain't got no sisters and brothers
> Ain't got no worth
> Ain't got no faith
> No God
> No Love

The translation shows a state of deprivement, described and lived by the voice of the immigrant. The writing of nouns as "home", "friends", "mother" and "father", always preceded by a denial, gives the receiver the imagination of a lost community, along with material, emotional and religious values. More than that, it conveys the feeling of a ruined destination, where the performative voice is explored, lonely and replaced in marginal conditions; consequences that can be attributed to the implementation of a choice, perhaps mistaken: the act of moving.

In foreign lands, the imigrant performer sings the insulation condition to which he is submitted to. In his country of origin he lived in "marginal" conditions, abroad such reality appears even worse and intensified. Far from family, the immigrant feels the absence of key attributes, which consisted of his formation and old living in the country of origin. The feeling of orphanhood before certain values is externalized and ratified by the end of the strophe from verses that emphasize a state of unbelief and lack of love: "I have no God/I have no love."

In the fifth and sixth strophes, the song remains in the denunciation tones to the global exploitation reality. By denouncing such a context, rap gives a warning to those who live and must act in the midst of such a situation. The verses state:

> This is still true today in 2009
> Only numbers grow,.ORG,.GOV.
> NGOs, UN
> Forget the movie
> It's just aspirins and vultures
> Go, change your vote for shoes or booze
> Who will save your skin is no vice or president
> Collor Collor, the highest offender
> Was a candidate again, in the recent past
> Go see... Sell what I can on the streets
> Collect cans to complement
> Nothing but bread, nothing but meat
> I'm at the point of throwing stones and letting alarm blair

In this excerpt, situations that relate to the practices of popular culture are mixed and at the same time, to the historical world, highlighting passages in the political scene of Brazil, represented from occurring partisan fight over the election period. This rap seeks to deconstruct the "metaphor of historical evolution" rooted in contemporary popular imagination.

In the fifth strophe, the song points to the temporal proximity of the events. The enunciator states "That's still true today in 2009," the timeframe that coincides with the time of production of the album "*Pássaro Imigrante*". The enunciator seems to associate the growth of financial figures to the proliferation of official entities linked to the government and of non-governmental entities. Such institutions, present in digital scope - as noted in the words ".org", and ".gov" that, in principle, should not aim at obtaining financial gain - arise, according to the inferences made during the performance, as explotative entities. At the final verses of the strophe - "Forget the movie/only aspirin and buzzard," the performative voice emphasizes, from metaphors, corporate and explotative action of capitalist agents, stressing "sick" times and full of "executioners" where the well-being is impossible.

In the sixth strophe specifically, the irony of the enunciating speech is notable. At this point, the song alludes to a very common behavior among Brazilians: the exchange of votes. "Go, trade your vote for shoes or booze/Who will save your skin is no vice or president"

The song guides so that there is a heightened perception of the behavior of politicians, many of them corrupt. Addressing the listener, the enunciator declares: "Who will save your skin is no vice or president." Note, in the following verse, the allusion to the surname of former Brazilian President Fernando Collor de Mello. The politician was removed from the presidency in 1992, after a request for impeachment, and was elected in 2006 as Senator of the state of Alagoas. In verses that bring to mind the lyrical association to a real context, of exploratory and corrupt nature, the consequence of which is evidenced by the increase in poverty and the marginalized strata, the song calls the listener to take a closer look, even towards the "other" similarly marginalized ("Go see... sell what I can on the streets/Gathering cans as complement"). Moreover, he emphasizes, once again, his own complaint potential, the core of his intentions: "Nothing but bread, nothing but meat/I'm at the point of throwing stones and letting the alarm blar."

From this "real picture" offered by the song, it is important to recall, once again, the theoretical position filed by Richard Schustermann (1998), when he advocates for the aestheticized reality. For the author, as stated earlier, exchanges between art and life are evident, as well as the correlations between aesthetics and ethics; art is an important element to which the property of reflective awakening is assigned, related to the "time of now".

In a remarkable passage of the work "*Living art: the pragmatist thought and popular aesthetic*", Schusterman manifests against the opposition between the ascetic life (grounded in ethical and spiritual rules) and the aesthetic life (where there are engagement correlations between the artistic practice and the social reality):

> This kind of life, of unity, centered, respectful of limits is sorted by Rorty as "asceticism" (R, 11), an unfavorable opposition to the "aesthetic life" he defends. But this feature is misleading and unfair. It is simply wrong to assume that a life that accentuates a strong unit and that adopts, certain limitations can not be an aesthetic life; that it can not be appreciated and lauded as aesthetically satisfying or even recommended with its aesthetic allure. (SCHUSTERMAN, 1998, p. 215-216).

Amid the body of analyzed strophess, the implicit enunciation of an invitation is clear, proposed by the art to receptors touched by it: the awakening to reality by identifying the means and forms that comprise it. In this way, the enunciator seeks to alert his listener so that they do not let themselves be deceived by pretentious schemes operative in their listening time.

The resulting perception of daily life is converted into meaning through language, in order to integrate the rapper substrate of truth being thus an object of poetic-musical creation. Thus, the aestheticization of contemporary reality, starts to act like a diagnosis that identifies the actions of the social environment, aspects detrimental to the interests and needs of the human community.

Established in performance, poiesis establishes thus a reflection on the socio-historical circumstances amid which it is established.

The closure of this performative rap starts from the chorus, here mentioned and analyzed. So, in the seventh strophe, the following content resurfaces:

> Chorus:
>
> Money's Jungle, tell me who is the first
> To surrender completely, body and soul
> Money's Jungle, tell me who is the first
> The surrender completely, no guilt or serenity
> Money's Jungle, tell me who is the first
> The surrender completely, no beef or trauma
> Money's Jungle, tell me who is the first
> Yeah...
> YOKA
> MSS

One factor that draws attention in this strophe is the verbal signature of the song. After the chorus, the enunciator says the album producer's pseudonym in which the song; "Yoka" is conveyed, plus the initial MSS that possibly refers to the group that performs; "Mamelo Sound System".

Exceção à Regra: the conscious resistance abroad

Performed by the São Paulo group Elo da Corrente, *Exceção à Regra* (Exception to the Rule) provides, once again, an example of performance whose purpose seems to be to give a kind of "aesthetic alert".

In the first transcribed strophe, in the enunciating voice, the purpose of the song can be perceived. At this time, the male and sober tone exposes the rapper's order to disseminate reason before his listeners:

> Spreading certainty through our ground
> giving life like a land used intelligently.
> From the fruit, a sweet taste that gets bitter at the end,
> Like a summer rain that turns into gale.

The first two verses, started under the gerund form, evidence one of the properties of rapper song performance: in which it is performed, being able to "spread certainties" through the "floor" of those who inhabit the oppressed ghettos and share the difficulties and ills created by the system on a global force.

To rap is attributed, at the beginning of the song, the property of providing "life" to these spaces, that under its affirmative influence, become comparable to the inteligent use of "land".

The metaphor of planting, present in the first strophe, ratifies the pedagogical function[23] often incorporated by rappers' songs. Note, in the third and fourth verses that integrate the strophe, the dubious form applied to the exercise of words that connote opposite impressions alluding, in some respect, feelings of positivity and negativity. The antithesis established by names and expressions - "bittersweet"- summer rain "gale"- dialogue with the contextual issues which originated the song, working thus the cognitive reality of the receiver.

The interpretation of the verse makes the poetic portrait of a "floor" filled with illusory properties clear, which attracts and punishes the oppressed classes to it recurringly. The passage in question, in this sense, carries the metaphor of the global scenario that, in its illusory image - "fruit sweet taste" - attracts the immigrants. These, at the proportion they experience the diaspora problems, intensify the negative opinions related to the experience in a foreign territory, so that, if at first the difficulties were seen as an ephemeral obstacle and easy overtaking - "summer rain"- gradually come to

---

23 See: MERCADAL, Trudy Sabbagh. **Hip Hop stories and pedagogy**. Available at: < http://web.mit.edu/comm-forum/mit4/papers/sabbagh.pdf>. Accessed: jul. 22th 2014.

be seen as serious issues - "gales" - that reverse the dream of a better life abroad, in finding a coercive reality, full of obstacles and existential difficulties.

> By the integrity of the window before the break,
> singular manifesto as the exception to the rule,
> Saint Jorge weapons in the body, bringing strength,
> sending ideas before anyone distorts them.

The song goes on and in the second strophe the idea of "transmitting a message "to receptors and listeners" remains. In the first two verses, we can see a justification attributed to rapper performance. The spoken song is meant to work in favor of the "integrity" set amid the social territory governed by neoliberal assumptions; being the sung word, in this regard, a "singular manifesto" that must remain "intact" and face segregation. The song is thus an "exception to the rule" of hegemonic discourse in the midst of this space.

Subsequently, the enunciator refers to the image of a body protected by faith. The allusion to St. Jorge conveys the idea of devotion, coupled with the attitude and thinking of those who have the courage to talk about the reality, and are not afraid to be punished for it. The sender wants to be the first to "have ideas" (musical message), before anyone else wrongly does, which is likely to create some kind of injury to the community.

The speech continues in order to give a tone of "sacred" to the knowledge it brings with it. In the third strophe, there is the realization that any sacrifice is valid before the "consciousness-word", externalized by the song and likely inspired by books, which "remain at the bedside table". The performative voice says in this sense:

> Strengthening the thesis, kink in the chair,
> Based upon the one that remains at the bedside table
> Of the Bed, from chaos to the mud that here extends,
> I go for the art that broke away from industry

Amid the chaos and mud-representations of difficulty in daily life - the performer relates his condition; not only to the purpose of describing it, but also to the intention to make it an example to listeners. In verses "Of the bed, from chaos and the mud that here extends/I go for the art that broke away from industry" note that the path of "art" is set as an escape condition and dispossession against the capital imperialism represented by the industry.

In the fourth strophe, the enunciating voice carries an allusion to Sierra Leone - a country which, although rich in diamonds and other minerals, remains as a nation in conditions of extreme poverty and inequality, in which slave practices are exercised, including those founded on exploitation of child labor. Through this reference, the enunciator is compared to a stone "human and precious", "diamond, such as those from Sierra Leone". But, contrary to what occurs in the aforementioned country, he will not submit to holdings of any species. In his speech, through the use of mixed rhymes, there are the following assertions:

> A diamond such as those from Sierra Leone,
> without the slavery that such land flies.
> illuminated hands, controlled minds, evil destroyer;
> not paid for their labor.

Note, in the midst of the fragment, the reference to a system ("evil destroyer") that "controls minds" and "illuminated hands". The verses protest before the "capital slavery" which explores the most of the people and does not recognize their right to due compensation. Cheap labor, huge profits. The systemic logic remains in focus in the fifth strophe. This time, the government's stance is emphasized:

> Senselessness such as the national government actions,
> enactments seem like plays.
> marginal life, we remain as dogs,
> in no man's land looking for our mothers.

The verses externalize the stance taken by the government, foolish in its actions; while also performative: political representation is attributed to the theatricality of actions that constitute the marginality, a necessary platform to the exercise of corruption.

The enunciator, while denouncing, confesses his state of abandonment, voiced by the absence of reference. "Marginal Life/ we remain as dogs/In no man's land/Looking for our mothers." The use of the first person plural - "our" - enshrines the understanding of a collectivized self-lyrical, representative of these "foreign bodies" and "social minority", whose origin usually constitutes ghetto ambientations, in which, besides the socio-economic segregation, the occurrence of estructured families is very common, evident in the nuclei where the mother, in general - and, due to different reasons - takes on the arduous task of raising her child(ren) alone.

The performance continues, and in the sixth strophe, the speech turns again to the first-person.

> Slowly, to avoid loosing my pace
> Unblinking, my way I do by myself
> Drive lines and like those who love what they do
> Sure of my space here I do what I know best

In the first verse "Slowly, to avoid loosing my pace", there is the implicit direction of "living in caution". The enunciator is not allowed the benefit of doubt, with regards to the construction of his path. The cautious impetus in making decisions, sung by the lyric voice, is the example of something that can achieve future realities. The song thus establishes itself as a tool, a voice preparing a way and at the same time, many ways. In this regard, we emphasize the verses: "I drive the lines as those who love what they do / Sure of my space here I do what I know best." The rapper song is the necessary tool to the lyrical voice that wants to institute the social debate. Leading the "lines" of this discussion, the enunciator declares appreciation for what he does and reveals "consciousness" both for the quality of his work, and the "space" that he occupies; the bottom of the pyramid.

In the seventh strophe, the use of speech as an ideological propagator is evident. The enunciative voice here aims to tell the consistency of his own mission:

> Being the exception to the rule, is the current mission
> So I fill my lungs and release my voice
> Loud and clear as in a sound of Mendes
> Burning a good one ... Then the police arrests

Here, the foreigner shows to have a "mission": to keep away from the systemic capital gear, "exception" among the masses. Noteworthy is the cunning with which he builds the enunciative performance. Again, the song is called as the current struggle and protest mechanism. Through it, the voice is released, "loud and clear." In the strophe in question, note the application of a metonymic process. When the voice utters: "Then I fill my lungs and release my voice/loud and clear/As in a sound of Mendes/Burning a "good" one/Then the police arrests"; highlights the image of the "inhaling". The enunciates portray in these terms, his own personality, of someone who inhales the poetic word, launching it on the environment throughout the aesthetic and transforming power provided by it. The poetic word "absorbed" by the self-lyrical concentrates ample power to denounce the injustices of the world and to call for the necessary revolution instigated by art.

Being "swallowed up" functions as an element that replaces the use of toxic substances - so common in young communities of the world. The performer, in stating the action of the absorbed and reverberated word, externalizes knowledge. If "burning a good" makes it a socially infertile attitude and subject to repressions - "Then the police arrests" - proposes the continuous use of word through the performance as proof of a more effective action, which serves the purpose of engaging aesthetics, whose concern is to shed awareness among the marginalized sectors and promote the transformation of the operative standards in society.

Also in this strophe, in which the use of poor and mixed rhymes is applied, our reading calls attention to the following verse: "As in a sound of Mendes". The reference seems to be an allusion to the rapper Crônica Mendes, Brazilian, born in Bahia and settled in São Paulo, whose work is known to present a politicized, and frequent criticism of the government, especially the government of São Paulo.

In the eighth strophe, the lyrical voice addresses his interlocutor- listener. The song says, in mandatory tones:

> It surprises you, but it is so obvious
> Each time in a different way, because time does not stop
> But look right, go beyond
> What they say is true and what is good

In the verse in question, the enunciator refers once again to the strong speech spread by the song. The evidence of the content of the verses is real, so that it "should not surprise" the receiver. There is an emphasis on the excerpt to the impromptu making of the song, "every time one way", because the temporal dynamics, permeated by actions and influences, requires such skill. The last two verses warn about the spread of false information. The enunciator advises doubt and attention to detail, he says, "But look right, go beyond / What they say is true and what is good."

The ninth and last strophe, again, the enunciator reinforces the "request" of caution to the receiver. Each shift in space - each "arrival" and/or each "match" - requires a specific approach, according to the verses:

> Watchful eyes to the nuances of life
> All your bids from arrival to departure
> I will make the best of my life to the end
> Head high is just what is expected of me

The poetic movement of the verses gives rise to the image of the "coming" and "going", which also characterizes the displacement of migration. In the rap, the construction of the final strophe confirms the purpose advocated throughout the song: that we must make use of wide rationality, when wanting to give body to works of "departures" and "arrivals". The guidance provided to an "imaginary other" are incorporated into the self-lyrical at the end of the last strophe - "I will make the best of my life to the end/Head high is just what is expected of me" - he says, using the first person present.

To the immigrant-listener, the voice in performance wants a single task, but a significant responsibility: to guide their own progress, with "watchful eyes", "head high" and willingness to improvise.

La Bala: urban violence in diaspora streets

"La Bala" is a song whose content aims to describe the scene of a murder. Right at the beginning of the song, in the first strophe, there is the description of the moments before the crime.

	Translation:
La pistola lo miraba fijamente bajo	The gun was staring at him
El manto brillo cromo de su veneno	The chrome cloak of its poison
Un disparo repentino	A sudden shot
Penetró cada partícula del aire	Penetrated every particle of the air
luego se cayó	Then he fell.

The performance gives the character killed a prominent place to the content narrated in the third person. The death at close range is described as something experienced by a man, inert against the personified weapon "staring at him" externalizing "the chrome cloak of its poison." To the descriptive foreshadow, the narrative-sung of the occurrence of a "snap shot" that "penetrates every particle of the air" follows. The fallen body, dying - before the eyes of the enunciator - suggests the implicit reflection of a cruel system, invisible, that "poisons" innocent citizens.

The first strophe is followed by the first chorus, in which the dead character appears as an innocent, a kind of martyr to shed his blood for many.

Translation:

Se derramó la primera gota ya por la cien (x3)	The first drop was spilled for one hundred (x3)
Por la cien	For one hundred.

In the third strophe, there is evidence of the fact of being the song built on a narrative psychological time. Having described the killing in the above verses again, the scene before death is described. The lyrics say:

Translation:

La muerte lo miró de forma desafiante	Death looked at him in a challenging way
Con la sangre entre los dientes	With blood between the teeth
Y una oscuridad reinante	And a reigning darkness
La bala entre tanto suspendida fija	The bullet, in this interval, suspended and fixed
Bailaba un asesinato girando sobre sí misma	Danced a murder, turning on itself
Se perdió de vista la vida con su pista	Lost sight of life and its track
Mientras un joven padece ante el deseo de conquista suelo	As a young man suffers on the desire to conquer the soil
De rodilla su beso cambia lentamente	On his knees its kiss slowly changes
Del rojo al hielo	From red to ice

Note the speech in flashback that, again, written in the third person, personifies death brought by the bullet. In it, death gets cruelty as a feature of its own "look", "challenging", having "blood between the teeth". Death is "dark", establishing a bad mood. In this passage, again it describes the scene prior to the shooting. The bullet "Suspended and fixed" "dances the murder" and highlights the orality of a rap metaphor for the bullet movement in the barrel of a gun.

The verse describes a body that loses its life slowly and with it also loses its dreams and plans for future days. "Lost sight of life and its track." The enunciative voice that matches the character described the young foreigner's figure, "who suffers before the desire to conquer the soil" and gradually loses its color - the red - of life, for ice - of death. "On his knees its kiss slowly changes/From red to ice", he says.

Following, the performance grants the "dead character" quality of angelic purity. It is the young dead person who becomes one more victim of "paper", or vulnerable in the face of systemic hardships governing large areas of the city.

	Translation:
Angelitos de papel se han perdido por babel	Paper angels were lost by Babel
¿Quién devolverá esta piel?	Who will return this skin?
La madre le suplica al coronel	The mother begged the Colonel
La muerte es un carrusel	Death is a carousel
Fúnebre en su vaivén	Funereal in its coming and going
Un juicio final cruel	A cruel judgment
El ángel le suplica al coronel	The angel pleads tothe Colonel

The city is translated metaphorically by the performer as a "Tower of Babel", a disagreement scenario and in several languages. Allusion of the rapper, perhaps, to the globalized territory witnessed by those immigrating, where death comes as constant, a "carousel", appropriating of many innocent lives. The song questions the legal social mechanisms, asking "Who will return this skin?". Noteworthy is also the mother figure pleading justice to authorities in favor of the dead child: "Mother begs to the colonel". Beside the maternal figure, an "angel" murdered also cries out for justice - "The angel begs to the colonel" says the performance. Note in the strophe the use of the rhymes ("Babel", "Carousel", "Colonel", "Cruel"), always placed at the end of each verse, in epistrophe.

The song continues and, as transcribed in the fifth strophe, we have again the description of the body: not fallen in agony, but already cold and torn apart by the fate it had.

	Translation:
Su mirada quedo congelada por el súbito	His gaze remained frozen by the sudden
Sonido pulsante que lo valió	pulsating noise that killed him
Hombre desplomado desangrado sin aliento	fallen man, bleeding, breathless
quedo pálida la vida le falló	Blanched, life failed him

The strophe shows the description of a body that, little by little, takes on the characteristics of death. "Fallen man, bleeding, breathless/Blanched, life failed him," says the enunciator at third person, without the use of rhymes.

The scene of the body in inertia is succeeded by the chorus that, in the sixth strophe, again, tells us about the martyr, uttering the following words:

Translation:

Se derramó la primera gota ya por la cien (x3)	The first drop was spilled for one hundred (x3)
Por la cien	for one hundred

After the chorus, we return to the scene of the mother, suffering, watching the corpse of her murdered son. Her name, Maria, reflects the simplicity of the anonymity of many other Marias, unknown and helpless in the face of ruthless urban setting, which kills innocent and does not measure consequences.

Anonymous and holy Mary, treated in the song through a common name, not without purpose, also refers to the name of the mother of God, according to the beliefs of the Catholic Church and the principles set out in the Bible. The verses transcribed in the seventh strophe, have the following contents:

Translation:

Aquel cuerpo sin vida era su hijo	That lifeless body was her son
María estupefacta	Maria was shocked
Cayó al piso	Fell to the floor
Su rostro deformado se convirtió en un grito	Her deformed face became a scream
Quedo solo un zumbido que significa (asesino)	Just a buzz that means (killer)
La hora del deceso marcaba por um beso del adiós	The time is marked by a farewell kiss
De la madre perdida en desconsuelo	Of a mother lost in disconsolate
Hizo llover al cielo	Like rain for the sky
Lágrimas del desierto y hasta la muerte	Desert tears and even death
Se quedo callada por respeto	Remained silent in respect

Note, therefore, that the song shows the perplexed farewell of a mother towards her child, now a body abandoned on the streets of some indifferent space. The content of the strophe comes down, then, to shock and silence of the farewell. "Maria shocked/fell to the ground/Her deformed face became a scream (...)".

"The time is marked by a farewell kiss," describes the lyrical voice in third person. In sensory and metaphorical construction, the rap describes the moment of farewell, as a moment surrounded by emptyness, before the biggest impact, caused by death: "The lost mother disconsolate/Like rain to heaven/Desert Tears and even death/Remained silent in respect."

Established the scene that describes the depth of the maternal pain at the loss of a child, the performance now is moving towards the end. In the eighth strophe the chorus arises again:

	Translation:
Angelitos de papel se han perdido por Babel	Paper angels were lost by Babel
Quien devolverá esta piel?	Who will return this skin?
La madre le suplica al coronel	The mother begged the Colonel
La muerte es un carrusel	Death is a carousel
Fúnebre en su vaivén	Funereal in its coming and going
Un juicio fina cruel	A cruel judgment
El ángel le suplica al coronel	The angel pleads to the Colonel

The chorus comes again as a fundamental part of the aesthetic rapper, questioning the cyclical deaths observed in the contemporary space. "Who will return this skin?" asks the insistent chorus, trying to be heard by someone who has the power of change.

Added now of a small verbalized extension, the chorus comes up with the intention to ratify the message turning, perhaps, more eloquent, the description of violence: ongoing problem, but which by its repeatability becomes, in the eyes of the mass, a common fact. The song is a warning!

	Translation:
Tiros suenan	Shots ring,
Sons de tiros	shots sounds
Muertes llevan	They bring death
Mortes conduzidas	Conducted deaths
Polvos queman	dusts burn
Pó queimaduras	Powder, Burning
Prakapampam(x4)	Prakapampam (x4)

"La bala" ends, certainly, with the provision of an alert. "Shots sound, sounds of shots/They bringdeaths/conducted deaths". This is an alert born of an observation: if there are shots in the city, there are deaths and those deaths are "carried" (read: "built").

The recording of this performance is made, no doubt, also as a lone cry or call for help: the system kills and every second innocents die.

Faced with the impossibility of taking concrete any action before the atrocities committed in the real world, the aesthetics of the song serve as an artistic alternative, noting the framework, calling for listeners, perhaps together, they can convert this reality.

Si te preguntan

"Si te preguntan" (If they ask you) is a song that is presented as an aesthetic-narrative invitation. By evoking Chile and Cuba (countries that are characterized by broad adherence to political positions of left), this rap purports to tell "another" history, ignored principle even by listeners for whom it is intended. A story set in peripheral ghettos where people live in conditions of marginalization and hopelessness. In this sense, we find the following discursive content, still in the first transcribed strophe:

Translation:

Yeah	Yes
La Aldea	The village
Ana Tijoux	Ana Tijoux
Cuba y Chille, siéntelo!	Cuba and Chile, feel them
Yo, yo, esta es otra historia	This is another story
En la memoria de otra esquina del planeta	In memory of another corner of the planet
Otra victoria sin gloria, escoria que cual espina penetra	Another victory without glory, slag that penetrates as a thorn
Otro sonido de metra que se siente	Another sound of machine gun that is felt
De otro jodido rincón que no visitó el presidente	From another fucked up corner that the president did not visit
Otros delincuentes tomando por asalto tu mente	Other offenders assaulting your mind
Armados con los problemas de su gente	Armed with the problems of their people
Otros que como tú cargan errores, sienten	Others lthat ike you carry mistakes, feel
Sobrevivientes, vividores, solo eso nos hace diferentes	Survivors, alive, only that makes them different
A lo más bajo vente	To the lowest, come
Donde se vive al día, tú dime un día	Where you live one day, tell me one day
en que no hay un fajo que cuentes, vente!	Where there is no beef to be told, go!
Donde vive esta mujer que te lo hace por dinero para que su hijo se alimente	Where lives this woman that Does it to you for money, to feed her child

The words spoken by Ana Tijoux are launched with a purpose: to remember the day by day of the ghettos and at the same time, describe it. At the beginning of the performance, the verses announce, through the narrative focus established in the third person singular: "This is another story/In memory of another corner of the planet." These are verses that actually perform an allusion to many, if not all, of the "periphery corners", spaces where routines are similar and its inhabitants too.

Different due to the depletion of dreams, the adherence to the crime as a survival tool, the living spaces of these cede the floor to rapper representation, who speaks on behalf of all. Along the rapper voice setting out the song the narrative and polyphonic-common issues emerge arising from many marginalized and territorialized layers in the global space.

Each foreign ghetto, in their own peculiarity, experiences "inglorious victories" and its forgotten due to being a "fucked up corner," that "the president has not visited". This experience generates the force required to produce the so-called "sounds of machine gun" – a representative expression used in reference to rappers purposes. Here, what Nascimento (Accessed on Sep 10th, 2014) calls the "warlike metaphors" incurs; i.e. the insertion of the discourse to the vital practical condition. Through the use of the word, the rapper plays its role in society, like that struggling in the midst of a war, composing the group that is doomed to "lose".

Through interspersed rhymes, the song speaks on behalf of many voices and realities and is established as a "tribute" to the "survivors", "from below"; those who are driven by feelings of historical and social order, and make of rap a necessary tool for "assaulting minds", guiding through words; as they assume, in the song, the role of alienation or simply shock.

Come meet the "lowest", challenges the music at the beginning, come meet the rap, "metric sound" different and full of utterances, which are made from a single song, established in one corner, but collectivized .

Once the invitation is established, the rap continues its narrative, describing not only the image of certain situations, but above all, using these to denounce the use of illegal practices in societies. The verses of the second strophe heading now to a hearer that ignores the reality of the ghetto, while they say:

	Translation:
Donde no vas pues dices que es peligroso el ghetto	Where you will not go, because you say that the ghetto is dangerous
La droga ahoga, pero no caen los que los introdujeron	The drug drowns , but those who introduced it do not fall

Las pandillas se matan, la policía maltrata	The gangs kill themselves, the police mistreats
Mientras la mafia real come con cubiertos de plata	While the real mafia eats with silverware
Es nuestra realidad, no sabemos de lujo	It is our reality, we know no luxury
Todo viene y se va, nadie controla el flujo	Everything comes and goes, no one controls the flow
Mucha necesidad dentro de poco espacio	Too much need in a short space
Vamos a más velocidad pues vivimos despacio	We go faster, because we live slowly
Vicios o socio no hay ley	Vices or partners, there is no law
Negocios, socio, no hay break	Business partners, no breack
Aleluya vivimos en la calle	Hallelujah, we live on the street
Nuestra casa es más grande que la tuya	Our house is bigger than yours

Isolated, the periphery is considered a "dangerous place", not frequented by wealthier layers. Using figures of speech like epistrophe ("It is our reality, we know no luxury/Everything comes and goes, no one controls the flow") and the antithesis ("Too much need within a short space"), and few rhymes ("luxury", "flow") - present both in the Spanish version, as in our rereading-translation ("street", "your"), the song reveals the experience of days, demonstrating to the "uncompromised look" that, in fact, the periphery is a place of "crime and drugs", but also of "short space", with "many needs" and "no law".

The sung narrative ironically describes the arrival of illegal substances to the periphery, which is given precisely by representatives of high society, those who "eat with silverware" and seek luxury from the exploitation of misery in the ghettos. The song denounces police action, stating in its verses that "the police mistreats", as in the ghetto there is no "law", the gangs are "killing themselves", the "drugs drown", but those really responsible for that "do not fall".

The rapper-performer sings under the observing condition. They sing reality, describing what is concrete or subjective; demonstrating the gaze born of the dark and hidden ghettos; for which no one wants to give attention and in which, no one wants to be.

The world in the eyes of the lyrical voice reverts in verbal picture, as the enunciator reveals a place corrupted by money. The world is a scene devoid of love and immersed in cold, a space that requires every day heroism of its people. In this sense, we present the third strophe.

	Translation:
Yo sé, que el amor... Se fue	I know that the love... Is gone
Cuando el dinero se pudrió de la fe	When money rotted faith
Que detrás de todo siempre hay interés	That behind it all there is always interest
Pero a pesar de todo me mantengo de pie	But still I remain standing
Firme! Que me mantengo! Todo el tiempo!	Firm! I keep! All the time!
Si te preguntan, di que somos de la calle!	If they ask, say we are from the street!
Cuba, Chile y América	Cuba, Chile and America
Cuba, Chile y América Latina	Cuba, Chile and Latin America
Santiago, la Habana, las capitales unidas	Santiago, Havana, as united capitals
Centro, sur cordillera o planicie valle	Center, south, range, valley
Que vaya caminando ya hacia la isla	Go walking to the island already
Desde el Malecón se abrirán las alamedas	From Malecón will open fairways
Se prenderán las velas y la luz	The candles will be lit and the light
Con sus estelas Centinelas sobre suelas,	With its Sentinels on soles
Secuelas sobre las huellas	Sequels on the footprints
Revueltas las escuelas, la cautela no da sueltas	Revolt schools, caution is not loose
Ella es la calle, ella es la madre	She is the street, she is the mother
Ella es la abuela de todos los pilares	She is the grandmother of all pillars
La que no te deja, ni menos te abandona	The one does not leave you or abandon you
Esquiva de forma agresiva, la salida más viva	Dodges aggressively, the most vivid escape

Explosiva de vida, sin normativas viva	Explosive of life, living without norms
Creativa y activa, de la calle más combativa	Creative and active, the most combative of the street
Que vio nacer en su manto, que vio caer a tantos, tantos	Has seen many being born in her cloak, she saw the fall of many, many
Que ningún canto alcanzaría para cuantos	That no corner would be enough for that many
Firme y fuerte por todos los ausentes	Firm and strong for all missing
Firme y fuerte por todos los presentes	Firm and strong for all present

In this third strophe, the narrative focus is reversed in the use of the first person. In the first verses of this strophe, the enunciator is discontent and resistant of the context that surrounds them: capitalist and cold. "I know that the love is gone/When money rotted faith/That behind everything there is always interest/But still I remain standing/Firm! I stay! All the time!" It says.

The collective voice provided to the verb appears through the mention of various Chilean and Cuban spaces and evoking the union of the peoples of Latin America. (Cuba, Chile and Latin America/Santiago, Havana and the united capitals/Center, South Range, Valley).

In the song, these territories have, as representatives, individuals that dominate and at the same time are confused with the public space ("if they ask, say you are from the street!")

The term "street" takes in this song, a subjective connotation, reinforced by the description set forth in anaphoras (An example is the final verses of the strophe: "Has seen many being born in her cloak, she has seen many fall, many many/No corner would be enough for that many/Firm and strong for all missing/Firm and strong for all those present").

You can understand the "street" as an environment punctually located in each of the cited territories, or even understand it as the "street of all the marginalized areas of the world", a metaphoric "street", where the concrete space becomes inhabited by the "children-migrants" in Latin America, underdeveloped strata of the American continent.

The union, which appears in the song as a kind of prophecy, also makes the basic point for the establishment of reflection among people. The marginalized people that "walk" towards the "islands" of isolation, may, as suggested by the song, open "avenues" of thought, becoming a kind of light, directed to those who ignore history.

It is noteworthy also in the third transcribed strophe, a certain praise and gratitude to the lessons learned from the experiences in urban environments. The "street" is the prototype of the mother, "school" of rioters, individuals who, by experience, have become sentinels of the world, always on alert to face exclusion mechanisms.

Urban soldiers are these individuals described as beings with an irreducible purpose: the fight against social injustice. And even before the representative strenght of an invisible and systematic power, they remain strong in fighting this condition.

The conscious resistance continues as a central and circular theme of the song, enshrining in its chorus in the fourth strophe.

Note, again, the enunciating consciousness of the consolidation of a centralized system, cold and selfish - Noteworthy at this point is the extent assumed by rapper critics, which may relate both to capitalist regimes, and in relation to Socialism in the case of Cuba[24], the nation mentioned along the music.

The enunciator shows that despite all the obstacles she "remains firm", calling attention to the source of her power, "the street".

---

24 On the verse "Desde el Malecón se abrirán las alamedas" (From the Malecón the boulevards Will be oppened), it is believed to allude to Cuba. The term "malecón" that, in spanish refers to the Idea of "pier" or "boardwalk" (SEÑAS, 2001), is also a known denomination for the rim of Havana, the capital of Cuba.

	Translation:
Yo sé, que el amor... Se fue	I know that love... Is gone
Cuando el dinero se pudrió de la fe	When money rotted faith
Que detrás de todo siempre hay interés	That behind it all there is always interest
Pero a pesar de todo me mantengo de pie	But despite everything I'm still standing
Firme! Que me mantengo! Todo el tiempo!	Firm! I keep! All the time!
Si te preguntan, di que somos de la calle!	If they ask, say we are from the street!

The street, place of impunity and sorrows, where crimes occur and punishments seem forgotten, it is always revealed as a propellant factor. The street is the metaphor of the encounter. It is in the street where the encounter happens between minority layers and their supporters. It is on the street where consciousness of the many difficulties and the need for resistance arises.

In the fifth strophe, the following lines appear:

	Translation:
Yeah, vengo de un lugar oscuro, sobrado de sombras	Yes, I come from a dark place, where the shadows are abundant
Donde la ley es no respetar la ley que pongan	Where the law is not to respect the law
Donde la injusticia oficial pisado se compra	Where injustice is purchased
Y verdad que gira inspira la mentira que nos ronda	And the truth that turns inspires the lie that haunts us
Mantén tu fe fuerte, no dejes	Keep your faith strong, do not allow
Que la fechorías espirituales te afecten	Spiritual crimes to affect you
Ni hagan efecto en tu alma, la infecten	Have no effect on your soul, infecting you
Friend sin frenar, inclina tu frente	Friend without stopping, lift your face
La vista pesa, la gente aprisa, va por la pista	The sight weighs, people rush, take the track
Y la humanidad solo en la plata piensa	And humanity only thinks about cash

Y en la street la triste tristeza
Sigue free, fría, y frívola
nos besa
Lava te que, la lava te
quema
Nada te queda, nada te queda
Acaba esa sed que acaba
tu sed
Escaba tu ser y clava tus pies
donde puedas
La sangre corre, errores no hay
quien borre
Forre esa y con responsabilidad
Y no respire hondo porque puede
caer como las torres
Y no resistirá ver que tu ser no se
deshonre
El fin esta, canta y un
gallo
La calle es un ring donde
King del King queremos ser tu
caballo
Sacan la mano a la velocidad del
rayo
Y más caro que un roll Roiz del
año te salen los fallos
Ana Tijoux hermana di tu
Si en Chile pagan en dólares y
cobran en club
Como el pana Mapocho lucho
para que escuchen mi voz
En un lugar donde corrupto
ahorita ya es hasta dios

And on the street the sad sadness
Remain free, cold, frivolous and
kisses us
Lava wants you, the lava that burns
you
Theres nothing left, nothing left for you
Quench this thirst that ends your
thirst
Escapes yourself, spiking its nails
where it can
Blood flows, no one can erase mis-
takes
Prevent yourself and with responsibly
And do not take a deep breath be-
cause it can fall like the towers
And will not bear to see no dishonor
of yourself
And the end is there, sings like a
rooster
The street is a ring where
King of Kings, we want to be your
horse
Theyremove their hand with light-
ning speed
And more expensive than a Rolls
Royce of the year, are your flaws
Tell your sister Ana Tijoux
In Chile they pay in dollars and
charge at the club
Like the friend Mapocho, I fight for
them to listen to my voice
In a place where corrupts will be up
to God soon enough.

In this strophe, the narrative focus remains in first person and has a lyrical voice that, in statement and in the use of anaphora ("where"), recognizes its place of origin and hopes for better days. In these terms the verses: "Yes, I come from a dark place where shadows are abundant/Where the law is not respected/Where injustice is purchased/And the truth that turns inspires the lie that haunts us/ Keep your faith strong [...]"

Interestingly, in this passage, is the evidence of a pedagogical attitude towards potential listeners who are on the street, living the situations described in the lyrics. Lines like "Do not let spiritual crimes affect you/Do not have an effect on your soul, infecting it/ Friend without stopping, lift your face" sound as a guide to individuals devoid of human frameworks and legal support.

The reality is described verse by verse, with words that show in synesthesia, the difficult reality that permeates the experience of minority layers: "The sight weighs, people rush, take the track/And humanity only thinks about cash/And on the street sad sadness/ follows free, cold, frivolous and kisses us/lava wants you/the lava that burns you."

Between the fourteenth and sixteenth verses of the strophe, the performance features an enunciator that encourages listeners - lost in the urban, systemic chaos. Noting the scene, the lyrical voice tell the elliptical interlocutor "There is nothing left/Nothing left for you" and asks that they "spike their nails" wherever they can. Although not specifically identified, the listener seems to be someone who the enunciator identifies with and cares about.

Among the seventeenth and twenty-first verses of the strophe, we see words that confirm the "guiding path" traced by her performative voice. It addresses the caller's figure, warning that errors are indelible marks, whose fatal consequences edge rancor and madness: "Blood flows, no one can erase mistakes/Prevent yourself [25]

---

25 The Spanish verb "forro"- that, on the mother language refers to the action of lining, coating (Senas, 2001) - also often used by the group language / slang to describe the idea of condom or condom. In this sense, the expression "to prevent," seemed to us the most appropriate for use in the stanza.

and with responsibility/And do not take a deep breath because it can fall like the towers/And will not bear to see no dishonor of yourself/And the end is there, singing like a rooster"(...)

Being careful is not enough for those who are subject to the system. The song alerts listeners to learn to behave before the fact, considering that the flighty inclusion among the "social game" can result in falls. The message highlights the idea that you have to be tough, have malice, faith and conscience not to miss, not to be vulnerable to destruction (Note, in this point, the reference established by rapper performance on the twin towers of the World Trade Center).

Among the twenty-third and twenty-ninth verses of the transcribed strophe, the expository voice takes on a collectivized character, showing a place of enunciation that is the voice of many. "King of Kings, we want to be your horse/They remove the hand with lightning speed," she says, expressing the will of collective invasion, against the territory dominated by the oppressors.

The performer, accordingly, declares herself as "sister" of these groups, alerting the street is a sort of "ring" where you have to fight against everything using the verb. From the comparison with a vehicle of the brand Rolls Royce, the song exemplifies how important it is to talk about the lived facts "and more expensive than a Rolls Royce of the year is the cost of your flaws."

The reference established by the song to one of the main Chilean rivers should be noted: Rio Mapocho; around which the city of Santiago arose and developed. Today suffering severe problems related to pollution and siltation, the river is an element, like the enunciative voice, that fights to ensure the survival and to reach some kind of representation. In these terms, Tijoux ratifies the challenge to remain "alive" in crash conditions, even if the times do not seem to have good conditions or solutions. "If Chile pays in dollars and charges at the club/Like the friend Mapocho, I fight for them to hear my voice/In a place where corrupt will be up to God soon enough".

About the existence of the Mapocho river, researchers Carlos Mello Garcias and Jorge Augusto Afonso Callado (2013) manifested, in the article *"Revitalization of Urban Rivers"*:

> The Mapocho River is located in the metropolitan area of Santiago, with springs in the city of Barnechea through several communities, including the cities of Providencia, Maipu and Santiago. Its extension is approximately 110km, and the drainage area of its basin is 4230km². Factors such as organic pollution from lack of sewage, the release of slurry due to inadequate disposal of solid waste, the lack of continuity in its channel and fragmentation of urban spaces related to the river are the main causes of degradation of the three parts of the Mapocho river. Among the consequences of degradation, are changes in biota and the lack of space and good quality of water to provide recreation and direct contact of the population with the river (GARCIAS; AFONSO, 2013, p. 137).

The completion of the message established by the musical text is given in the sixth and final strophe when, once again, we see the conscious chorus:

	Translation:
Yo sé, que el amor... Se fue	I know that love... Is gone
Cuando el dinero se pudrió de la fe	When money rotted faith
Que detrás de todo siempre hay interés	That behind it all there is always interest
Pero a pesar de todo me mantengo de pie	But despirte everything I'm still standing
Firme! Que me mantengo! Todo el tiempo!	Firm! I keep! All the time!
Si te preguntan, di que somos de la calle!	If they ask, say we are from the street!

Si te preguntan appears as the conscious presence of a rapper-composer offering through aesthetic a picture of her time, while creating, from the established soundscape, conditions for which there is identification of her hearers and they find there, within the content sound, the orientation of "non-succumbing" to global pressures, they can find in their own exclusion ghettos, the motivation for resistance.

Χαιρετισμός: Salute to the parents

The "*Χαιρετισμος*" song (which means "compliance" in Greek) is the "flagship" of the *Αλάνα* CD. The translation process of the song reveals a grateful speech and recognition of parental figures, seen as courageous and resilient in the face of an oppressive system.

Satirizing the religious bourgeois reality condensed in Orthodoxy, MC Yinka creates a chorus in which the image of the saints revered by the Greeks is replaced by the parents, representative metaphor of all kinds of immigrants, consisting of people and stories that share the dream of leaving a country destroyed by the colonizers, in favor of a country which brings them better survival conditions. In this sense, the lyrical voice tells us in chorus, under the narrative focus in the first person singular, the first transcribed strophe:

	Translation:
Ρεφραίν- 2Χ	Chorus- 2x
Χαιρετώ με σεβασμό τον δικό σου αγώνα	I salute with respect your struggle
Παίρνω φως και τραγουδώ την δικία σου εικόνα	I light a candle and sing your image

The continuity of the song is done in an almost epic tone, of a narrative poetry. In the second strophe, one notices the presence of a contemporary look that reinterprets the past, seeing this, as evidence of a capitalist exploitation before which the first immigrants fought. In this sense, the lyrics say:

Αδέσποτες ψύχες ψαχνοντάς
για νέους ήλιους .
Σημαδεμένες από του κόσμου
το απαρτχαϊτ
Από γενοκτονίες οικονομικές,
κρίσεις ,κλεμμένα εδάφη
ήρωες που το χέρι της δύσης
τους 'εχει αρπάξει, τον πλούτο
γυρνάνε σελίδα, ψαχνοντάς να
βρουν ονόμα στο όνειρο τους
να του λούσει μια ηλιαχτιδα,
σε αυτή την πατρίδα, τους
είδα, να
επιβιώνουν με μέσα μηδαμίνα
για να κερδίσουν την παρτίδα.
αρχές δεκαετίας 80 είδα το
φως , οι γόνεις μου οι πρώτοι
μου μετανάστες
και είδα πως το σύστημα δεν
ήταν έτοιμο να του αγκαλιάσει
αλλά και ανίκανο το ηθίκο
τους να σπάσει και έτσι
συνέχισαν
πάνω από δύνες προκαταλήψεις
να μου χαμογέλανε
κοίτα τους, κοίτα τους .

Translation:

Souls aimlessly looking for new
horizons
All marked by the ills of
the world
Slaughters, economic crises,
stolen lands
Heroes who stole the glory from
them- the leaders stole everything
They turn the page trying to find
a name for their dreams.
Trying to have a ray of sunshine
in the country they have
chosen
Fighting with their minimum
strength to get a homeland
In the 80's I came into the world,
my parents were the first immigrants
And I realized that the system was
not ready to embrace them,
Nor to make them
give up.
They continued on great difficulties, with smiles.
Look at them, look at them.

Note that the lyrics are between the description of the past and the realization of the present. Thus, the first verses describe a not too distant past, in which the first immigrants left their countries in search of better living conditions.

In the first seven verses of this stanza, this search is told through a narrative focus established in the third person singular:

Souls aimlessly looking for new horizons / All marked by the ills of the world / Slaughters, economic crises, lands stolen / Heroes who stole their glory, the leaders stole everything / They turn the page trying to find a name for their dreams./ Have a

ray of sunshine in the country they have chosen / Fighting with
their minimum strength to get a homeland (...).

The description of the experience of the diaspora is evident
through these first verses, led by beings, regardless of nationality,
that have common characteristics: being "rudderless", "colonized",
"extorted", "abused", those who leave their places of origin and use
their "little strength" to go on in search of "sunshine" to be able "to
name their dreams".

From the eighth to the twelfth verse of the strophe, the enunciator tells its origins in the narrative focus of the first person singular. Belonging to the second generation of immigrants, highlights
the fact that MC Yinka really belongs to such a group. The lyrical
voice performs a reinterpretation of the official historical facts, seeing in the face of diaspora a scenario of exploitation to which his
predecessors had to sustain, successfully making it so bravely per-
sisting in the face of difficulties.

Attempts to overcome every obstacle faced, however, are described by the lyrics as a foreseeable end. At the eyes of the lyrical
voice, suffering and persistence of the displaced at the country chosen, would be an inevitable result, once the country held no conditions for the reception of these "new people", either with to prevent
them from resisting. "And I realized that the system was not ready
to embrace them / Nor to make them give up / They continued on
great difficulties, with smiles," he says.

The lyrical voice calls attention to this resistance: "Look at
them, Look at them," he says, noting the existence of faces scarred
by the stigma, but serene and smiling, at the possibility of finding
a "thread" of hope in their destinations.

The song has a musical moment that, in a way, accompanies
the historical time. The narrative song establishes a twenty-year
jump, going from the description of the "birth of the rappper-
voice, in the 80's, to the address the social context established in
the 2000's".

The rapper-observer sees a country of social injustice and prejudice, where immigrants are just pieces for the proper functioning of the capitalist system. So the third strophe:

Ελλάδα 2000 και βάλε οι
μετανάστες αδύναμοι κρίκοι
στην κοινωνική αλυσίδα από
ξενομάνης ξενόφοβους
που φωνάζουν εξω οι ξένοι σαν
να είναι η ουσία της ζωής τους,
από αυτό δεμένοι. Το δυσκίνητο
κράτος, αργοπορήμενα
διευθέτησε το θέμα,
νομιμοποιήσης και ετσι οι
οικονομίκοι
μετανάστες πλέον,
τροφοδοτουν το σύστημα της
δικιάς τους
αποξενώσης, τα παιδιά τους
γέννημα θρέμμα Έλληνες,
δεν γράφονται στα
δημοτόλογια και μόλις γίνονται
18
τους ζητάνε άδεια παραμονής
σαν να έχουν έρθει πριν ένα
χρόνο
στον τόπο αυτό.
η ατιμωρησία, και η ανόχη δίνει
έδαφος σε άναδρους φασίστες.
Να κάνουν πεσίματα σε
ανυπεράσπιστους πακιστάνους
και μικροπωλήτες
Επίθεσεις ρατσιστίκες αμέτρητες.
Ανεξιχνίαστες υποθέσεις
νεκρών μεταναστων σε χέρια
αστυνομίκων

Translation:

Greece 2000 and they put immigrants in fragile rings
In a society that is afraid of foreigners and is xenophobic
They shout, out foreigners!
It is the essence of their lives
As if it was their fault ...In this country without production
The themes on legalities and economic issues are transferred
And so immigrants feed the system.
Alienation. Their children born and raised in Greece,
When they turn 18,
they are asked for a license to stay
As if they had just arrived
In this place
Impunity and intolerance give way to the fascists.
To punish Pakistan and the small Asia.
many racial problems.
Cases unresolved, dead immigrants in the hands of the police.

Μέσα σε σκοτείνα δωμάτια	In dark rooms, beatings and
ξυλοδάρμοι και κυνηγητα	harassment.
και η πολίτεια το βλέμμα της	And the city is balanced
αλλόυ να πέτα ,	as it can
εμπόριο ξένης σάρκος,	Trade of foreign meat, women
διακίνηση γυναικών	trafficking
που θέλουν να εργάστουν και	Who want to work and now get
τώρα σε βρώμικα	dirty
στενα την αθωότητα τους	Sell their innocence
πούλουν.	

As we can see, the findings of the poetic rapper show the existence of immigrants as slaves or social prisoners. Using the narrative focus in the third person, the enunciator describes a context that gave birth to exploitation and xenophobia: "Greece 2000 and they put immigrants in fragile rings/In a society that is afraid of foreigners and and is xenophobic/They shout: out foreigners! It is the essence of their life/As if the fault was theirs (...) In this country without production/Themes about legalities and economic issues are transferred/And so immigrants feed the system". Note that the verses demonstrate the lack of belief in the country described, considered by the performative voice as something "unsolved".

Greece, where the parents of Afolanios also immigrated, author of the song in question, is described in performance as a space guided by exploratory-capitalist logic, a logic that "feeds" off foreign labor. In the verse, the rapper seems to perform the trajectory: the residence permit requested to Manolis in the real world - and repeatedly mentioned in interviews - is now sung by MC Yinka, in striking verses that say: "Their children are born and raised in Greece/When they turn 18, they asked for license to stay/As if they just got/to this place".

The performer mentions the presence of "Pakistani" immigrants and from "Little Asia", assessing the fate of those who just wanted to work and "succeed in life", but found more difficult ways than expected. "Food" for a system that does not care to regularize the situation of workers from other countries, such immigrants are described as being subject to an oppressive reality, guided by extreme intolerance.

The space described by the song interposes the image of bigoted natives, especially those who exercise police action and clandestinely oppress and assassinate immigrants. To emphasize that sense, the following passages: "Cases unresolved, dead immigrants in the hands of the police/In dark rooms, beatings and persecution/And the city balances as it can/trade of foreign meat, trafficking women/Who want work and now get dirty/sell their innocence".

Also is highlighted in this section is the reference to foreign women, despised by the lawful mechanisms of the Greek labor system, who need to "sell their innocence", in the "dirty and dark alleys" of the country.

The song reaches the end, once again, with a refrain in recognition of those who immigrated and faced the hardships of an unknown nation.

	Translation:
Ρεφραίν- 2X	Chorus- 2x
Χαιρετώ με σεβασμό τον δικό σου αγώνα	I salute with respect your struggle
Παίρνω φως και τραγουδώ την δικία σου εικόνα	I light a candle and sing your image

Note that, again under the narrative focus established in the first person, the performer honors the struggle of their ancestors and also of all immigrants, who put on equal foot against the representative images of Orthodox saints that are seen as deserving of respect and admiration.

Άφρικα: *African history, sung in rapper beats*

"*Αφρικά*" is a song that explicitly lends itself to tell a story. Camouflaged by a tone of fiction, the narrative uses imaginary descriptions to have concrete facts that refer to fundamental issues originating of the reasons that drove (and drive) many African immigrants to submit to the conditions of the diaspora.

	Translation:
Άλλη μία ρυθμίκη ιστόρια θα πω για μια Πριγκηπέσα που εκροσωπούσε το χορό	I'll tell a rhythmic story Of a princess who represents the dance
Το ρυθμό και τον πλούτο το βασίλειο της ξακουστο	The famous palace by its wealth and function
Γιατί ητάν άγρια όμορφο άφρικα το όνομα της	Its beautiful and wild name was Africa
Η ματία της ήτανε γιορτή και από πολλούς μνηστήρες	Represented treasures for many candidates
Ποθήτη γύρω της πάντα μαζέμενοι αυλικόι και πριν πάρει απόφαση	Courted by the palacians, but before settling for one
έπαιρνε από αυτούς συμβουλή	She received several advice from them.

In the very first strophe the intention of the lyrics assigned to the song is noted, to "tell a rhythmic story", the story of a princess very "rich", called "Africa". Under the narrative focus established in the first person singular, the voice performs a metaphorical reference to the African continent, a factor that allows the receiver the association between the lyrical and the real story. Africa is a territory described in the song as being subject to exploitative nations "palatial candidates" that by understanding it as a "treasure" of extreme value several disputes are undertaken around this.

A closer look allows us to infer that the strophe is a historical reference which refers to the process of colonization crossed by the African continent. Referring to the "princess" Africa, the lyric voice describes several suitors that could be understood as the nations who tried to colonize the continent. In this sense, they sing the verse: "Her beautiful and wild name was Africa/treasures represented for many candidates/courted by the palacians, but before settling for one/She received advice from many of them." The idea of a "metaphorical body", related to the colonizing process established on the African continent, appears ratified by the second strophe, that tells us:

	Translation:
Μόλις την έβλεπα στο μυαλό μου έφερνα γόνιμες περιοχές Αγάθες μορφές ανθρώπους με αρχές και παραδόσεις Κρουστά και τελέτες Το βασίλειο της ήταν κάτω από την μεσόγειο βασίληάδες Ψάχνανε τρόπο για να γευτούν τα κάλη της μαυρής θέας Για αυτό πλησιάσανε τους αυλικούς που ήταν πονήροι Και καιροσκόποι ,πίσω από την πλάτη της αυτοί κάνανε συνοικέσια Πήραν τα λέφτα και πουλήσανε την άφρικα φθηνά Και αυτή έγινε πόρνη αδηφάγων τεράτων που την ρουφούσαν σαν Κυφήνες.	When I saw her, she reminded me of fertile regions Sincere face of people with principles and customs Percussion and ceremonies, Her reign was less powerful than the reigns of the Mediterranean They looked for a way to taste the flavors of the black goddess So they went to meet the sagacious palacians. Shrewd and opportunists who, without her consent, made arrangements They received money and sold Africa cheap She turned into a prostitute for hungry beasts that feed ifrom her Like parasites

The enunciator, in this verse describes the observation of a fertile region, particularly in the conservation of cultural practices on the local tradition. "When I saw her, she reminded me of fertile regions/Sincere face of people with principles and customs/Percussion and ceremonies", he says.

However, the "rich" and "fertile" continent happens to be described, from the fourth verse on, as well as something fragile to face "powerful kingdoms of the Mediterranean". The fragility of the "African Princess" and "her kingdom" has given way to greed and later exploitation. Describes, in this sense, the lyrical voice. "Shrewd and opportunists who, without her consent, made agreements/received money and sold Africa cheap".

Metaphors aside, it is known that, in real life, the continent suffered the colonizing presence of explorers who came from different countries (Portugal, Britain, Spain, Holland, etc.). The intense harassment of the African land, culminating in the division of the continent in 1884.

In the article "*Africa, a changing continent - The third wave of democratic transitions and some political impacts of globaization in non-democratic states*", the researcher Alberto Manuel Vara Branco (2006, p. 63) reports, include how this process was:

> The scramble for Africa begins, in fact, with the Berlin Conference (1884), which established standards for the occupation. At the beginning of World War I, 90% of the land was already under the domination of Europe. The sharing was done arbitrarily, not respecting the ethnic and cultural characteristics of each person, which contributed to many of the current conflicts on the African continent. Other European countries also seek to dominate Africa, such as France, Belgium and Italy. Portugal's share continues with Cape Verde, Sao Tome and Principe, Saint John the Baptist of Ouidah, Guinea-Bissau, Angola and Mozambique. After the sharing resistance movements occured. However, many of the manifestations were strongly suppressed with violence by settlers.

In the third strophe, the chorus comes. In it, the lyrical voice emerges repeating the word "Africa", as if it cried out, nostalgic for an imaginary continent. The song that seems to start in fragments of an ascending scale, kicks to the last syllable spoken, which might suggest a kind of "sadness" sung by the receiver. The word Africa extends in sound prolongations that in our translation gain the "body" of the ellipsis.

Ρεφραίν- 2x	**Translation:** Chorus- 2x:
Αφρικά ... Αφρικά ...	Africa... Africa...

The idea of a nostalgia regarding the nation - of a mother decimated by foreigners is sustained in the fourth strophe when the foreigner shows deep sorrow to observe the devastation caused by foreign people.

	Translation:
Μέτα από καιρό την είδα, μία ρακέντητη πριγκήπισα	After some time I saw her, Princess ragamuffin
Στημένη και ρημαγμένη πλέον στο έλεος των αυλίκων	Destroyed and set on the charity of palacians
Που γίνανε διαχειριστές στο βασίλειο της	Who became administrators of her kingdom
Η πάλε ποτέ θέα δεν εμπνέει πλέον τους υπηκόους της	The goddess no longer inspires her subjects
Δεν πιστευούν πια στον πνεύμα της , για αυτό	They do not believe in her spirit
Και αγκαλιάσανε την ανασφάλεια και πηδήξανε Στο πλοίο της ξενιτιάς .	And so they embraced insecurity They jumped on a ship for a foreign trip
Μόλις την βλεπω μου έρχεται στο μυαλό η ασθένεια	As soon as I see her, memories of diseases come to me
Μου έρχεται στο μυαλό οι εμφύλιες διαμάχες	Memory of the civil wars
Μου έρχεται στο μυαλό η ανέχεια μια μορφή	Memory of misery and the image
Τσακισμένη από δυνάστες	Busted by the despots

The "African Princess" now "ragamuffin" and "destroyed" is administrated by the "palacians" and for being "exploited", no longer arouses the desire for new "pretenders", nor the admiration of her "subjects". In a game of alliteration and metaphors, the song describes Africa post-colonization, which comes down to a scenario of conflict and "insecurity", "unhealthy" reality brought by the colonizers. The sounds, almost imperceptible, sometimes resemble a piano; for others, a oquestra. These are sounds that give way, throughout the performance, to homesick and resentful words, representative of feeling and memory of those who left their homeland and form today the aesthetic of history itself. Using the cohesion mechanism "anaphora", thus the lyrical voice states that: "The memory of the civil wars come to me/The memory of misery and the image/Busted by the despots."

In the fifth strophe something unexpected comes. It shows a kind of expository expansion of aesthetics in the analysis, in the sense that they - having been devoted to narrate the history of the African continent through the oppressed look - dedicate its final verses to other "princesses" also devastated through colonizing attitudes. The verses of this strophe state:

	Translation:
Αλλό ένα τραγούδι για τις περιοχ'ες που καταπατήθηκαν	This is another song for devastated places
Για τις πριγκηπησες που την λάμψη τους έχασαν , για τις αποικίες	For the princesses who have lost their luster
Που μέτα από την ανεξαρτησία έπεσαν στα χέρια εθνοπατέρων	For the territories that after independence fell into the hands of usurpers
Καταχραστών που αρνηθήκανε την εξέλιξη της ίδιας τους της χώρας	Who refused the progress of their own country
Στο όνομα του κέρδους και της διαφθοράς,και για να ναI πάντα καλά	For profit and corruption, to be always well
Του κόσμου τα αφεντικά,υποβαθμισμένα όνειρα και αντιλήψεις τρίτου κόσμου Τουριστικά θέρετρα.	The owners of the world... Destroyed dreams... Third World Perceptions tourism resorts, wonderful resorts,
θέαμα για ανυποψίαστους που αλλάζει	unsuspecting of change
Με ένα κουμπί και για τους μετανάστες μια ξεχασμένη γη...	As if in the push of a button, immigrants from a forgotten land

For the princesses who have lost their "luster", "for the usurped territories", "for the resistance to corruptions filed" and many others "immigrants" singing their "forgotten land", the song presents the spokesman of the colonized nations, of similar historical past. "To the Agents of capital, 'unsuspecting', seems to incur in a subliminal message: that the 'immigrants' from a 'forgotten land' can orchestrate 'the change', quickly, as in a "pushing a button".

Rich in alliterations and metaphors, from the beginning to the end of its length, the lyrics of "Αφρικά" come to the end of this transcript, once again, with the exposure of the chorus, in which the sender claims for their imagined homeland.

Ρεφραίν- 2x	**Translation:** Chorus- 2x:
Αφρικά ... Αφρικά ...	Africa... Africa...

"Αφρικα": it is undoubtedly a tribute both to the colonized nations, as to their children - and those in native soil, or deterritorialized, recalling the origin and their country in diaspora sensations.

Shock: the doctrines of shock and the angry intolerance of marginal masses

Composed and the performed by Ana Tijoux, "Shock" is a song that, in a way, externalizes the onset of a forceful reaction from the marginalized sectors, in relation to the systemic-capitalist apparatus. In the first strophe, performed by the enunciator, there is the finding of a conductor speech, coming from the totalitarian system controller.

Translation:

Venenosos tus monólogos	Poisonous are your monologues
Tus discursos incoloros	Your speeches are colorless
No ves que no estamos solos	Don't you see that we are not alone
Millones de polo a polo	Millions from pole to pole
Al son de un solo coro	At the sound of one choir
Marcharemos con el tono	We will march with the tone
Con la convicción que	With the conviction of
Basta de robo!	Enough theft!

With the narrative focus established in the first person plural, and using poor rhymes, the enunciator starts issuing its verses describing and at the same time adjectifying, the hegemonic discourse: "Poisonous are your monologues/Your speeches are colorless". In direct reference to the system, asks: "Don't you see that we are not alone?" and states then and predictably, the union between similars. "Millions from pole to pole/We will march with the tone/With the conviction of enough theft."

Tired of systemic usurpation, the enunciator pounces to refuse the social situation in which she seems to be immersed. With the identification of certain characteristics of the order - the wealth, the political leadership and the hypocritical word - comes the second strophe, when there is the abandonment of a subservient speech in favor of refusal to stagnation.

Translation:

Tu estado de control	Your state of control
Tu trono podrido de oro	Your rotten golden throne
Tu política y tu riquesa	Your politics and your wealth
Y tu tesoro no!	And your treasure, no!
La hora sono! La hora sono!	The time came! The time came!
No permitiremos mas, mas	We will not allow more, more.
Tu dotrina del shock!	Your doctrine of "shock"
La hora sono, la hora sono	The time came, came!
Dotrina del shock 2x	Doctrine of "shock" 2x

As an "awakening", the enunciator performs the desire for action. In the strophic construction - riddled with metaphors, anaphora, assonance and alliteration - the self-lyrical utters lines like "Your rotten golden throne/Your politics and your wealth/And your treasure. no!" [26-27] , under which she demonstrates the perception of malfeasance and social injustice, opposing the submission to the active position. Repeatedly, the expository voice sends back "The time came" by establishing a metaphorical reference to this critical awakening and active stance taken by the minority classes.

In the third strophe, what we see is an utterance which states the critique of the capitalist reality established globally. The rulership of the world is attributed to few and what you have, via performance, is the denunciation of one regency that emerges in guidelines compared to fascism.

Translation:

No hay países solo corporaciones	There are no countries, only corporations
Quien tiene más, más más acciones	Who has more, more and more shares
Trozos gordos, poderosos	large pieces, powerful
Decisiones por muy pocos.	Decisions by very few
Constituición pinochetista	Constitution of Pinochet
Derecho opus dei, libro fascista	"Opus dei" rights, fascist book
Golpista disfrazado de un indulto elitista	Coup leaders disguised as an elitist reprieve
Cae la gota, cae la bolsa	Drops fall, drops the stocks
A torna se torna la maquina rota	The decision is made, the machine, broken
La calle no calle, la calle se raya	The street does not shut, the street scratches itself
La calle no calla debate que estala.	The street does not shut, the debate explodes
Todo lo quitan, todo lo venden	They take everything, they sell everything

---

26 Our highlighting
27 Style figures also present at the spanish version.

Todo se lucra, la vida, la muerte	Everything is profit, life, death
Todo es negocio como tu todos	Everything is business, like
Semilla, Pascuala, métodos y	you, all
coro	Seed, Pascuala, methods and
	leather

Assuming a tone essentially descriptive and accumulative - as the information comes in an "almost chaotic" way, at great speed in singing performance - the strophe has the narrative focus set on the third person singular.

In the first two verses, the use of parallel rhymes, the enunciator issues a statement: "There are no countries, only corporations/ Who has more, more and more actions." The idea related to the cancellation of the nations is based on the finding of voracity exerted by the capitalist system.

This perception changes a bit when we move to the analysis of the passage established between the third and seventh verses. Note, by the established terms, that the critical sense in the face of oppression experienced due to the neoliberal systematic is mixed with historical knowledge that, in a way, is also responsible for their exile, led by rapper Ana Tijoux and transferred in performance, as noted from the appreciation of the verses.

In this sense, the enunciator says "large pieces, powerful/ Decisions by very few/Pinochet Constitution/"Opus dei" rights, fascist book/Coup leader disguised as an elitist reprieve." The establishment of direct criticism against the Catholic Church is evident- who, by means of pardons, have been forgiven of the atrocities committed "in the name of God" - and the government of former General Augusto Pinochet (1915-2006), who was the front of Chile, between the years 1973 and 1990. Capitalist reality, placed next to Pinochet's action, are equal in the eyes of the enunciator, the dynamics of fascism. The projection of real life is noted, established in the song, in dialogy, as it was during the government of Pinochet, as explained above, that the parents of performer Ana Tijoux had to leave Chile, under the condition of political exiles.

Amid complaints, the strophe emphatically carries the theme of awakening, revealing a song immersed in wide emotional charge and based on feelings arising from the autobiographical trajectory that was composed.

From the eighth to the eleventh verse, it is instituted by the fictionality of singing the description of actions correlated to the revolutionary act. Remarkable, in the strophe, is the attention to language, full of anaphora, metaphors and alliteration; able to properly describe the revolutionary process. On the verse "Drop fall, drops the stocks" it uses the term stocks as a metaphor of social economic hegemony that is dissolving, i.e. "falling". The notion of this "fall" is maintained in the course of the following verses, which retain the sense of "breaking a gear" or "machine", which gradually crumbles. The decision is made that the machine is broken/The streets do not shut, the streets scratches itself/The streets do not shut, debate that explodes[28-29]"

Aware of all the corruption and injustice, those doomed to marginality condition, regardless of the territorial position they occupy in the world, take to the streets in "debates", struggling to "break the machine", understood, for purposes of this analysis, as "capital machine", i.e. operant capitalism in the world, in the analyzed song receives scathing criticism against the unceasing interest in getting the most value.

The musical performance attests to the birth of the revolution, while the self-lyrical assumes the voice in leadership. In front of a large mass of the marginalized, she walks demonstrating commitment and certainty of an effort that will not be discharged in vain. Between the twelfth and fifteenth verses, she describes the revolution that occurs in a mixed way to describe the capitalist operation. Through examination of verses "They take everything, They sell everything/Everything is proft, life and death/Everything is business

---

28 Our highlighting.
29 Style figures also present at the spanish version.

like you all / Seed, Pascuala, methods and leather" notes a kind of "lyrical-explanation" established by collectivized voice.

It is clear, on the fifteenth verse, which seems to be a reference established by the song to the young Chilean songwriter (and singer) Pascuala Ilabaca (1985-). Known for performing folk music, in which she operates with the accompaniment of accordion and piano, Pascuala is one of the members of the group Sama di (which means "trance state" or "spiritual evolution"[30]), ethnic music, known to compile and perform repertoires of several territoriality, such as Africa, Latin America, Arabia and Europe (MUSICA POPULAR cl., accessed on Aug 10th 2014)

Transcribed in the fourth strophe, note the repetition of the chorus:

	Translation:
Venenosos tus monólogos	Poisonous are your monologues
Tus discursos incoloros	Your speeches are colorless
No ves que no estamos solos	Don't you see that we are not alone
Millones de polo a polo	Millions from pole to pole
Al son de un solo coro	At the sound of one choir
Marcharemos con el tono	We will march with the tone
Con la convicción que	With the conviction that
Basta de robo!	Enough theft!

Attesting to the strength of her group before the centralizing-government actions, the performative voice acts in "leadership" as if to lead a revolution. The song gives the receiver the idea that, in favor of the revolution, "anything goes". Ownership of the capital system values is valid, to the acquisition of a resistance posture and, above all, the confrontation of all "fighting". Life is valid, as well as death, the struggle for recognition, the achievement of rights on behalf of all.

In the appreciation of the song arises the fith strophe, with the following verses:

---

30 Our translation.

	Translation:
Golpe a golpe, beso a beso	Blow by blow, kiss by kiss
Con las ganas y el aliento	With desire and encouragement
Con cenizas, con el fuego	With ash, with fire
Del presente con recuerdo	From the present, with memories
Con certeza y con desgarro	With certainty and with fret
Con el objetivo claro	With the clear objective
Con memoria y con la historia	With memory and history
El futuro es ahora!	The future is now

The verbal momentum in the performing verses rescues the memory of an oppressive past, in order to establish the change. Within the certainty of a future - present, has the image of a spokeswoman of marginalized layers.

This, through its verses, awakens the encouragement and action of those with whom she shares existential realities and identity aspects. "With a clear objective" built from the "memory", a propelling factor for confronting the "hits" and the quest for "victory". The song describes the "desire" and "encouragement" existing in a desired revolution, feelings transmitted through the practice of musical appreciation and subject therefore to materialize.

The transcription process goes on and got to the point where the song describes in further deepening one "critical eye" and "introspection", released by the enunciator about the world in which it operates. The enunciator, in these terms, finds to be in the midst of a sizable trial process. A marionette manipulated by power and its agents; she compares the day-by-day to a "test tube", aspects that can be observed on the sixth strophe, with the verses:

	Translation:
Todo este tubo de ensayo,	All this is a test tube,
Todo este laboratorio que a diario,	All this is a laboratory for everyday,
Todo este fallo, todo este económico modelo condenado de dinosaurio.	All this fails, All this is a doomed and jurassic economic model

Todo se criminaliza	Everything is criminalized,
Todo se justifica en la noticia,	Everything is justified by the news,
Todo se quita	Everything is removed,
Todo se pisa	Everything is stepped on,
Todo se ficha y clasifica.	Everything is stored and classified,
Pero...	But ...
Tu política y tu táctica,	Your politics and your tactic
Tu típica risa y ética.	your typical laugh and ethic
Tu comunicado manipulado	Your manipulated communication ...
¿cuantos fueron los callados?	How many were muted?
Pacos, guanacos y lumas,	Cops, stupid and batons,
Pacos, guanacos y tunas,	Stupid cops and students
Pacos, guanacos no suman.	stupid cops do not add up
¿Cuantos fueron los que se robaron las fortunas?	How many got away with fortunes?

Ironically, the performer uses the song to question the ethics in which the system is operated. The verses denounce the actions of an archaic and repressive system, although global and unified in which the masses are judged and punished by the maximum rigor of the laws. The strophe is built, from the first to tenth verse, with the use of anaphora that realizes truths about the system. "This is all a test tube/All this is a laboratory for everyday/all this is failure (...)"

Thus, through the enunciator, we see the realization of a failed and corrupt system, information handler and which "adds" nothing to the development of humanity. There is an explicit reference to the student struggle, which appears illustrated in vehemence by the song [31] "Cops, stupid and batons/stupid cops and students/stupid cops do not add up." To the system and its agents, the enunciator asks, in the thirteenth and seventeenth verses: "How many

---

31 It is noteworthy that over the song, highlighted the use of the term "guanacos" usually used to refer to a mammal, whose presence is typical in some regions. It was discovered during investigations that this is a word that can take connotative meanings. In this regard, by way of explanation, we reproduce the following entry - "Guanaco, a.i. s (zool) Guanaco, ruminant mammal used as a beast of burden in the southern Andes; (Fig.) Simple, silly, stupid."(ORTEGA, 1982, p. 1444).

were muted"?/"How many fled with the fortunes"?

The performance comes to an end with the repetition of the chorus, coincidentally also the first verse of this song. The seventh strophe, once again confirms the idea of boosting a social movement in resistance:

	Translation:
Venenosos tus monólogos	Poisonous are your monologues
Tus discursos incoloros	Your speeches are colorless
No ves que non estamos solos	Don't you see that we are not alone
Millones de polo a polo	Millions from pole to pole
Al son de um solo coro	At the sound of one choir
Marcharemos con el tono	We will march with the tone
Com la convicción que	With the conviction that
Basta de robo!	Enough theft!

As noted, biopower consciousness is in Schock, the propelling factor of symbolic confrontation promoted by the rapper's aesthetic. This aesthetic has in its interior, the certainty of the existence of transnational order problems. Moreover, it seems to tell the composition of the lyrics, with a persuasive enunciation; which tries to awaken in the receiving subject some kind of practical reaction, able to subvert and change the current capitalist machinery in the world.

To take the throne or advise, the word: the rap, libertarian aesthetic of the voice in fury

This section is made of interpretative analysis of songs that, in general, deal with the possibility and attempt to reverse social problems, from the rapper's word. These are songs that describe and denounce, showing the resentment of the excluded and their attempt to be represented politically and actively through the word, also object disseminating knowledge. In this sense, the section will start from the "*Αλάνα*" analysis, a song produced and performed by the Greek rapper MC Yinka.

Αλάνα: the denounce of the system and rescue through the voice

"*Αλάνα*" (or Alana in English) is a song whose purpose is also related to denouncing oppression and codes imposed by the neoliberal system, while exalting the power of verbal aesthetic in accomplishing this task.

In the interpretation of this study the hypothesis that the title of the song is possibly a variant of gender on the term "alano" remains, which means:

> Alano [lat.Alanu]. Sm 1) Individual of the Alans, barbarous people of Asian origin established in Sarmatia, between the Sea of Azov and the Caucasus and that in the fifth century invaded and dominated, Gaul and Iberia. Aj. 2. Related to this people. (FERREIRA, 2010, p. 88).

This hypothesis comes from the perception that the discursive content developed in the song attributes to the voice the function to "invade" territories already colonized by the dominant forces and to dominate them, spreading among them a kind of "aesthetic orientation", aimed to clarify about the facts that permeate the reality and the mechanisms that operate in it.

The song begins with an introductory sound basis, in discrete volume. After 0:20 (twenty seconds) of introduction the rapper presence comes, less melodic and more spoken. The sound of speech is opposed to the sound of the base, providing from the beginning of the song, a sensory feature that attests scenario of the voice that "came to shout".

The first strophe reveals an utterance devoted to foster in its recipients, the conscience of a "society of the spectacle", whose operation generates harmful effects to humans. This is a society that disintegrates, hurts and dampens human dreams, but even so, is coveted and pleasing to many, due to the "illusions of the material order" that it generates.

Translation:

Καλώς ήλθες στην ενότητα που σβήνουμε στείρες στιγμές	Welcome to the section that erases sterile times
Στιγμές Που είσαι εγκλωβισμένος στους τέσσερις τοίχους του νου	Moments that are trapped in the four walls of the mind
Που- χωρίζει ότι η καρδιά ότι η καρδία ενώνει	That separates what the heart unites
θα αγκαλιάσεις, αγαπήσεις ότι σε πορώνει	You shall love and embrace what hurts you
ο ήχος γίνεται βίωμα και αγγίζει ψυχές	The sound turns into life and touches the souls
μαρτυρά και δίνει φωνή σε βουβές κραυγές	Accuses and gives voice to the silent screams
ζούμε σε τεμπέλικες μέρες, το ηθικό θέλει	We live in lazy times, moral is what pushes
σπρώξιμο.φάστ-φούντ προτάσεις και πέρα κάνει	Wants Fast-Food, makes suggestions, recommendations
το ψάξιμο το δέσιμο ψάχνω με υγιείς καταστάσεις	Looking for statements and salutes
που λένε να δεις την πραγματικότητα σε άλλες διαστάσεις	They say they see the reality in other dimensions
παραστάσεις ψυχαναγκασμού, θέλω να κράξω και τα σενάρια	Performances and obsession, I want to scream scenarios
που γράφουν για μένα χωρίς	that speak of me without me Writing letters about me without burning me

εμένα να κάψω ,να γράψω στίχους
που ζουν ,δεν μιζεριάζω που
θέλουν ένα ποτήρι κρασί
να σε κεράσουν, στο θέατρο της
ζωής δεν υποκρίνονται
μεσ' στο παράλογο της απλώς
αφήνονται

Writing verses of life without
misery, for those who want a
glass of wine
In the theater of life one does
not pretend
Is simply carried away

The pretentious immediacy, arbitrariness and social segregation described in the song are factors that support the contextualizing routines of any capitalist society and, in a wayevidencing the presence of an unquestioning, "lazy" population.

In this sense, the enunciator - which in the case of narrative structure oscillates between first and third person singular - gives an invitation to reflection, catering mainly to the excluded layers to most capitalist social practices. In the first verse, the listener has the impression of entering into another environment, the musical environment of the rapper, space with specific ideological political purposes, of stopping the alienating and unfruitful effects arising from the capitalist process. The enunciator says in that sense on the first four verses: "Welcome to the section that erases sterile moments / moments that are trapped in the four walls of the mind/ That separates what the heart unites (...)"

The musical space is also a transformer space which "gives life" and "touches souls", providing silenced with the possibility of voice. In the seventh to tenth verses, the capitalist scheme is described in detail by the lyrical voice, which states in ironic tones: "We live in lazy times, moral is what pushes/Want Fast-Food, make suggestions, recommendations/Looking statements and salutes/They say they see reality in other dimensions."

The time narrated by the song is a lazy time, possessor of a determinist and Americanized speech. A discourse that requires the consumption and living standards. Given this capitalist speech, the enunciator interposes his will to be declared between the eleventh and fifteenth delivered verses: "I want to shout scenarios that speak of me without me/That write letters about me without burning me/

write verses life without misery, for those who want a glass of wine/ in the theater of life one does not pretend/just gets carried away." The will specified is a will to subversion. The song, in this sense, states that it is directed to those who "want a glass of wine"- i.e. the deprived of the power consumption of basic human rights and the possibility of speech. The lyrical voice, through rap, gives the right to "scream" reality, externalizing the risk of being censured, merged with the will necessary to express their reasons.

Ratifying something common to "style conscious rap music inserts the rapper's voice as a way to subvert the system.

The performer, through his art, flees the use of any kind of mask and through the song itself, justifies his position: "In the theater of life one does not pretend/just gets carried away."

The lyrical voice calls for continuing protests, asking those who sing to not let themselves be discouraged by possible repressions. The chorus, on the second strophe has the following words:

	Translation:
Ρεφραίν - 4x:	Chorus- 4 x:
Μην σταματάς ,μην σταματάς να παίζεις	Do not stop, do not stop playing Friend, break and if you fall, do
Φίλε να τα σπας και εάν πέσεις	not demote
κάτω μην κολλάς	You are in the alley (Alana)
Είσαι στην αλάνα	

Directed to those who "inhabit the becos"- forgotten territories of exclusion - the song calls for resistance and lends itself to break any socio-economical boundaries imposed. The continuity of the song is done with an alternance of the narrative axis. The lyrical voice is built again in first person and describes possible connections between existential uncertainties of the excluded and the role played by music in the process. In this sense, the third verse strophe tells us:

Είμαι μια ψύχη που κυνηγά
ώρες διαύγειας
Ώρες που βρίσκω απαντήσεις
σε ερωτήσεις και λύσεις
Σε γρίφους στίχους σε ύμνους.
Έμπνευση μέσα από ήχους
ώρες που το αίσθημα ξεχείλιζει
κ έρχομαι πιό κοντά
σε άτομα που αγαπώ ,είμαι
τύπος που αναπολώ εξιστορώ
σε μένα βιώματα μου και βλέπω
το αντίκτυπο που έχει ο χρόνος
σε εμάς χρωματιστή κλεψύδρα
και κάθε χρώμα μια περίοδος
χρόνια χαμένα ή κερδισμένα
στην προσπάθεια να αποδείξεις
ότι μπορείς συνειδητοποιείς,
συνειδητοποιείς,
συνειδητοποιείς
γεννίεται η αποκάλυψη και
πρέπει να την δεχτείς.
καμμία φορά δεν χώρα στο
μυάλο μου το ποσό διαφέρει
ο ένας με τον άλλον μα το
δέχομαι γιατί αυτό είναι η ουσία
και η ομορφία του κοσμού , μα
βλέπω το ρατσισμό να
βασίζεται στο αντίθετο .μιλώ
για την ψυχολογία που χτίζεις
τη συνείδηση που γυμνάζεις
κάθε στιγμή που νίωθεις οτι
αλλάζεις
για το πόσο διαβάζεις τη σκέψη
σου και για το πώς και πόσο σε
ψάχνεις.

Translation:

I am a soul that seeks hours of
lucidity
Hours to find answers for
problems and solutions
Charades, verses of hymns,
inspired by the sounds.
Times in which feeling
overflows
I get closer to the
people I love.
I experience, I see the impact
of time on the color of the
hourglass
Each color a period
years lost or added in an effort
to prove
That you realize,
realize,
realize
Sometimes discovery
happens
But your mind does
not stand
I do not understand that much
difference between them
But I accept because this is the
reason and the beauty of the
world
But I see the racism that is
based on opposite
I speak of the psychology that
is built on the conscience,
Who knows your thoughts
and how much you search for
yourself

The realization of the song shows the establishment of a search. The lyrical representation of the rapper voice reverberates reflections from groups in marginal situations, seeking an understanding of themselves and the operational context of the world in which they live. Between the first and sixth verses uttered, the enunciator undertakes a self-definition process by which this search becomes clear, externalized in emotional tones. "I am a soul that seeks hours of lucidity/hours to find answers for problems and solutions/Charades, hymns verses, inspired by the sounds/Times in which feeling spills over/I come closer to people I love./I do experiences, I see the impact of time on the color of the hourglass (...)"

As noted, the experience of singing in performance is reversed, exactly, within this search space, which shows the attempt of translation, it seems, of the very time the rap song occurs. The enunciator, who sees the "impact of time on the color of the hourglass" deposits in music all his doubts and, through it, seeks to prove that he "sees" the social effects of his time.

Assuming the discomfort of not understanding the existence of differences in the contemporary scene, the enunciator externalizes the acceptance of plural time, governed by various prejudices instilled by the systemic logic in the face of human consciousness. In this sense, there is the final stretch of the verse in question, between the tenth and the sixteenth verse, by which the enunciator declares:

"Sometimes the discovery happens/But your mind does not support/I do not understand that much difference between them/But I accept because this is the reason and the beauty of the world/But I see the racism that is based on the opposite/I speak of psychology that builds on consciousness/Who knows your thoughts and how much you search for yourself."

Built by the application of anaphora and metaphors, the verse in question demonstrates the sadness of the state in which differences - supposedly motivated by the "reason" and "beauty" of the world - become appropriated by the logic of racism, proposed by a system that controls consciousness and builds opinions.

Turning to the fourth strophe, it appears that the note of neoliberal logic, established by the enunciator, has lost strength as he tells us about the potential of singing.

Through singing, he escapes oppression and reaches "clarity". The freedom provided by singing is metaphorically equated to the comfort of a fetus during the pregnancy. In this way, the fourth strophe reads:

	Translation:
Είμαι εδώ ελεύθερος πιά σαλεύω σαν βρέφος μες την κοιλία Κυλιέμαι κάτω χορευώ με την σκέψη , αφεντεύω στην, μαγεία της Αγάπης. Καθώς χαλαρώνω και εκτιμώ αυτά που έχω Αντέχω ακόμα ,γιατί τα όρια δεν είναι στη γη είναι στον Ουρανό εκεί ψηλά ψύχη και σώμα θέλουν να εκτονωθούν Καταστάσεις και πρόσωπα να ερωτευτούν Η παίδικη μας χαρά αντανακλά την αλλή ζώη Που ζούμε μες τα όνειρα . Είκονες σε ψηφιδωτά και παλάτια σκαλιστά Με μίκρους ήρωες και ξύλινα σπαθιά φωνάζω δυνατά Φωνάζω δυνατά μα δεν βραχνιάζω πιά	Here I am free, protected, baby in the womb I roll, dance with the thought Thus I relax and appreciate what I have Hold still, because the limits are not on earth, they are in heaven. Up above body and soul want to disarm Situations and people want to love Happy childhood reflects the afterlife We live in dreams Images in mosaics and carved palaces With young heroes and wood swords, I shout I shout aloud, but do not get hoarse

The verses record the freedom granted by the song. "Here I am free, protected, baby in the womb," says the performative voice, demonstrating to occupy a peculiar place of enunciation. The "mother's womb" externalizes the existence of a protective space of nutrition, before the social and historical life. In this place thought flows and incite resistance which becomes the ultimate purpose of all the performed action, this purpose assumed by the expository voice.

Situations and people want to love
Happy childhood reflects the afterlife
That we live in dreams

Images in mosaics and carved palaces
With young heroes and wood swords, I shout
I shout aloud, but do not get hoarse

Demonstrating a certain spirituality and belief, the voice of enunciation is thus determined to transcend the difficulties existent in space. Thus he believes that he will find the bounties offered by other life. Resistance therefore, starts from the exercise of faith, voiced by the enunciator - this occurs mainly between the fourth and fifth verse, when he tells us: "Hold still, because the limits are not on earth, they are in heaven./Up above, body and soul want to disarm."

The lyrical voice thus demonstrates that the realization is possible only in a spiritual territory, definitive in determinations. The desired love for people, situations of peace, will only be possible, according to the song, in metaphysical dimensions.

The voice- rapper insists, shouting their wishes and complaints, describing moments that he associates with happiness: the "childhood", the "dreams", the "young heroes", "wood sword". Note the persistence of the enunciator, to the extent to which he is not allowed to be mute, not allowed to become "hoarse". On the contrary, he remains optimistic in relation to the emergence of new times.

Alana's speech comes to an end with one more repetition of the chorus cited above. The fifth and final strophe, tells us:

	Translation:
Ρεφραίν- 4x	Chorus- 4x:
Μην σταματάς ,μην σταματάς να παίζεις	Do not stop, do not stop playing
Φίλε να τα σπας και εάν πέσεις κάτω μην κολλάς	Friend, break and if you fall do not demote
Εϊ! Είσαι στην αλάνα	You are in the alley (Alana)

The "broken" reference, draws attention in the song. The slang is used in the song to refer to the existence of their own performance. The act of breaking is shown, at the "eyes" of the lyric voice as necessary and therefore sustained by the rapper speech. The "broken" cannot stop.

Using the vocative "friend", the song asks the listener not to succumb to the difficulties; and at the same time it gives some sense of belonging (You're in the Alley [Alana]); making it possible to identify the awareness of belonging to a group or tribe rapper, able to subvert the capital logic.

Unite

"*Unite*" is a hybrid construction consisting of several languages and the three performed rappers' voices MC Beto, responsible for sayings in Portuguese and Sat-Skill and Pay-Ment, singing in Japanese. Throughout the song, they oscillate in using both the Japanese language as well as the Portuguese and English languages. In addition, each verse has the presence of a different rapper voice, allowing the participation of all the components of the group Tensais MCS in the unfolding of musical narrative.

In "*Unite*", the song takes on an aggregative approach, seeking to unite similar identities externalized by foreign-Brazilian communities, rooted in Japan. The performance begins with a brief melodic introduction. In the sound's base comes the gentle sound of a piano. The introduction - which suggests the presence of a similar musical cell used in the jazz and Bossa Nova - is stopped abruptly after six seconds, with the incisive rapper voice input, which gives:

フック

Translation:

Chorus 4 x- All:

マイク、ケーブル、２ターン
テーブル HeyYo!! ３ MC此処に
あらわる
マイクロフォンチェック１２
１２
調子どうだ！手を上げろ！
É "nois" na fita, aqui presente chega!
Se for "pra" somar "cola", mas se
vacilar "poca"

Microphone, cables, two DJ
tables, it's all right Hey Yo!Three
MC testing the microphones 1
and 2 and 1 and 2.
How is the tone, raise your
hands!
These are us, here it comes!
If you're gonna add up, come.
But if you're not, piss off

As we can see, the first transcribed and translated strophe simulates a process of montage of the musical equipment. The rapper announces that it is "all right" - microphone, sound mixer, DJ - and makes an alert invitation to listeners: "If you're gonna add up, come. But if you're not, piss off."

The only ones welcome to the performance are those that lend themselves to add value to it. The rest, as you see, are at the outset "asked to leave the performance space", even before the performance begins.

The song goes on to establish direct references to the foreign community rooted in Japan. In the transcribed/translated second strophe there is mention of the presence of Japanese descent Brazilian immigrants. It says:

(MC Beto)
300 mil gaijin a toda parte que se
vá
É assim tem burajirujin
Ayase, Chi, Terao, Tsuruma, Chogo
Higashi kaigan, Chigasaki, Tsurumi, Kanto

Translation:

(MC Beto)
300,000 foreigners everywhere
you go
It has Brazilian
Ayase, Chi, Terao, Tsuruma, Chogo
Higashi kaigan, Chigasaki, Tsurumi, Kanto

Cara de japonês, e dai o que é que tem.	Japanese face, so what?.
Se "pra" eles estrangeiro, latino, nanbei !	If for them they are foreign, Latin, panamericano!
Discriminado é, ou alvejado	Is discriminated, or targeted
Imigrante, sou latino doidão, "cê" tá ligado?	Immigrant, I am the crazy Latin, you know?

After emphasizing the foreign presence, the enunciator, cites several surnames of Japanese origin - *Ayase, Chi, Terao, Tsuruma, Chogo, Higashi, Kaigan, Chigasaki, Tsurumi and Kanto* - and alerts: despite having a "Japanese face," such characteristic is of no use to the Brazilian immigrant who is considered a foreigner, Latin American, suffering because of this, a number of existing prejudices in the diasporic day-by-day. "Japanese faces so what?/If 'to' them they are foreign, Latin, panamericano!/Is discriminated, or targeted", says the enunciator, confirming his opinion.

The strophe, which is constructed from internal and parallel rhymes, is also a structure devoted to identity affirmation. In the eighth and final verse there is the following statement: "Immigrant, i'm the crazy Latin, you know?".

The enunciator, addressing the figure of a hidden interlocutor, seeks to call their attention ("you know?") for a feature that he believes is inherent to him, "crazy". By classifying himself as "crazy", the enunciator allows us to draw inferences regarding the image he has of himself: an immigrant willing to creatively confront all obstacles and difficulties that life abroad interposes him.

Among the daily difficulties described by the song, is the presence of "false friends", narrated in the third strophe. These, in a cowardly way, cross the moral principles, breaking with what preaches the so-called "good education". The strophe has the following words:

(Sat-Skill)
背後からバッサリ斬りつける
刀　あっさり卑怯千万打つ輩
未熟なハンターはあんたじゃ
ないか？　刃からこぼれ落ち
る涙
伝統もなくぜ　世相めっぽう
胡散臭ぇ中でも捨てんなリス
ペクト
風貌違えど俺等は兄弟

Translation:
(Sat-Skill)
Stabbed in the back with a knife by a coward "friend". Who will be missing is you, friend. The blade cries, a sad social situation, breaking what we call good manners (tradition). Do not miss the respect you have inside, outside we are different, but inside we are all brothers.

Sat-Skill – rapper's voice is responsible for the verses in question - describes the lack of nobility of attitude, alerting the listener to equality among humans, often forgotten/deprecated due to other differences in physical or economic-social order.

The guidance set out in the verse above shows, especially given the last verse, the pedagogical aspect of the performance. To the hidden interlocutor, the enunciator proposes a lesson that will certainly be absorbed by the speaker-listener: "Do not miss the respect you have inside, outside we are different, but inside we are all brothers."

The song goes on like a speech, describing a kind of climax of revolting, which is given by the succession of obstacles to which the foreigner is submitted. The feeling of exclusion has thus violent potentialities, however, instead of becoming harmful to the surrounding context, it is reversed only in performance. It says in the verses of the fourth transcribed/translated strophe, performed by Pay-Ment rapper:

(Pay-Ment)
四六時中溜まったストレス開放
　大量摂取　覚醒する細胞
行っとく）感染するドーピング
（Hip- Hop）隅々までハーコー
にコーティング

Translation:
(Pay-Ment)
The stress that was accumulated for a long time was released, It was climbing trhough the cells
What served as the anesthesia was the Hip-Hop, healed all wounds and clothed me with a protective layer..

モノホンだけのソウル嗅ぎ
つけ　狂犬だらけのホール
が実現
Yes Yes Y'all や SAYHOO 木霊
し　マイクにかえすUniteの証

The soul snuffed only by the monophones and realized a hall full of rabies
Yes Yes Y'all and SAYHOO Spirit and return to microphone Proof of Unite

The resentment generated by the daily experiences ends up being sublimated[32] from the activities offered by the Hip-Hop Movement (dancing, singing, graffiti, manipulation/creation of sounds). The sense of identification and belonging to the group/community becomes a consequence of the characteristics attributed by the song, to the Hip-Hop Movement.

At the "eyes" of the performance, Hip-Hop is "healing", "union" and "security", posture ratified by the provision of the second and third verses. "What served as the anesthesia was Hip-Hop, healed all wounds, united and clothed me with a protective layer" Continuing the analyzed song, once again, comes the chorus, established in the sixth strophe transcribed / translated.

Translation:

フック

Chorus 4x:

マイク、ケーブル、２ターン
テーブル　HeyYo!!　３MC此処に
あらわる
マイクロフォンチェック１２
１２
調子どうだ！手を上げろ！
É "nois" na fita, aqui presente chega!
Se for "pra" somar "cola", mas se vacilar "poca".

Microphone, cables, two DJ tables, it's all right HeyYo!! Three MCS testing the microphones 1 and 2 and 1 and 2.
How is the tone, raise your hands!
These are us, here we come!
If you're gonna add up, come. But if you're not, piss off.

Integrating the Hip-Hop Movement becomes something absolutely fundamental to their survival and integrity. As the song

---

32 See footnote 06.

is performed and repeated, it shows how to take on a mission: to engage the performer and listener, each time more into generating meanings, establishing the gregarious feeling that, in practice, it seeks to expand the number of members belonging to that ideological sector of the Hip-Hop community, of which he is part of.

The verses of the seventh transcribed/translated strophe seem to adhere to this line of reasoning.

(Sat- Skill)

五臓六腑　染みわたるHip-Hop１語１句　息吹き込めるヒットマン
７５型の言霊はいかが？国境をまたぎ壊すテリトリーストリートから右に左に耳から脳へ方々をRockOn
俺らはアジアのメッセンジャー　ラスト侍、起こすビックサプライズ

Translation:

(Sat- Skill)

The internal organs are "invaded" by the Hip-Hop, and breathing depends on each word of prayer in that song. Do you like the talk of the hood? Across the street that cuts the nation, looking right then left to the people who are listening, pay close attention, these are the last Samurai messengers of Asia, surprise!

In the strophe in question, performed by Sat-Skill, there is the dependence of respiration (biological function) in relation to the performance of singing. Rap is inserted in this sense, as a communication tool that spreads it through the country. The verse throws a question: "Do you like the talk of the hood?", prompting the audience to pay attention to the words of rappers, brave messengers, last "samurai" warriors in Asia.

Rap retains the insightful mission of guiding. To listeners, it is proposed to clarify every day issues, introducing practical changes of beneficial nature in their lives. The song suggests the existence of a world with a prevailing Manichean logic. Being a part of rap's teaching is to be vulnerable to bad influences; while following it means to walk the path of good.

The eighth transcribed and translated strophe is performed by the rapper Pay-Ment:

(Pay-Ment)

頭の中酸欠寸前　溜め込んだ
煙　吐き出すぜ
腐った奴のどす黒い空気　ば
っかじゃ正気も鋭利ます凶器
ストリートかませアクション
　悪路駆け抜けー蓮托生
雑草みてぇな前評判　覆すダ
ークホースが最強

Translation:

(Pay-Ment)

I will put out all the smoke that was messing up my mind
If you keep storing all that, that bad people transmit your sanity and good sense will not be enough to take you to a good path. You are going to look like a weed, which does not serve as a good example to anyone

The above once again, confirms the position taken by rap through the "performer's look". The enunciator, under the narrative focus established in the first person, expresses the representation given to the act of singing. "I'll put out all the smoke that was messing up my mind," says the enunciator, revealing to see the performance as a "safety valve" in the face of the issues that oppress them. It is through music that one transcends reality. The verses that follow alert the listener about the failed forms filed against the conduct of life. "If you keep storing all that, which bad people transmit, your sanity and good sense will not be enough to put you in a good path" (...) The verse suggests, therefore, that each person willing to listen and follow the guidelines established by rap take the option to walk the path of "good", serving as an example to those that, per chance, are still unaware of such guidelines.

The ninth transcribed/translated strophe brings verses that propose the assertion and identity reinforcement, from the union between similar.

Junto e misturado, mesclado e dechavado.
Bolado na letra no papel com os aliados
Se porque aqui não tem paga pau
Imi wakaru ka doidão? Não, wakaranai!

Translation:

Together and blended, mixed and jumbled...
Rolled in the letter on the paper with the allies
Total Firmness, Chill and for real.
It is because there are no suckers here
Do you understand, stoned? I do not understand.

Burajiru furusato, sutoritto soda-chi.	I'm from Brazil, raised on the street.
Sonkei to kenkyou, hito no ashi wo fumanai	I am humble, I don't step on any-one.
Waru sou dakara tte kobinai	I only seem to be evil

Reading the verses proposes that for the composer rapper, being together is to be in improving condition. The voice suggests that writing is an act of courage, reflection or proper "association" to the others. He says: "Blended, mixed and jumbled/Rolled in the letter on paper with the allies." Note that the poetic musical composition is something that is described as part of a "collectivized" voice, a self-standing lyric rolled, or concerned with problems that are not exclusive to them, but also part of the social body it integrates.

The performative voice takes on the stereotypical closed face "I only seem to be evil," which is justified by the difficult history and socioeconomic status he inhabits. "I'm from Brazil, created on the streets./I am humble, I don't step on anyone "- he justified, while claiming his own identity. The enunciator, by transiting between languages and cultural habits, affirms to be Brazilian, humble and owner of an established training "on the street", where they do not apply the demagogic processes, so there were no suckers.

The 10th, 11th and 12th strophes emerge in scattered verses, delivered respectively by Pay-Ment, Sat-Skill and MC Beto. These verses tell us, in order:

	Translation:
（ブリッジ） キック、バスとスネアのタイミングで間髪いれずかますライミング	(Pay-Ment) Take a chance on the speed of a trap and of a bus, but be careful not to lose your head.
MC Beto: Certo camarada ta no rap na jornada a cara é se unir sem maldade e pal-haçada	MC Beto: Okay buddy it is in the rap, on the journey, the thing is to unite without malice and buffoonery

(Sat-Skill)
腹から吠えろ　オリジナルイェロー　中指立てな　エンターティナー
（３人）
国境を越えた３人のファイター　止まらねぇ　飛ばせ弾丸ライナー

(Sat-Skill)
It's a howl that comes out of the belly, original of an artist.

This is the cry of three people who crossed the nation, we will not stop!

The verses that lead to the end of the song propose counseling "signed" by an aesthetic produced by foreigners and for foreigners. The enunciator merges with the voice of those who composed it. To the listener tips are offered that pervade boldness, caution and honesty. Rap is defined as a "howling", a "journey", something that will help their listeners "not to lose their head". The song, therefore, is stated as a scream, invasive in crossing the nation, incessantly, for the purpose of guiding and perhaps reversing the conditions that dictate the rules of social functioning.

The Unite performance is topped with the words of the chorus, presented in the 13th transcribed/translated strophe.

Translation:

（フック）

(Chorus)

マイク、ケーブル、２ターンテーブル Hey Yo!! ３MC 此処にあらわる
マイクロフォンチェック１２１２ 調子どうだ！手を上げろ

Microphone, cables, two DJ tables, it's all right Hey Yo! Three MC testing the microphones 1 and 2 and 1 and 2.How is the tone, raise your hands!

É 'nois' na fita, aqui presente chega!
Se for 'pra' somar 'cola', mas se vacilar 'poca'.

These are us, here we come!
If you're gonna add up, come. But if you're not, piss off.

The self-affirmative refrain (and present throughout the song) reinforces its purpose of gregarious aesthetics, whose strength is established from the union between those who share identities and experiences, sometimes considered "minorities" in front of their own social bodies.

マイクロフォン戦士 *Microfone Soldier*

"Microphone Soldier" is also a song that deals with the importance of "speaking" through aesthetic rap. In this performance - started with a hybrid sound basis on which typical musical elements of forró and samba, rhythms known in Brazil are applied - MCS Beto and Pay-Ment act alongside Japanese MCS guests - Akig, Tahkick, Masahiro, Kazuki, IB and Runboo. The performance is also part of a multi-lingual production, as in the song the presence of Japanese, Portuguese and English are noted.

The group, born in the *Kanagawa* province - located south of Tokyo - already in the first strophe, makes statements that refer to the origin and purpose established by the formation of MCS.

The first transcribed/translated strophe has the following message:

（Pay-Ment）
湘南アンダーグラウンドぶっといパイプ　ヴァイブス連結
ぐっと良いパイプ吸う
燃やせたいまつ　あげろ戦火
ドープなこいつで火種点火
とうに限界超え　尚、吐き出す声　１３４号方面　Check It Out!
俺等無敵なマイクロフォンソルジャー　明日なき道を掴み取る猛者

Translation:
（Pay-Ment）
To the south in the underground there is a thick tube, with a good vibe, feel that vibe. Set fire to the things you hate, let's make a war, we will burn this shit down. Let's go over the limit, we will release our voice, feeling the road 134! Check it out! Me and my invincible microphone, we will tread our way!

The lyrics support the fact that in the southern ghettos - where immigrants live and sections of the population are excluded, art is made with the intention to transcend boundaries. The song involves in orality and music, a fact voiced in the first verse. Faced with a "good vibe", the voice, in an appealing tone, persuades an invitation to party: "(...) feel that vibe," he says.

Paradoxically, the microphone is good energy to those who appreciate and practice the art of rap, it is like taking a gun meant for functionality. The microphone is something that announces the beginning of a war, positioning those in marginal conditions and who have a coping attitude towards the system, after suffering the consequences of impropriety (administrative, legislative and executive), present both in the country of origin, and in the country of destination. The second verse stands out in this sense when the expository voice imperatively states: "Set fire to the things you hate, let's make a war, we will burn this shit down," urging the ocult interlocutor (and also the listener) to rebel in establishing an "aesthetic war".

In the third verse the reference to the sung word stands as a form of freedom. Assuming the first person plural, in a collectivized speech, the enunciator says:

"We will exceed the limit, we will release our voice, feeling the road 134" in verses that address in some way, leaving the "ghetto", in favor of a "range" of freedom. It is noteworthy in this regard to also mention National Route 134, the road that connects the city of Yokosuda to the municipality of Oiso, both located in the province of Kanagawa – a place inhabited by the immigrant rappers on the performance in question.

The song is described as an instrument of freedom. While denouncing dislikes and disaffects, it also creates an "aesthetic war" and gives power to the rapper – an unshakable hero - by using the words and holding the microphone - the ability to go further and build his own "path".

In the second transcribed/translated strophe comes the voice of Akig. At this point of the song, the discursive approach continues dealing with the art of the rap. According to the enunciator, it is a simple art, but endowed with feelings and transforming power.

（Akig）
モクモク上げな狼煙　ウォー
イウォーイ上げときな拳
腕の落書きはマスターピース
　よりアチー魂の日本人　ガ
キの頃からのダチ
マジ半端ねぇステージ　体感
で満タンだエナジー
スペシャルワンピースAkig
鷲づかんじゃうMIC

Translation:
(Akig)

The rocket that rises fast, the hand that trembles in time to make it go up. The scrawl made by hand, that may have more feeling than a masterpiece that artists do out there. A friendship from childhood times, a special piece, Akig hold that microphone!

As it is built, the song reinforces the bonds of friendship. Ties that can be understood as something established both among those who composed it and among those who perform or appreciate it, at the proportion in which it is performed. Although they have never met before, fans of the song have each other, and towards the performers, a shared identity, able to provide, therefore, the establishment of a fraternal, friendly vision. Thus, the rap is consolidated as an identitary strengthening and unifying gregarious element.

Due to the high emotional charge that it holds, the rapper song gains the ability to be dissipated. The enunciator attests the MC's awareness regarding this fact and the nervousness of performing it. The song, as it is performed, flies away, like a "rocket", spreading counter-hegemonic words and thoughts. Performer's consciousness about art practice is emphasized in the strophe. Through the appreciation of the passage, it appears that rap is something simple, minimalist. However, compared to the so called "high art", it may be surprising, taking into account its persuasive potential. In this sense, the enunciator says: "The scrawl of a hand may have more feeling than a masterpiece that artists make" - equating "to rapping" the existence of a scrawl, simple but holder of a important aesthetic power, sentimental and transforming. The transmission of the song between the performers is done simultaneously to cement friendship. Giving voice "to his friend" is also granting the right to sing. The song is thus the right to talk...

"A friendship from childhood times, a special piece, Akig hold this microphone," is uttered by all other performers at the end of Akig singing, in a voice that is no longer just one and gains again the collectivized tone.

In the third transcribed, translated strophe, the chorus comes up:

（フック）

Translation:
(Chorus)

Japanese	Translation
マイクで前へ　マイクのウォーリア　マイクで前へ　マイクでWo!Wo!	Take this microphone and come "to" the front, microphone soldier, take that microphone and come "to" the front, yell with the microphone Wo Wo.
前行くぜ　前行くぜ　前行くぜ　前行く！　Wo!Wo! x2	I will go to the front, I will go "to" the front, I will go to the front, I will go to the front Wo, Wo! x2
マイクで前へ　マイクのウォーリア　マイクで前へ　マイクでWo!Wo!	Take this microphone and come "to" front, microphone soldier, take this microphone and come "to" front, yell with the microphone Wo!Wo!
前行くぜ　前行くぜ　前行くぜ　前行く！　前行く　前行く　マイクロフォンソルジャー	I will go to the front, I will go to the front, I will go to the front, I will go to the front Wo! Wo! Microphone soldier.

In imperative tones, the enunciator determines the ocult interlocutor to "take the microphone", establishing what can be inferred as being in fact "the aesthetic war" proposed by the song. Personified, the microphone becomes a "soldier". To it the ability to "carry forward" is given for those who use it and those who believe in it. Note the repetition of the words "I will go to the front, I will go to the front, I will go to the front, I will go to the front Wo, Wo!", reinforcing the idea of a transforming art, the power of art.

The microphone is given the task of rescuing the ghetto's word and identities; and the duty to propose a symbolic war and modify the social context.

Concern for the freestyle, a practice of free establishment of rhymes, is also noted in the lyrics under study. In the fourth strophe, the enunciator recounts the importance of music as a form of expression.

(Tohkick)
マイクロフォンウォーリア
俺語を網羅　曖昧の裏側のフ
ォントを描写
握るクリスタルカイザー　炭
酸なら断然コーラだ　マイク
コントローラー
信念断片数珠繋ぎ　本日も潮
騒に胸騒ぎ　変わり映えなき
素晴らしき１日
国境ジャンル無視　言葉遊び

Translation:
(Tohkick)
The microphone soldier describes what I mean, shows the side of me I keep hidden. The cup that I hold is made of glass, if it is a soda, it is certainly Coca-Cola. Each has believed in one thing, and today as always, the waves bother me. This is a words game.

The microphone reverts the meaning of all grievances carried by the foreign. Through it, he escapes oppression and silencing. "The microphone soldier describes what I mean, it shows that side of me that I keep hidden", notes the *performer* through the song.

The strophic sequence continues, making clear the fact that it is only a "words game", it is possible to infer some meaning. The word carried by the rapper in a broader perspective, can be considered as "glass", a "cutting" instrument intended to tear patterns and socially established "pre-conceptions". It can also be seen as a "container", the word carries with it the memory and history of the ghettos, spaces often "invisible" to the richest eyes within the capitalist system. Its essence is valuable and perhaps, therefore, by drawing a comparison to soda, the rapper references a well-known brand (Coca-Cola), perhaps the most enjoyed and present in the segment.

Simulating the occurrence of a battle of rhymes, the music is continued. In the fifth transcribed/translated strophe, there is the performance of MCs Beto and Masashiro.

	Translation:
(Beto & Masahiro)	(Beto & Masahiro)
Então me passa o microfone	So pass me the microphone
Te provo que não sou clone	I will prove that I am not a clone
Vai função pique misoshiro e feijão	Go bro, chop, fermented soy broth and beans
Arigatou "pros" senshi que "tão" presente aqui	Thanks to the warriors that are here
Forma a banca dos guerreiros latinos e nihonjin	Form the stage for the Latin and Japanese warriors
Pode chegar, "só" não desarrumar que "tá" firmeza	Come here, "just" do not mess up that it is all good
Respeito é a chave,cadeado é "nois" na cena	Respect is the key, the lock is us in the scene.
Hip-Hop universal se manifesta em você	Universal Hip-Hop is manifested in you
A rua te olha e os pivetes se espelham em quem?	The street looks at you and the boys look up to who?
Somos querreiros do mic wowo kotoba de strick	We are soldies of the mic wowo Street on words
Quebrando as barreiras do som com a força do flow	Breaking the sound barriers With the force of the flow

To take the microphone is to show personality. The enunciator therefore suggests the presence of a cocky rapper/songwriter, with his own opinion and refuses to be only a copy ("clone").

Individual words in Japanese and Portuguese suggest also in verse, the encounter between cultures, the occurrence of which is given exactly in the Hip-Hop movement. Note, for example, the reference to two popular dishes the nations addressed in performance: the missohiro (fermented soy broth), derived from Japan; and beans, a food of Brazilian cuisine.

Through song, one of music's forms, a "universal language", Latin and Japanese are integrated, "warriors of sound", agreed by the respect and stimulated by the word. Building examples for the younger of same origin, they intend to break borders with the courage of those who have the "possession of the microphone", gun ammunition of words.

In the fifth transcribed/translated strophe, the personification of the object continues which allows the realization of the song: the microphone "sees" and "talks" about the world; he is "strong", a "Warrior" and "essential" to those who need some way to tell the foreigner reality of the ghettos. The verses performed by MC Kazuki contains the following message:

(Kazuki)
マイクロフォンソルジャー
常にチャレンジャー　リズム
刻むライムメッセンジャー
ワイドビジョン　カラーと線
　変幻自在に描くから
まさに突き抜ける様な青い空
　ためた力　吐き出すから
刺激が欲しけりゃもっと来
な！　放つパワー　常に俺流

Translation:

(Kazuki)
Microphone soldier, he tries, he is our messenger that makes rhythm Sees the world through different eyes, different color, conveys all that we want to say, all the accumulated anger on the chest.
He is strong, microphone soldier!

Singing becomes a way of subverting the oppressive system. Any other alternative would be socially censored, "cut" without mercy. Ratifying this reasoning, the performer songs IB, sings the sixth transcribed/translated strophe:

(IB)
ちいっと失礼　御用改め
手向かえば容赦なく斬り
つける　無用にはびこる
過激な不逞見つけ　抜刀
　すかさず応戦　いざOk
俺等に任しておけ
到底俺を斬れるわけもね
え　家に帰るか刀を置け
　赤バッチ相手なんじゃ
しゃーねぇーなー

Translation:

(IB)
That's a bit offensive, review your intentions, if I turn my back they would certainly cut me off without loyalty. The trick is to find the weak spot To attack. At the time everything goes right, you can leave it to me There is no reason to cut me off, so put thisblade away and come back "to" home.
I have no time for idiots.

The song allows the expression of feelings, sometimes even offensive. The impetus encouraged by the song allows the rapper to refer to his opponents as "idiots". It allows the performer to not care about the criticisms and oppressing mentions, allowing him to continue. When looking at the self-enunciation, the music becomes freedom and possibility. In the face of the oppressors, power agents, the enunciator offers an alternative to survival, he says: "The trick is to find the weak point to attack."

This alternative, of course, is the rapper art through which you can freely speak without censorship. Given this conviction, the enunciation continues: "At the time everything goes right, you can leave it to me/There is no reason to cut me off, so put that blade away and come back "to" home/I do not have time for idiots", prompting the possible repressor of the fact of being expressly disregarded.

Approaching the end of the song, it is possible to note that the song itself is instituted as an alternative before its performers and listeners.

After traveling a long musical journey, the enunciator reaches its destination. In the seventh transcribed/translated strophe are the following verses:

Translation:

(Runboo)
無我夢中で走り続けた三千里　完全にOn　決めるRockOn　吠えるHeadsどう？
絡める景色はWhat's Colorだ　From湘南C.I.C Show Me上げるぜVIP
ふところBIG　その場でE感じ　分かり合えるぜHomies

(Runboo)
With ecstasy, I ran 5000 kilometers, sure I'm on, I choose the Rockon, what about those heads, barking? What color was this landscape? Southern. Show me. Let's raise our voice in this place, with feeling. I can understand, bros.

The song's path brings a landscape from the south, that is, *Kanagawa*. "What color was this landscape? Southern", says the enunciator. The voice of enunciation that questions also offers answers. It is aware of the new style - in slang called *Rockon* (rock-on) - which lends itself to be a "cry" to rely on feelings converted to aesthetics, to denounce social and territorial problems. By performing their rap, the performer also establishes an invitation from the own lyrics: "Let's raise our voices in this place, with feeling / I understand, bros." The call to verbalization said through aesthetic and sensations, therefore walks beside the finding of the understanding. Note that from the statement in the first person "I can understand" the voice of enunciation dialogues with the caller-listener, a form of focused stimulation to the ability of understanding, suggesting thus the educational and engaging potential of the song, which chronicles life, but also raises awareness and encourages reflection on the part of its listeners.

The song uses the chorus at the end of the performance. In the eighth transcribed/translated strophe, it has:

（フック）	**Translation:** (Chorus)
マイクで前へ　マイクのウォーリア　マイクで前へ　マイクで WO!WO!	Take this microphone and come "to" the front, microphone soldier, take that microphone and come "to" the front, with the microphone shout Wo Wo. x2
前行くぜ　前行くぜ　前行くぜ　前行く！×2	I will go "to" the front, I will go "to" the front, I will go "to" the front, I will go "to" the front Wo, Wo!
マイクで前へ　マイクのウォーリア　マイクで前へ　マイクで WO!WO!	Take this microphone and come to the front, microphone soldier, take this microphone and come "to" the front, with the microphone shout Wo!Wo!

前行くぜ 前行くぜ 前行く ぜ 前行く！ 前行く 前行 く マイクロフォンソルジャ —	I will go "to" the front, I will go "to" the front, I will go "to" the front, I will go "to" the front. Wo! Wo! Microphone soldier.

Microphone soldier is thus a song of invitation. It is proposed to awaken young listeners to the world, attentive to the questions of his time and, more than that, able to have the word, sung as a guiding factor in his days and encouragement necessary for survival in exile.

Π άνω από το νέφος: looking beyond, to move on

"Π άνω από το νέφος" ("Above the Clouds", in English) is another song with evidences of libertarian nature. In it, the performer appears as someone who sees the world clearly, being aware of all its devices, misdeeds and segregations. Similarly to someone who is part of this scenario - and that, for that reason, is able to look "outside" - the rapper/performer criticizes the system and society, claiming to use the sung word to stay "ahead".

In the song, the voice input is made almost at the same as time the entrance of the almost implied musical base. In a strong and passionate tone, the Yinka performer starts the message with the following verses, transcribed and translated, in the first strophe:

	Translation:
Πίο ψήλα ναι X 4	Always on top, yes! X4
Στην κορύφωση παντά στην συνθέση	Always in the heights, that order
Στους αδεσποτούς καιρούς εκθέτω την επιτήδευση	In unordered times I demonstrate malingering
Δικηγόροι του διαβόλου κάνουν αγόρευση και	devil's advocates make speeches
στολίζουν με τα λόγια τους	And embelishing, with their words,

την γενική την ύφεση
είναι η ψυχή στο στόμα .αυτή
κίνει το σώμα
και αυτό με τη σείρα του
ξορκίζει τις σκέψεις τα δαιμόνια
νεκρός ή ζωντανός να'σαι
θα ορμίσουνε τα όρνια με
φάτσες αγγελίκες
για να σου μασήσουνε τα χρόνια
ψάξε να βρεις το θέμα
ακού το Σάουντρακ της εποχής
η ενορχήστρωση του δείχνει
μία παράφωνη εικόνα
αποθημένα σκόρπια από
σκορπιους ανθρωπους
που οι ευαισθησίες
περιορίζονται στον μικρόκοσμο
τους
λάτρες του θεαθήναι και του
μικρού ΕΓΩ τους.
Θρέφουν κάθε μέρα τον
αδηφάγο υλισμό τους
Του ζώνουνε τα φίδια και ζουν
στα αποκαϊδια
Παρ όλα αυτά όμως σώζουν τον
καθωσπρεπισμό τους

the general decrease
With the soul in mouth- it
moves the body,
and he in turn frees thoughts
and demons,
wether alive or dead
Monsters with angelic
faces will attack
To chew their years
Try to find the theme
Listen to the soundtrack of
that time
The sounds of the orchestra
show a distorted image
A bunch of scorpions
A bunche of people-scorpions
And the sensitivity is reduced
to their small worlds
Narcissists with their little ego
Daily feed their greed
The snakes sorround them all
the time
They live in the ashes
But despite that, they save
their "dignities"

The performance begins with lines that resemble a war cry or title: "Always to the top, yes!/Always on the heights, this order", says the self-lyrical, depicting the presence of an enunciator inviting voice that suggests to the listener the construction of a new order, with other guidelines and other times. The repetition of four times in the two verses, reveals the insistence of the affirmative idea.

After about forty seconds of the start of the performance the verses begin which describe the daily life, as seen by the foreigner's eyes.

The enunciator, structured in the third person, establishes the existence of a demagogic "order", that testifies to his posture. The words "in unordered times I demonstrate malingering" can refer to an interpretation of duality in nature. In a literal sense, one could say that these verses relate to social life in a chaotic space. To live with hierarchies of demagogic operation, the rapper/lyrical voice also assume a position of social staging. If, however, considering the possibility of a metaphorical statement, it would be possible to infer that the music itself, in a symbolic context, is free of oppressive law; a kind of created space "for" and "to" otherness, capable of allowing the voice that performs the daily simulacra of production, worked from the irony ("sham") as a stylistic feature.

A possibly purposeful ambiguity leads to the interpretation of a verse, both metalinguistic and libertarian ("With the soul in the mouth/it releases thoughts and the living-dead demons").

The word spoken by the rapper in the performance is the same exalted by the enunciator. The word is matched by the issuer, to the condition of soul. The word crops up feelings and forgotten desires, coming possibly from an intense process of anguish and oppression.

The word is the liberating element of body and spirit. From it, the rapper-performer finds himself far from preconceptions and reproaches and can finally say what he thinks.

In the eyes of the enunciator, the exercise of power is described as something that occurs in disguised form through "angelic covers" that hide bad essences. The enunciation is put in alert condition, also alerting the receiver to signal the existence of true "monsters-human" angelic faced owners, whose intention is only to explore the subaltern masses. "They will attack/to chew their years", he says.

Based on injunction purposes, the text lends itself to guide the listener. The "orchestra" mentioned in the verses comes as an allusion to a dominant and illusory discourse, to which listeners should not submit to. "The sounds of the orchestra show a distorted image/A lot of scorpions/A lot of people-scorpions" warns the enunciator. In this sense, it is also proposed to the interlocutor to listen to the sounds of his time, find his path and not to be dictated by a hegemonic discourse. "Try to find the theme/Listen to the soundtrack of that time," he says, offering hearing and vision, while connecting senses that will serve to understand the days in society.

Like a *flaneur* who walks through the city recording his impressions, the rapper performs in lucidity condition, coming from a look able to identify the prevailing evil in the social context. The reality comes described in a manichean way. The rapper talks to his people - similar in color, pattern, or purpose - giving the existential setting a divided space between the coexistence of two groups: one to which the word integrates and directs; and "other", which is excluded and which assigns executioner characteristics. The ironic reference of the rapper to the second niche is noted in this sense, which although essentially surrounded by bad energy, ("The snakes around them all the time / They live in the ashes") is presented to other people's eyes as something good, since it is operated by "narcissists" forces, driven by "greed", they can "save their dignity".

The description of the societal context has continued in a chorus which is shown as an example to the listeners of foreign layers, stimulated to "see beyond". In this sense, the verses of the second transcribed/translated strophe say:

	Translation:
Ρεφραίν - x2	Chorus-2x:
Ρίμες πάνω από το νέφος πετώ	I throw rhymes over the dark clouds
Για να κρατήσω το όραμα καθαρό	To make the landscape clearer
Διαχρονικές αξίες αναζητώ	Seeking eternal values
Μια ματιά γύρω σου να ρίξεις ζητώ	I ask you to look around

The cloud, metaphor of the illusion generated by a capitalist / global stage, is something that overshadows the community's sight and therefore must be dissipated. As an example to be followed, an existential model, the rapper takes the first person narrative and declares how his own way of acting was built. By looking beyond ("above the clouds"), the rapper produces the aesthetics of "rhymes" and such aesthetics, more than the "closed" top values, configured as path in the search for truth. At the end of the chorus the displacement of the narrator stands out. Turning to the third person, the enunciator determines in guidance to the listener: "Look around you."

The song that lends itself to guide maintains its purpose in the third transcribed/translated strophe, when the verses state:

	Translation:
το νέφος είναι των μεταναστών η γκετοποίηση	The clouds are the ghettos of immigrants
όλων των μνηστήρων εξουσίας η μπατσοποίηση	The cloud is the corrupt policing of the suitors of power
ανθρώπινων δικαιωμάτων η ιδιωτικοποίηση	It is the privatization of human rights
και σε πονήρους ανήθικους δρόμους η μύηση	And initiation into immoral ways
η μυθικοποίηση του λάΙφ στάΙλ	The soul who has learned to
και προσώπων που μέσα τους ο ναρκισίσμος κυλάει	want the superfluous And now dances the dance of
η ψυχή μας που έμαθε να λαχταράει το περιττό	trades
και τώρα χορεύει του εμπόριου το χόρο	Impacts, ephemeral messages distorted signals, vagabonds who hunt their prey
κολλήματα, εφήμερα μηνύματα ,παραμορφωμένα	Experiments with humans The owners of power do
σήματα. Λαμόγια που κυνηγάνε θυμάτα	Wanting to take on a second personality
πειράματα ανθρώπους σε άνθρωπο ,και φύση και τωρα	Paranormal
η παραφύση έγινε δεύτερη φύση	Fags, whores in action And solidarity will cry
Καβατζόπουστες εν δράσει και αλληλεγύη θα κλάψει	You are fighting someone else's battles
Αλλονών τους πολέμους πολέμας,το συμφέρον θα λάμψει	The interest will shine
Παραθύρια,στου νόμου τα τσαντήρια, κάνουν χατήρια	Windows in the tents of law They do favors to companies
Σε εταιρείες ενώ αύτες τσαλακώνουν της γης τη μοίρα..	While they knead the fate of the planet

In this strophe, the message makes it clear that the fact of allowing it to "be in illusion" is a kind of imprisonment. Using metaphors, the lyrical voice defines the nature of the cloud, it provides: "The clouds are the ghettos of immigrants/The cloud is the corrupt policing of the suitors of power/is the privatization of human rights/And the initiation immoral ways/the soul that has learned to want the superfluous/And now dance the dance of the trades. "Before the verses, it is possible to infer, therefore, that being surrounded by the "cloud" would be the same as being present in society under a state of alienation; not realizing the arbitrariness of power and allowing it to keep operating without any questions.

In this sense, the criticism of globalization and capitalism stands out. Dance the "dance of trade", means letting yourself be carried away by shallow and futile routines, it is synonymous of a position taken in a vulnerable condition before the experiments filed by the owners of "power".

When reporting the capitalist scenario where the enunciator lives, there is a warning to the listener: "You are fighting someone else's battles"; and argues in the verse, issues related to the exploration of otherness and corporatist domain.

The awakening to the situation that the experience is given in a global society in which the games of interest and manipulation of the "planet" by some companies predominate, it is possible only in the function of a "another look" assumed by performer/voice station. Through the word, the rapper subverts and avoids the effects of capitalism on himself. His argument is required and made possible only by the fact that there is a proposition: to see "beyond".

In the fourth transcribed/translated strophe, you have the following message:

Translation:

Πίο ψήλα ναι Χ 4	Always on top, yes! 4x
Πάνω από το νέφος είδα τύπους	Above the clouds I saw power-
με σθένος	ful people
Που ζουν ένα βίος σαν έπος	Living a grand life
λεοντόκαρδοι	Who keep the order as the
Που φύλουν το δίκαιο σαν κόρη	apple of their eye
οφθαλμού σαν βρέφος	Who keep the order as a
Νιώθουν ότι έχουν το χρέος σε	newly born
αυτούς που ζούνε στο σκότος	They feel they have the duty
Να ρίξουν άπλετο το φως και	and the right over those who
αυτοί να γίνουν χείμαρρος	live in darkness
Βλέπω αύτους που αλλάξαν και	To whom they can throw a lot
αποβάλλαν το αδικαιολόγητο	of light
μένος	That can turn into stream
Και είδα ότι με εμπρηστίκες ιδεές	I see those who have changed
δεν πρέπει να είσαι ταυτισμένος	And they threw away the
Νιώθω περήφανος γιατι εκε;i	anger, for no reason
πάνω γνώρισα το γένος αυτών	I also saw that you can not
που τα μάτια	identify with incendiary ideas
Χάμογελαν γιατι μπρόστα	But I feel proud because from
κοίταν,	above the clouds
Ξανάγεννημένος στο λύρικο	I met the generation of those
παιχνίδι εκστασιασμένος	whose eyes smile by looking
Λέξεις φώτος να αναζήτω όταν	ahead
νιώθω ενταφιασμένος	Born again, enraptured in
Είναι ρουκέτες οι ρίμες και σε	a lyrical game, looking for
αύτες πάνω είμαι δεμένος	words of light
Και μάζι με αύτες σκίζω τα μαύρα	While I feel suffocated
σύννεφα πάντα φορτισμένος	

Insistent, the performer repeats "always on top, yes", and emphasizes the need to establish a different look on the daily facts. "Above the cloud" the enunciator sees the manipulative actions of rulers and politicians, kidnappers of order and economic power. In the first verses of the strophe in question, in the first person, the rapper provides: "Above the clouds I saw powerful people/Living a grand life/That keep the order as the apple of their eye (...)/ They feel they have the duty and the right over those who live in darkness (...). Following that, the behavioral change of people is portrayed who by chance have abandoned the indignation, motor of rappers songs: "I see those who have changed/And threw away the anger, for no reason," says the voice of enunciation.

This, even in an ironic way, shows a complacent tone about those who oppose the message of the music. "I also saw that you cannot identify with incendiary ideas," he says. Not being allowed to identify with the incendiary ideas means "fear" in a broader sense. Fear for possible repression... Whether in the material, physical, psychological, economic or family context in the case of the possibility of violence come to be established towards any loved one. The phrase that describes the "not being able" suggests, in this sense, the existence of cowardice found from the "abandonment of anger" or of the rapper practice.

The verse continues, and between the twelfth and fifteenth verse, "being above the clouds" takes on another meaning: that of inspiring. The enunciator says: "(...) from above the clouds/I met the generation whose eyes smile to look forward/Reborn, enraptured in a lyrical game, looking for words of light/While I feel suffocated." Note, therefore, that "above the clouds" occurs during the meeting of the enunciator with past generations; these, that from the sky, see the evolution of time, obtained with the contribution of their struggle. Generations that include the words of the current rapper, in awe, and that drive the "heroes" of today to continue their way, however difficult they may seem.

The fantasy performed turns into thinking, demonstrating the action of the performer as something that stems from one's belief, whether in relation to their ancestors, or even in terms of their own actions, present or future.

The speech contained in the song comes to an end with the provisions in the fifth strophe. In this, there is a second chorus, that thus provides:

Ρεφραίν- 2x:	**Translation:** Chorus- 2x:
Ρίμες *πάνω από το νέφος πετώ* *Για να κρατήσω το όραμα* *καθαρό* *Διαχρονικές αξίες αναζητώ* *Μια ματιά γύρω σου να ρίξεις* *ζητώ*	Rhymes games over the dark clouds To make clearer the landscape Seeking eternal values I ask you to look around

The performance ends, therefore, with a statement made by the performer: the rhyme, or rap is the vital motivation of the one who performs. For the song and from the song, he survives. The song, therefore, is an instrument of daily struggle. With it is possible to fight for better days, overcoming obstacles "ripping dark clouds". The song motivates the rapper and keeps him "energized" to move forward. To the listener, the performance leaves only the request to "look around" to finally learn to see the reality.

Επαναστατικο ταξίδι: a rebellious and learning journey through music

"*Επαναστατικο ταξίδι*" (or "Rebelious Journey") is an intertextual song that performs the idea of learning from the word. The beginning of the performance in question has the narrative focus in the first person plural. In the first transcribed/translated strophe, the performer - as a spokesman for black layers in the global diaspora, represents a desire of this group in question. Note thus, the following message:

	Translation:
Θέλαμε να κρατήσουμε τον	We want to keep alive the rythim
ρυθμό ζωντανό να νιώσουμε	of life
Πώς είναι να 'σαι ανθρωπος	Feeling what it is like to be people
και όχι παράσιτο	and not parasites
Θέλαμε να κρατήσουμε τον	We want to keep the rythim of life
ρυθμό ζωντανό να νιώσουμε	alive
Πώς είναι να 'σαι ανθρωπος	Feeling what is like to be people
και όχι παράσιτο	and not parasites

Note that, assuming the first person plural, the enunciator externalizes the purposes of a group. The repetition of the statement "We want to keep the rythim of life alive/Feeling what it is like to be people and not parasites" seems to refer exactly to the transforming purpose of rapper performance, active *praxis*, which chronicles the life at the same time of improving it.

As if narrating a story elapsed in an oneiric space, the performer reports the occurrence of some meetings that would have given him important lessons about making revolution.

Within the second strophe, the verses thus provide:

	Translation:
Για άλλη μια φορά βρέθηκα στην	Again I felt on the street
οδό των ονείρων	of dreams
Να παρελαύνω με πάθος και δίψα	Receiving with passion and thirst
για κάτι νέο	something new
Ο δρόμος με οδήγησε σε ένα τόπο	The path led me to a
που με ενέπνεε	place inspiring
Γιατί εξέπεμπε ένα μεγαλείο και	Through which went beyond a hap-
το σώμα μου ένιωθε	piness that my body felt
Τις δονήσεις το ανεξήγητο ρίγος	With the inexplicable force, shivers
γινόταν πίο ισχυρό	grew stronger
Αγωνιούσα για το τι θα βρω μέσα	Agonized and seethed inside me what
μου έβραζε	i would find
η απορία του τι εστί επανάσταση,	The answer to what is revolution,
λες να βρω στο τόπο αυτό	would I find it in this place?
απάντηση να μια μορφή με ματία	Along the way I met a gaze con-
επιβλητική,	vinced and proud

και στάθηκα αμέσως μπροστά της με προσοχή μου λεέι "Εγώ είμαι ο Τσε και εκπροσωπώ την γροθία στους δυνάστες και ακόλουθοι μου όλοι είναι επαναστάτες ταξιδευά πολύ και είδα την φτώχεια μπροστά μου ζωντανή πολλών είδων αρρώστιες σε χώρες που είχαν έλλειψη κάθε μέρα τρεφόμουν με την αλληλεγύη και την ισότητα και πάλευα για αυτήν την πραγματικότητα"	I stopped in front of him and he calmly told me: I am Che and I present my strength to dictators, all who follow me are revolutionary. I traveled a lot and saw poverty before me very poor countries with various diseases, missing every- thing Every day I fed from equality and fraternity I fought for this reality

Describing the moments leading up to the "meeting" with the Cuban leader Ernesto Guevara de la Serna - known as "Che Guevara", the enunciator shows great anxiety ("With the inexplicable force, shivers grew stronger") and claims that the place of meeting was an interior space ("agonizing and seething inside me that I would find / the answer to what is revolution, would I find it in this place?").

Immersed in their subjectivities, he mentions the meeting with "Che", who teaches him the provisions of the revolution. He highlights in this sense, the affirmative speech of an imaginary character ("I am 'Che' and present my strength to dictators, all those who follow me are revolutionary").

The performer theatricality takes on, with the speech of the "poetic-character" "Che", the function of narrating achievements of a Revolutionary hero. Under the voice of "Che" the story of someone who traffics in diverse spaces witnessing the reflections of social segregation has been told. In the face of poverty, disease and lack of moral and material conditions, necessary for survival, the character states: "Every day I fed from equality and brotherhood / I fought for this reality."

The continuation of the song is done with the return of the performer, in the third strophe, it is proposed to describe his reaction to this "meeting".

τον είδα να
δακρύζει γιατί όταν μίλαγε
ένιωθες το συναίσθημα
και την πίστη να ξεχειλίζει και
τότε του είπα ότι ακόμα
και σήμερα εμπνέει του
αγωνίστες για αυτούς που
θέλουνε
νέες εποχές, είπε ότι για να
αλλάξεις τα πράγματα
θέλει πειθαρχία
οργάνωση,θυσίες αφοσίωση
γνώση και παιδεία
ητάν σαν μεγάλος αδερφος
του είπα χαίρε τον αγκάλιασα
και συνέχισα
ακάθεκτος το ταξίδι να με πάλι
σαν ιχνηλάτης στην έρευνα
ξερόντας ότι στον τόπο αυτό
θα βιώσω συγκίνηση και χαρά

Translation:
I saw him
With crying eyes as he spoke pouring emotion and feeling
And loyalty the point of overflowing.
To him I said that, today, he inspires those who struggle and want new times
I learned that to change the situation it was necessary
Obedience, organization, sacrifice, dedication, education and knowledge.
It was as if he was my older brother, I said goodbye and continued.
Impetuous on the trip, and again a locator in research
Knowing that this was the place where I could find excitement and joy.

The description of a "great plan" that the enunciator's meeting provides with the revolutionary "Ché Gevara" is also, as noted, a kind of space of knowledge. There, the enunciator reports having become aware of a number of attributes necessary to change the situation. The song says in this regard: "I learned that to change the situation it was necessary:/Obedience, organization, sacrifice, dedication, education and knowledge."

After dismissing the character "Che Guevara", the lyrical "impetuous" voice follows his way of search and exploration, fiction, if seen in the light of the performed orality itself, but able to convert into reality, is prepared for consideration of the listener. The song path thus has its purposes to take, clearly, guidance through the aestheticized word.

In the fourth transcribed/translated strophe, the new meeting comes: this time with black leader Martin Luther King and the members of the Black Panther party.

λίγο μετά καθώς
περιπλανιόμουν άκουσα
κραυγές
και της μοίρας μου το
πλήρωμα περίμενα.

(Απόσπασμα ομιλίας Μάρτιν
Λούθερ κίνγκ)

*Into a beautiful symphony of broth-
erhood. With this faith we will be
able to work together, to pray together, to struggle toget her, to go to
jail together, to stand up for freedom
together, Knowing That We will be
free one day.*

Μπροστά μου στάθηκαν
μαυροφορεμένοι αδερφοί
και σηκωσάν την μαύρη του
γροθιά ψηλά με πυγμή
μαζί τους είχαν ένα ιερέα
ντυμένο στα άσπρα
φιλήσυχο ειρηνικό που έλαμπέ
σαν τα άστρα
ητάν οι μαυροί πάνθηρες και
ο μάρτιν λούθερ κίνγκ και το
μανιφέστο
μπροστά μου έτοιμο να
ανοιχτεί ένιωθα οτι ήμουν σε
ιεροτελεστία
τις πεποιθήσεις τους έπρεπε να
μου πουν πάση θυσία

Translation:

Later in this adventure,
walking aimlessly, I
heard shouts
My crew had the expected destination

*(Extracted from the speech of Mar-
tin Luther King)*

*Into a beautiful symphony of broth-
erhoodWith this celebration we can
work together, to pray together,
to struggle together, to go to jail
together, to stand up for freedom
together, Knowing That We will be
free one day.*

In front of me came bereaved
brothers
And they lifted up with strength
their black handles
With them was a white
priest
Serene and smooth- in peace,
shining like the stars
They were the Black Panthers,
Martin Luther King the manifesto
In front of him, ready to
be openI felt as if I was in a religious ceremony.
Its resolutions should tell me
anyway

Once again, there is a kind of suspense before the actual description of the meeting. The narrative of the "shouts" intensify
such tone, creating a greater expectation on the part of the listener.
At this time of performance, the enunciator seems to integrate the
audience that is about to witness one of several speeches by Luther
King, during the 1960's.

Thus, at the 01:40 mark of the performance, you can see through the intertextuality, that it is the I have a Dream speech delivered by the leader, in 1963, in Washington, USA. The event marked the struggle for civil rights in the country and had as main objective the eradication of racism. At such a time of musical performance, the voice of the enunciator gives way to the voice of Martin Luther King himself who, through the sampler, now also integrates the song. In his speech, King preaches the struggle and the union of the leading group in the name of freedom.

The scenario is the arrival of the enunciator amid an area already populated by a multitude of "blacks". After the speech of Luther King, the poetic voice returns to the scene. The self-lyrical, then it integrates the audience. He identifies himself to the place and the audience that "sees", referring to it as a whole consisting of "brothers". The description is of a scene in which the audience shows full agreement in relation to the words of their leader and the willingness to reverse the social framework of the country.

In this sense, the context is portrayed by the enunciator, describing the sign of approval: "raised their black hands". The performance, to allude to the existence of a more egalitarian society, also indicates the presence of a Catholic religious leader who, dressed in white, joins the protestant crowd, expressing support for the fight for human rights in peaceful coexistence.

In the crowd, the enunciator ritually sets waiting for guidelines aimed at him from Luther King. Such guidelines arise in the fifth strophe of the song, when taking the King's personality, the performer says:

	Translation:
Ὑπήρξαμ σκλάβοι για χρόνια μας	We were slaves for many years,
είπαν τελείωσε η δουλεία	they say slavery is over
και ακόμα όμως, είχαμε δεσμά	However we are still connected
ένα ολόκληρο έθνος στο	An entire country suffering,
περιθώριο να πονά	

και την κοινωνική αλλαγή να
ζητά, θέλαμε να κρατήσουμε τον
ρυθμό ζωντανό
να νιωσουμε πως είναι να σαι
ανθρωπος και όχι παράσιτο και
έτσι το κίνημα
των δικαιώματων δούλευε για το
πρόοδο της φυλής ξεπερνώντας
εμπόδια εκείνης της εποχής

asking for social change.
We want to keep the
rythim alive
Work for the progress of
the race
Overcoming all the
difficulties of the time

In his speech, King's character attests to what continues today, many of the obstacles against which he fought at the time in which he lived. The black leader presents a link between the past days and the present day and encourage his recipient, stating that it is still necessary to fight so that the collective objectives are achieved. "We want to keep the rythim alive/work for the progress ofthe race/ overcoming the difficulties of the time."

In the sixth strophe, we have once again the presence of the enunciator-traveler who, again, says goodbye to the personality that is speaking. Describing the scene of farewell, the enunciator summarizes everything he learned from Martin Luther King.

ο Κινγκ μου είπε για να αλλάξεις
το σκηνικό
πρέπει να έχεις όραμα, όνειρο,
στόχο. σκοπό τους είπα
ευχαριστώ γιατί με γέμισαν
και αυτοί πάλι με την γροθία ψηλά
με χαιρέτισαν.
Συνέχισα την πορεία μου
περήφανος γιατί ζούσα μεγάλες
στιγμές
Ναι ήτανε γεγονός, όλοι αυτοι μου
δώσαν τροφή για σκέψη
Μια εικόνα επαναστατική που το
μονοπάτι μου θα φέξει

Translation:
The King told me to
change
the scene
I must have vision, dream,
goal and direction
I thanked him and they
greeted me with raised fist
I continued my route,
proud, lived there great
moments
Yes, it was right, everyone
gave me food for thought
A revolutionary image that
will light my way

Ένιωθα ευφορία σαν να μουν
μεθυσμένος στο μονοπάτι της
χαράς
Εκστασιασμένος. ήμουν
συνεπαρμένος από ήχους
ψυχεδελικούς

I felt euphoric, drunk in
the way of joy
Enraptured, listening melodies, psychedelic sounds

The performance describes a learning process given in terms of the encounter between the character, "enunciator-traveler" and icons of the world's revolutionary history.

By promoting the encounter between the enunciator and several revolutionary characters consecrated by history, the external subject-poetic purposes with his speech: to establish, from the rapper aesthetic, representing a reactionary and subversive identity to the system, the assumptions that can radiate and become the consolidation of a collective consciousness identity to emerge among the marginalized layers.

The path preformed through the song is the same crossed by the listener at the time of musical enjoyment. As while listening to rap, the listener starts to receive guidance, noting that the fight is relevant and that they need the "dream", the "goal" and "direction".

The performance which chronicles a man enraptured by the guidelines he received and the touching melodies in his way is the same that gives the song the property of metalinguistic and motivational purposes.

The authenticity of the "journey" described in the song appears attested in the last strophe of the song, when he says:

Translation:

Αυτούς που βλέπεις παραμύθια
σαν τους ακους και τους είδα
Μπροστά μου ήταν απίστευτο
ο μαϊλς ντέϊβις και ο τζίμι
χέντριξ να
Τζαμάρουν, πιο κει ο σαλβατόρ
νταλί να εμπνέται και να
ζωγραφίζει αυτό

These you see, telling
stories I heard and saw.
In front of me in disbelief,
I saw Miles Davis and Jimi
Hendrix
Walking further along the
Salvador Dali painting with
inspiration

251

Που βγάζει η τελετή. αυτοί μου
μίλησαν μονό με τα όργανα
τους
μου είπαν οτι ακολουθήσαν
την ψυχή τους και όχι την
γενία τους
Γιατί οι εποχές είχαν τρόπους,
μόδες τάσεις.και στεγανά που
Πρέπει να τα σπας σαν να είναι
δεσμά, τζάμαρα μαζί τους
Έχωσα μια ρίμα που ήταν
ατελείωτη σαν το πνεύμα ολων
αυτών που
Γνώρισα.στο Επαναστατικο
ταξίδι

Where ended the irony -
They spoke with their instru-
ments
They spoke that they were ac-
companied by their souls and not
their decendência
Because times have modes, fash-
ions, trends and fetters
Things must be broken, as the
handcuffs
I made a rhyme to
infinity
Endless as the souls of those I met
During this rebel trip

Near the end of the performance, the enunciator quotes important characters of art history. Miles Davis, Jimi Hendrix, Salvador Dali... Members of revolutionary movements that, through aesthetics, were keen for the breakdown of social and artistic paradigms. People who have shown to be ahead of their times, who followed their "souls" and used art to comunicate. On behalf of these people, the enunciator justified his rhyme and declared to be in a "rebel trip".

Sacar La Voz (Release the voice): verses in fight preaching non-muting and redemption

"Sacar la voz" is a song of invitation. The performance of its verses leads the listener to abandon the areas of (dis)comfort and muting, urging them to be represented, denouncing injustices and above all to fight for better living conditions in society. The first strophe of the transcribed/translated song carries the following content:

Translation:

Respirar para sacar la voz	Breathe to release the voice
Despegar tan lejos como un	Take off as far as a
águila veloz	swift eagle
Respirar un futuro esplendor,	Breathing a splendorous future
cobra más sentido si lo creamos	makes more sense if we both
los dos.	create it
Liberarse de todo el pudor, tomar	Get rid of all the shame and take
de las riendas, no rendirse al	the reins, not surrendering to the
opresor.	oppressive
Caminar erguido, sin temor,	Walk erected without fear breathe
respirar y sacar la voz.	and release the voice
Uhh, uhh, uhhh (x2)	Uhh, uhh, uhhh (x2)

Note that the enunciator performs a kind of gregarious preparation. The rap establishes through the voice before the systemic-capitalist fact a symbolic clash situation, also describing this reality in simulacrum.

To perform the clash, he narrates a situation in which some attributes are shown as fundamental: it is necessary to divest in conscience of any tie and raise courageously in confronting the oppressor, "release the voice" to fight in aspirations for better days. The creation of a splendid future is a collective creation. In this sense, the enunciator makes use of expressions and verbs like "take the reins", "create", "take off"; that translate in claims, the desire for union, conditioned by the constructivist objective of new days in society.

After subsequent statements made by the application of the infinitive mode, the enunciator goes to propose a self-description, by which their own existential conditions are put in evidence, since the text is to be delivered in the first person. In the second strophe, the narrative focus turns to the performing character who carries out the following definitions:

Translation:

Tengo los bolsillos vacíos, los labios partidos, la piel con escamas, cada vez que miro hacia el vacío.	I have empty pockets, chapped lips, skin with scales, every time I look into the void
Las suelas gastadas, las manos atadas, la puerta de entrada siempre tuvo el cartel, que dijo que estaba cerrada.	The sole of my shoe worn, hands tied, the gateway always had a sign that said it was closed
Una espina clavada, una herida infectada, entramada, una rabia colmada, en el todo y en la nada.	A spine spiked, an inflamed wound, resistant anger at the height of everything and nothing
El paso torpe, al borde, sin acorde, cada vez que pierdo el norte, tengo la pérdida del soporte.	A unsteadily step on the edge without chord, every time I lose the north I have lost support
El tiempo que clava, me traba la daga, me mata, filuda la flama, sin calma, que de las manos se me escapa.	The time plunges, the knife locked in me, kills me, the flame without calm that escapes from my hands
Pero, tengo mi rincón florido, sacar la voz, no estoy sola, estoy conmigo.	But I have my flowery corner, release the voice, I am not alone, I am me
Liberarse de todo el pudor, tomar de las riendas, no rendirse al opresor. Caminar erguido, sin temor, respirar y sacar la voz.	Get rid of all the shame and take the reins, not surrender to the oppressive. Walk erected without fear, breathe and release the voice
Uhh, uhh, uhhh (x4).	Uhh, uhh, uhhh (x4)

Note in the strophe, the description of an experience filled with hardship, both moral, and material and psychological. In financial terms, the enunciator reports the lack of opportunities as a constant factor in his routine. A factor that prevents even the realization of plans and envisionment of achievements in future times. Citing chapped lips, perhaps by the cold, and the body with scales emphasizing where this last bone or keratin structure, designed to provide protection to the body of many animals. The enunciator sees himself as a socially stigmatized element and bound to a series of denials, then explained in the first verses of the strophe: "The soles of my shoes worn, hands tied, the gateway always had a sign that said it was closed."

In the absence of perspectives and existential uncertainty, imposed by his stigma condition, he is in permanent state of defense before the world and makes his "wounds" a boost for the reaction. Dominated by anger, flame without calm that escapes his hands, it is precisely singing that the enunciator recounts the discovery of a path and a motivation to continue: "But I have my flowery corner, release the voice, I am not alone, I'm with me."

The image given by the enunciator to the song, is of something necessary to days spent in pain. Thus, in the view of the enunciator, in the face of mistreatment and oppression, it is through the song that he can find a possible way to freedom.

In the third transcribed/translated strophe, the enunciator reveals how this process takes place, in full adherence to the song. The verses state:

	Translation:
Tengo el amor olvidado, cansado, agotado, botado. Al piso cayeron todos los fragmentos, que estaban quebrados.	I have forgotten love, tired, exhausted. Fell to the ground all the pieces that were broken
El mirar encorvado, el puño cerrado, no tengo nada, pero nada, suma en este charco.	The curved look, the clenched fist, I have nothing more, but nothing adds anything to this puddle
La mandíbula marcada, palabra preparada, cada letra afilada, está en la cresta de la oleada. Sin pena ni gloria, escribiré esta historia, el tema no es caerse, Levantarse es la victoria.	Scarred jaw , prepared word, each letter is sharp, on the crest of the wave. Without pain or glory, I will write this story, Falling is not failing, but rising is victory
Venir de vuelta, abrir la puerta, estar resuelto, estar alerta.	Return again, open the door, be determined, be alert
Sacar la voz que estaba muerta, y hacerla orquesta	Raise the voice that was dead and turn it into orchestra
Caminar, seguro, libre, sin temor, respirar y sacar la voz.	Walk, safe, free, without fear, breath and raise the voice
Liberarse de todo el pudor, tomar de las riendas, no rendirse al opresor. Caminar erguido, sin temor, respirar y sacar la voz.	Get rid of all the shame and take the reins, do not surrender to the oppressive. Walk raised without fear breathe and release the voice
Uhh, uhh, uhhh (x4)	Uhh, uhh, uhhh (4x)

By contrasting a number of ideas, the enunciator shows certain insensitivity towards their surroundings. The feeling of exhaustion - physical and psychological- makes possible only one reaction possible: singing pure, free of any kind of censorship or canst.

Without "sorry" or "glory", the rapper wins the freedom to open all doors; the same ones that previously had been closed. The song, in this sense, is a necessary path for the reversal of social roles and consequent achievement of "victory". Prompting the receiver to think through the ideas disseminated in the content of the song, rap brings the message that we need to rescue people from muteness, make them fight.

The fight in this case is only possible from the union between the similar. On the verse "Release the voice that was dead and turn it into orchestra", the gregarious idea should be noted, once again. By joining his voice to the voice of his fellow men, the enunciator gives the word the potential for transformation. Becoming an "orchestra", the word gained the strength to fight for a more just society, to promote the revolution and preach to guarantee the rights to marginalized groups.

Attention is drawn at this time in the performance – at about 02:40 after the start of musical performance – to the transformation given in the sound basis acompannying the rapper's voice. This base, which at the beginning of the song brought mimesis sampled small chords performed on a keyboard/piano, reaches its peak at this time. Music plays a crescendo in terms of dynamics, which accompanies the verbal progression of the words as the song unfolds. What previously represented soft touch keys, begins to mimic at this point, the presence of a great orchestra, in which the rubbed string instruments assume the melody.

At 03:15 draws attention a sound on the background, like a noise, presented through the possible recycling towardst the rapper musical beat. In this section, on the background, the sound is simulating an ancient radio transmission in wheezing words that say, in the fourth strophe:

	Translation:
El tiempo clava la daga	Time plunges the dagger
Haga lo que haga uno	Whatever you do
Estraga oportuno	Spoil an adjustment
Tú no cobras lo que el tiempo	You do not charge what time
paga.	pays
Estraga saga tras saga	Spoils, saga after saga
Raspa con su amarga espátula	Scrapes with its bitter spatula
Huérfano se hace de brújulas	Orphaned is made of compasses
Y lúcidamente en celo	And lucidly in fervor
Blanca el arma, blanco el pelo	White weapon, white hair
Su blanca cara de crápula	His scoundrel white face
"Ésta" dice un espinela	"This one" said a spinel
La que Violeta cantaba	The Violet sang
La de la sílaba octava del pateador	The eighth syllable of the "kicker"
Vieja escuela.	Old School
Y lo que duela, que duela	And what hurts, let it hurt
Si es que tiene que doler	If it has to hurt
La flama sin calma que arder	The flame without calm That has
tenga	to burn
Que siga ardendo	Let it continue burning
Que siga fosforeciendo	Continue phosphorescing

The above section carries a number of metaphors. In the early verses a clear reference is made to an inevitable massacre, promoted by the systemic time. The recorded voice says: "Time plunges the dagger/Whatever someone does/You do not charge what time pays". In this passage, the allusion to a system that oppresses is clear, regardless of the actions taken by the men who inhabit it. It oppresses, damages and establishes daily sagas, which are reversed in subjectivities of distress experienced as a "dagger" individually in each existence.

On the sixth to the eighth verse, the expository voice takes on an imperative tone: "Scrap with his bitter spatula/Orphaned is made of compasses/And lucidly in the fervor"; entailing a possible reaction by the oppressed population. The excess of systemic guidelines ("compasses") is reported in the recording as the consequence of a feeling of helplessness ("orphans"). This, in turn, causes a "revolution", made in a "lucid" and ardent way - "in fervor".

It is a fact that poetry is also present in the electronic base, in this case, acting as a kind of "special effect" against the rapper macro-context.

Through ninth to the fourteenth verse, recording behaves as if to expose the systemic actions taken at any time and almost imperceptibly, abstractly, "white". "White weapon, white hair/Your scoundrel white face," says the recording. Further, there is the given content in the eleventh and twelfth verse: "It is, said a spinel Violet singing."

The reference to spinel-stone, often synthetic, commonly confused with ruby - may be a metaphor in relation to the neoliberal system; that under a first look keeps the possibility of precious opinion and persuaded by its beauty, but by further "reading" it proves to be essentially false. Personified, the spinel is directed to Violeta. At this point, it is believed to be an explicit reference to Violeta Parra.

Composer dedicated to popular music, Parra became known for the content of her songs, whose approach was always dedicated to the issues of social engagement and struggle of the oppressed working class, one of her hit songs, *"Volver a los 17"*, has been recorded by the Brazilian artist Milton Nascimento.

By exposing, through the verses, the image of a "singing" spinel Violeta by eighth syllable of a *"pateador"* – an animal that kicks a lot, or a player whose job is done by "kicking" - recorded in metaphors, tells us about the systemic persuasion before the popular classes fighters; an attempt that, at first glance shows seductive and bright as a spinel, but that truly keeps in itself the obscure intentions of a *"pateador"*, a "student" of an "old school".

From the fifteenth to the twenty-first verse of the strophe in question, the idea of the revolution arises: "And what hurts, let it hurt/If it has to hurt/The flame without calm/That has to burn/Let it continue burning/Continue phosphorescing/If it has to phosphoresce." Reading these statements transmits to the one who reads the epic sense given the tone of the recording. To achieve change, the fight is necessary, the confrontation is necessary, it is necessary to "let it hurt"... And aware of that notion, the voice that launches its message to "listeners" of an "imaginary radio", "the performed the song", as opposed to resorting to any subterfuge, remains in combative stance. If you have to hurt, "let it hurt" he says, expressing the certainty of a non-repentance. The voice recorded transmits to its "listeners" the lesson, that the fight for better days should continue in momentum and power, that reversed feelings of "distress" and "anger", "flame without calm", are the will of transformation.

The performance of the song reaches the end on the fifth transcribed/translated strophe, in which the lines confirm the view of strength, suggesting imagery metaphor of "strength". However, the existence of a human being could suggest here the allusion of a marginal human, "hanged" by the oppression of the capitalist system that contextualizes its existence - gives way to the song, that, "hanging" on a string, disseminates verses of exciting and educational character. Words that keep in itself the war potential of the revolution, engagement.

	Translation:
En un cordel, a colgar la copla,	On a rope hung the song that
que el viento mece,	scaled the wind
Que pocas veces merece.	That rarely deserves
Cada pena, suelta voz, cada	Each pen, release the voice, every
tos	cough
Pensando en sacar la voz.	Thinking of releasing the voice
Uhh, uhh, uhhh (x2).	Uhh, uhh, uhhh (x2)

Words are allowed practically anything. The word "few" times is penalized, it is a libertarian instrument and it takes courage to use it in order to get social victory.

The message set by recording *"Sacar la Voz"* goes back to the idea of belief in social struggle - as a combative, necessary and urgent way to achieve the "light" metaphor related to necessary and urgent social transformations: "Let it keep phosphorescing / If it has to phosphoresce".

"Sacar la Voz", in short, is a song that preaches non-mutance. The union of the marginalized is represented by this rap which, in turn, also stimulates the gregarious feeling in its listeners, serving as

a stimulus so that, in obstinacy, "release their voice", claiming their rights and spreading their duties in society.

If you don't believe feat: the attitude of men, the use of the belligerant word

Performed by the London group Partnership of Sound the song. "*If you don't believe feat*" is another rapper song that puts the power of the word in the hope for social revolution.

The song begins with a very smooth and almost imperceptible piano sound base. After three seconds of recording, the sound of the piano is broken and we can see the intertextuality proposed by the sampler: a kind of epigraph disposed towards the music, comes the passage of a constant dialogue of the documentary *Jazz*, directed by Ken Burns (2001). In the passage, composer Duke Ellington has a conversation with a reporter, about the inspiration to write songs.

> \- Where did you get your ideas from?
> \- The ideas? Oh man, I get a million dreams
> It's all I do is dream all the time
> \- I heard you play piano...
> \- No, no, this is not piano. This is dreaming

Twenty one seconds after the musical performance started, comes the resounding voice of the enunciator, performed by several voices, and again accompanied by a sound base, only this time it was electronic, more intense and (dynamically) stronger. At such time, in the second strophe there are the following verses:

> Life life life (life)
> Can be impose in heaven ...
> In a jar without an opening composed in haze
> Will not tell you once you're so close in there,
> Opposed in there dedicate the space
> You're choking back the tears as you're talking on the atmosphere

Despair, sat around the cheer (cheer?) (Yeah!)
Acting like this world is theirs
They've been doing this for years
Even centuries, feature sensory
Caught sex with more sex
We all said picking up the pen and pad
And write to inspire
You'd like to wear the mad
Matter of fact I'm rather glad
There is heinous, heinous set the hatred

Through the performance, there is the simulacrum of a dialog situation between the enunciator and an interlocutor, the latter invisible in the scene (it is known that he is there, although he is not given the voice of performance at any time, either is a name conferred). This interlocutor, to whose personality existential angst characteristics and suspension status of fugue are attributed - which are mixed feelings of joy and despair typical of the condition of a drug addicts, receives from the enunciator stories about the systemic usurpation held on to over the centuries, and more than that, the invitation to a wake in fury.

When referring to the system, the enunciator denounces the injustice, that he felt, throughout history. "They have done this for years/centuries even, feature sensory."

Furthermore, he draws attention to the motivating principles of his own speech. "We all talk using pen and pad / And write to inspire." The writing here mentioned, metalinguistically, proposes a reference to the act of composition, which is aimed at inspiring his listeners. The importance of the word and its practical intention is remarkable throughout the performance.

In the analyzed strophe the impetus given to the spoken word is clear too. It is rhymed on paper, but spread through singing, and incites imaginary and real interlocutors to taking certain attitudes. In this case, an action also based on feeling. "You should wear the rage," says the performer, spreading his lyrical voice. The feeling of anger would thus give the imaginary receiver an advice in the fictional poetic plan, but also put an idea to the listener's reflection, that by keeping in touch with the performed song, would be vulnerable to the influence of reflection.

The song invites the listener to leave the state of inertia, going to intervene in their own reality. By this logic, follow the lines of the third strophe are performed:

> Back in the yard you can better play it
> Keep me waiting for the day the mad is elevating
> Relegating
> The hole jump
> You face the consequence of yapping
> Rap has the ways, you can't see what is happening
> You have Vaseline
> Better draw your sorrow with the half glass of rain
> … And it's left, let us see if they can help
> … The same clause, the vow that spare you the mental break
> down
> The fate frowns around us
> Getting straight, get ever to waste no less astound us
> … None of your boxes nor chains can abound us
> I'm busting out of the chains
> Like that you caged
> Filled with rage I'll be your powerman
> Now this world's my stage
> I feel the microphone juice moving through my veins
> Rendering me insane as I feed off all MC remains
> I never stay in lanes, my parchment is DVA
> And eradicate… Only a beat can medicate
> I sing to hit ups to medicate but their illness prevails
> Riding roughshod and career enough rails to tell tales
> Some slingers are itchy fingers looking at dead ringers
> Through their eyes, we hate lingers
> Are such souls, long cold, so bring them to the fold
> Rebounded to teach non-believers to do as they're told
> Cause for too long, I kept my mouth simple

> What is found around are superfights, now you can swivel
> From de middle to the front, to the rear
> Like my neighbour's Matt murder boy, I have no fear

By inviting the imaginary interlocutor to come back to court, i.e. the citizen and revolutionary activity, leaving drug addiction, the enunciator is shown avid for the occurrence of furious expression, provided by rap. "Keep me waiting for the day when the great raging will awaken/Apart walk up/Skip the Hole"

The enunciator demonstrates his imaginary interlocutor the social resistance to the practice of rap. "You pay the price for being disapproving/Rap has these things," he says.

But, he warns too, about the fact of not seeing things, for being under the effects of drugs ("Do you have Vaseline?" he says.). Suggesting a possible resistance from the imaginary interlocutor, the enunciator quips "You better draw your suffering with half a glass of rain/And then abandon it (...) Let's see if so they can help (...)", and goes on to criticize the resignation assumed by this interlocutor.

Resignation in "downcast countenances" is seen as a possible comfort zone, which saves the subject of visibility and critics. Contrary to submission, the enunciator determines "Go ahead (...) And do not miss". Submission imprisons and the prisoner is the party to which the enunciator addresses. "I'll be your superman/ Now the world is my stage," he says.

Again, the revolutionary dimension of the rapper word is portrayed in the song. Born between MCS, the song comes from a great sense of fury. In music, this song is matched to a drug and an alert. "I sing to call you and medicate/But your disease is still prevalent," he says.

Condemning the disposal of those who are adopting the path of drugs to escape reality, the enunciator lends himself to recover "lost souls". In this regard, it is believed there is also in the passage in question, an allusion to the existence of gang fights, responsible for what the enunciator calls "fights for nothing", exemplified by the murder illustration of a neighbor called "Matt".

By despizing the violent reality space provided by gangs and drugs, the poetic voice describes his path and points the process that culminated in choosing another path. In the fourth performed strophe, we have the following speech:

> I stand for many years, seen tears
> Wiped the cheer clear a fruit boy clears
> A bad man's tears
> So I raised no ears,
> My throne is follicly challenged
> I keep scalps visible to all those who would fashion
> Any hopes to dethrone
> Any hopes to debone
> Any hopes to bright wide
> And any hopes to go home.
> Any hopes to feel safe.
> Any hopes to get mended
> Any hopes That You had will now be ended.
> Done, done, done, done, done, done, done
> And if you do not believe, just watch me
> You better watch me, yes just watch me, yo
> If you do not believe, better watch me, yo, just watch me
> Well, you better watch me, yo
> And if you do not believe, you better watch me, yes, you better watch me, yo, just watch me
> And if you do not believe, you better watch me, yes, just watch me, yo, better watch me, yo

The reading of the verse in question reveals an enunciator that, having been in coping conditions related to various life situations, was carried away by the influence of his surroundings. "I did not realize" he says.

The bald head becomes an identity mark before his peers, people of "style". Keeping hopes, the enunciator externalizes his foreign condition, revealing the desire to return "home" and feel "safe".

In using the rapper word, he considers any dream as previously implemented. Everything is "done".

The performance concludes with a finding made by the enunciator and delivered face by his imaginary interlocutor: "And if you do not believe, just watch me/You'd better see me, yeah, just watch."

Considerations on a different track and (in) definitely [instrumental]

Among the tracks that make up the record "*Pássaro Imigrante, Definitivamente [Instrumental]*", may be the one to arouse greater cuiriosity in this analysis process. Although its title may refer to the idea of a music devoid of the presence of vocals, the appreciation of the track, imediatly shows us otherwise.

The song begins with a sound base of mysterious texture, which will accompany it, without oscillations, to its end. Little more than a second after the beginning of the performance, there is the voice of the poet Carlos Drummond de Andrade. Drummond, in this track, takes the place of performative voice, reciting initially two strophes of the poem *"Procura da Poesia"*.

> Do not make verses about events.
> There is no creation or death before poetry.
> Before it, life is a static sun,
> Neither heats nor lights.
> Affinities, birthdays, personal incidents do not count.
> Do not do make verses with the body,
> this excellent, complete and comfortable body, so averse to lyrical effusion.
> Your drop of bile, your grimace of joy or pain in the dark
> Are indifferent.
> Do not reveal to me your feelings,
> that prevail of misunderstanding and try the long journey.
> What you think and feel, this still is not poetry.

Part of the work "*A Rosa do Povo*" [33] (1945), "*Procura da poesia*"[34] was consecrated in history as an important modernist poem. Through it, there is the exercise of metalanguage, since the poem provides reflections on the very poetic production.

The analysis of the strophe shows the presence of a self-lyrical that, determined to guide his imaginary interlocutor, provides advice regarding the creation of poems. By conjugating verbs from the imperative mood ("do not do", "do not betray"), Drummond refers to the existence of poetry as something that is not done in the hasty and shallow way of descriptions. "What you think or feel, it still is not poetry," notes the lyrical voice.

The intention of the poet to address issues relating to political and social themes emerges in "*A Procura da Poesia*", coated with aesthetic concerns. Drummond seems to realize that poetry should not be produced (or read) while an objective text. On the contrary, it should be worked artistically, without giving up the exercise in lapidating the word, nor inspiration.

On the article "*A poética prescritiva de Carlos Drummond de Andrade*", the researcher Luiz Roberto Zanotti (2009, p. 133) discusses this question:

> For Drummond, poetry can not be seen as an objective, a mere circumstantial attribute: "I do not think poetry is a

---

33 Of great impact, the "Rosa do Povo" is among the works of Carlos Drummond de Andrade that more explicitly reveals the aspect of socio-political engagement, developed by the author. Flocking poems contrary to the ideology preached by Getulio Vargas and the Estado Novo - regime which ruled in Brazil at that time - the work was of great impact. About the importance assumed by this production, the author Jaime Ginzburg elaborates: "The Consecration of Rosa do Povo", specifically, indicates an ability to cope with extreme challenges. Besides having a keen sense of the contradictory movements of the historical context in which they defined their production conditions, Drummond had, in his experience as a columnist and as a poet, a difficult thought autonomy to constitute, in a period as violent as the "Estado Novo". (GINZBURG, 2002, p. 144).

34 Annex GG.

means to communicate anything, but that itself is something that communicates" (DRUMMOND cited SANT'ANNA, 1992, p. 195). Following this reasoning, around a poetry set to the proper "poetry", one can also see that there is a fusion of subject and object proposed by Drummond that eliminates any possibility of an objective reading of his poetry, as the poet puts the reader in the text, so that is bound (crossed) by the poem. Thus understood, poetry is a search that is performed while the search itself.

Negations in verse conceal certain lyric irony that wants to ratify the urgency of creative devices before the poetic approach to every day issues. Poetry is, so to speak, a kind of trajectory which seeks something; a route to be traveled, both for the one who writes it - and wants to find the ideal way to implore the record of his words - and by the one that reads and wants to understand it.

The continuity of the poem, though not about the song in question, suggests the need for a patient work done over the word, so that it ceases its "dictionary state" and, regardless of the subject to which it is intended, passes to the condition of poetry.

"Penetrate dully in the realm of words/There are poems that expect to be written/There is calm and freshness intact in the surface/They are alone and silent in dictionary state" - has one of the strophes that give continuity to the poem.

Drummond defends, then, a "creative coexistence" of the poet with the word. A life that makes possible the appropriation and implementation of any theme to the literary condition. The poet must, therefore, feel the "realm of words", hear them silently, to rescue them from their denotative meanings and revert them to the condition of art. We must therefore carry out a "lucid magic", on which refers Marlene de Castro Correia in the work "*Drummond: A Mágica Lúcida*"

> Writing poetry is to fight with words (...) to manage them in a specific way, updating their expressive potentialities, combining them with such effectiveness that they acquire

meaning of fullness. Poetry is defined, therefore, as a combinatorial operation of words and configuration of a form. Consequently, the first task of the poet is the significant enrichment of the language. (CORREIA, 2002, p. 15).

In the track *"Definitivamente"* [Instrumental], what we see is the occurrence of a meeting made possible by the performance of the canonical poetic (represented by Carlos Drummond de Andrade) and rapper poetic whose presence is the implicit, done only by the continuous electronic base, followed by the voice of Drummond.

The track seems to transmit to the listener of the performance that rap is indeed [and "definitely"], a form of poetry; something that is guided in a creative way, by the themes of every day life; serving as a tool to change it, transform it.

In this sense, it is inferred that the rapper, like the modernist poet, is a guy who "gets" the universe of words and "rhymes" them, resuming, today, the purpose of engagement preached by the Modernists; as he also elaborates in poetic performance, recurrent issues to social contemporary context.

The recording containing the voice Drummond is sustained until the 43 seconds of performance. After this, the utterance is stopped , and the performance remains, only with an isolated instrumental supporting base.

The instrumental track continues practically apart until the end of the track, when at 03:00 the exposed idea is confirmed. The voice of Drummond uttering the following verses arises again in the mix:

> Your ivory yacht, your diamond shoe,
> Your mazurkas and mistakes, your family skeletons
> disappear in the time lapse, is something snotty.

This time, what we see at the end of the track is a kind of message directed to the social aristocracy. No one is better than anyone... And everything disappears, in "the time lapse."

A Intersemiotic proposal: reading videoclips

Fundamental considerations on the intersemiotic translation

The intersemiotic translation consists of a proccess related to transformation. As was previously provided, through this process verbal signs are obtained from non-verbal signs.

When faced with the challenge of undertaking a intersemiotic translation, the researcher should therefore extend the range of their concerns, in addition to the oral language or written word. In intersemiotic translation other elements are also taken into account - sonic textures, images, color, editing, etc. - That, like the verbal content, also communicates.

Based upon the theory of Charles Peirce on "General Theory of Signs" Plaza (2003) takes concepts that see the idea of sign, as an element that "(...) is something to someone, it is addressed to someone (...) creates in one's mind an equivalent sign, or perhaps more developed." (PLAZA, 2003, p. 21).

According Plaza (2003), in relation to the object to which they refer, the signs can be classified according to the nature. Thus, in relation to the object to which it relates, a sign can be: an icon, an index or a symbol. In this sense, Plaza (2003, p. 21-22) offers us the following explanation:

> ICONS: are signs that operate by the similarity in fact among its qualities, its object and its meaning. The icon, in relation to its Immediate Object is a quality sign, and the meanings that it is about to set off, are mere feelings such as the feeling aroused by a piece of music or artwork.
>
> INDEXES: they operate primarily by the contiguity of its Dynamic object due to being related to it when compared to

the real. The index, in relation to its Immediate Object, is a sign of an existing one.

SYMBOLS: they operate first of all, by institutive contiguity, seized from their material part and its meaning. Determined by its Dynamic object only in the sense of being interpreted, the symbol depends on a convention or habit. The symbol, in relation to its Immediate Object, is the sign of the Law.

Considering the property of signic transcreation, Plaza (2003) confirms the lack of watertight categories. For the author, the same sign can assume iconic, indexical and symbolic functions in relation to the object to which it refers. In this sense, citing Peirce, he concludes: "The most perfect of signs are those that are amalgamated in proportions as equal as possible" (PEIRCE, cited PLAZA, 2003, p. 22).

Translations, as well as associations evidenced from the signs are, according to Plaza (2003), guided by the Legissígno category, another Piercian notion, this time based on the sign-law idea. According to Plaza, the Legisigns: "Allow establishment of a semiotic order that makes us differentiate between what is the same, similar and what is different, providing thus the conditions for the establishment of a synthesis" (PEIRCE, cited PLAZA, 2003 p. 22).

Identified by Plaza, (2003) three categories are assigned to legissígnos: The Transducer Legisigns, the Paramorfism Legisign and the Legisign as optimization.

The Transducer Legisigns constitute a category in which "(...) we pass from one order to another order tending to (...) keep the energy load of the original sign, that is, to keep the invariant equivalence". (PLAZA, 2003, p. 72).

The Paramorfism Legisign, admits the multiplicity of forms, occurring when "(...) the legisign becomes responsible for paramorfism as diverse structure, but with the same meaning (...). In relation to the paramorfism Legisign, Plaza afirms that this category provides (...) the conditions to establish the comparative study of the arts, seen as more significant comparison of form and less as a content comparison." (PLAZA, 2003, p. 72).

Legisign as Optimization, establishes a "(...) the optimization process (...) which consists of a method by which a process continuously adjusts to obtain better results, and this is done analytically."(PLAZA, 2003, p. 72)

Inspired by the piercian theory, its signs and its laws, Plaza creates a characterization for intersemiotic translations. Although not considered as fixed a parameter, such a classification would serve in the manner of a guiding element, available to translation processes. Thus, he classifies intersemiotic translation into three types, namely: iconic, indicial and symbolic translation.(PLAZA, 2003)

Regarding the first, Plaza (2003) points out that this is a category for which the attribute of similarity between the structure matrix (original) and derived structure (translated) is present. According to the author:

> Iconic Translation: This is guided by the principle of similarity of structure. We have, thus, an analogy between immediate objects, equivalence between the same and the alike, which show the changing life of semiotic transformation. The iconic translation is able to produce meaning as qualities and appearances, similarly (...) In this type of translation, it is essentially about facing the untranslatable of the Immediate Object of the original through a transducer sign of law. It can be distinguished, thus iconic translations of isomorphic and paramorphic character, in a metaphoric appropriation of these coming from notions of chemistry and physics. (PLAZA, 2003, p. 89-90).

Considering the iconic translation as transcreation - "(...) devoid of dynamic connection to the original which it represents (...) going (...) simply that the meanings produced by their material qualities are reminiscent of the original, once they have been created in order to provide sensations similar to this" (PLAZA, 2003, p. 93). The author questions the differentiation procedures applicable between concepts involving the original and the copy, authenticity and originality; and claims that this kind of translation holds a very strong aesthetic load.

Plaza (2003) discriminates also the existence of the other two sub-categories, differentiating them from the association deriving concepts of chemistry and physics: isomorphic character (in which we highlight the similarity between the structures) and paramorphic character (in which highlight the different format structures). The second category proposed by Plaza (2003), in the study of intersemiotic translation is the indicial translation. This category is guided by "transposition into", expressing a relation of "cause and effect" or "contiguity by reference" between the translation and the original. By launching its concept about this translational classification, he states:

> The indicial translation is guided by contact between the original and the translation, there is continuity between the original and translation. The original's immediate object is suitable and transferred to another medium. In this change there is the transformation of quality of the immediate object, as the new medium semanticizes the information it conveys. In operation one can shift the whole or part. (PLAZA, 2003, p. 89-90).

Regarding the operating possibilities inherent to this category Plaza (2003) distinguishes, again, the existence of two groups: the homeomorphic translation and the Metonymic translation.

The first group, following the notion of homeomorphism, due to topology, Plaza (2003) claims to have the correspondence between the original and the translation elements." Two homeomorphic sets have the same topological invariants." (PLAZA, 2003, p. 90).

On the second group, Plaza (2003) states that it consists of a practice whereby the notion of homeomorphism is explored partially; with only segments of the original in the translation. Such a practice would incur, according to the author, in exploring the design of metonymic displacement, alternative to the notion of contiguity.

Unlike the iconic translation, which exerts its action by analogies between it and the original's immediate objects, indicial translation saves by the new medium, traits related to the text-matrix. Faithful to the original aesthetics, indicial translation guards the possibility to "crystallize" it in different ways, simultaneously preserving, the notions of contiguity and innovative meanings. Thus, he states: "These translations are characterized as syntactic assembly (reference by means) and semantic assembly (reference by contiguity), meaning that it indicates the physical contact relationship with the object, more than transposing by invention." (PLAZA, 2003, p. 90)

The third category established by Plaza (2003) is the symbolic translation. Through this type, the connection between the objects will occur through conventions that will determine its significance. Metaphors, symbols and other signs of conventional character are used, in this sense, in order to undertake a search for references to which prior knowledge is assumed. As pointed out, "in this case, the translation is a transcoding." (PLAZA, 2003, p. 90)

The intersection between different languages - verbal, photographic, musical, filmic, television, pitctoric, etc. - and the effect produced by these new settings - holders of hybrid forms and purposes - is what will govern all the motivation of intersemiotic studies.

Translating the information transmitted through the contemporary technology, full of possibility and character of signs, is the underlying purpose of Plaza's theory (2003). Contrary to establish other theoretical perspectives related to translation - embodied from the ideal of fidelity to the original text - intersemiotic translation is guided by the possibility of creative reinterpretation, dialogue between the signs and the historical re-writing. Using the words of Plaza, we can define the purpose of this field of study:

> (...) Penetrate the bowels of different signs, seeking to to illuminate their structural relations, as are those relationships that are most popular when it comes to focus on the elements governing the translation. Translate creatively is primarily, es-

tablishing intellective structures aimed at the transformation of forms. (PLAZA, 2003, p. 71).

In the course of this thesis the attempt to intersemiotically read four videoclips related to immigrant rapper production will be performed. As previously mentioned - based on theoretical foundation provided by intersemiotic translation - some thoughts on the works *"Sacar la Voz"* (2012), *"Shock"* (2011); *"Pássaro Imigrante"* (2011); *Το Κέρμα* (2010) will be woven.

Among the various possible forms of translation in this study, we identified the transient occurrence of two processes reported by Plaza (2003), namely:

1) Transcreation related to the iconic translation that identifies this process, depending on the fidelity externalized by the studied videoclips, to transpose, through specific signs, the materiality, of the content of the songs sung in the study; 2) Transcoding inherent in symbolic translation, since in some parts of the videoclips studied metaphors and symbols show up, whose presence requires prior knowledge or research established on the subject, so that the receiver-interpreter can understand them in their fullness.

Before, however, we expose the reading about the pre-selected videoclips, which will be established by some notes that deal with the social history of the genre in question and may contribute to a deeper understanding of the objects of study here in evidence.

In this way, therefore, the next research section will be dedicated to establishing considerations about the audiovisual music video genre.

Understanding the music video: from the beginning to contemporaneity

With origins in the avant-garde films of the early twentieth century, the music video is a television genre of great popularity in the contemporary context.

Yet in the decades of 20's and 30's the first cinematographic manifestations came towards synchronization between sound and image. According to Soares in the work "*Videoclipe: o elogio da desarmonia*"(2012, p. 21), the elaborate film projections in this period were accompanied by music, the very choice of them, something exercised depending on the image - "(...) the choice of the score was related to the content of the images shown," confirms the author.

Soares explains, also, about the jazz influence in relation to audiovisual productions, since the genre, until then, sought to consolidate in the music market, becoming a valuable production, a real "source" for editing filmed musical numbers. In this sense, he says:

> Between the 20's and 30's, jazz, then a musical genre that was trying to "raise" its legitimacy, had become a source for the production of filmed numbers, especially by artists such as Duke Ellington and Woody Herman. In 1927, *"The Jazz Singer"* starred in theaters with Al Jolson, first musical film in the history of cinema. (SOARES, 2012, p. 21)

Over time, the number of situations in which the "video" and the "audio" elements were filmically correlated increased. In the 40's, for example, the filmmaker Oskar Fischinger designed the opening sequence for Disney's Fantasia, "(...) a film that would build a deep kinesthetic relationship between music and image in cartoons" (SOARES 2012, p. 21).

Already in the mid-50's, with the arrival of television, the presence of musical-imagistic production was also remarkable. The program *Paul Whiteman's Teen Club* on the ABC network is noteworthy in that period. Since then, film and television went to play important roles in the dissemination of the musical numbers, "feeding" the music industry.

By way of illustration, Soares (2012) cites the rock inclusion in American society when, in the midst of traditionalism, the trajectory of diverse artists emerged:

Numbers like Bill Haley and The Cornets singing Rock Around the Clock in the film Blackboard Jungle, of Richard Brooks, began a fruitful relationship between film and music, which would consecrate, especially the name of an artist: Elvis Presley. With the amount collected in Elvis Presley movies, director Richard Thorpe (Jailhouse Rock) produced musical numbers effectively geared to highlight artists, as ensures Grimalt, was one of the means responsible for Rock insertion in the sphere of the conservative american society consumption(...) In 1964, the film A Hard Day's Night, with The Beatles and directed by Richard Lester, has given way to what Durá-Grimalt calls "a close precedent of the videoclip." (SOARES, 2012, p. 22-23).

Regarding the appearance of the videoclip in the format, researchers Marildo Nercolini and Ariane Holzbach Diniz (2009), in the article *Videoclipe em tempos de reconfigurações*, argue that there is controversy regarding the date of emergence of this product. According to them, despite the non-passivity against the merits of the case the 70's are generaly considered as such date.

According to the researchers, the production-milestone in the history of the videoclip is "*Bohemian Rhapsody*", by the band Queen classified as the first music video, a designation atributted by the "*New Musical Express*" (NME3) is an important European musical reference. According Nercolini and Hozbach (2009), this videoclip presented special effects and a well-defined script. Having been shown in several television shows, "*Bohemian Rhapsody*" - was then called a "promotional video" – and had the distinction of the fact that it was "primarily designed to release the song in the media".

Regarding the nomenclature "videoclip", back to the words of Smith (2012), when the term came to be used only in the 80's, a time that also marked the consolidation of this product by the recording industry. Referring to this fact, he explains:

> The popularization of the videoclip took place, especially in the 80's through the creation of Music Television, MTV - a

television station that was first cable and then open, dedicated to continuously show videoclips. The very nomenclature that defines the video already has the characteristic: the idea of speed, of favorite structures. At first, the clip was simply called musical number. Then, it received the name of promo, a direct allusion to the word "promotion". Only from the early 80's it finally reach the term "music video". Clip, which means "cutting" (newspaper, magazine, for example), clamp or clip, rightly focuses on the business side of this audiovisual. (SOARES, 2012, p. 32)

Over time, the videoclip was consecrated as a popular audiovisual genre, of rapid production and editing, reaching an extension of approximately three minutes. Through the videoclip, informed performances became widespread through the mixture of musical and visual elements, focused on the exposure of the song, narrated or scripted, in order to express specific stories, parallel to the performance of the song, established not only through the association between imagistic language and the musical content - made up of words and music - but also adorned by the applicability of specific aesthetic features such as ambient sounds, images, gestures, editing effects... Elements that are not always present in CD or MP3 recordings, but that arise immersed in the body of audiovisual, working or not for the success of a performance.

Goodwin (1992) elaborates that, historically, the studies related to the videoclip always privileged imagistic aspects, so they were restricted to investigations related to the field of music. In 1992, he noted:

> The iconography of pop music has been often disregarded.The implications of the pop music gender are constantly overlooked or neglected in this way, the videos are read as if its generic meaning was based only on film meanings (...) (GOODWIN, 1992, p. 4).

The author refers to "(...) deaf methods "and critics without ears (...)" (GOODWIN, 1992, p. 5) to identify the uniqueness of the dominant conceptual fields in the study of the video; suggesting the need for the emergence of a "musicology image" to be present in the investigations that deal with this musical product.

From the time of Goodwin's findings(1992) until today, other temporal and spatial changes, propitiated shifts around not only the videoclip, but the audiovisual genre as a whole. Thus, it is highly important to consider the fact that music, image and lyrics go together, as constituents of a hybrid cultural event that should no longer be seen in isolation, the way in which it is possible to omit one of its elements, in relation to others.

The passing years brought new proposals that were gradually integrated into the videoclip. Initially, this consisted of a "homogeneous" and "commercial" whole, in relation to the dissemination and "sale" of the artistic image - in which luxurious scenarios appeared, usually intended to the persuasion from the kinesthetic diffusion of feelings of freedom. Already in the mid-90's the situation was different. With the result from that time, the commercial purpose gives way to video art, a factor that adds stylistic changes from the assembly of the videoclip. In this sense, Machado (2000, p. 175) exemplifies:

> (...) When a Polish artist like Zbigniew Rybczynski, with a long history of experimentation in film and video, performs a clip as Imagine (1987), he is no longer thinking about a disc promotion or Jonn Lennon's music (in fact, he was not even hired or paid for it), but rather to develop, from some ideas already contained in the Lennon song, a true experimental video in the clip format. At other times, even working in order labels - as The Original Wrapper (1986) for Lou Reed and in Oportunities (1986) for the Pet Shop Boys - the videoclip appears clearly to Rybczynski as an opportunity to explore new ideas within the audiovisual universe. Some videoclips are unapologetically poetic constructions in the best tradition of video art.

Considering the heterogeneity of these productions, Machado (2000) proposes a classification for videoclips. According to the author, such productions can be basically classified into three groups or categories, he explains:

> The first, most primitive of all, it is what makes the ordinary promotional clip, mere illustration of a pre-existing song. With this group is not worth wasting time. The second (...) comprises a whole community of filmmakers coming from the film or experimental video industry and that, together with composers and boldest interpreters, managed to turn this TV format in a wide range and open to the reinvention of audiovisual. But there is still a third group (...) is the one who sees the clip as a form of full and self-sufficient audiovisual, able to give a more modern response to the secular pursuit of a perfect synthesis of image and sound. This third group is formed by another type of directors: they are usually musicians, as well as to account for the entire composition and interpretation of their musical pieces, they also face themselves the visual design of the clip. (MACHADO, 2000, p. 182).

The video clips to which we have proposed a reading proccess - this action driven by the assumption that these are audiovisual products that ratify the performed content through the orality of the songs - part, in our view, from the third category.

In the interpretations proposed by this chapter changes crossed by this audiovisual "product" over time are taken into account, whether they are related to the production, editing or placement of it.

Currently, videoclip aesthetic features, alongside the marketing intentions, a sense of reality and its various worldly contextual aspects, so that it becomes possible to observe also, through such productions, the picture of misery and the problems related to violent global poverty, already mentioned in this work.

About the constitution of the videoclips, it is necessary to note that such works, if they appeared before as the arbitrariness of isolated productions by large multinational music industries, today, thanks to the new possibilities that permeate in the Web 2.0, they can also be prepared in an amateur way (homemade) and without requiring high budgets for productions.

In addressing the new modifier productions of the consolidated Mass Culture, researchers Ludmila Santos and Luisa Procnik recall the importance of Youtube (Accessed on December 1st 2011)

> In February 2005 is based on the Internet the great facilitator of the dissemination of video over the network, the YouTube.com.The English term tube is used informally in relation to television. The slogan of the site, Tube yourself (something like "telecast yourself"), is an example of the receiver search for the power of the word, which previously belonged only to large media companies and were conveyed only by the traditional media such as television, radio and newspapers printed.

From the sound point of view, there are also important changes. Not only does it have the harmony of tonal sounds, but also the presence of specific technological features capable of editing, and producing increasingly latent effects. Noises associated with the text, seem to offer certain forcefulness to hybrid phonographic products, above all, it can be configured also as a potential simulacrum of days spent by recipients and enunciators and perhaps more than that; while a recording instrument of an era in which we are all inserted.

Given these brief considerations about the "videoclip" phenomenon, the next section will attempt to analyze the four pre-selected videoclips, namely: "*Sacar la voz*" (2012), "*Shock*" (2011); "*Pássaro Imigrante*" (2011); "*Το Κέρμα*" (2010).

Sacar La Voz (Release the Voice)

"*Sacar La Voz*" is an audiovisual production that begins synchronicized with the song. The piano sounds simulated by electronic beats contrast with the rapper's image in performance who over the first five seconds of the videoclip, remains silent. Wearing simple clothing (cap, plaid shirt and jeans) and carrying a few Accessesories (bracelets and earrings), Ana Tijoux conveys the image of a lonely person, with a lost look, in displacement.

Early in the audiovisual performance, the video draws attention to the dialogue between music and the editing process. Note, in this sense, the presence of "filters" is what allows the recipient the impression of being in front of a hybrid production.

At the same time that the video conveys the notion of something "old", in black and white. It shows, also, in the first images, the applicability of a contrast overexposure, while "small imagistic cuts" remain simultaneous to the musical beat.

At 00:06 the image of Ana Tijoux is replaced by another scenario: a simple house, situated probably in a suburban neighborhood. The image is colored, while the overexposure contrast remains. In this sense, the scenario assumes prominence in relation to the initial images in black and white.

The footage gives the receiver the existence of an intention: the "penetration" in the routine of that residence in focus, a fact that is confirmed by the display of subsequent images: the room of a couple, a baby and a basket of bread.

At the 00:12, the video resumes the performer's image. In this excerpt the verbal discourse of the song starts. The external image of the same foregoing scenario: under the black and white texture, in close-up the image of Ana Tijoux is shown; this time singing.

The song follows in performance, while the images alternate. At 00:16 it displays the image in silhouette and black and white contrast of two people in an altercation. The scene suggests a fight similar to boxing, since the participants display the size of the sport's typical gloves. At 00:18, still in black and white, a quick "cut" in editing, focuses on the image of a plate, possibly in wood: emphasizing the words *Radio 1 de Mayo,* an established reference to the homonymous radio station, located in Chile.

Built in the 90's, the station's principle is the interest and political participation of the popular classes; beyond the struggle against neoliberalism. The reference to the *Radio 1 de Mayo* ratifies the political and ideological purpose of the song that begins, factor to be confirmed by the rest of the performance's studio (RADIO PRIMEIRO DE MAYO, Accessed on Jul. 31st 2014)

At 00:20 the image of a square draws attention. In it, there are several flags waving. On this fragment, a special effect editing is used: the saturation of a color image amid the rest of the visual context, established under the texture in "black and white" - Note that although the image displays, the square happens in devoid of a color mode, the flags are colored. Another aspect that draws attention is the fact that those flags are representative of Chile, country of origin of the rapper in performance.

The continuity of the videoclip is done through the images alternation: between the image of Tijoux singing, and images of the urban day-by-day. Whether inside the simple houses or in the public space of the city, what is portrayed through the videoclip in question is the existence of an oppressed social group.

Amid the crowds, a succession of images: entire families, adults, children, merchants, musicians... Individuals who inhabit different "every days", but keep one thing in common: the muting and the daily struggle. This fact is proved by the representation of these characters: all depicted with a red ribbon tied on the lips, behind the head - most of the time, these characters appear working on their professional duties; while muted by the red cloth imagistic element, saturated in color, the result of the previously mentioned editing effect.

Of everyday scenes addressed by videoclip, some, in particular, attract the attention of the critical receptor.

At 00:52, for example, the closed plan focuses the image of a single citizen in fighting position. With the mouth shut and wearing a black shirt, the guy looks at the camera, with an expression of determination. A quick cut editing inserts him in a little more complete scene at 00:53, when in a more open plan, he is shown an environment that resembles a square: in it, the same individual appears.

This time in combat. The image, which shows the characters half-length in fighting, is followed by a cut to 00:54 when, once again, the plan closes showing the opponent's features of an individual that externalizes obstinacy and dresses a Puma's brand shirt, sign that can play in the context in question a dual role: while it is an allusion to capitalism, it also depicts the bravery of the citizen. This citizen is a simple man who, like many other men, faces daily obstacles and violence filed by the neoliberal system.

Such an intention is ratified along the execution in this videoclip. By way of illustration, there is the scene of a crowded bus stop, at 00:56.

The scenes are displayed in sync with the discursive content of the song; which at this point focuses in the self-description of the enunciator: "I have empty pockets, chapped lips, skin with scales, every time I look into the void/The soles of my shoes are worn out, hands tied, the gateway always had a sign that said it was closed/a spine spiked and an inflamed wound, resistant anger at the height of everything and nothing."

The combination of music and imagery content allows us, in this sense, to perceive it as the self-description proposed by the song, *a characteristic inherent to the community.* The enunciator in this sense, sings on behalf of many oppressed citizens and at the same time, operative - as they are not subject to stagnation and contentment.

In sequence, the video goes in sync to the verbal content delivered by the song. The images alternate between displaying the performer (Ana Tijoux) and urban routines, starring a muted anonymous - representation which remains established by the red scarf, highlighted by the aforementioned overexposure effect on contrast. The recurrance of the red collor in the scarf image calls the attention of the receiver. It is possible to infer that the use of an accesseory in this color - the same used by the communist or socialist ideological inspiration movements - is a possible performative allusion to urban guerrilla or revolution.

At 01:01 there is a reference to *break* – a street dance, one of the elements that integrates the Hip-Hop Movement.

At 01:13 another highlight arises in relation to the visual music content transmitted by the production. At this point, the image of a violinist in advanced stage of pregnancy appears. She appears simulating an instrumental performance.

The image display coincides with the musical content running - on this stretch, the electronic base remains isolated from verbal rapper speech, simulating an orchestrated performance, in which the melodic content is "assigned" to a small group of stringed instruments.

The scene reflects the individual struggle, which makes this a period when attempting to transition is established: the "deconstruction" of a society immersed in segregation and violence of all kinds , and a "set" of a future context, molded by egalitarian and just bases. It also proves that this rap is a hybrid song, in which mixed elements are traditionally linked to scholasticism in a socially considered "higher" culture and elements of popular culture. In this regard, it highlights, on the one hand, the image of the aforementioned violinist in "performance" (01:13), associated with the presence along the song, of orchestral sounds; and on the other, *break* dancers images (01:03) and a musical group - also in performance - typical of the Andean culture (01:47). The latter even seems to strengthen this link between tradition and modernity that the atino rap usually present in its productions.

At 01:27 there is another proof of this mentioned hybridity. After they have left their daily struggle functions in isolation, anonymous people are gathered at one point of the city, still featuring the red scarf in muting signal. There is a grand contemporary *ballet* shown, which coincides with the "orchestrated" background over which the verbal content of the rapper's refrain is developed: "Breathing to release the voice/Lift flight as far as a swift eagle."

The ballet scene seems to give rise to the existence of an implicit lesson being broadcast by the videoclip: that the fight should not be individual, but rather collective. The production in this sense conveys the idea that only through the joining of individual forces the implementation of the "revolution" and the "deconstruction" of forces touting the neoliberal macro system becomes possible.

In the following video section, there are references to daily muted individuals. At 01:44, there is the image of an anonymous, in front of an old television. Attentive, he watches the testimonial of two men of simple appearance, which prove to be affiliated with the "revolutionary movement".

In 01:47 the image of street musicians is folllowed by that of activists and, again, at the 01:57 count there is a reference to the *Radio Primero de Mayo*.

This time, the studio is led by individuals also connected to militancy. Note, once again, the presence of red cloth on their faces.

The impression conveyed to the audiovisual's receptor is an image of the militant organization that gradually dominates the territories - including the media spaces, most often conducted by alienating logic of the masses - a gregarious movement and counter-hegemony.

The idea of dominating the spaces is confirmed when at the 03:13 mark, the *ballet* performance appears once again, consisting of anonymous people. In this excerpt, the orchestral sound base mingles with the sound of a radio broadcast - which, by analyzing the videoclip, is attested to be an allusion to the activity carried out by *Radio Primero de Mayo*. The ballet resembles a revolutionary movement - resistance and turmoil are performing through the dancer's bodies. The dance takes place at the same time the radio words are transmitted, expressing, at 03:15, a message to its recipients. "Time plunges the dagger/Whatever a person does/Spoils an adjustment."

After the display of *ballet,* the image again takes its focus in the person of Anna Tijoux. In the passage, the performer says the following verses "On a string hung the song that rarely deserves."

At 03:45 begins, in a closed plan, the image of anonymous individuals who, one by one, remove their red scarfs - as the song flows.

Thus, little by little, the actors involved in the music video, remove their scarfs, freed from muting and oppression. The mask that mutes them is the color red, a revolutionary and liberating color.

Its edition and effects confirm this fact, especially at this point of the videoclip. The imagery of the depicted scenario is as follows: each mask removed, faces and bodies - that previously appeared in black and white tones are gradually gaining color, as they get rid of that accessesory.

This "action" suggests, through a metaphor of imagery, the reflection of the rapper singing, the revolutionary aesthetic object, that would be a kind of output to the days of oppression. Music raises awareness. Through its actions, they are designed and earn the chance to come to fruition. The song brings those who mechanically did not understand the meaning of their routines back to life. It encourages the thought that, in turn, it incites action. Hence the great contribution of music, while also an element to awaken political and social positions.

The audiovisual performance comes to an end approximately at the 04:12 mark, leaving a moral legacy to the receiver: that only through the union of minority forces, it is possible to transform the social concept.

After establishing considerations of "*Sacar La Voz*", we will proceed to analyze another production launched by Ana Tijoux: the videoclip "*Schock*".

Schock

Among the videoclips studied in this research, perhaps "*Schock*" is one of the most complex ones. This is due to the production and editing motivations that enable the convergence of a parallel narrative to that established by the performed song in orality, whose contents or verses, were previously analyzed.

In this sense, more than faithfully illustrating the words of the song - until then reduced to audio - the video lends itself also to show a narrative content based on real contemporary events, reported by the international media: the actions related to the Chilean student struggle, the occurrence of which began in April 2011.

In relation to this movement, researchers Lara Antonia Garcia de Melo Alvares and Natalia Monzón Montebello (2013) have manifested in the Article "The student movement of 2011 and the Legitimacy Crisis of the Chilean political system", that explains:

> On April 28, 2011 thousands of students took to the streets of Santiago, protesting the cost of higher education and the consequent high level of student debt. This was the first march of a series that would continue in the coming months, reaching mobilization of approximately 700,000 people in demonstrations spread throughout the country on August 04 of that year, calling for the fall of the "Pinochet education". Across the country, students organized themselves to express their discontent, and the paralyzation of schools, came to last four months. The main complaint of the protesters was the structure of the educational system market, which treats education as a commodity and not as a right, turning it into an agravator of social differences in the country, rather than a mechanism of social ascencion.(ALVARES; MONTEBELLO, 2013, p. 1).

The representation of the student struggle is clearly shown to the viewer at the beginning of the videoclip, an aspect that emphasizes the dialogic potential of the studied production. The short audiovisuals are established in the manner of a documentary. This style certainly endows the production of greater proximity to the real history, displayed in simulacrum, that is, there is a real immanent effect on the production.

At 00:01 white characters arranged on a black background contextualize the receiver, as they exhibit the following words: "Chile 2011".

After establishing the spatiotemporal context of the videoclip, which lasts until the 00:14 mark, the following message appears, also encoded by written white characters arranged on a black background:

Miles de jóvenes se han tomado sus colégios y universidades, exigiendo al gobierno uma educación gratuita y de calidade, despertando a um país enterro.

Paros y huelgas han marcado um ãno repleto de la criatividade constructiva de uma geración que se há atrevido a luchar por la gratuidade del conocimiento.

Thousands of young people took their colleges and universities, demanding from the government a free and quality education, raising an entire country.

Stoppages and strikes marked a year of constructive creativity of a generation that dared to fight for the gratuity knowledge [35] .

After viewing the text fragment, the continuity of the video starts with the testimony of a boy, at the 00:15 mark.

The "character" - that we do not know for sure if real or not - utters the following words: "Nosotros los estudiantes no olvidamos nuestro ser Mapuche" ("We, the students, we have not forgotten our Mapuche[36] essence [37] ").

Noticing the speech of that "student character", the allusion draws attention to "Mapuche" communities, composed of natives inhabiting different regions of Chile and parts of Argentina.

According to researcher Elba Soto (2004) in her doctoral thesis *"In Search of Social Change: Dreams and Struggles of Mapuches in Chile"*, the term "Mapuche" means "people of the land" and refers to the indigenous communities that inhabit different territories of the country, such as the VIII Region of Bio Bio, IX Region Auracania, X Region (Lagoas), Region Pre-Cordillera and the Andes.

---

35 Our translation.

36 "Ma-pu-che: 1. Adj-s. form. (* Índio) coming from Arauco, Chile: Mapuches are also called Araucanians. Mapuche -2- LING. * Language of the Indians of Arauco, Chile: it ~ Amerindian language. Mapuche. "(SEÑAS, 2001, p. 801).

37 Our translation.

According to the researcher, the diversity observed by geographical distance does not prevent the ideological identification of the community, which self-recognizes themselves as "Mapuche". In these terms, the researcher explained:

> Although geographic diversity involves a series of distinct differences between these Mapuche territories such as, for example, climate, soil, customs arising from these geographic differences, etc., it is necessary to emphasize that all these groups are identified as Mapuche, as belonging to one people. All these regional differences are not as relevant, taking into account that within each region different situations are encountered; for example, there are families who no longer speak the Mapuche language, while others in the same region, maintain, with vigor, the language and many of the traditions of this people. In this sense, despite the different assimilation processes, experienced in each of the regions, the Mapuche unite around the conviction of belonging to a specific social formation, resisting all attempts to destroy them and deny them as a people. (SOTO, 2004, p. 23).

According to Soto (2004), in Chile, the Mapuche are one of the most significant ethnic minorities in poverty. Historically known for acting in the resistance against the Spanish Colonial logic - such as the Arauco War, which began in the sixteenth century and lasted for about three hundred years - the Mapuche people resists to this day and struggles for identity and cultural recognition.

According to Soto (2004), there are currently frequent clashes between the Mapuche and the Chilean State, consolidated in "white and European" ideals.

> The Mapuche issue is politically placed as follows: Chilean society has within it a distinct ethnic society with historical and cultural rights of its own. In this context, all the policies have been guided by the criteria of integrating the Mapuche into the national life, a subordinated and partial integration that implies the abandonment of their rights as a people. (SOTO, 2004, p. 24).

Citing Begoa and Valenzuela, researcher Soto (2004) also takes up the following passage:

> (...) The history of relations between Chilean society and Mapuche society can be summed up in the ongoing attempt of the state and the dominant society to prevent the real existence of a culturally different society within the country, and, on the other hand, the indigenous' resistance to fade (BENGOA; VALENZUELA, cited SOTO, 2004, p. 24).

The speech in reference to the Mapuche people demonstrates an existing identification by the student leaders, in relation to the strength of purpose and counter-hegemonic conduct, brought by the indigenous-Mapuche community, throughout history - and whose origins allude to the process of colonization of the country.

The "spokesman" character of the students in his brief speech, attests the purposes of resistance to State actions. In allusion to the the Mapuche ideal, established by a community composed of culturally distinct peoples and separated by geographical area, but integrated by the ideas of group equality and struggle for collective rights - in a way also coincides with the ideological rapper's discourse proposed, in contemporary times, by immigrants located in different parts of the world. Regardless of the regions where it is produced, the speech carries questions that show plurals and at the same time common to minority layers, making up a transnational ideological macro-recognition. The student struggle, the Mapuche struggle, the aesthetic struggle established by foreign rap identify and sympathize in an ideal collective macro that seeks fairer social realities, to be implemented and enjoyed in near future.

In the video, the reference to the student movement, associated with the "character-student" testimony is missing in the recorded audio version of the rap.

Reading the videoclip brings attention to such issues as a kind of supplement to the song. It is until 00:19 that the voice of Ana Tijoux can be heard performing the rap *"Schock"*. "Poisonous your monologues/Your speeches incoloros/Can't you see that we are not alone"

At 00:19 the image of a young woman singing the lyrics appears. Serious face, framed by a hooded sweatshirt, foreshadows an aesthetic message coming from a dark environment. In the surroundings, broken glass (00:21) suggest a ghetto space, forgotten or unknown by those who make up the most affluent classes and ignored by those who make up the dominant sectors. Also, on parallel images of other "young-singers", who engage in "supporting characters" positions, assist in the conduct of the "song-engaged".

The portrait of the young singer, constantly overlaid by a series of images, representative of the student demonstrations and taken from academic spaces by the Chilean youth. The first, portrays at 00:23, the front of an institution called Liceu ML Amunatequi. There is a large banner hanging on the building; curious passers and young people holding placards are portrayed, while persuading the vehicles passing by. It is not possible to read the text on the banner and the poster.

In editing the existence of a filter is noted, capable of establishing a color gradient effect. You can see an orange tone at the bottom of the images, stronger and "lively". This tone gradually disperses when on the upper half of the screen, producing a yellowish effect, "colder" with respect to color perception.

This effect is a constant throughout the videoclip. At 00:25 the focus of the film is limited to display, in close-up, a painted message on the wall: Educacion no es un acto inocente (Education is not an innocent act[38]), signaling the collective perception that the poor quality of education offered by the government reveals an arbitrary intention to create an apathetic population group before the various State directions filed against the social reality.

Between 00:26 and 00:28 a sequence of images is established, in which students are depicted linked to different institutions. Each of them appears in isolated frames, holding a wooden board on which the following information appears carved: student's name and educational institution to which they belong to: Gabriel

---

38 Our translation.

Sepulveda- Liceo Artistico (00:26), Antonia Liceo Emanuel Salas (00:27) and Lagarto- Liceo Amunategui (00:28) are some of the sections covered by the videoclip.

Student profiles are preceded by several images that interchangeably depict the young singer (the same as at the beginning of the videoclip), and images related to the performance of the student movement. Chairs and piled furniture, graphited walls and the image of the very young protagonists: Dever- Liceo M. Cervantes (00:32); Francia Garate- Liceo A131 (00:33), who stands out by using a white mask, showing her mute condition and the registration of her name, established by gluing red letters cut into cardboard and pasted on the wall of the place in which she is; Patricia Nahuelnir - Apoderada (also portrayed at 00:33). The image of this character also draws our attention: an older woman, perhaps representing the figure of a teacher or student's mother. On the nameplate, Patricia does not have the name of a school, but the noun "apoderada", which in English means "person with authority to speak on behalf of others" or "attorney"[39].

At 00:38 another image takes prominence. The simulation of a kind of press conference arises, where several cameramen are portrayed shooting before the young leaders. "The audio remains running musical content, interspersed with different images. Now the portraits of young singers appear - especially of the one occupying the "leading role" in the video, appearing to replace the performer Ana Tijoux; sometimes the spaces are portrayed as taken by the Movement too. Note that the presence of the "young-singers", replacing the performer/composer reverts in an allusion to the seizure of power by the students. The youngsters command everything, including the "song". The presence of the "young-singers" makes us sure of the potential related to the aesthetic-revolutionary representation, which is simulating the "student revolutionary seizure" at the same time that it provides support.

---

39 Our translation.

At 00:43 images begin to appear of people who explicitly express support for the movement depicted. The scene is the same: a character carrying a wooden board on which their identification is inscribed - Max Viv ar- Apoyo a los estudiantes (00:43); Damian Contreras- Ex Dirigiente Aces (00:45).

Already at 00:46, when the music sets the chorus - The time has come! The time has come!/We won't allow anymore/Your doctrine of shock!/The time has come, The time has come!/Doctrine of shock 2x - The external image of the word Schock arises, as if being designed in bright letters on a wall. At this point, we see the use of other resources related to the videoclip: on a black background, the word Schock appears on the screen in the middle of a series of "scratching". Such scratchings, typical of old movies, can metaphorically represent the socio-systemic segregation, set and practiced in national scenarios through the action of the various power agents.

Regarding the editing, the video follows, from beginning to end, the beat of the music, through quick cuts and superimposed images - always depicting the making of spaces and the unique identification of each of the students and their supporters. At 00:53 it draws attention to the image of a girl, a supporting character, who briefly takes on the role of singer - surrounding this character is broken glass, again contextualizes the environment, emphasizing the issue of "scratch-metaphor", a possible allusion to the image of social segregation.

Among the images portrayed the inscriptions made on posters, banners and paintings, set on different walls are emphasized. Some of these inscriptions followed here, translated: (00:47) - "It is better to die standing, than live kneeling"; - "Turn off the TV" (00:48); (00:56) - "Income Card: Limitless Slavery" - (01:02) - "Since when did we become so cowardly to not defend ouselves." Cervantes school. (01:19) - "Our triumph: The Revolution of Consciousness." - LEA. En Toma 2011 (01:24) - "they are afraid because they know that we are not afraid." LEA En Toma, 2011. - (01:52) - "Students are the yeast that will give flavor to the bread that will come out of the oven." (2:00) - "Being young and not revolutionary is a contradiction."

Among the posters, banners and inscriptions displayed by the videoclip, it must be emphasized that those who explicitly state references to capitalist exploitation context usually come accompanied by images or phantasmagoric illustrations that embody the interpretation of systemic reality, as a monstrous kind, to which destructive intentions are attributed - in this sense, two illustrations relating to the above arranged quote stand out: "Turn off the TV" (0'48") and "Income Card: Limitless Slavery"(0'56").

Military, media and political actions appear side by side, through images that overlap following the musical beat. The importance of editing in this sense is notorious next to the beat, it creates a peculiar rhythm: the change of images accompanying the music beat. There is in this regard, the establishment of two cadences dialoguing with each other, which are a set of sound and image, able to materialize the critical intent of the videoclip, to promote resistance to the systemic-capitalist apparatus.

At 02:01 is an image that emphasizes this question. Comes a specific character which resembles a president or dictator. Accompanied by his aides, he enters the Liceu dependencies. His image and actions are preceded and are almost simultaneous to the portrait of the young resistance, relentless in physical and aesthetic actions. The song remains even before the leader who assumes the figure of the oppressor.

Among the 02:09 and 02:22 mark, the song is stopped. A short montage is made up, which again establishes the documentary style. In this section various student's testimonials are displayed, whose translation and description of associated images is established below:

- Between 02:09 and 02:11: The scene depicts a young man who appears in front of a graffitied wall. The drawn image is of a man holding a type of hammer. The design also suggests the representation of a fight. In front of the graphite, the character makes the following statement: "We want to eradicate education as a business. Education should be a social right."

- Between 02:13 and 02:15: The pictured environment seems to be the inside of an academic institution. In this context, it shows the image of a boy, lying, using a white mask; for us, representative of the social muting, contested by the videoclip. In testimony, this character makes the following observation: "This social movement becomes greater every day."

- Between 02:16 and 02:22: The pictured environment seems to be the balcony of a house. The testimonial of a young woman appears who standing, explains: "It's not just a movement of people in the streets protesting, but also to create an awareness and commitment among those involved."

The student image is interleaved with a poster in which, below the figure of a traffic signal the following words appear: "No law will bury public education." While the poster is displayed, the statement is continued in audio.

At 02:22, the song is taken up in the follow-up "music video model". The editing remains with the original style. Characters that portray young students and individuals in solidarity, with respect to the fight established by the student movement, are shown on the image. All carrying wooden boards, which contain individual identities. Editing cutouts overlap those images to specific actions related to the movement. The notion of a scenario is provided which gradually gets dark. Pictured are several inscriptions on the walls (texts and drawings) and signs emanating messages in support of the movement. Among the texts in evidence, some assume prominence portraying resistance practices filed against the centralizing measures of the government, directed mainly to the field of education.

- At 02:26, writting is set on the wall, bearing the words: "I declare myself guilty of being born in this system. Fight it to the end!".

- 02:53, a grand sign, in which the words are written: "On hunger strike for education day".

-02:53 A graphic pastiche (poster), which is represented by the image of a member of the Ku Klux Klan - racist and criminal organization, founded in the United States at the end of the nineteenth century- torturing someone. It is noted in part that there is a dollar sign drawn on the hood of this character.

From the point of view of reception the capacity of audiovisuals to display the poster in question can be seen in superimpose practices and temporality, which will allow for different readings of history.

Alluding to the existence of an ancient criminal organization (whose work, remains to this day) and assigning it to the representation of dollar sign - symbols referring to the neoliberal system and its economic-capitalist reality - the image enables the emergence of reflections different in relation to the traditional narrative, with respect to matters relating to the present, society and the general history.

The videoclip "allows", the receiver to see and conjecture around what is "not visible" (AUMONT, 1993), what usually goes unnoticed, either because of ignorance rooted by force of hegemonic traditional narratives or even troubled everyday dynamics. Like other media devices, audiovisual therefore provides interpretations of systemic objectives which determine the gear of society and thus creates "(...) fictional environments in which spheres of power, historically specific, become visible" (SHOHAT; STAM, 2006, p. 145).

The imagistic passage in question is revealed in the light of the interpretation set out in this study, as a way to alert and bring awareness to potential receivers so that they are not fooled by the promises of the capital, governed by the larger goal of profit and devoid of any precautions correlated to non-oppression.

- At 02:56, there is the image of the Chilean flag, tainted by a stamp in which the symbol (R) appears; which makes us infer that it's meant to be a symbol related to the revolution proposed by the student movement. This image is preceded by images of the arrival of the military, coupled with the idea of repression. At 03:02 there is the picture of the young resistance and the clash locked to those who represent power.

Arriving at the end of the video segment in which the notion of overlapping images remains, there are actions associated with the individual presentation of the militants and their supporters, a scene surprises. At 03:11 Ana Tijoux's image arises that under the condition of supportive to the cause, she appears holding a plate labeled "*Apoyo a Los Estudiantes*" (I support the students).

From start to finish, the video constantly goes on, always following the same idea. Inscriptions, all the time, attract the attention of the receiver.

- At 03:13 the image of a wall, with the following words written: "*El motor de la historia es la lucha de clases*" (The motor of history is the class struggle).

- At 03:16, another wall on which the phrase: "*Revolucion Compañeros*" (Revolution, brothers) is inscribed.

The video ends with the identification of the young student who began the performance of the song, taking over from Ana Tijoux as the main performer during entire videoclip. At the 03:42 mark the "character" is filmed in silence - the song continues running, although only as a musical background of the videoclip. Like other "characters portrayed", the young woman appears carrying a wooden board which states the proper identification: Javiera Toro-Liceo Artistic Exp.

The closing of the videoclip is between 03:44 and 03:46, when once again the word Schock in bright letters appears, the title of the rapper's song. Under the black background, and again filled with "scratchy" effects established by the editing, the image precedes the technical specifications of the product.

"*Schock*" is an audiovisual that records the struggle of students in favor of a quality public education. The imagistic content associated with the lyrics on performance is a final product that takes the role of a bridge to the aesthetic field, a small sample of the numerous and violent social conflicts existing in real life.

It is relevant in this regard to recall the argument of Ivana Bentes (2003), in the Article "*Estéticas da Violência no Cinema*". According to the researcher, violence is a way of thinking of the present, since the beginning of audiovisual language, but that currently intensifies in its projections, manifesting at the same time, under the political and aesthetics forms (catharsis).When talking about productions that follow, this line tells us:

> It is through violent images that the new marginalized hurt and violate the world that has rejected them, it is through images that they are demonized by the media, but also by the image that they appropriate media and its resources of seduction, glamourization, performance and spectacle, in order to exist socially. (BENTES, 2003, p. 6).

In fact, the video "works" as an aesthetic "reply" to the administrative malfeasance affecting the Chilean educational sector; and the repressions carried out before the student community, the government, in its control mechanisms and maintenance of order: "No longer allow your shock doctrine" - "shouts" all the time in the production.

Analyzing the videoclip Schock allows us to see that a production-aesthetic can establish dialogue and identification before social issues for the territory in which it is produced. By supporting the production of a videoclip which establishes an overlay to that emanated narrative only by the performance of the song, the Franco-Chilean rapper takes the engagement before the social issues that take place within her country of origin, demonstrating support for the student movement. Moreover, while she tells us about a national-Chilean question, it also critically portrays, especially through the images, the harm brought by capitalism and history.

Once launched in the cyberspace, Schock reveals a critical eye that can "shape memory" (SHOHAT, STAM, 2006) and the thought of being sympathetic to the performed cause and/or having similar stigmas. The audiovisual production is, therefore, something that inspires, while "escapeing" the goals and standards set by traditional narratives, hegemony, centralized and usually of European or North American heritage.

Communication is established, thus, as a "line of flight", a "transformation", escaping to vertical and homogeneous standards advocated by the mass media. These "new" forms of representation, made possible by the use of alternative media, can lead to one conclusion: that the overall effects of neoliberalism often are felt and experienced, similarly, in the various territories of the world.

Shohat and Stam (2006) remind us of the importance of the identity assumed by the media today. The researchers state that:

> Contemporary media form identities; in fact, many would argue that they are very close to the identities' production center. In a transnaciona l world, characterized by global movement of images and sounds, goods and people, they have huge impact on national identity and sense of community. By promoting interpretations between distant people, the media "deterritorialize" possibilities to imagine a community life. And if, on the one hand, they can destroy communities and incorate loneliness to turn viewers into isolated consumers or self-sufficient monads, they can also promote the sense of community and alternative affiliations. As the media can promote the otherness of certain cultures [..] they can encourage multicultural connections.(SHOHAT; STAM, 2006, p. 27-28.).

It is through the point of view of dispossession, mentioned by Shohat and Stam (2006), that this analysis, of the *"Shock"* video is established. We found that the production keeps the political purpose of differentiated aesthetic, demonstrating the fractional and authentic face of the "society of the spectacle". Aesthetic that target "other" publics, perhaps non-privileged socio-economically; that act in order to externalize and incite factors such as creativity, strength, identity recognition and revaluation of values.

Set out the considerations of this production, we will move to the next item of our work, which is the analysis of the music video: *"Pássaro Imigrante"*.

Pássaro immigrante

Rails and movement contextualize a train ride. The internal transport image intercalates the figure of a man, always lost in the urban chaos. The closed plan provides the image of half the body of the character. Dressed in a gray blouse, he is lost in the environment, whose photograph shows to be a subway station. The video display externalizes, an initially artisanal means of production. The camera in hand and the application of filter effects during the edition, give to the audiovisual an aspect of aging, characterized by certain spots in the statement of the slightly distorted images.

The scene, silently extends to the 00:20 mark when this same man, accompanied by a sound base, opens the song. Closed up, the camera focuses on him: a lone passenger in the midst of urban chaos, shown through the edition, sometimes in and sometimes out of the train.

Synchronic to the performance in orality, the video content confirms the song as a sung presentation of consciousness, expressed through the image of a immigrant obstinate before the foreign territory in which he is.

Devoid of any inserts or legend, the discursive content of the song - which was fully transcribed and analyzed throughout the research - shows the presence of a versified orality, in which the enunciator manifests from metaphors, anaphora, and in most often, using rhyme. In this sense, there is the opening words of the song:

> I come from the immense blue, this land promises
> Here I am one more, against the puppets
> Ducks go south, parrot repeats
> My nest I will build, do not meddle
> My freedom I myself generate
> My passport is a mere detail zero
> From those I consider sincere, I do not hope
> They cut my wings, I recover

The body of the song reveals, side by side in the image, the certainty of loneliness of immigrants in the urban context and the necessary will to overcome all obstacles through work and faith.

The metropolis is a scenario of many dangers: easy women, bad influences, drugs and charlatans. The song tells an insistent life, of those who need to have a "wise mind" and an "Eagle gaze" to live immersed in difficulties that reveal the preconception of the country in which he has decided to inhabit.

Walking inside a train, says the enunciator, free bird "You search your flock/Your race ignores you/Always rebuffing you/ Some kind of Captivity".

Excluded by "humans" of little "humanity", the performer appears lonely too amidst the audiovisual simulacrum and remains so for most of the video. The image of the character-rapper singing his message, contrasts compared to other train passengers. The bank in which the performer appears to be sitting, has an empty seat. All static sign of indifference, before the "musical trip". Only at the count 01:14 mark, this place is occupied by two seconds when there is an individual accommodated who appears singing the chorus with the main performer of the videoclip (MC Indigesto).

Everything seems to show an old context. This impression is confirmed when, between the time-code 01:16 and 01:19 the use of masks editing feature used to insert cuts amid the main imagistic text - images of old news are displayed, probably related to the experience abroad.

In 01:26 the camera's focus gets cut up. The scene is the exterior image of the moving train itself. The feeling of aging now mixes the idea of separation: although the enunciator talks from inside the said means of transport, he does not seem to be integrated to that. From the train he sends a message to the world, whose blurred and representative image by the "sign-train" refers to the texture of the mass alienation.

In the section that extends between 01:28 and 01:30 another section calls attention: the focus on the security monitor, inside a subway station; followed by a window image, expressing the view from within the train. In this stretch, the "immigrant trip" is translated by the videoclip. The application of filters makes the scene slightly dark and the footage shows having been performed from the use of a camera with very low quality; typical characteristics of old equipment.

Semantically, we could infer that the bothersome and relatively poor image has been used on purpose, as a kind of "translation" of the territory assigned to the marginalized voice: the place of the ghetto, the "ignored", where aesthetics are "dirty" and "indefinite", a result of a controlled non-recognition. Under the latter, once again, we emphasize the presence of the monitor, refering to the ubiquitous mechanisms of control, active front of the whole social context.

Between the timecodes 01:42 and 01:46 the audio quality is transformed into an effect. The sound that was clear before, appears compromised in this passage, showing the likeness of an archaic radio broadcast. Virtually serving a noise function before the totality of the sound is presented, this stretch ratifies the reference to the archaic again, as the only possibility of minority classes and at the same time, susceptible to the element of strangeness to interpretant postures.

Imagistic scraps demonstrate the inflated metropolis of people running in all directions. The exterior urban setting is toggled with the interior of the station. The MC is seen sometimes in and sometimes out of the subway station, always running, always controlled, always alone; with a vague and wandering gaze.

The song goes on and, amid the big city, the effort of the immigrant is as valuable as the currency. Repeatedly the voice of the MC sings: "Blood, sweat and tears are more than oil."

From 02:17 the edition shows an MC walking around town while singing. The stretch from 02:15 to 02:25 is noteworthy in this segment. Observant, the MC finds himself amid a protest. The image shows the clustering of militant people carrying flags in protest, but also military action through the use of pumps and trucks, showing the repressive and violent attitude of the power agents.

With the lost and apprehensive look amid such a scene, the character searches for a direction to follow. Although he appears silent on the image, on the background of the performance, the song remains. Then comes the chorus of the song on the background, a summary of immigrant daily life, insistence before the unknown city. In the clip, the chorus is added to the intertextual phrase "loneliness terrifies" performed in a melodic mode compared to other verses.

Chorus 2x:

Better one in the hand than two in the bush
In a distant world
Nothing is as before
Time to break away from the pack
Up and above
Immigrant bird

At 02:29, the walk gives way to a race. The MC, now with a desperate look, crosses the city, terrified and always chased by black pigeons, associations established before in the music that suggest the representation of vultures, carrion birds that, in the song, symbolically appear as references to the systemic-capitalist image.

The edition remains displaying clippings related to news and life of the city. At 02:31 "the background music is muted. There is only the image of the MC running, his frightened features and monitoring of the musical beat. At 02:39, in open - plan, you can see the full picture of the character-performer. We can see in this passage the full clothing he uses: gray knitted sweater, blue jeans and sneakers, simple clothing, also characteristic of other rappers.

The context continues until the 02:50 timecode when the MC falls on a demarcated area. The body of the scene lying on the ground and inert is contrasted by the image of a lake; representing a prime area of the city. The water, full of swans swimming, translates the landscape of big cities and their sectioning: while lives are snuffed out in the forgotten ghettos, the white-bourgeois routine proceeds in its normal course of indifference.

Surrounded by curious and inert onlookers, the body of the MC character is attacked, at 03:00 by "vultures", filmed in defocused mode and in black and white colors which, in a more extensive visual interpretation, could confirm the aforementioned metaphor of a devouring capitalist system.

After the analysis, it is concluded that the process translated into image-video, ratifies the verbalized content of the song and its purpose: to raise awareness and show the world the ills and difficulties that permeate the foreign experience across the globe.

To Κέρμα (Coin)

When analyzing *"To Κέρμα"* immediately, at the first second, the impression one has of what one will watch comes as if running from a typical old movie projector. This perception comes both from the noise, common to machines of this kind, and from the preview image when you have the display of the MC-performer's face, centered on a kind of frame, at the time count of 00:01.

In sequence, we have, at 00:02, the same frame with the image of the MC, but with a kind of subtitle, which states the title of the audiovisual track. In 0:03 simulating the typing performed by a typewriter, the signature of the artist performer arises: MC Yinka. By typing, letter by letter, in white tones over black background, focus the attention of the listener-spectator creating, like an epigraph, tension and expectation for the establishment of initial contact in relation to the performed aesthetic content .

At 0:10 the performance effectively starts. The electronic beat, associated with some vocal sounds delivered by the performer correspond to the musical background of the following scenario: sitting in a living room, MC Yinka appears in front of a TV. When operating the remote control repeatedly, which entails an understanding there on the scene, the theatricality of a dissatisfaction with the media content, the MC ends up quitting this monitoring, turning the device off, which can be found at the timecode 00:20.

The scene, which suggests a kind of critical-aesthetic in the face of the alienating power exerted by the massive communication apparatus, which has as an output the exit of the performer from this context. Leaving the comfort zone of the living room, the rapper starts, at 00:21, the performance of spoken song, which takes place in sync with the performed content image.

The context externalizes a combative and conscious aesthetic stance. Refusing the domination of hegemonic ideologies, the issuer sends his message. The videoclip aesthetics assumes then a certain constancy in the image/sound texture: with a black background and focus on the light falling on the performer, the product demonstrates the intention to set the receiving attention before the song. More than any aesthetic shell, what matters is what is being said, i.e. the message.

This fact coincides with the poetic-narrative theme. If we think of the song in its entirety, we are provided, by the title, a reference to a game of "heads or tails". Pragmatically, the "coin" remains "in the air" and is referenced as such in the rapper's song, which also wins "invisible allusions" established by the image shown. Noteworthy are accordingly specific stretches - as initiated in 0:25 when the lens is blurred around the imagistic frame, except for the hands of the singer, calling the viewer's attention to the movement of the fingers, drawing the hand "in air". The meta-language established between the sung orality and imagery of the performance favors the concentration of the listener/viewer.

The idea of clarifying the message is shown at 01:04 when there is an image overlay; so the rapper appears duplicate, simulating a conversation with himself. The content of the conversation is output by the music, which in this stretch leads to the interpretation of self-questioning: - Do we live or just exist?/- Truth! Have we found you or do we know you?/Articulate or just talk?/Study or just read? Regarding the "two" characters performing this scene, we emphasize one fact: the image of the speaker comes in a slightly larger size of that in which the receiver displays it. Also drawing attention, are the colors of the shirts used by the performer: the version that "speaks" uses blue; counteracting with the version that is "listening", in which the rapper uses red.

From this passage the song is edited in parts in which either the enunciator appears singing to wearing a red shirt, or a blue one; which demonstrates, once again, an allusion to the game "heads or tails", thus demonstrating the two sides of a coin.

At 01:37 there is the use of a kind of security camera positioned in the direction of the transmitter of the performance. The image view of the black and white tones gives the context an aura of mystery and investigation. In 01:43 an editing feature gives the picture a stormy aspect. The hands of the issuer under the special effect, leave stains on the screen and the impression of being several hands. The turmoil aspect coincides with the reference to the media made in the song - "Screen Characters, athletic idols, examples/ bright retouched faces falling/Over the lustful eyes of lies show," says the issuer, alluding image and voice to the issues of exhaustion by the excess of information and ideological manipulation.

Regarding the use of images, at 02:08 a small change is noted. On the background of the performer, the video externalizes a parallel scenario: the image of an army walking in arms, associated with landscapes on fire. The scenes in the background appear out of focus - this, in turn, still focusing on the performer, who promotes the idea that the scenario exists only to illustrate an obscure reality of terror; and the song is always put under a condition of greater importance than the content viewed through the videoclip. In this section the cuts in the edition also draw attention. If before, in a way, they were presented synchronously to the musical beat, in this passage they take place at a slightly higher speed.

At 02:52 when the rapper's song externalizes complaints to the mechanisms of order, we emphasize these in the verses: "peace, order and security, military helmets/Maintainers of the blue order, servants of civilians/ Superheroes with cover and sword/fight daily to ensure justice "- there again the sync editing and the singing voice.

Although the musical beat remains the same, we note in sequence several cuts, established one after the other, associated with some flash effects on the image. Regarding the latter, we highlight the scene recorded in 03:11, when the effect in flash dialogues also with the sung content: "tear gas, panic" says the voice , while the image is in instability intentions.

The edition in this sense gives, through the videoclip, a certain synesthesia, approaching the receiver to the violent intensity of the narrated actions, the implementation of which is attributed to the presence of power agents.

The editing intensifies in effects on the extent to which the videoclip is nearing the end. Approximately at 03:17 cuts intensify, even at the end, after several repetitions of the chorus: "See See the truth as you want/The coin is in the air, heads or tails?" is said by the enunciator. The final thirty seconds, above all, demonstrate the acceleration of cuts, so that they accompany the musical beat, even in the absence of spoken words.

After establishing the analysis of the "*Το Κέρμα*" (2010) videoclip, we will now turn to the final considerations of this work.

Final considerations

This work took on the challenge of trying to understand the foreign aesthetics, represented by the immigrant rapper song, produced in our time: A time guided by the neoliberal logic and use of technological increasingly advanced devices... Where social differences are shown as glaring to the point of living together side by side, constituting a problem that, as the system, is also global.

Based on this finding, we searched the internet for immigrant rapper productions, from different artists and different regions: MC Yinka (Africa/Greece), Ana Tijoux (Chile/France); Yoka (Brazil/World) and Tensais MCS (Brazil/Japan). After meeting their works, we have selected sparse songs. Productions that, as previously exposed throughout the work, despite having been recorded in CDS-Vinyl, gained wide dissemination through the cyberspace through their digital versions, availability for free to download or offered for sale online.

Such productions, similar to what is known in general terms for "ideological rap", kept, in the light of the investigative process, which was the preparation of this research, as a challenging way to traditionalists standards for the production of songs.

Among the characteristics presented, they have shown to be hard-hitting in verbal aspect and hybrid framework in musical sphere, as they showed full effects of which were remarkable cultural references that come from multiple traditions, implemented in conjunction with electronic databases, able to ratify the technological presence already entrenched throughout the world on these contemporary times. More than that, such songs suggested the need to become known, since they seemed to be important reasons for organizing potential discussions on campuses.

In addition to these similarities, these productions also possessed another feature: extense lyrics propagated without the use of inserts containing the written record of their official discursive content. The absence of these records was given in both placements via the internet, as in the productions themselves - CDs and Vinyl.

To establish a more complete and thorough understanding around the discourse of these songs; and with the help of native speakers and experts, we set out to accomplish the transcription, translation and interpretation of them.

As contextual factor base for this process, we established the rescue of important philosophical and cultural theories related to various axes of themes - for example, globalization, cultural translation, issues related to foreignness, structural poverty, art and performance.

We use in this sense, the thoughts of authors such as Zygmunt Bauman (1999), Roger Haesbaert (2009), Julia Kristeva (1994), Mike Davis (2006), Stuart Hall (2007), Hommi Bhabha (2007), Patrice Pavis (2010), Mikhail Bakthin (1979; 1992), Richard Schustermann (1998) and Richard Rorty (2005;2007) - the latter two even exponents of neopragmatist philosophy, contemporary philosophical current, through which the ideological rap is constituted as a major aesthetic-dialogic production, established from the experiences inherent to social groups considered as minorities, providing clarification on the political and gregarious positioning of these same groups.

In order to verify, in practical terms, the existence of this dialogue and associate it to the globalized reality and its consequent structural poverty - after the theoretical exposure - we, then, proceeded the interpretative analysis of selected songs.

Given the finding of common-themes, the lyrics, already translated and transcribed, were separated and analyzed in four thematic subsections, so called: 1) In the crowd, another one wants to be someone "who am I and who are you" regarding statements and identity perceptions within foreigner rapper songs. 2) Among the capital jungles, acculturation, violence and resistent faith: the system, the origins and the holy sung by the immigrant mass; 3) To cross borders, guide or simply survive: the rap word, libertarian aesthetic of conscious and abandoned voices, and 4) Considerations on a different track and (in) "Definitely [Instrumental]".

Thus, within these categories analysis-interpretation was made and the thematic grouping of songs, a process that could prove, in the midst of selected performances, the dialogism theorized by Bakhtin (1979;1992), and the "aestheticization of ethics" advocated in neopragmatist precepts of philosophy; both inherent characteristics to immigrant rappers performances.

Located in different parts of the world, foreign rappers-appearing to have been similarly affected by the experiences set forth in their routines - transfer to the musical discourse the experience of new-diasporas, guided by mechanisms of exclusion, denial and identity negotiations; and experienced and supported by multiple behaviors conducted by sentimental sensorialities involving discomfort, anger, longing, despair, disbelief and at the same time hope for better days.

From these experiences, the foreign rapper also transforms the song into a guiding tool, aimed at others who live or think in similar exile conditions. Revolutionary, the immigrant rapper song makes up the ideological type, operating thus on the social pragmatics. Note that the elaborative action and enforceability of these songs always part of an emotional-border state, as such, productions arise from the threshold between feelings of anguish and oppression caused by living in society, and the will to survive and construction, was also born in this context.

Thus, the assessment of a foreign rapper song materializes as a "manual" for survival in exile and living with global practices, as proposed through promoting politicized resistance actions, possible feelings erupt from the union between individuals convicted by the neoliberal system to marginality condition.

In each of the analyzed productions, it was possible to realize the strict selection of vocabulary intended to integrate the rapper speech. Such discourses take place amid the realities of migrating from which many hardships emanate when composers empower the word and put the condition of "materiality towards a reflective function", thus generating combative and evaluative performances of reality. From the sung word memories and positions echo, often seeking reform of deeply rooted values in society; precepts that ratify the segregation and exclusion proceedings before the neoliberal spaces. The song is, therefore, an active instrument for building a great social reform.

In this sense, the song while music in confirming what is signaled by José Miguel Wisnik in The Sound and Sense: "(...) music speaks as the horizon of society and the subjective vertex of each one (...) The music rehearses and anticipates those changes that are taking place, which will happen, or should take place in society. " (WISNIK, 2009, p 13).

The intend of engagement, present in rap songs, intensifies in perceptions when we read the recorded video performances. Thus, after the section in which we have established the translation and interpretive study of songs in audio, we analyzed four audiovisual productions related to some of the rappers songs, selected to compose the thesis of this study.

Thus, we sought to analyze Sacar la voz (2012), Shock (2011); Pássaro Imigrante(2011); Το Κέρμα (2010), in order to identify how the imagistic content associated with assemblies and effects established by edition, enabling a macro understanding of the communication established at first instance by the performance in recorded audio.

Analyzing the videos, taking into account the possibilities of semiotic translation, enabled us to establish a more critical exercise. We realized in each of the four productions, that the effects related to the issue, which associated with the displayed image (often, too, in the form of a theatrical performance), reinforcing the content of the lyrics and confirming our thesis that foreign rap, following assumptions of the ideological rapper, tells of historical issues and territorial experiences in the present reality, addressing problems like: structural poverty characterized by disrespects of social, economic and humanitarian order; and experiences, in this case analyzed, by immigrants and their descendants.

In this research immigrant productions from diverse territorialities were studied, which describe similar situations and permeated by shared sensorialities. Audios and specific subjectivities externalize videos that exceed in intensity the provisions of content in ordinary practice of ideological rap-anxiety, loneliness, anger, criticism of centralizing realities, capitalism, globalization; strengthening identity, union between the marginalized layers, remembrance and recognition of culture and family history. All these feelings and purposes gain weight when living in exile, the flashpoint of labor exploitative practices, feeling the gaping societal prejudices, nostalgia. A weight that originates in the oppression of every day absurd practices, a weight that leads to revolt and reverses into art.

The aestheticized revolt in rap becomes thus under the baton of critical foreign-looking, a sort of driving force, determined by a transformative ideal. At the same time that it punctuates individualized political-territorial issues, it sympathizes with the struggle of other minority groups and is spread due to the technological facilities of our time.

Although set apart, in relation to the physical space in which they are made, such immigrant productions have familiar themes - inherent in these territories own production and enunciation origin. These are productions that, above all, depict the societal context of the present world; depositing in our "multiterritories" digital aesthetic documents certifying and socializing the transformative intentions of those in exile; constituting a kind of cry that calls for change. A cry that, at the look of a reader-translator may suggest the possibility of new connections and cultural exchanges, provided by the virtual union forces that are shown engaged in conducting a passionate ideological purpose: the revolution in universal scope.

References

ANTISERI, Dario; REALE, Giovanni. História da Filosofia: de Freud à atualidade. Vol. 7. São Paulo: Paulus, 2011.

ALVARES, Lara Antonia Garcia de Melo; MONTEBELLO, Natália Monzón. O movimento estudantil de 2011 e a crise de legitimidade do Sistema Político Chileno. Disponível em: <http://www2.espm.br/sites/default/files/pagina/lara_antonia_alvares_-_ii_semic_2013_0.pdf.>. Acesso em: 31 jul. 2014.

APPLE, Michael; TEITELBAUM, Kenneth. John Dewey. Disponível em http://www.fundaj.gov.br/geral/educacao_foco/dewey.pdf. Acesso em Acesso em 04. fev. 2014.

ARISTÓTELES. Arte retórica e arte poética. Rio de Janeiro: Ediouro, 1990.

AUMONT, Jacques. A imagem. Campinas, SP: Papirus, 1993.

BAKTHIN, Mikhail. Marxismo e filosofia da linguagem. São Paulo: Hucitec, 1979.

_____. Estética da criação verbal. São Paulo: Martins Fontes, 1992.

BARBOSA, Ana Mae. John Dewey e o Ensino da Arte no Brasil. São Paulo: Cortez, 2002.

BARTHES, Roland. Aula. São Paulo: Cultrix, 2004.

BAUMAN, Zygmunt. Globalização: as consequências humanas. Rio de Janeiro: Zahar, 1999.

BENJAMIN, Walter. O narrador: considerações sobre a obra de Nikolai Leskov. In:

_____. Obras escolhidas: magia e técnica, arte e política. São Paulo: Brasiliense, 1994.) p. 197-221. (Obras Escolhidas; v. 1).

_____. Magia e técnica, arte e política. São Paulo: Brasiliense, 2004.

BENTES, Ivana. Estética da violência no cinema. Revista Semiosfera, Rio de Janeiro, ed.especial, p. 1-8, dez. 2003.

HABHA, Homi K. O local da cultura. Belo Horizonte: UFMG, 2007.

BORGES, Ana Isabel; NERCOLINI, Marildo José. Tradução cultural: transcriação de si e do outro. Terceira Margem, v. 7, n. 8, p. 138-154, 2003.

BOSCO, Francisco. Cinema canção. In: NESTROVSKI, Arthur (Org.). Lendo Música: 10 ensaios sobre 10 canções. São Paulo: Publifolha, 2007.

BUORO, Anamélia Bueno. O olhar em construção: uma experiência de ensino e aprendizagem da arte na escola. São Paulo: Cortez, 2000.

BURKE, Peter. Hibridismo cultural. São Leopoldo: UNISINOS, 2006. (Coleção Aldus).

BURKE, Peter; HSIA, R. Po-chia (Org.). A tradução cultural nos primórdios da Europa Moderna. São Paulo: UNESP, 2009.

CAMPOS, Augusto. Entrevista a João Queiroz. [20--]. Disponível em: <http://www. Academia. Edu/379271/sobre_ tradução_ intersemiótica>. Acesso em: 30 mar. 2013.

CANCLINI, Néstor Garcia. Consumidores e cidadãos: conflitos multiculturais da globalização. Rio de Janeiro: UFRJ, 1995.

_____. Culturas híbridas: estratégias para entrar e sair da modernidade. São Paulo: USP, 2008.

CÂNDIDO, Antonio. Dialética da malandragem: caracterização das Memórias de um
Sargento de Milícias. In: ALMEIDA, Manoel Antônio. Memórias de um Sargento de Milícias. Rio de Janeiro: Livros Técnicos e Científicos, 1978.

CARLSON, Marvin. Performance: uma introdução crítica. Belo Horizonte: UFMG, 2010.

CASTELLS, M. A sociedade em rede. 11. ed. São Paulo: Paz e Terra, 2008.

CHEVALIER, Jean; CHEERBRANT, Alain. Dicionário de símbolos. 13. ed. Rio de Janeiro: José Olímpio, 1999.

COHEN, Renato. Performance como linguagem: criação de um tempo-espaço de experimentação. São Paulo: Perspectiva, 2002.

CORREIA, Marlene de Castro. Drummond: a magia lúcida. Rio

de Janeiro: Jorge Zahar, 2002.

CORNELIS, de Wall. Sobre Pragmatismo. Tradução de Cassiano Terra Rodrigues. São Paulo: Loyola, 2007

CUNHA, Marcus Vinícius da. Educador e filósofo da democracia. Educação, História da Pedagogia, fascículo 6, p. 6-17, dez. 2011.

DAZZANI, Maria Virgínia Machado. Rorty e a Educação. Belo Horizonte: Autêntica, 2010.

DAVIS, Mike. Planeta favela. São Paulo: Boitempo, 2006.

DELEUZE, Gilles.; GUATTARI, Félix. Mil platôs: capitalismo e esquizofrenia. São Paulo: Editora 34. 1997. v. 5.

DEWEY. John. Experiência e Educação. São Paulo: Companhia Editora Nacional, 1974.

_____. Experiência e Natureza. São Paulo: Abril Cultural, 1980.

_____. Meu Credo Pedagógico. Tradução: Bruna Gibson. Disponível em http://docslide.com.br/documents/23016719-john-dewey-meu-credo-pedagogico.html. Acesso em 04 fev.2014.

DONKIN, Richard. Sangue, suor e lágrimas: a evolução do trabalho. São Paulo: M. Books do Brasil, 2003.

DURKHEIM, Emile. Sociologia, Pragmatismo e Filosofia. Tradução: Evaristo Santos. Porto Portugal, Portugal: Rés Editora. Lda. S. D

FERREIRA, Aurélio Buarque de Holanda. Alano. In: DICIONÁRIO AURÉLIO ILUSTRADO. Curitiba: Positivo, 2010. p. 88.

_____. Limbo. In: DICIONÁRIO AURÉLIO ILUSTRADO. Curitiba: Positivo, 2010. p. 1266.

_____. Pirâmide. In: DICIONÁRIO AURÉLIO ILUSTRADO. Curitiba: Positivo, 2010. p. 1642.

_____. Samurai. In: DICIONÁRIO AURÉLIO ILUSTRADO. Curitiba: Positivo, 2010. p. 1884.

FINNEGAN, Ruth. O que vem primeiro: a palavra, a música ou a performance? In: MATOS, Cláudia Neiva de; TRAVASSOS,

Elizabeth; MEDEIROS, Fernanda Teixeira (Org.). Palavra cantada: ensaios sobre poesia, música e voz. Rio de Janeiro: 7 Letras, 2008.

FRYE, Northrap. Quarto ensaio: crítica retórica: teoria dos gêneros. In: _____. Anatomia da crítica. São Paulo: Cultrix, 1973.

GARCIAS, Carlos Mello; AFONSO, Jorge Augusto Callado. Revitalização de rios urbanos. Revista Eletrônica de Gestão e Tecnologias Ambientais (GESTA), v. 1, n. 1, p. 131-144, 2013. Disponível em: <http://www.portalseer.ufba.br/index.php/gesta/article/download/7111/4883>. Acesso em: 01 set. 2014.

GINZBURG, Jaime. Drummond e o pensamento autoritário no Brasil. In: WALTY, Ivete; CURY, Maria Zilda (Org.). Drummond: poesia e experiência. Belo Horizonte: Atlântica, 2002.

GILROY, Paul. O Atlântico Negro: modernidade e dupla consciência. São Paulo: Ed 34, 2001.

GLISSANT, Édouard. Introdução a uma poética da diversidade. Juiz de Fora: UFJF, 2005.

GOMES, Tiago de Melo. Gente do Samba: malandragem e identidade nacional no final da Primeira República. 2007. Disponível em <http://www.revistatopoi.org/numeros_anteriores/topoi09/topoi9a7.pdf.>. Acesso em: 08 jul. 2014.

GOODWIN, Andrew. Dancing in The Distraction Factory: Music, Television and Popular Culture. Minneapolis: University of Minnesota, 1992.

GROOVE, George; SADIE, Stanley. Dicionário Grove de música. Edição concisa. Rio de Janeiro: J. Zahar, 1994.

HAESBAERT, Rogério. O mito da desterritorialização: do "fim dos territórios" à multiterritorialidade. 4. ed. Rio de Janeiro: Bertrand Brasil, 2009.

HALL, Stuart. Da diáspora: identidades e mediações culturais. Belo Horizonte: UFMG, 2003.

_____. A identidade cultural na pós-modernidade. Rio de Janeiro: DP&A, 2007.

HERMANN, Nadja. Ética e estética: a relação quase esquecida. Porto Alegre. EDIPUCRS, 2005.

HOLZBACH, Ariane; NERCOLINI; Marildo José. Videoclipe em tempos de reconfigurações. Revista Famecos: mídia, cultura e tecnologia, v. 1, n. 39, 2009. Disponível em: <http://revistaseletronicas.pucrs.br/ojs/index.php/revistafamecos/article/view/5841/4235>. Acesso em: 31 jul. 2014.

HONNETH, Axel. Luta por reconhecimento: a gramática moral dos conflitos sociais.são Paulo: Ed. 34, 2003.

INDIGESTO. Pássaro imigrante. Disponível em: <https://www.youtube.com/watch?v=YC586ECtsz8 >. Acesso em: 12 ago. 2011.

JAKOBSON, Roman. Linguística e comunicação. 24. ed. São Paulo: Cultrix, 2007.

JAZZ. Direção: Ken Burns. Produção: Ken Burns; Lynn Novick. Los Angeles: Home Video, 2001. 1 DVD (1140 minutos).

JUNIOR, Paulo Ghirandelli. História Essencial da Filosofia. Vol. 4. São Paulo: Universo dos Livros, 2010.

KRISTEVA, Julia. Estrangeiros para nós mesmos. Rio de Janeiro: Rocco, 1994.

MACHADO, Arlindo. A televisão levada a sério. São Paulo: Senac, 2000.

MATOS, Cláudia. Acertei o milhar: samba e malandragem no tempo de Getúlio. Rio de Janeiro: Paz e Terra, 1982.

MERCADAL, Trudy Sabbagh. Hip Hop stories and pedagogy. Disponível em: <http://web.mit.edu/comm-forum/mit4/papers/sabbagh.pdf>. Acesso em: 22 jul. 2014.

MONDARDO, Marcos; HAESBAERT, Rogério. Transterritorialidade e antropofagia: territorialidades de trânsito numa perspetiva brasileiro-latino- americana. 2010. Disponível em: <http://www.uff.br/geographia/ojs/index.php/geographia/article/viewFile/378/297>. Acesso em: 29 mar. 2013.

MORAES, Alexandre de. Direito constitucional. 11. ed. São Paulo: Atlas, 2002.

MUSICA POPULAR. CL. Pascuala Ilabaca. Disponível em: <http://www.musicapopular.cl/3.0/index2.php?op=Artista&id=2471>. Acesso em: 10 ago. 2014.

NASCIMENTO, Jorge. Cultura e consciência: a "função" dos Racionais MC's. Z Cultural: Revista Virtual do Programa Avançado de Cultura Contemporânea, v. 5, n.3, 2011. Disponível em: <http://www.pacc.ufrj.br/z/ano5/3/index.php>. Acesso em: 10 set. 2014.

_____. O Titanic afundou: poesia e cultura, rap e sociedade. Contexto: Revista do Programa de Pós-Graduação em Letras, n. 19, p. 213-248, 2011.Disponível em: <http://publicacoes. ufes.br/contexto/article/view/6567>. Acesso em: 10 set. 2014.

_____. Mó mamão, só catá, demorô, ó só: traduzindo o rap dos Racionais MC's. In: SALGUEIRO, Wilberth; SOUZA, Marcelo Paiva de; CARVALHO, Raimundo (Org.). Sob o signo de Babel: literaturas e poéticas da tradução. Vitória: Flor&-Cultura, 2006. p. 111-123.

NOVAES, José. Um episódio de produção de subjetividade no Brasil de 1930: malandragem e Estado Novo. Psicologia em Estudo, Maringá, v. 6, n. 1, p. 39-44, 2001. Disponível em: <http://www.scielo.br/pdf/pe/v6n1/v6n1a05.pdf>. Acesso em: 20 set. 2014.

ORTIZ, Fernando. Contrapunteo cubano del tabaco y el azúcar. Front Cover. Cuba: Fundacion Biblioteca Ayacuch, 1999.

PAVIS, Patrice. A encenação contemporânea. São Paulo: Perspectiva, 2010.

PAZ, Octávio. Signos em rotação. 3. ed. São Paulo: Perspectivba, 2005.

PIMENTA, Rita. Investigação, educação e democracia. Educação, História daPedagogia, fascículo 6, p. 64- 73, dez. 2010.

PLAZA, Júlio. Tradução intersemiótica. 2. ed. São Paulo: Perspectiva, 2003.

PORTAL DA PSIQUÊ. Sublimação. Disponível em: <http:// www.portaldapsique.com.br/Dicionario/S.htm>. Acesso em: 13 jun. 2014.

PROCNICK, Luísa; MATOS, Ludmila Santos. Vídeos amadores, poder e vigilância em Foucault. In: INTERCOM – SOCIEDADE BRASILEIRA DE ESTUDOS INTERDISCIPLIN-

ARES DA COMUNICAÇÃO, 32., 2009, Curitiba. Anais..., Curitiba: INTERCOM, 2009. Disponível em: <http://www.intercom.org.br/papers/nacionais/2009/ resumos/R4-2231-1.pdf>. Acesso em: 1 dez. 2011.

POGREBINSCHI, Thamy. Pragmatismo: Teoria social e política. Rio de Janeiro, Relume Dumará, 2005.

PORTO, Leonardo Sartori. Filosofia da Educação. Rio de Janeiro, Jorge Zahar, 2006.

QUEIROZ, Amarino Oliveira de. Griots, cantadores e rappers: do fundamento do verbo às performances da palavra. In: DUARTE, Zuleide (Org.). África de Áfricas. Recife: Programa de Pós-graduação em Letras, UFPE, 2005. P. 11-12. (Coleção Letras).

RADIO PRIMEIRO DE MAYO. Disponível em: <http://radio1demayo.blogspot.com.br/p/historia.html>. Acesso em: 31 jul. 2014.

RAMA, Angel. Transculturación narrativa en América Latina. 2. ed. Buenos Aires: El Andariego, 2007.

RANCIÈRE, Jacques. A partilha do sensível: estética e política. 2. ed. São Paulo: Editora 34, 2009.

RECUERO, Raquel. Redes socias na internet. Porto Alegre: Sulina, 2009.

RORTY, Richard. Pragmatismo e política. São Paulo: Martins Fontes, 2005.

_____. Contingência, ironia e solidariedade. São Paulo: Martins Fontes, 2007.

_____. A Filosofia e o Espelho da Natureza. Lisboa: Dom Quixote, 1988.

_____. Verdade e Liberdade. Disponível em https://ghiraldelli.files.wordpress.com/2008/07/rorty_verdadeliberdade.pdf . Acesso em 14 de março de 2014.

ROVIGHI, Sofia Vanni. História da Filosofia Contemporânea: do século XIX à neoescolástica. 3. ed. São Paulo: Loyola, 2004.

SANTAELLA, Lucia. Culturas e artes do pós-humano: de cultura das mídias à cibercultura. São Paulo: Paulus, 2003.

SHOOK, John. Os pioneiros do pragmatismo americano. Rio de Janeiro: DPeA, 2002. O

TRIVINHO, Eugenio. A dremocracia cibercultural: lógica da vida humana na civilização mediática avançada. São Paulo: Paulus, 2007.

SANTOS, Boaventura de Sousa. Os processos da globalização. In: _____. (Org.). A globalização e as ciências sociais.3. ed. São Paulo. Cortez, 2005.

SANTOS, Milton. Por uma outra globalização: do pensamento único à consciência universal. 20. ed. Rio de Janeiro: Record, 2011.

SANTIAGO, Silviano. O cosmopolitismo do pobre: crítica literária e crítica cultural. Belo Horizonte: UFMG, 2004.

SAYAD, Abdelmalek. A imigração ou os paradoxos da alteridade. São Paulo: EDUSP,1998.

Schusterman, Richard. Vivendo a Arte: o pensamento pragmatista e a estética popular. São Paulo: Editora 34, 1998.

SEÑAS: dicionario para la enseñanza de la lengua española para brasileños. Universidad de Alcalá de Henares. São Paulo: Martins Fontes, 2001.

SHAW, Lauren. Song and social change in America Latina. Texas: Lexington Books, 2013.

SHETARA, Mano. 450 anos levando coice de burro. In: C., Tony . Hip hop a lápis: o livro.São Paulo: CEMJ, 2005

SHOHAT, Ella; STAM, Robert. Crítica da imagem eurocêntrica: multiculturalismo e representação. São Paulo: Cosac Naify, 2006.

SHUSTERMAN, Richard. Vivendo a arte: o pensamento pragmatista e a estética popular. São Paulo: Editora 34, 1998.

SILVA, Tomaz Tadeu. A produção social da identidade e da diferença. In: SILVA, Tomaz Tadeu da; STUART, Hal; WOODEWARD, Karthry (Org.). Identidade e diferença: a perspectiva dos estudos culturais. 11. ed. Petrópolis: Vozes, 2012.

SOARES, Thiago. Videoclipe: o elogio da desarmonia. João Pessoa: Marca da Fantasia, 2012.

SOTO, Elba. Na busca de uma mudança social: sonhos e lutas Mapuches no Chile. 2004. 126 f. Tese (Doutorado em Educação) - Programa de Pós-Graduação em Educação. Universidade Estadual de Campinas. Faculdade de Educação, Campinas, SP, 2004. Disponível em: <http://www.bibliotecadigital. unicamp.br/document/?code=000303181&fd=y>. Acesso em: 31 jul.2014.

SUDA, Joyce Rumi; SOUZA, Lidio de. Identidade social em movimento: a Comunidade Japonesa na Grande Vitória (ES). Psicologia & Sociedade, v. 18, n. 2, p. 72-80, maio/ago. 2006. Disponível em: <http://www.ufrgs.br/seerpsicsoc/ojs/viewarticle.php?id=17>. Acesso em: 14 jul. 2104.

TATIT, LUIZ. Cancionistas invisíveis. Disponível em: <http://www.luiztatit.com.br/artigos/artigo?id=29/Cancionistas-Invis%C3%ADveis.html>. Acesso em: 30 jul. 2013.

TAYLOR, Charles. A necessidade de reconhecimento. In: _____. A ética da autenticidade. São Paulo: Realizações, 2011, p. 51-61.

TIJOUX, Anita. Sacar La Voz (ft. Jorge Drexler). Disponível em: <https://www.youtube.com/watch?v=VAayt5BsEWg Sacar La voz>. Acesso em: 12 ago. 2011._____. Shock. Disponível em:<https://www.youtube.com/watch?v=177-s44MSVQ>. Acesso em: 12 ago. 2011.

_____. To Kerma. Disponível em: <https://www.youtube.com/ watch?v=BFKAftDYJvg>. Acesso em: 12 ago. 2011.

TOMAS, Lia. Música e filosofia: estética musical. São Paulo: Irmãos Vitale, 2004. (Conexões musicais)

TRIVINHO, Eugênio. A dromocracia cibercultural: lógica da vida humana na civilização mediática avançada. São Paulo: Paulus, 2007.

VALVERDE, Monclar. Mistérios e encantos da canção. In: MATOS, Cláudia Neiva de;

TRAVASSOS, Elizabeth; MEDEIROS, Fernanda Teixeira de. Palavra cantada: ensaios sobre poesia, música e voz. Rio de Janeiro: 7 Letras, 2008.

WILLIAMS, Raymond. Marxismo e literatura. Rio de Janeiro: Zahar, 1979.

WISNIK, José Miguel. A vida é crise: entrevista com José Miguel Wisnik. Concedida a Lisandro Negueira em 29 de setembro de 2012. Disponível em: <http://lisandronogueira.com.br/2012/09/29/a-vida-e-crise-entrevista-com-jose-miguel-wisnik>. Acesso em: 15 set. 2013.

_____. O som e o sentido: uma outra história das músicas. 2. ed. São Paulo: Companhia das Letras, 2009.

ZANOTTI, Luiz Roberto. A poética prescritiva de Carlos Drummond de Andrade. Revista de Literatura, História e Memória: Inter-relações entre a literatura e a sociedade, v. 5, n. 6, p. 129-136, 2009. Disponível em: <http://e-revista.unioeste.br/index.php/rlhm/article/download/3133/2469>. Acesso em: 10 out. 2014.

ZUMTHOR, Paul. Introdução à poesia oral. São Paulo: Hucitec, 1997.

_____. Performance, recepção, leitura. 2. ed. São Paulo: Cosac Naify, 2007.

Συνεντεύξη με τον MC YINKA, για τα παιδιά της δεύτερης γενιάς μεταναστών. Disponível em: <http://ergatiki.gr/index.php?option=com_k2&view=item&id=9096%3Ai1101&Itemid=62.> Acesso em: 30 jan. 2014.

Exhibits

ANNEX A
TRANSCRIPTS
(TENSAIS MCS- CD
MESTISOUL)

MESTISOUL
(TENSAIS MCS)

Mestisoul, o puro sangue brasileiro
'Tá' na cara, 'tá' na cor que
Descende o mundo inteiro
Se você ama esse país solta a voz brow!
Soul brasileiro, sou brasileiro sou!

Salve, Salve Jean Charles, nosso mártir na
Inglaterra
Brasileiro quer trabalho, então parte 'pra'
outras terras
Legal ou não? É o jeitinho brasileiro!
Exportamos mão de obra 'pro' mundo
inteiro
Em todos continentes estamos presentes
Com a cultura que se expande e consequen-
temente
O futebol, nossa marca registrada
Cinco estrelinhas ,marca muito respeitada
O nosso som, a nossa ginga e a nossa
malandragem
O nosso rango, as nossas minas e toda
aquela paisagem
O nosso jeito modesto e bastante acolhedor
O brasileiro mostra as garras é nos momen-
tos de dor
A nossa arte, está presente e sendo preser-
vada
A capoeira e a bossa 'tão' muito bem repre-
sentada

ANNEX A1
TRANSLATIONS
(TENSAIS MCS-CD
MESTISOUL)

MESTISOUL
(TENSAIS MCS)

Mestisoul, pure Brazilian blood
'it is in the face, it is in the color that
Descends the whole world
If you love this country, release your voice
'brow'!
Brazilian Soul, I am Brazilian, I am!

Hail, Hail, Jean Charles our martyr in
England
Brazilian wants to work,so he goes to other
lands
Illegal or not, it is the Brazilian way!
We Export labor work to the world

In all continents, we are present
With the culture that expands and
consequently
Soccer, our trademark
Five stars, a very respected brand
Our sound, our swing and our trickery

Our food, our girls and all that landscape

Our modest and quite welcoming ways
The Brazilian shows their claws in the times
of pain
Our art is present and being preserved

Capoeira and bossa are very well represented

Song of the Displaced

O Hip- Hop, o Funk e o Rock
Pouco a pouco se tornam a MPB Jovem
Mestisoul, o puro sangue brasileiro
'Tá' na cara, 'tá' na cor que
Descende o mundo inteiro
俺は日本人mas sou brasileiro támbem!
Soul brasileiro, sou brasileiro sou!

FAVELA育ち 桜色MESTISOULどこま
で揺らす気 お熱いのは好き 踊り明
かす夜 真っ赤なリオ 伝統のSAMBA
極上の音色
FAVELA 育ち 侍MESTISOUL どこま
で揺らす気 お熱いのは好き 踊り
明かす YO毎度LATINO 灼熱のsound
めっぽうあちぃーの
Mestisoul, o puro sangue brasileiro
'Tá' na cara, 'tá' na cor que
Descende o mundo inteiro
Se você ama esse país solta a voz brow!
Soul brasileiro, sou brasileiro sou!

Seja do sul ou do norte, interior ou capital
Do sertão ou do cerrado ou do litoral
Da Floresta Amazônica ou do Pantanal
Minha alma clama e grita por você que é
eternal
Diz 'pra' mim se você não é brasileiro?
Verde e amarela gravada no seu peito!
Botando azul e branco são as cores da
nação
Da bandeira que eu amo e respeito de
coração
E vai além da imaginação e da criação
Mistura de sangue, de raça, cor
Arte, cultura, filosofia
É 'nois' sofredor!
Apesar do sofrimento é alegre no viver
Supera as dificuldades com sede de vencer
A malandragem 'tá' no sangue e o samba
no pé
Conquistando seus sonhos com garra e fé!

Hip-Hop, Funk and Rock
Gradually become the new MPB
Mestisoul, pure Brazilian blood
It is in the face, it is in the color that
Descended the whole world
I'm Japanese, but I am also Brazilian!
Brazilian Soul, I am Brazilian, I am!

Favela, a samurai warrior who grows as a
Mestisoul
Feel the rhythm of the beat, the vibe is so
good, that Samba from Rio
Has become a tradition, everyone likes it.
Favela grows with the color of a cherry-tree.
Mestisoul, feel the rhythm of the beat, this
vibe is so good …Yeaah, every time the Latin
makes a hot sound to delight.
Mestisoul, pure Brazilian blood
'it is in the face, it is in the color that
Descends the whole world
If you love this country, release your voice
'brow'!
Brazilian Soul, I am Brazilian, I am!

Be from the South or North, countryside or
capital
The Hinterland or Cerrado or the coast
The Amazon forest or the Pantanal
My soul cries and screams for you, that is *eternal*
Tell me if you are a Brazilian?
Green and yellow engraved in your chest!
Adding Blue and white, these are the nation's
colors
Of the Flag that I love and respect with all my
heart
And it goes beyond imagination and creation
Mixing of blood, race, color
Art, culture, philosophy
These are us, sufferer!
Despite the suffering, they are joyful in living
Overcome the difficulties with a will to win
The trickery is in the blood and the samba is
in the foot
Conquering their dreams with determination
and faith!

Mestisoul, o puro sangue Brasileiro
Tá na cara, tá na cor que
Descende o mundo inteiro
俺は日本人mas sou brasileiro também!
Soul brasileiro, sou brasileiro sou!

Mestisoul, pure Brazilian blood
It is in the face, it is in the color that
Descended the whole world
I'm Japanese, but I am also Brazilian!
Brazilian Soul, I am Brazilian, I am!

Favela育ち 桜色Mestisoulどこまで揺
らす気 お熱いのは好き 踊り明かす
夜 真っ赤なリオ 伝統のSamba 極上
の音色
Favela 育ち 侍Mestisoul どこまで揺ら
す気　お熱いのは好き　踊り明かす
YO毎度Latino灼熱のsound めっぽうあ
ちぃーの

Favela, a samurai warrior who grows as a
Mestisoul
Feel the rhythm of the beat, the vibe is so
good, that Samba from Rio
Has become a tradition, everyone likes it.
Favela grows with the color of a cherry-tree.
Mestisoul, feel the rhythm of the beat, this
vibe is so good ...Yeaah, every time the
Latin makes a hot sound to delight.

日本と地球の真反対 だが兄弟目指
すとこ変わんない　距離は遠くない
音楽繋ぐ輪国境越え広がるひたすら
FAMILIA になってもう4年目 TENSAIS
伝える全身全霊
発信地湘南からホットなラテンナンバ
ーが登場だ
SAMBA, CAPOEIRA, FORRÓ, MPB.
調子よく踊ろうベイベ 君は素敵
なBrasileira 世界一のDanceまさに
Cinderela, Cachaça で乾杯 Made in Real
Brasil 万歳 Favela から真実のコール ヤ
ッベーな　Brasileiro　の　Soul

Brazil and Japan may even be in opposite
positions on the globe, but the will to be
brothers does not change. The distance is
not that big for music, it can get easily to
the two nations. It 's been four years that
we are a family and Tensais do not get
tired of fighting. They come from South
America, these warm traditions, Latin
traditions.
Samba, Capoeira, Forro, MPB.
Let's dance Baby, you're a beautiful
Brazilian, the princess of dance, may even
be a cinderella.Let's toast with a 'cachaça',
typical of Brazil. From favela it is possible
to hear a chorus that says, "Vixe! I am
Brazilian, I am"

Mestisoul, o puro sangue brasileiro
'Tá na cara, 'tá na cor que
Descende o mundo inteiro
Se você ama esse pais solta a voz brow!
Soul brasileiro, sou brasileiro sou!
Mestisoul, o puro sangue brasileiro
'Tá na cara, 'tá na cor que
Descende o mundo inteiro

Mestisoul, pure Brazilian blood
It is in the face, it is in the color that
Descended the whole world
If you love this country, release your voice
brow!
Brazilian Soul, I'm Brazilian!
Mestisoul, pure Brazilian blood
It is in the face, it is in the color that
Descended the whole world

俺は日本人mas sou brasileiro também!
Soul brasileiro, sou brasileiro sou!

I'm Japanese, but I am also Brazilian
Brazilian Soul, I am Brazilian, I am!

ANNEX B TRANSCRIPTS (TENSAIS MCS- CD *MESTISOUL)*

SAMURAI MALANDRO (TENSAIS MCS)

OH LALIA OBA!
OH LALIA OBA!

切り捨てごめん 要らぬ世の中世渡り
上手もストリートのマナー
コンクリート サバンナの檻に解き放た
れた侍五人
本当のフィールドで見せるテクニック
オリジナルスパイス
効かすエスニック 剣は抜かぬが言葉
で切る
舌を巻く話術で×かける魔術

O papo é o seguinte, o mano aqui também
gosta de requinte
Mas viver tipo malandro é todo dia tá no
pinch!
Malandragem é saber viver!
É dedicar o seu tempo ao que cê gosta de
fazer
Dançar, curtir, sorrir, beijar, brincar!
Mas a vida não é só isso, tem que saber
levar!
Dificuldade... Em qualquer lugar do
mundo tem
Mas quem ama a si e aos outros até que
vive bem!
É só saber chegar e também sair
Respeitar a igualdade é evoluir
Não sou mais do que ninguém, só quero
conquistar.
O que um sorriso e um abraço pode me
proporcionar!
A felicidade pra Malandro é amar e ser
amado

ANNEX B 1- TRANSLATIONS (MCS TENSAIS CD *MESTISOUL)*

SAMURAI TRICKSTER (TENSAIS MCS)

OH LALIA OBA!
OH LALIA OBA!

Sorry for my way of speaking, it is the fault
of this world that deceives us.
Five samurais trying to escape a concrete
cage.
Exerting the technique to show what you
really are, the original essence, their ethnicity,
what you can not demonstrate
You can even cut the air with the sword, but
the words cut and hurt more than the blade.

Here is the thing; the brother here also
likes refinement
But living like a trickster is to be in the
pinch everyday!
Trickery means knowing how to live!
Means dedicating your time to what you
like to do
Dancing, chilling, smiling, kissing, playing!
But life is not only that, you must know
how to do it
Difficulty... Anywhere in the world has it
But those who love themselves and others
kind of live well
It is all about knowing how to get there,
and how to leave
Respecting equality means evolving
I'm not more than anyone else, I just want
to conquer.
What a smile and a hug can provide me

Happiness, to the trickster, is loving and
being loved

E tá junto da Família e dos Aliados
E como bom malandro só pra te lembrar
Eu trabalho pra viver, não vivo pra trabalhar!

And being with the family and allies
And as a good trickster, only to remember you
I work to live, I do not live to work!

Um rapaz perdido no mundão vai saber?
Sabe chegar e se envolver!
Imigra pro outro lado do Planeta
As estrelas que me guiam
Presente, o samurai de bombeta!
Salve, salve, pro guerreiros estão de pé!
Na nobreza de viver de se esquivar da má fé
Sou samurai ocidental, bom malandro

What will a lost boy in this big world know?
Know how to arrive and get involved
Immigrates to the other side of the planet
The stars are what guide me
Present, the samurai bombeta!
Hail, Hail, to the warriors that are standing!
The nobility of living, of dodging bad intentions

マランドロは平成ジゴロクジチュウ転がす 俺のベロ とびっきり良い女もいいん
な 超魅了する調味料は賞味期限なしの少々危険なsambaの香がプンプンするぜ 可愛いカナリヤかなり鳴いてる そろそろここらで 頂き

I am the Western Samurai, a good trickster
The trickster is a gigolo of the present times.
My tongue calls for a 'good woman'.
I am fascinated and this fascination is endless.Little by little I feel the samba smell in the air
As if it were a beautiful canary singing

Fala ae mano?
E ai santista, beleza?!
E esse Vasco, vai ou não vai?
'Tá' lindo, mas deixa isso 'pra' lá!
O bacalhau e o peixe...
Nós dois somos do mar!
O Mar, misterioso mar...
Opa! Eu conheço essa música!
Império serrano!
Diz ai Kta Brasil, de que pais você é?
Japão, mas minha alma é brasileira!

Whats up man!
Whats up Santista, all good?!
And that Vasco, will win or not?
It is going well, but nevermind!
The cod and the fish ...
We're both from the sea!
The Sea, the mysterious sea ...
Man!I know this song!
Imperio Serrano!
Tell me, Kta Brazil, what country are you from?
Japan, but my soul is Brazilian!

俺はBrasileiroだしJaponêsだぜ!!
描き始めるあふれ出す色

I am Brazilian, but I'm Japanese!
The colors overflow when I start to draw

Calor Humano.
熱く友情

Human heat
Human Heat

Disciplina
騒ぐ情熱
Respeito e Humildade
大きな心

Discipline
An unsettle passion
Respect and humility
A good heart

奇跡起すぜ、Gingaでゆらすぜ!
O malandro vem sambar
O dança o nosso samba

Vem 'pra' beira do mar
Vem coração ver o 青空
Malandragem e saber viver
Faço tudo por você
Vejo o sol amanhecer
間違いないぜ俺に掛けな
Quero apenas ser feliz
Faço tudo por você
Vem coração ver o 青空 。

Let's make a miracle happen! With swing
we will rock!
The trickster comes to samba the dance,
our samba
Come to the seaside
Come heart, come and see the blue sky
Trickery means knowing how to live
I do everything for you
I see the dawning sun
It is a sure thing, trust me, I just want to
be happy
I do everything for you
Come heart, come and see the blue sky

ANNEX C TRANSCRIPTS (TENSAIS MCS- CD *MESTISOUL*)

UNITE (TENSAIS MCS)

（フック）
マイク、ケーブル、2ターンテーブ
ル HeyYo!! 3 MC此処にあらわる
マイクロフォンチェック1212調
子どうだ！手を上げろ！
É 'nois' na fita, aqui presente chega!
Se for 'pra' somar 'cola', mas se vacilar
'poca'.

（MC Beto）
300 mil *gaijin* a toda parte que se vá
É assim tem *burajirujin (brasileiro)*
Ayase chi, terao, tsuruma, chogo.
Higashi kaigan, chigasaki a tsurumi, kanto.
Cara de japonês, e dai o que é que tem.
Se para eles estrangeiro, latino, nanbei!
Discriminado é, ou alvejado.
Imigrante sou latino doidão, 'cê' ta ligado?

ANNEX C 1 - TRANSLATIONS (TENSAIS MCS CD *MESTISOUL*)

UNITE (TENSAIS MCS)

Chorus 4 x- All:
Microphone, cables, two DJ tables, it's
all right Hey Yo! Three MC testing the
microphones 1 and 2 and 1 and 2.
How is the tone, raise your hands!
These are us, here it comes!
If you're gonna add up, come. But if
you're not, piss off

（MC Beto）
300,000 *f*oreigners everywhere you go
It has Brazilian
Ayase, Chi, Terao, Tsuruma, Chogo
Higashi kaigan, Chigasaki, Tsurumi, Kanto
Japanese face, so what?.
If for them they are foreign, Latin, panamer-
icano!
Is discriminated, or targeted
Immigrant, I am the crazy Latin, you know?

（SAT-SKILL）

背後からバッサリ斬りつける刀　あっさり卑怯千万打つ輩
未熟なハンターはあんたじゃないか？　刃からこぼれ落ちる涙
伝統もなくぜ　世相めっぽう胡散臭ぇ中でも捨てんなリスペクト
風貌違えど俺等は兄弟

（PAY-MENT）

四六時中溜まったストレス開放　大量摂取　覚醒する細胞
行っとく）感染するドーピング
（Hip-Hop）隅々までハーコーにコーティング
モノホンだけのソウル嗅ぎつけ　狂犬だらけのホールが実現
Yes Yes Y'all や SAYHOO 木霊し　マイクにかえす Unite の証

（フック）

マイク、ケーブル、２ターンテーブル HeyYo!! ３MC 此処にあらわる
マイクロフォンチェック１２１２調子どうだ！手を上げろ！
É 'nois' na fita, aqui presente chega!
Se for 'pra' somar 'cola', mas se vacilar 'poca'.

（SAT-SKILL）

五臓六腑　染みわたる Hip-Hop １語１句　息吹き込めるヒットマン
７５型の言霊はいかが？国境をまたぎ壊すテリトリー
ストリートから右に左に耳から脳へ方々を RockOn
俺らはアジアのメッセンジャー　ラスト侍、起こすビックサプライズ

（PAY-MENT）

頭の中酸欠寸前　溜め込んだ煙　吐き出すぜ
腐った奴のどす黒い空気　ばっかじゃ正気も鋭利ます凶器

（SAT-SKILL）

Stabbed in the back with a knife by a coward "friend".
Who will be missing is you, friend. The blade cryes, a sad social situation, breaking what we call good manners (tradition).Do not miss the respect you have inside, outside we are different, but inside we are all brothers.

（PAY-MENT）

The stress that was accumulated for a long time was released, It was climbing trhough the cells.What served as the anesthesia was the Hip-Hop, healed all wounds, united and clothed me with a protective layer.

Chorus 4x:

Microphone, cables, two DJ tables, it's all right HEY YO!Three MCS testing the microphones 1 and 2 and 1 and 2. How is the tone, raise your hands! These are us, here we come! If you're gonna add up, come. But if you're not, piss off.

（SAT-SKILL）

The internal organs are "invaded" by the Hip-Hop, and breathing depends on each word of prayer in that song.Do you like the language of slang? Across the street that cuts the nation, looking right then left to the people who are listening, pay close attention, these are the last Samurai messengers of Asia, surprise!

（PAY-MENT）

I will put out all the smoke that was messing up my mind
If you keep storing all that, that bad people transmit

ストリートかませアクション　悪路
駆け抜けー蓮托生
雑草みてぇな前評判　覆すダークホ
ースが最強だ

Your sanity and good sense will not be
enough to take you to a good path. You are
going to look like a weed, which does not
serve as a good example to anyone

(MC Beto)
Junto e misturado, mesclado e dechavado.
Bolado na letra no papel com os aliados
Firmeza total, tá suave na moral.
Se porque aqui não tem paga pau
Imi wakaru ka doidão? Não, wakaranai!
Burajiru furusato, sutoritto sodachi.
Sonkei to kenkyou, hito no ashi wo
fumanai
Waru sou dakara tte kobinai

(MC Beto)
Together and blended, mixed and jum-
bled..
Rolled in the letter on the paper with the
allies
Total Firmness, Chill and for real.
It is because here there are no suckers
Do you understand, stoned? I do not
understand.
I'm from Brazil, raised on the street.
I am humble, I don't step on anyone.
I only seem to be evil

（ブリッジ）
(PAY-MENT)
キック、バスとスネアのタイミング
で間髪いれずかますライミング

(PAY-MENT)
Take a chance on the speed of a trap and
of a bus, but be careful not to lose your
head.

(MC Beto)
Certo camarada 'ta' no rap na jornada
a cara é se unir sem maldade e palhaçada

(MC Beto)
Okay buddy it is in the rap, on the journey, the thing is to unite without malice
and buffoonery

(SAT-SKILL)
腹から吠えろ　オリジナルイェロー
中指立てな　エンターティナー
（3人）
国境を越えた3人のファイター　止
まらねぇ　飛ばせ弾丸ライナー

(SAT-SKILL)
It's a howl that comes out of the belly,
original of an artist.
This is the cry of three people who crossed
the nation, we will not stop!

（フック）
マイク、ケーブル、2ターンテーブ
ル HeyYo!! 3MC此処にあらわる
マイクロフォンチェック1212調
子どうだ！手を上げろ！
É 'nois' na fita, aqui presente chega!
Se for 'pra' somar 'cola', mas se vacilar
'poca'.

(Chorus)
Microphone, cables, two DJ tables, it's
all right Hey Yo! Three M C testing the
microphones 1 and 2 and 1 and 2. How is
the tone, raise your hands!
These are us, here we come!
If you're gonna add up, come. But if you're
not, piss off.

ANNEX D
TRANSCRIPTS (TENSAIS MCS- CD *MESTISOUL)*

マイクロフォン戦士
MICROFONE SOLDIER

（PAY-MENT)
湘南アンダーグラウンドぶっといパ
イプ　ヴァイブス連結ぐっと良いパ
イプ吸う
燃やせたいまつ　あげろ戦火　ドー
プなこいつで火種点火
とうに限界超え　尚、吐き出す声
１３４号方面　Check It Out!
俺等無敵なマイクロフォンソルジャ
ー　明日なき道を掴み取る猛者

（AKIG)
モクモク上げな狼煙　ウォーイウォ
ーイ上げときな拳
腕の落書きはマスターピース　より
アチー魂の日本人　ガキの頃から
のダチ
マジ半端ねぇステージ　体感で満タ
ンだエナジー
スペシャルワンピースAKIG　驚づか
んじゃうMIC

（フック)
マイクで前へ　マイクのウォーリア
マイクで前へ　マイクでWO!WO!
前行くぜ　前行くぜ　前行くぜ　前
行く！×2
マイクで前へ　マイクのウォーリア
マイクで前へ　マイクでWO!WO!
前行くぜ　前行くぜ　前行くぜ　前
行く！　前行く　前行く　マイクロ
フォンソルジャー

ANNEX D 1-
TRANSLATIONS (MCS TEN-SAIS CD *MESTISOUL)*

マイクロフォン戦士
MICROPHONE SOLDIER

（PAY-MENT)
To the south in the underground there is a
thick tube, with a good vibe, feel that vibe.
Set fire to the things you hate, let's make a
war, we will burn down this shit.
Let's go over the limit, we will release our
voice, feeling the road 134! Check it out!
Me and my invincible microphone, we will
tread our way!

（AKIG)
The rocket that rises fast, the hand that
trembles in time to make it go up.
The scrawl made by hand, thaat may have
more feeling than a masterpiece that artists
do out there. A friendship from childhood time, a special piece, Akig hold that
microphone!

(Chorus)
Take this microphone and come 'to' the front,
microphone soldier, take that microphone and
come 'to' the front, yell with the microphone
Wo Wo.
I will go to the front, I will go to the front, I
will go to the front Wo,
Wo!X2
Take this microphone and come 'to' front,
microphone soldier, take this microphone
and come 'to' front, yell with the microphone
Wo!Wo!
I will go to the front, I will go to the front, I
will go to the front, I will go to the front Wo!
Wo! Microphone soldier.

Song of the Displaced

（TOHKICK）

マイクロフォンウォーリア　俺語を
網羅　曖昧の裏側のフォントを描写
握るクリスタルカイザー　炭酸な
ら断然コーラだ　マイクコントロ
ーラー
信念断片数珠繋ぎ　本日も潮騒に
胸騒ぎ　変わり映えなき素晴らし
き１日
国境ジャンル無視　言葉遊び

（TOHKICK）

The microphone soldier describes what I
mean, shows the side of me I keep hidden. The glass that I hold is made of glass,
if it is a soda, it is certainly Coca-Cola.
Each has believed in one thing, and today
as always, the waves bother me. This is a
words game.

（BETO＆MASAHIRO）

Então me passa o microfone
Te provo que não sou clone
Vai função pique misoshiro e feijão
Arigatou 'pros' senshi que 'tão' presente
aqui
Forma a banca dos guerreiros latinos e
nihonjin
Pode chegar, 'só' não desarrumar que tá
firmeza
Respeito é a chave, cadeado é 'nois' na cena
Hip-Hop universal se manifesta em você
A rua te olha e os pivetes se espelham em
quem?
Somos querreiros do mic wowo
kotoba de strick
quebrando as barreiras do som
com a forca do flow

（BETO＆MASAHIRO）

So pass me the microphone
I will prove that I am not a clone
Go bro, chop, fermented soy broth and
beans
Thanks to the warriors that are here
Form the stage for the Latin and Japanese
warriors
Come here, 'just' do not mess up that it
is all good
Respect is the key, the lock is us in the
scene.
Universal Hip-Hop is manifested in you
The street looks at you and the boys look
up to who?
We are soldies of the mic wowo
Street on words
Breaking the sound barriers
With the force of the flow

（KAZUKI）

マイクロフォンソルジャー　常にチ
ャレンジャー　リズム刻むライムメ
ッセンジャー
ワイドビジョン　カラーと線　変幻
自在に描くから
まさに突き抜ける様な青い空　ため
た力　吐き出すから
刺激が欲しけりゃもっと来な！　放
つパワー　常に俺流

（KAZUKI）

Microphone soldier, he tries, he is our
messenger that makes rhythm
Sees the world through different eyes,
different color, conveys all that we want
to say, all the accumulated anger on the
chest. He is strong, microphone soldier!

（IB）

ちいっと失礼　御用改め手向かえ
ば容赦なく斬りつける　無用には

（IB）

That's a bit offensive, review your
intentions, if I turn my back they would

びこる
過激な不逞見つけ　抜刀　すかさず
応戦　いざOk俺等に任しておけ
到底俺を斬れるわけもねぇ　家に
帰るか刀を置け　赤バッチ相手な
んじゃ
しゃーねぇーなー

(RUNBOO)
無我夢中で走り続けた三千里　完全
にOn　決めるRockOn　吠えるHeads
どう？
絡める景色はWhat's Colorだ　From湘
南C.I.C　ShowMe上げるぜVIP
ふところBIG　その場でE感じ　分か
り合えるぜHomies

（フック）
マイクで前へ　マイクのウォーリア
マイクで前へ　マイクでWO!WO!
前行くぜ　前行くぜ　前行くぜ　前
行く！×2
マイクで前へ　マイクのウォーリア
マイクで前へ　マイクでWO!WO!
前行くぜ　前行くぜ　前行くぜ　前
行く！　前行く　前行く　マイクロ
フォンソルジャー

certainly cut me off without loyalty. The
trick is to find the weak spot
To attack. At the time everything goes right,
you can leave it to me
There is no reason to cut me off, so put
thisblade away and come back 'to' home.

(RUNBOO)
I have no time for idiots.
With ecstasy, I ran 5000 kilometers, sure
I'm on, I choose the Rockon, what about
those heads, barking? What color was this
landscape? Southern. Show me. Let's raise
our voice in this place, with feeling. I can
understand, bros.

(Chorus)
Take this microphone and come 'to' the
front, microphone soldier, take that microphone and come 'to' the front, with the
microphone shout Wo Wo.
I will go 'to'the front, I will go 'to'the front,
I will go 'to' the front, I will go 'to' the
front Wo, Wo!X2
Take this microphone and come to the
front, microphone soldier, take this microphone and come 'to' the front, with the
microphone shout Wo!Wo!
I will go 'to' the front, I will go 'to' the
front, I will go 'to' the front, I will go 'to
'the front. Wo! Wo! Microphone soldier.

ANNEX E
TRANSCRIPTS
(CD PÁSSARO IMIGRANTE)

PÁSSARO IMIGRANTE
(INDIGESTO)

Venho do imenso azul, essa terra promete
Aqui sou mais um, contra os marionetes
Os patos vão pro sul, papagaio repete
Meu ninho eu construo, não se intromete
Minha liberdade eu mesmo gero
Meu passaporte é mero detalhe zero
Dos que considero sincero, não espero
Cortam minhas asas ,me regenero

Quero visão de campo , olhos de águia
Ter a mente sábia, não cair na lábia
Pois bico sujo trouxe como que se fosse
Bico doce ,cujo, desses fujo do refúgio

O pássaro peregrina,pela noite e matina
Desvia em cada esquina das aves de rapina
Cantos de todos cantos, prantos eu ouço
tantos
Janto de vez em quando, mando versos
pros santos

Refrão 2x:
Mais vale um na mão que dois voando
Num mundo distante
Nada é como antes
Hora de se desprender do bando
Pro alto e avante
Pássaro imigrante

Solidão apavora
Você busca seu bando
Tua raça te ignora, sempre te urubuzando
Espécie de cativeiro, tu já tá cativando

Belas elas chegam com suas plumas
Suas turmas

ANNEX E 1
TRANSLATIONS
(CD IMMIGRANT BIRD)

IMMIGRANT BIRD
(INDIGESTO)

I come from the immense blue, this land
promises
Here I am, one more, against the puppets
Ducks Go to the south, the parrots repeat
My nest I will build, do not meddle
My freedom I, myself, will generate
My passport is a mere detail, zero
From those I consider sincere, I do not expect
They cut my wings, I recover

I want a wide sight, eyes of eagle
Having a wise mind, not falling into lies
'Cause dirty beak brought as if it were
sweet beak, from these refuges I flee

The bird wanders, through night and
morning
Dodges raptors in every corner
Corners of all corners, I hear so many tears
I have dinner once in a while, I send verses
to the saints

Chorus 2x:
Better on in the hand than two in the bush
In a distant world
Nothing is as it was
Time to break away from the pack
up and above
immigrant bird

Loneliness strikes
You search your pack
Your race ignores you, always rebuffing you
Some kind of captivity You're already
Captivating

Beautifull, they arrive with their feathers
Your crowd

Nessa que tu se acostuma a não ter só uma	With those you get used to not having only one
Cansado de dar rasante em maré revolta	Tired of grazing revolt tides
Na onda do calmante várias piriquitas soltas	In the wave of soothing, many loose birds
Mas se tu cola agora, vê se tu colabora	But if you come now, try to collaborate
Não pula da cartola, teu truque aqui não rola	Do not act as the boss, your tricks do not work here
Melhor bico calado,nada de asinhas de fora	Best to be with your mouth shut, no wings out
Se tu quer cantar de galo, tu vai cantar na gaiola	If you want to sing as a cock, you will sing in a cage

Não vou ter pena de quem me depena, Abutres!
Quem te diz que te dá alpiste de ti se nutre.
Sangue, suor e lágrimas são mais que petróleo
Criam corvos que te comem os olhos

I will not feel sorry for anyone who plucks me, Vultures!
Those who claim to feed you with bird-seed, actually feed from you.
Blood, sweat and tears are more than oil
They create crows that eat your eyes

Refrão 2x:
Mais vale um na mão que dois voando
Num mundo distante
Nada é como antes
Hora de se desprender do bando
Pro alto e avante
Pássaro imigrante

Chorus 2x:
Better one in the hand than two in the bush
In a distant world
Nothing is as it was
Time to break away from the pack
Up and above
immigrant Bird

ANNEX F
TRANSCRIPTS
(CD PÁSSARO IMIGRANTE)
SELVA DO DINHEIRO
(*MAMELO SOUND SYSTEM*)

ANNEX F 1
TRANSLATIONS
(CD IMMIGRANT BIRD)
MONEY'S JUNGLE
(*MAMELO SOUND SYSTEM*)

Verso Gorila Urbano:

Gorila Urbano Verse:

Seja papa-anjo, nêgo, ou papa-defunto
O negócio é o negócio, o que importa é quanto eu junto
Quanto eu janto, e se eu levanto tanto é o

Be a craddle robber, bro, or a undertaker
Business is business, what matters is how much I earn
How much dinner I have, ad how much I

Song of the Displaced

assunto
Sempre, em todo canto, até mesmo no
conjunto
Musical, mas na real
Só pelego paga-pau é quem me leva a mal
Quando eu digo: 'meu pecado não é
capital'
Bow Wow Wow*, tô sossegado, na moral
E se insiste em me dizer que o cifrão é o
novo Deus
Então tá bom: os meus são ateus
De Osasco a São Mateus, o que eu quero
mesmo é ver os
Mano e as mina dar adeus
À dor de ser tratado à tapa
Enquanto corporação ianque, china, ou
japa
Devasta e saqueia o solo brasileiro
Só o que resta é tacar fogo no vespeiro

raise. That is what matters
Always, everywhere, in every corner,
Musical, but for real
Only suckers take me wrong
When I say, 'My sin is not capital'
Bow Wow Wow, I'm chilling, for real
And if you insist on telling me that the
dollar sign is the new God
So okay: mine are atheists
From Osasco to São Mateus, what I really
want is to see
The bros and the girls say goodbye
To pain of being treated like shit
While corporations from the US, China,
or Japan
Devastate and plunder the Brazilian soil
All that remains is to set fire in the hor-
net's nest

Refrão:
Selva do dinheiro, me diz quem é o
primeiro
A se entregar por inteiro, de corpo e alma
Selva do dinheiro, me diz quem é o
primeiro
A se entregar por inteiro, sem culpa ou
calma
Selva do dinheiro, me diz quem é o
primeiro
A se entregar por inteiro, nem treta ou
trauma
Selva do dinheiro, me diz quem é o
primeiro
É…

Chorus:
Money's Jungle, tell me who is the first
To surrender completely, body and soul
Money's Jungle, tell me who is the first
The surrender completely No guilt or
serenity
Money's Jungle, tell me who is the first
The surrender completely, no beef or
trauma
Money's Jungle, tell me who is the first
Yeah…

Verso Lurdez Da Luz:
Ain't got no home
Ain't got no shoes
Ain't got no money
Ain't got no class
Ain't got no friends
Ain't got no school
No mother
No father
Ain't got no sisters and brothers
Ain't got no worth

Lurdez Da Luz Verse:
Ain't got no home
Ain't got no shoes
Ain't got no money
Ain't got no class
Ain't got no friends
Ain't got no schooling
No mother
No father
Ain't got no sisters and brothers
Ain't got no worth

Ain't got no faith
No God
No Love**
Isso ainda é real hoje em 2009
Só números que crescem, . ORG, .GOV
ONG, ONU
Esquece o cinema, é só aspirina e urubu
Troca logo o seu voto por sapato ou
aguardente
Quem salvará sua pele não é vice ou
presidente
Collor, Collor, o mais alto delinquente
Se recandidatou em um passado recente
Vai vendo… vendo o que tiver no engar-
rafamento
Junto latinha como complemento
Nada além do pão, nada além da carne
Tô pra tacar pedra e deixar soar o alarme

Refrão:
Selva do dinheiro, me diz quem é o
primeiro
A se entregar por inteiro, de corpo e alma
Selva do dinheiro, me diz quem é o
primeiro
A se entregar por inteiro, sem culpa ou
calma
Selva do dinheiro, me diz quem é o
primeiro
A se entregar por inteiro, nem treta ou
trauma
Selva do dinheiro, me diz quem é o
primeiro
É…
*citação de "Atomic Dog", do George
Clinton

**citação de "Ain't Got No / I Got Life",
da Nina Simone

Ain't got no faith
No God
No Love
This is still true today in 2009
Only numbers grow,.ORG,.GOV.
NGOs, UN
Forget the movie
It's just aspirins and vultures
Go, change your vote for shoes or booze
Who will save your skin is no vice or
president
Collor Collor, the highest offender
Was a candidate again, in the recent past
Go see… sell what I can on the streets
Collect cans to complement
Nothing but bread, nothing but meat
I'm at the point of throwing stones and
letting alarm blar

Chorus:
Money's Jungle, tell me who is the first
To surrender completely, body and soul
Money's Jungle, tell me who is the first
The surrender completely, no guilt or
serenity
Money's Jungle, tell me who is the first
The surrender completely, no beef or
trauma
Money's Jungle, tell me who is the first
Yeah…
Yoka
MSS

ANNEX G
TRANSCRIPTS
(CD PÁSSARO IMIGRANTE)

ANNEX G 1
TRANSLATIONS
(CD IMMIGRANT BIRD)

EXCEÇÃO À REGRA
(ELO DA CORRENTE)

EXCEPTION TO THE RULE
(ELO DA CORRENTE)

(CAIO)
Espalhando uma certeza pelo chão da
gente,
dando vida como a terra usada inteligen-
temente.
Do fruto o sabor doce que se amarga no
final,
feito chuva de verão que se transforma em
vendaval.

(CAIO)
Spreading certainty through our ground
giving life like a land used intelligently.
From the fruit, a sweet taste that gets
bitter at the end,
Like a summer rain that turns into gale.

Pela integridade da vidraça antes da
quebra,
manifesto singular como a exceção da
regra,
As armas de Jorge no corpo, trazendo
força,
mandando idéias antes que alguém as
distorça.

By the integrity of the window before the
break,
singular manifesto as the exception to the
rule,
Saint Jorge weapons in the body, bringing
strength,
sending ideas before anyone distorts
them.

Reforço a tese, se retorça na cadeira,
embasado pelo que permanece na cabeceira
da cama, do caos a lama que aqui se
estende,
vou pela arte que da indústria se despren-
de.

Strengthening the thesis, kink in the chair,
Based upon the one that remains at the
bedside table
Of the Bed, from chaos to the mud that here
extends,
I go for the art that broke away from
industry

Um diamante como os de Serra Leoa,
sem o escravagismo que tal terra sobrevoa.
Mãos iluminadas, mentes controladas, mal
assolador;
não remuneradas pelo seu labor.

A diamond such as those from Sierra
Leone,
without the slavery that such land flies.
illuminated hands, controlled minds, evil
destroyer;
not paid for their labor.

Insensatez como em ações do governo
nacional,
encenações parecem peça teatral.
Vida marginal permanecemos como cães,

Senselessness such as the national government actions,
enactments seem like plays.
marginal life, we remain as dogs,

na terra de ninguém à procura de nossas mães.

in no man's land looking for our mothers.

(PITZAN)

Devagar que é pra não perder o passo
Sem pestanejar, meu caminho sou eu mesmo que faço
Conduzo as linhas como quem ama o que faz
Certo de meu espaço aqui faço o que sei mais

(PITZAN)

Slowly, to avoid loosing my pace
Unblinking, my way I do by myself
Drive lines and like those who love what they do
Sure of my space here I do what I know best

Ser da regra a exceção, é a missão de agora
Então encho o pulmão e boto a voz para fora
Em alto e bom tom como num som de Mendes
Queimando um do bom... aí os home prende

Being the exception to the rule, is the current mission
So I fill my lungs and release my voice
Loud and clear as in a sound of Mendes
Burning a good one ... then the police arrests

Você se surpreende, mas tá tão na cara
Cada vez de um jeito porque o tempo não para
Mas repara bem, vá mais além
do que dizem que é verdade e o que é de bem

It surprises you, but it 'is so obvious
Each time in a different way, because time does not stop
But look right, go beyond
What they say is true and what is good

Olhos atentos às nuances da vida
Todos seus lances da chegada à partida
Farei da minha vida o melhor até o fim
De cabeça erguida é só o que esperam de mim

Watchful eyes to the nuances of life
All your bids from arrival to departure
I will make the best of my life to the end
Head high is just what is expected of me

ANNEX H
TRANSCRIPTS AND TRANSLATIONS
(CD IMMIGRANT BIRD)
IF YOU DO NOT BELIEVE FEAT
(PARTNERSHIP OF SOUND)

- Where did you get your ideas from?
- The ideas? Oh man, I get a million dreams
  It's all I do is dream all the time
    - I heard you play piano...
- No, no, this is not piano. This is dreaming
  Life life life (life)

Can be impose in heaven ...
In a jar without an opening composed in haze
Will not tell you once you're so close in there,
Opposed in there dedicate the space
You're choking back the tears as you're talking on the atmosphere
Despair, sat around the cheer (cheer?) (yeah!)
Acting like this world is theirs
They've been doing this for years
Even centuries, feature sensory
Caught sex with more sex
We all said picking up the pen and pad
And write to inspire
You'd like to wear the mad
Matter of fact I'm rather glad
There is heinous, heinous set the hatred

Back in the yard you can better play it
Keep me waiting for the day the mad is elevating
Relegating
The hole jump
You face the consequence of yapping
Rap has the ways, you can't see what is happening
You have Vaseline
Better draw your sorrow with the half glass of rain
... And it's left, let us see if they can help
... The same clause, the vow that spare you the mental break down
The fate frowns around us
Getting straight, get ever to waste no less
astound us
... None of your boxes nor chains can abound us
I'm busting out of the chains
Like that you caged
Filled with rage I'll be your powerman

Andressa Zoi Nathanailidis

Now this world's my stage
I feel the microphone juice moving through my veins
Rendering me insane as I feed off all MC remains
I never stay in lanes, my parchment is DVA
And eradicate... Only a beat can medicate
I sing to hit ups to medicate but their illness prevails
Riding roughshod and career enough rails to tell tales
Some slingers are itchy fingers looking at dead ringers
Trough their eyes, we hate lingers
Are such souls, long cold, so bring them to the fold
Rebounded to teach non-believers to do as they're told
'Cause for too long, I kept my mouth simple
What is found around are superfights, now you can swivel
From de middle to the front, to the rear
Like my neighbour's Matt murder boy, I have no fear

I stand for many years, seen tears
Wiped the cheer clear a fruit boy clears
A bad man's tears
So I raised no ears,
My throne is follicly challenged
I keep scalps visible to all those who would fashion
Any hopes to dethrone
Any hopes to debone
Any hopes to bright wide
And any hopes to go home.
Any hopes to feel safe.
Any hopes to get mended
Any hopes that you had will now be ended.
Done, done, done, done, done, done, done
And if you don't believe, just watch me
You better watch me, yes just watch me ,yo
If you don't believe, better watch me, yo, just watch me
Well, you better watch me, yo
And if you don't believe, you better watch me, yes, you better watch me, yo, just watch me
And if you don't believe, you better watch me, yes, just watch me, yo, better watch me, yo

ANNEX I
TRANSCRIPTS
(CD PÁSSARO IMIGRANTE)

ANNEX I 1
TRANSLATIONS
(CD IMMIGRANT BIRD)

DEFINITIVAMENTE [IN-STRUMENTAL] -BASE SONORA SOB TRECHOS DO POEMA A PROCURA DA POESIA- CARLOS DRUMMOND DE ANDRADE - YOKA

DEFINITELY [INSTRUMENTAL] –SOUND BASIS IN POEM EXCERPTS "THE PURSUIT OF POETRY"- CARLOS DRUMMOND DE ANDRADE - YOKA

Não faças versos sobre acontecimentos.
Não há criação nem morte perante a
poesia.
Diante dela, a vida é um sol estático,
Não aquece nem ilumina.
As afinidades, os aniversários, os incidentes pessoais não contam.
Não faças versos com o corpo,
Esse excelente, completo e confortável
corpo, tão infenso à efusão lírica.

Tua gota de bile, tua careta de gozo ou de
dor no escuro
São indiferentes.
Nem me reveles teus sentimentos,
Que se prevalecem do equívoco e tentam
a longa viagem.
O que pensas e sentes, isso ainda não é
poesia.
Teu iate de marfim, teu sapato de diamante,
vossas mazurcas e abusões, vossos esqueletos de família
desaparecem na curva do tempo, é algo
imprestável.

Do not make verses about events.
There is no creation or death before
poetry.
Before it, life is a static sun,
Neither heats nor lights.
Affinities, birthdays, personal incidents
do not count.
Do not do make verses with the body,
this excellent, complete and comfortable
body, so averse to lyrical effusion.

Your drop of bile, your grimace of joy or
pain in the dark
Are indifferent.
Do not reveal to me your feelings,
that prevail of misunderstanding and try
the long journey.
What you think and feel, this still is not
poetry.
Your ivory yacht, your diamond shoe,
Your mazurkas and mistakes, your family
skeletons
disappear in the time lapse, is something
snotty.

ANNEX J
TRANSCRIPTS –
(MC YINKA–CD AΛANA)

ANNEX J 1
TRANSLATIONS -
(MC YINKA CD AΛANA)

KEPMA (Mc Yinka)

Στην ζουγκλά του μπέτον ζω
Αφροέλλην ανυπήκοος οικονομίκος
μετανάστης
Γέννημα θρέμμα Αθήνων κεντρικά εκεί
που ο κοσμός
Ζει πυκνά δεν παρατηρεί,ξέρει καλά ομώς
να κοιτά.
Καθώς κινούμε στα στένα της πόλης
μπορεί. να μου την πέσουν
Φασίστες, μπορεί. στο λεωφορείο να μου
πουν
''εδώ είναι Ελλαδα γύρνα πίσω'' η να με
κοιτάξουν παράξενα
Μόλις με ελληνίδα ξεμυτίσω.
Η άλλη όψη είναι να μου πουν
'' EΪ ΓΙΟ!!! Μαν εσείς οι μαύροι τα σπάτε!!
Έχετε ρυθμό!
Δεν με νοιάζει εάν έχετε νιονιό σας έχω δει
στην τι-βι και αύτο μου αρκεί μου
Βγάζετε κάτι το θεαμάτικο!!!βλέπω βίλλες
καζίνα τσιφλικάδες να πλουτίζουν
Να πέρνανε φίνα και από την άλλη
συνταξιούχοι σε καραντίνα , καμμένα
Δάση μια ντουζίνα . νταβατζιλίκι φόροι.
Και η ακρίβεια να σε κάνει να ζεις
Τσίμα –τσίμα ζούμε ή απλώς υπάρχουμε? .
αλήθεια! Σε βρίσκουμε ή σε μαθαίνουμε?
Μίλαμε ή απλως αρθρώνουμε? Μελετάμε ή
απλώς διαβάζουμε?

KEPMA (MC Yinka)

Natural African-Greek economic immi-
grant
Born and raised in Central Athens, there
Where people live crowded
Does not notice, but can see.
While I wander through the city's alleys,
Fascists may surround me.
Can tell me, inside the bus:
- Here is Greece, go away and go back to
your country -
And look at me strangely
Especially if I go out with a Greek girl
On the other side of the coin, they say:
- "Oh, son; Oh man, you blacks rock!You
have rhythm!
I do not care if you stink.I watch you on
TV. This is enough for me.
You make beautiful things. I see man-
sions, casinos, rich farmers
Living in luxury; and on the other hand,
retirees surviving
burned forests, huge taxes and famine
compels you to live
- Do we Live or simply exist?
- Truth! Do we find you or know you?

Do we articulate or just talk?
Do we study or just read?

Ρεφραίν -2x:
Δες την αλήθεια οπώς θες
Το κέρμα είναι στον αέρα. κορώνα ή
γράμματα?

Chorus -2x:
See the truth as you wish
The coin is in the air, heads or tails?

Δες την αλήθεια οπώς θες
Το κέρμα είναι στον αέρα .κορώνα ή
γράμματα?
Τηλεοπτίκες περσόνες αθλητικά είδωλα,

See the truth as you wish
The coin is in the air, heads or tails?

screen characters, athletic idols, examples

πρότυπα
Γυαλιστέρα πρόσωπα ρετουσαρισμένα για
να πέφτουν
Πάνω τους λάγνα βλέμματα του θεάματος
τα ψέμματα
Γίναν οι δίκες μας αλήθειες και όμως μέσα
σε βρώμικα
Δωμάτια δοθήκανε και επίπεδα ανεβήκανε.
Αναβολίκα
Ρουφήξανε φουσκόσανε. Πουλήσανε την
ψύχη τους στο
Διάλο και όμως ευημερήσανε, πολλά τα
θέλω αναγκές πολλές
Τη σύγχρονη εποχή δουλεύεις για να θες
και ας σε κυνηγάνε οι
Οφείλες, προτεραιότητα είσαι για
εταιρείες διαφημιστικές
Που μελετάνε την ψυχή σου και σε κάνουν
την κρίση σου να καις
Τα όμορφα χωριά όμορφα καίγονται.
πέφτουν βομβές και μέτα πεφτούν
καρβέλια
Πολιτικοί σε συνόδους δίνουνε τα χέρια,
και ο κόσμος γλέντιαει μέσα στα πεδία
Μάχης με κομμένα χέρια.κατώ από το
τράπεζι ,πίσω από την βιτρίνα , τι κρύβει
Το προσωπείο τι λένε τα ψήλα τα
γράμματα.

Ρεφραίν- (2x)
Δες την αλήθεια οπώς θες
Το κέρμα είναι στον αέρα. κορώνα ή
γράμματα?
Δες την αλήθεια οπώς θες
Το κέρμα είναι στον αέρα .κορώνα ή
γράμματα?

Ησυχία τάξη και ασφάλεια , πηλίκια
νηφάλια
Οργάνα της τάξης υπηρέτες των πολίτων,
μπλε
Σουπερ ήρωες με μπέρτα και ασπίδα
Δίνουν μάχες καθημερίνα για να
επικράτησει το δίκαιο
ΟΥΠΣ τρέλες σφαίρες βλέπω στα
εξαρχεία, θέλω να πάνε στον
Ουράνο μα... βρίσκουν ψάχνο μια 15χρόνη

Bright faces, retouched after falling

Under the lustful eyes of the show of lies
They have become our own truths, but with-
in dirty rooms
They gave up, climbing social scales
Stalling, they sucked excuses and were full

They sold their souls to the devil

And still they thrived, I want a lot, I need a
lot
Today, you work, and by working generate
benefits
And leave the hunters of debt chasing you
It is the priority, it is advertising
No one looks at the human side, but build
the judgment to burn you
Small and beautiful villages burn
Bombs fall and then bread falls

Politicians in Congress hold hands
And the world is partying in the fields
Battles with cut on the table
Behind the window that hides
The mask, they say, plays high cards

Chorus -2x:
See the truth as you wish
The coin is in the air, heads or tails?
See the truth as you wish
The coin is in the air
Heads or tails?

Peace, order and security, military helmets

Maintainers of the blue order, servants of the
civils
Superheroes with cape and sword
They struggle daily to ensure justice

Crazy bullets want to go to heaven

But they find a 15 year-old soul that went to

ψυ χή πήγε στο ουράνο
Πάνω από τα δακρυγόνα και τον πάνικο
ευκολή ζωη γρήγορα όλα τα
Κομφόρ.
Όμορφες χρωματιστές τροφές αυτοκίνητα
με πολλές στρόφες
Εργοστάσια πολυεθνικές αχρείαστες
συσκευες ΝΑΙ από όλα έχει
Ο μπαχτσές .
Ο κάρκινος έχει πλέον χίλια πρόσωπα,
πιτσίρικια χτυπάνε κάρτα
Και δουλεύουν 15ωρα , η γη ένα
θερμοκήπιο μη αναστρέψιμη κατασταση
Στενεύουν τα περιθώρια.

Ρεφραίν (2x)
Δες την αλήθεια οπώς θες
Το κέρμα είναι στον αέρα. κορώνα ή
γράμματα?
Δες την αλήθεια οπώς θες
Το κέρμα είναι στον αέρα .κορώνα ή
γράμματα?

heaven
tear gas, panic
On the other hand, easy life, all the
comfort
Beautiful engines, colorful foods, fast cars
Factories, multinationals, beautiful
packaging
Yes,everything is in the garden
Cancer has a thousand faces, children hit
the card
And they work 15 hours, the world
moves, but nothing changes
Spaces shrink

Chorus -2x:
See the truth as you wish
The coin is in the air, heads or tails?
See the truth as you wish
The coin is in the air
Heads or tails?

ANNEX K
TRANSCRIPTS –
(MC YINKA–CD ΑΛΑΝΑ)

ANNEX K 1
TRANSLATIONS -
(MC YINKA CD ΑΛΑΝΑ)

ΧΑΙΡΕΤΙΣΜΟΣ (MC YINKA)

SALUTE (MC Yinka)

Ρεφραίν (2x)

Chorus- 2x

Χαιρετώ με σεβασμό τον δικό σου αγώνα
Παίρνω φως και τραγουδώ την δικία σου
εικόνα
Χαιρετώ με σεβασμό τον δικό σου αγώνα
Παίρνω φως και τραγουδώ την δικία σου
εικόνα

I salute with respect your struggle
I light a candle and sing your image

I salute with respect your struggle
I light a candle and sing your image

Αδέσποτες ψύχες ψαχνοντάς για νέους
ήλιους .
Σημαδεμένες από του κόσμου το
απαρτχαΐτ
Από γενοκτονίες οικονομικές, κρίσεις

Souls aimlessly looking for new horizons
All marked by the ills of the world
Slaughters, economic crises, stolen lands
Heroes who stole the glory from them- the
leaders stole everything

,κλεμμένα εδάφη
ήρωες που το χέρι της δύσης τους 'εχει
αρπάξει, τον πλούτο
γυρνάνε σελίδα, ψαχνοντάς να βρουν
ονόμα στο όνειρο τους
να του λούσει μια ηλιαχτιδα, σε αυτή την
πατρίδα, τους είδα, να
επιβιώνουν με μέσα μηδαμίνα για να
κερδίσουν την παρτίδα.
αρχές δεκαετίας 80 είδα το φως , οι
γόνεις μου οι πρώτοι μου μετανάστες
και είδα πως το σύστημα δεν ήταν έτοιμο
να του αγκαλιάσει
αλλά και ανίκανο το ηθίκο τους να
σπάσει και έτσι συνέχισαν
πάνω από δύνες προκαταλήψεις να μου
χαμογέλανε
κοίτα τους, κοίτα τους .

They turn the page trying to find a name
for their dreams.
Trying to have a ray of sunshine in the
country they have chosen
Fighting with their minimum strength to
get a homeland
In the '80s I came into the world, my
parents were the first immigrants
And I realized that the system was not
ready to embrace them,
Nor to make them give up.
They continued on great difficulties, with
smiles.
Look at them, look at them

Ελλάδα 2000 και βάλε οι μετανάστες
αδύναμοι κρίκοι
στην κοινωνική αλυσίδα από ξενομάνης
ξενόφοβους
που φωνάζουν εξω οι ξένοι σαν να είναι η
ουσία της ζωής τους,
από αυτό δεμένοι. Το δυσκίνητο κράτος,
αργοπορήμενα
διευθέτησε το θέμα, νομιμοποίησης και
ετσι οι οικονομίκοι
μετανάστες πλέον , τροφοδοτουν το
σύστημα της δικιάς τους
αποξενώσης , τα παιδιά τους γέννημα
θρέμμα Έλληνες ,
δεν γράφονται στα δημοτόλογια και μόλις
γίνονται 18
τους ζητάνε άδεια παραμονής σαν να
έχουν έρθει πριν ένα χρόνο
στον τόπο αυτό.
η ατιμωρησία, και η ανόχη δίνει έδαφος
σε άναδρους φασίστες.
Να κάνουν πεσίματα σε ανυπεράσπιστους
πακιστάνους και μικροπωλήτες
Επίθεσεις ρατσιστικές αμέτρητες.
Ανεξιχνίαστες υποθέσεις νεκρών
μεταναστών σε χέρια αστυνομίκων
Μέσα σε σκοτεινά δωμάτια ξυλοδάρμοι
και κυνηγητα
και η πολίτεια το βλέμμα της αλλού να
πέτα ,

Greece 2000 and they put immigrants in
fragile rings
In a society that is afraid of foreigners and
is xenophobic
They Shout, out foreigners!It is the essence
of their lives
As if it was their fault ...In this country
without production
The themes on legalities and economic
issues are transferred
And so immigrants feed the system.
Alienation. Their children born and raised
in Greece,
When they turn 18, they are asked a
license to stay
As if they had just arrived
In this place
Impunity and intolerance give way to the
fascists.
To punish Pakistan and the small Asia.
many racial problems.
Cases unresolved, dead immigrants in the
hands of the police.
In dark rooms, beatings and harassment.
And the city is balanced as it can
Trade of foreign meat, women trafficking

εμπόριο ξένης σάρκος, διακίνηση
γυναικών
που θέλουν να εργάστουν και τώρα σε
βρώμικα
στενα την αθωότητα τους πούλουν.

Ρεφραίν (2x)
Χαιρετώ με σεβασμό τον δικό σου αγώνα
Παίρνω φως και τραγουδώ την δικία σου
εικόνα
Χαιρετώ με σεβασμό τον δικό σου αγώνα
Παίρνω φως και τραγουδώ την δικία σου
εικόνα

Who want to work and now get dirty
Sell their innocence

Chorus- 2x
I salute with respect your struggle
I light a candle and sing your image
I salute with respect your struggle
I light a candle and sing your image

ANNEX L
TRANSCRIPTS –
(MC YINKA–CD ΑΛΑΝΑ)

ΑΦΡΙΚΑ (MC YINKA)

ANNEX L 1
TRANSLATIONS -
(MC YINKA CD ΑΛΑΝΑ)

AFRICA [ΑΦΡΙΚΑ]
(MC YINKA)

Άλλη μία ρυθμίκη ιστόρια θα πω για μια
Πριγκηπέσα που εκροσωπούσε το χορό
Το ρυθμό και τον πλούτο το βασίλειο της
ξακουστο
Γιατί ητάν άγρια όμορφο άφρικα το όνομα
της
Η ματία της ήτανε γιορτή και από πολλούς
μνηστήρες
Ποθήτη γύρω της πάντα μαζέμενοι αυλικόι
και πριν πάρει απόφαση
έπαιρνε από αυτούς συμβουλή

Μόλις την έβλεπα στο μυαλό μου έφερνα
γόνιμες περιοχές
Αγάθες μορφές ανθρώπους με αρχές και
παραδόσεις
Κρουστά και τελέτες Το βασίλειο της ήταν
κάτω από την μεσόγειο βασίληάδες
Ψάχνανε τρόπο για να γευτούν τα κάλη της
μαυρής θέας
Για αυτό πλησιάσανε τους αυλικούς που
ήταν πονήροι
Και καιροσκόποι ,πίσω από την πλάτη της
αυτοί κάνανε συνοικέσια
Πήραν τα λέφτα και πουλήσανε την

I'll tell a rhythmic story
Of a princess who represents the dance
The famous palace by its wealth and
function
Its beautiful and wild name was Africa
Represented treasures for many candi-
dates
Courted by the palacians, but before
settling for one
She received several advice from them.

When I saw her, it reminded me of fertile
regions
Sincere face of people with principles and
customs
Percussion and ceremonies,
Her reign was less powerful than the
reigns of the Mediterranean
They looked for a way to taste the flavors
of the Black Goddess
So they went to meet the sagacious
palacians.
Shrewd and opportunists who, without her
consent, made arrangements

Song of the Displaced

άφρικα φθηνά
Και αυτή έγινε πόρνη αδηφάγων τεράτων
που την ρουφούσαν σαν
Κυφήνες.

Ρεφραίν
Αφρικά ...
Αφρικά...

Μέτα από καιρό την είδα, μία ρακέντητη
πριγκήπισα
Στημένη και ρημαγμένη πλέον στο έλεος των
αυλίκων
Που γίνανε διαχειριστές στο βασίλειο της
Η πάλε ποτέ θέα δεν εμπνέει πλέον τους
υπηκόους της
Δεν πιστευούν πια στον πνεύμα της , για
αυτό
Και αγκαλιάσανε την ανασφάλεια και
πηδήξανε
Στο πλοίο της ξενιτιάς .
Μόλις την βλεπω μου έρχεται στο μυαλό η
ασθένεια
Μου έρχεται στο μυαλό οι εμφύλιες διαμάχες
Μου έρχεται στο μυαλό η ανέχεια μια μορφή
Τσακισμένη από δυνάστες.

Αλλό ένα τραγούδι για τις περιοχ`ες που
καταπατήθηκαν
Για τις πριγκηπησες που την λάμψη τους
έχασαν , για τις αποικίες
Που μέτα από την ανεξαρτησία έπεσαν στα
χέρια εθνοπατέρων
Καταχραστών που αρνηθήκανε την εξέλιξη
της ίδιας τους της χώρας
Στο όνομα του κέρδους και της
διαφθοράς,και για να ναI πάντα καλά
Του κόσμου τα αφεντικά,υποβαθμισμένα
όνειρα και αντιλήψεις τρίτου
Κόσμου ,τουριστικά θέρετρα.θέαμα για
ανυποψίαστους που αλλάζει
Με ένα κουμπί και για τους μετανάστες μια
ξεχασμένη γη…

Ρεφραίν

Αφρικά...
Αφρικά...

They received money and sold Africa cheap
She turned into a prostitute for hungry
beasts that feed ifrom her
Like parasites

Chorus- 2x:
Africa...
Africa...

After some time I saw her, Princess
ragamuffin
Destroyed and set on the charity of
palacians
Who became administrators of her
kingdom
The goddess no longer inspires her
subjects
They do not believe in her spirit
And so they embraced insecurity
They jumped on a ship for a foreign trip
As soon as I see her, memories of diseases
come to me
Memory of the civil wars
Memory of misery and the image
Busted by the despots

This is another song for devastated places
For the princesses who have lost their
luster
For the territories that after independence
fell into the hands of usurpers
Who refused the progress of their own
country
For profit and corruption, to be always
well
The owners of the world ...Destroyed
dreams....Third World Perceptions
tourism resorts, wonderful resorts, unsuspecting of change
As if in the push of a button, immigrants
from a forgotten land

Chorus-2x

Africa...
Africa...

ANNEX M
TRANSCRIPTS –
(MC YINKA–CD ΑΛΑΝΑ)

ΑΛΑΝΑ *(MC YINKA)*

Καλώς ήλθες στην ενότητα που σβήνουμε
στείρες στιγμές
Στιγμές Που είσαι εγκλωβισμένος στους
τέσσερις τοίχους του νου
Που- χωρίζει ότι η καρδιά ότι η καρδία
ενώνει
θα αγκαλίασεις, αγαπήσεις ότι σε πορώνει
ο ήχος γίνεται βίωμα και αγγίζει ψυχές
μαρτυρά και δίνει φωνή σε βουβές
κραυγές
ζούμε σε τεμπέλικες μέρες, το ηθικό θέλει
σπρώξιμο.φάστ-φούντ προτάσεις και πέρα
κάνει
το ψάξιμο το δέσιμο ψάχνω με υγιείς
καταστάσεις
που λένε να δεις την πραγματικότητα σε
άλλες διαστάσεις
παραστάσεις ψυχαναγκασμού, θέλω να
κράξω και τα σενάρια
που γράφουν για μένα χωρίς εμένα να
κάψω ,να γράψω στίχους
που ζουν ,δεν μιζεριάζω που θέλουν ένα
ποτήρι κρασί
να σε κεράσουν, στο θέατρο της ζωής δεν
υποκρίνονται
μεσ' στο παράλογο της απλώς αφήνονται

Ρεφραίν - 4 x

Μην σταματάς ,μην σταματάς να παίζεις
Φίλε να τα σπας και εάν πέσεις κάτω μην
κολλάς
Είσαι στην αλάνα

Είμαι μια ψυχή που κυνηγά ώρες διαύγειας
Ώρες που βρίσκω απαντήσεις σε
ερωτήσεις και λύσεις

ANNEX M 1
TRANSLATIONS –
(MC YINKA–CD ΑΛΑΝΑ)

ALANA [ΑΛΑΝΑ]
(MC YINKA)

Welcome to the section that erases sterile
times
Moments that are trapped in the four
walls of the mind
That separates what the heart unites
You shall love and embrace what hurts
you
The sound turns into life and touches the
souls
Accuses and gives voice to the silent
screams
We live in lazy times, moral is what
pushes
Wants Fast-Food, makes suggestions,
recommendations
Looking for statements and salutes
They say they see the reality in other
dimensions
Performances and obsession, I want to
scream scenarios that speak of me without
me
Writing letters about me without burning
me
Writing verses of life without misery, for
those who want a glass of wine
In the theater of life one does not pretend
Is simply carried away

Chorus- 4 x:

Do not stop, do not stop playing
Friend, break and if you fall, do not
demote
You are in the alley (Alana)

I am a soul that seeks hours of lucidity
Hours to find answers for problems and
solutions

Song of the Displaced

Σε γρίφους στίχους σε ύμνους. Έμπνευση
μέσα από ήχους
ώρες που το αίσθημα ξεχείλιζει κ έρχομαι
πιό κοντά
σε άτομα που αγαπώ ,είμαι τύπος που
αναπολώ εξιστορώ
σε μένα βιώματα μου και βλέπω το
αντίκτυπο που έχει ο χρόνος
σε εμάς χρωματιστή κλεψύδρα και κάθε
χρώμα μια περίοδος
χρόνια χαμένα ή κερδισμένα στην
προσπάθεια να αποδείξεις
ότι μπορείς συνειδητοποιείς,
συνειδητοποιείς, συνειδητοποιείς
γεννίεται η αποκάλυψη και πρέπει να την
δεχτείς.
καμμία φορά δεν χώρα στο μυάλο μου το
ποσό διαφέρει
ο ένας με τον άλλον μα το δέχομαι γιατί
αυτό είναι η ουσία
και η ομορφία του κοσμού , μα βλέπω το
ρατσισμό να
βασίζεται στο αντίθετο .μιλώ για την
ψυχολογία που χτίζεις
τη συνείδηση που γυμνάζεις κάθε στιγμή
που νίωθεις οτι αλλάζεις
για το πόσο διαβάζεις τη σκέψη σου και για
το πώς και πόσο σε ψάχνεις.

Είμαι εδώ ελεύθερος πιά σαλεύω σαν
βρέφος μες την κοιλία
Κυλιέμαι κάτω χορευώ με την σκέψη ,
αφεντεύω στην ,μαγεία της
Αγάπης. Καθώς χαλαρώνω και εκτιμώ αυτά
που έχω
Αντέχω ακόμα ,γιατί τα όρια δεν είναι στη
γη είναι στον
Ουρανό εκεί ψηλά ψύχη και σώμα θέλουν
να εκτονωθούν
Καταστάσεις και πρόσωπα να ερωτευτούν
Η παίδικη μας χαρά αντανακλά την αλλή
ζώη
Που ζούμε μες τα όνειρα .
Είκονες σε ψηφιδωτά και παλάτια σκαλιστά
Με μίκρους ήρωες και ξύλινα σπαθιά
φωνάζω δυνατά
Φωνάζω δυνατά μα δεν βραχνιάζω πιά

Charades, verses of hymns, inspired by
the sounds.
Times in which feeling overflows
I get closer to the people I love.
I experience, I see the impact of time on
the color of the hourglass
Each color a period
years lost or added in an effort to prove
That you realize, realize, realize
Sometimes discovery happens
But your mind does not stand
I do not understand that much difference
between them
But I accept because this is the reason and
the beauty of the world
But I see the racism that is based on
reverse
I speak of the psychology that is built on
the conscience,
Who knows your thoughts and how
much you search for yourself

Here I am free, protected, baby in the
womb
I roll, dance with the thought

Thus I relax and appreciate what I have

Hold still, because the limits are not on
earth, they are in heaven.
Up above body and soul want to disarm

Situations and people want to love
Happy childhood reflects the afterlife

We live in dreams
Images in mosaics and carved palaces
With young heroes and wood swords, I
shout
I shout aloud, but do not get hoarse

Ρεφραίν - 4 x:	Chorus- 4 x:
Μην σταματάς ,μην σταματάς να παίζεις Φίλε να τα σπας και εάν πέσεις κάτω μην κολλάς Εϊ !!! Είσαι στην αλάνα	Do not stop, do not stop playing Friend, break and if you fall do not demote You are in the alley (Alana)

ANNEX N TRANSCRIPTS – (MC YINKA–CD ΑΛΑΝΑ)

ANNEX N 1 TRANSLATIONS (MC YINKA–CD ΑΛΑΝΑ)

ΠΑΝΩ ΑΠΟ ΤΟ ΝΕΦΟΣ (MC YINKA)

Πίο ψήλα ναι x 4

Στην κορύφωση παντά στην συνθέση
Στους αδεσποτούς καιρούς εκθέτω την επιτήδευση
Δικηγόροι του διαβόλου κάνουν αγόρευση και
στολίζουν με τα λόγια τους την γενική την ύφεση
είναι η ψυχή στο στόμα .αυτή κίνει το σώμα
και αυτό με τη σείρα του ξορκίζει τις σκέψεις τα δαιμόνια
νεκρός ή ζωντανός να'σαι
θα ορμίσουνε τα όρνια με φάτσες αγγελίκες
για να σου μασήσουνε τα χρόνια
ψάξε να βρεις το θέμα
ακού το Σάουντρακ της εποχής ,
η ενορχήστρωση του δείχνει μία παράφωνη εικόνα
αποθημένα σκόρπια από σκορπιους ανθρωπους
που οι ευαισθησίες περιορίζονται στον μικρόκοσμο τους
λάτρες του θεαθήναι και του μικρού ΕΓΩ τους.

ABOVE THE CLOUDS [ΠΑΝΩ ΑΠΟ ΤΟ ΝΕΦΟΣ] (MC YINKA)

Always on top, yes! x 4

Always in the heights, that order
In unordered times I demonstrate malin-gering
devil's advocates make speeches
And embelishing, with their words, the general decrease
With the soul in mouth- it moves the body, and he in turn frees thoughts and demons, wether alive or dead
Monsters with angelic faces will attack
To chew their years
Try to find the theme
Listen to the soundtrack of that time
The sounds of the orchestra show a distorted image
A bunch of scorpions
A bunche of people-scorpions
And the sensitivity is reduced to their small worlds
Narcissists with their little ego
Daily feed their greed
The snakes sorround them all the time
They live in the ashes
But despite that, they save their "digni-ties"

Θρέφουν κάθε μέρα τον αδηφάγο υλισμό
τους
Του ζώνουνε τα φίδια και ζουν στα
αποκαΐδια
Παρ''όλα αυτά όμως σώζουν τον
καθωσπρεπισμό τους

Ρεφραίν x2

Ρίμες πάνω από το νέφος πετώ
Για να κρατήσω το όραμα καθαρό
Διαχρονικές αξίες αναζητώ

Μια ματιά γύρω σου να ρίξεις ζητώ

το νέφος είναι των μεταναστών η
γκετοποίηση
όλων των μνηστήρων εξουσίας η
μπατσοποίηση
ανθρώπινων δικαιωμάτων η
ιδιωτικοποίηση
και σε πονήρους ανήθικους δρόμους η
μύηση
η μυθικοποίηση του λάιφ στάιλ
και προσώπων που μέσα τους ο
ναρκισίσμος κυλάει
η ψυχή μας που έμαθε να λαχταράει το
περιττό
και τώρα χορεύει του εμπόριου το χόρο
κολλήματα, εφήμερα μηνύματα
,παραμορφωμένα
σήματα. Λαμόγια που κυνηγάνε θυμάτα
πειράματα ανθρώπους σε άνθρωπο ,και
φύση και τωρα
η παραφύση έγινε δεύτερη φύση.
Καβατζόπουστες εν δράσει και αλληλεγύη
θα κλάψει
Αλλονών τους πολέμους πολέμας,το
συμφέρον θα λάμψει
Παραθύρια,στου νόμου τα τσαντήρια,
κάνουν χατήρια
Σε εταιρείες ενώ αύτες τσαλακώνουν της
γης τη μοίρα.

Πίο ψήλα ναι x 4

Πάνω από το νέφος είδα τύπους με σθένος

Chorus-2x:

I throw rhymes over the dark clouds
To make the landscape clearer
Seeking eternal values
I ask you to look around
The clouds are the ghettos of immigrants
The cloud is the corrupt policing of the
suitors of power
It is the privatization of human rights
And initiation into immoral ways
The soul who has learned to want the
superfluous
And now dances the dance of trades
Impacts, ephemeral messages
distorted signals, vagabonds who hunt
their prey
Experiments with humans
The owners of power do
Wanting to take on a second personality
Paranormal
Fags, whores in action
And solidarity will cry
You are fighting someone else's battles
The interest will shine
Windows in the tents of law
They do favors to companies
While they knead the fate of the planet

Always on top, yes! 4x

Above the clouds I saw powerful people

Που ζουν ένα βίος σαν έπος λεοντόκαρδοι
Που φύλουν το δίκαιο σαν κόρη
οφθαλμού σαν βρέφος
Νιώθουν ότι έχουν το χρέος σε αυτούς
που ζούνε στο σκότος
Να ρίξουν άπλετο το φως και αυτοί να
γίνουν χείμαρρος
Βλέπω αύτους που αλλάξαν και
αποβάλλαν το αδικαιολόγητο μένος
Και είδα ότι με εμπρηστίκες ιδεές δεν
πρέπει να είσαι ταυτισμένος
Νιώθω περήφανος γιατι εκε;ι πάνω
γνώρισα το γένος αυτών που τα μάτια
Χάμογελαν γιατι μπρόστα κοίταν ,
Ξανάγεννημένος στο λύρικο παιχνίδι
εκστασιασμένος
Λέξεις φώτος να αναζήτω όταν νιώθω
ενταφιασμένος
Είναι ρουκέτες οι ρίμες και σε αύτες πάνω
είμαι δεμένος
Και μάζι με αύτες σκίζω τα μαύρα
σύννεφα πάντα φορτισμένος

Ρεφραίν x2

Ρίμες πάνω από το νέφος πετώ
Για να κρατήσω το όραμα καθαρό
Διαχρονικές αξίες αναζητώ
Μια ματιά γύρω σου να ρίξεις ζητώ

Living a grand life
Who keep the order as the apple of their
eye
Who keep the order as a newly born
They feel they have the duty and the right
over those who live in darkness
To whom they can throw a lot of light
That can turn into stream
I see those who have changed
And they threw away the anger, for no
reason
I also saw that you can not identify with
incendiary ideas
But I feel proud because from above the
clouds
I met the generation of those whose eyes
smile by looking ahead
Born again, enraptured in a lyrical game,
looking for words of light
While I feel suffocated

Chorus- 2x:

Rhymes games over the dark clouds
To make clearer the landscape
Seeking eternal values
I ask you to look around

ANNEX O
TRANSCRIPTS –
(MC YINKA–CD AΛANA)

TO ΕΠΑΝΑΣΤΑΤΙΚΟ ΤΑΞΙΔΙ
(MC YINKA)

Θέλαμε να κρατήσουμε τον ρυθμό ζωντανό
να νιώσουμε
Πώς είναι να 'σαι ανθρωπος και όχι
παράσιτο

Θέλαμε να κρατήσουμε τον ρυθμό ζωντανό
να νιώσουμε
Πώς είναι να 'σαι ανθρωπος και όχι παράσιτο
Για άλλη μια φορά βρέθηκα στην οδό των
ονείρων
Να παρελαύνω με πάθος και δίψα για κάτι
νέο
Ο δρόμος με οδήγησε σε ένα τόπο που με
ενέπνεε
Γιατί εξέπεμπε ένα μεγαλείο και το σώμα μου
ένιωθε
Τις δονήσεις το ανεξήγητο ρίγος γινόταν πίο
ισχυρό
Αγωνιούσα για το τι θα βρω μέσα μου
έβραζε
η απορία του τι εστί επανάσταση, λες να βρω
στο τόπο αυτό
απάντηση να μια μορφή με ματία επιβλητική,
και στάθηκα αμέσως μπροστά της με
προσοχή μου λεέι
"εγώ είμαι ο Τσε και εκπροσωπώ την γροθία
στους
δυνάστες και ακόλουθοι μου όλοι είναι
επαναστάτες
ταξιδευά πολύ και είδα την φτώχεια
μπροστά μου ζωντανή
πολλών είδων αρρώστιες σε χώρες που είχαν
έλλειψη
κάθε μέρα τρεφόμουν με την αλληλεγύη και
την ισότητα
και πάλευα για αυτήν την πραγματικότητα''

ANNEX O 1
TRANSLATIONS–
(MC YINKA–CD AΛANA)

THE REBELIOUS JOURNEY
[TO ΕΠΑΝΑΣΤΑΤΙΚΟ ΤΑΞΙΔΙ]
(MC YINKA)

We want to keep alive the rythim of life
Feeling what it is like to be people and
not parasites

We want to keep alive the rythim of life
Feeling what is like to be people and not
parasites
Again I felt on the street of dreams
Receiving with passion and thirst some-
thing new
The path led me to a place inspiring
Through which went beyond a happiness
that my body felt
With the inexplicable force, shivers grew
stronger
Agonized and seethed inside me what i
would find
The answer to what is revolution, would I
find it in this place?
Along the way I met a gaze convinced and
proud
I stopped in front of him and he calmly
told me:
I am Che and I present my strength to
dictators, all who follow me are revolutionary.
I traveled a lot and saw poverty before me
very poor countries with various diseases,
missing everything
Every day I fed from equality and frater-
nity
I fought for this reality

τον είδα να
δακρύζει γιατί όταν μίλαγε ένιωθες το
συναίσθημα
και την πίστη να ξεχειλίζει και τότε του είπα
ότι ακόμα
και σήμερα εμπνέει του αγωνίστες για αυτούς
που θέλουνε
νέες εποχές , είπε ότι για να αλλάξεις τα
πράγματα θέλει πειθαρχία οργάνωση , ,θυσίες
αφοσίωση γνώση και παιδεία
ητάν σαν μεγάλος αδερφος του είπα χαίρε τον
αγκάλιασα και συνέχισα
ακάθεκτος το ταξίδι να με πάλι σαν ιχνηλάτης
στην έρευνα
ξερόντας ότι στον τόπο αυτό θα βιώσω
συγκίνηση και χαρά,

λίγο μετά καθώς περιπλανιόμουν άκουσα
κραυγές
και της μοίρας μου το πλήρωμα περίμενα.
(απόσπασμα ομιλίας Μάρτιν Λούθερ κίνγκ)
Into a beautiful symphony of brotherhood
With this celebration we can
work together, to pray together, to struggle togeth-
er, to go to jail together
Defend freedom together, and maybe one day we
will be free

Μπροστά μου στάθηκαν μαυροφορεμένοι
αδερφοί και σηκωσάν την μαύρη του γροθιά
ψηλά με πυγμή
μαζί τους είχαν ένα ιερέα ντυμένο στα άσπρα
φιλήσυχο ειρηνικό που έλαμπέ σαν τα άστρα

ητάν οι μαυροί πάνθηρες και ο μάρτιν λούθερ
κίνγκ και το μανιφέστο
μπροστά μου έτοιμο να ανοιχτεί ένιωθα οτι
ήμουν σε ιεροτελεστία
τις πεποιθήσεις τους έπρεπε να μου πουν πάση
θυσία

"υπήρξαμ σκλάβοι για χρόνια μας είπαν
τελείωσε η δουλεία
και όμως ακόμα, είχαμε δεσμά
ένα ολόκληρο έθνος στο περιθώριο να πονά

I saw him
With crying eyes as he spoke pouring
emotion and feeling
And loyalty t the point of overflowing.
To him I said that, today, he inspires
those who struggle and want new times
I learned that to change the situation it
was necessary
Obedience, organization, sacrifice, dedi-
cation, education and knowledge.
It was as if he was my older brother, I said
goodbye and continued.
Impetuous on the trip, and again a loca-
tor in research
Knowing that this was the place where I
could find excitement and joy.

Later in this adventure, walking aimlessly,
I heard shouts
My crew had the expected destination
(Extracted from the speech of Martin
Luther King)
Into a beautiful symphony of brotherhood
With this celebration we can
work together, to pray together, to struggle
together, to go to jail together
Defend freedom together, and maybe one
day we will be free

In front of me came bereaved brothers
And they lifted up with strength their
black handles
With them was a white priest
Serene and smooth- in peace, shining like
the stars

They were the Black Panthers, Martin
Luther King the manifesto
In front of him, ready to be open
I felt as if I was in a religious ceremony.
Its resolutions should tell me anyway

We were slaves for many years, they say
slavery is over
However we are still connected
An entire country suffering, asking for

Song of the Displaced

και την κοινωνική αλλαγή να ζητά,θέλαμε
να κρατήσουμε τον ρυθμό ζωντανό
να νιωσουμε πως είναι να σαι ανθρωπος
και όχι παράσιτο και έτσι το κίνημα

των δικαιώματων δούλευε για το πρόοδο
της φυλής ξεπερνώντας
εμπόδια εκείνης της εποχής" ο
Κινγκ μου είπε για να αλλάξεις το σκηνικό
πρέπει να έχεις όραμα, όνειρο, στόχο.
σκοπό τους είπα ευχαριστώ γιατί με
γέμισαν
και αυτοί πάλι με την γροθία ψηλά με
χαιρέτισαν.
Συνέχισα την πορεία μου περήφανος γιατί
ζούσα μεγάλες στιγμές
Ναι ήτανε γεγονός , όλοι αυτοι μου δώσαν
τροφή για σκέψη
Μια εικόνα επαναστατική που το
μονοπάτι μου θα φέξει
Ένιωθα ευφορία σαν να μουν μεθυσμένος
στο μονοπάτι της χαράς
Εκστασιασμένος .ήμουν συνεπαρμένος
από ήχους ψυχεδελικόυς

Αυτούς που βλέπεις παραμύθια σαν τους
ακους και τους είδα
Μπροστά μου ήταν απίστευτο ο μαϊλς
ντέϊβις και ο τζίμι χέντριξ να
Τζαμάρουν,πιο κει ο σαλβατόρ νταλί να
εμπνέται και να ζωγραφίζει αυτό
Που βγάζει η τελετή . αυτοί μου μίλησαν
μονό με τα όργανα τους
μου είπαν οτι ακολουθήσαν την ψυχή
τους και όχι την γενία τους
Γιατί οι εποχές είχαν τρόπους, μόδες
τάσεις.και στεγανά που
Πρέπει να τα σπας σαν να είναι δεσμά
τζάμαρα μαζί τους
Έχωσα μια ρίμα που ήταν ατελείωτη σαν
το πνεύμα ολων αυτών που
Γνώρισα.στο ΕΠΑΝΑΣΤΑΤΙΚΟ ΤΑΞΙΔΙ...

social change.
We want to keep the rythim alive

Work for the progress of the race

Overcoming all the difficulties of the time
The King told me to change the scene
I must have vision, dream, goal and
direction

I thanked him and they greeted me with
raised fist
I continued my route, proud, lived there
great moments
Yes, it was right, everyone gave me food
for thought
A revolutionary image that will light my
way
I felt euphoric, drunk in the way of joy

Enraptured, listening melodies, psychedelic sounds

These you see, telling stories I heard and
saw.
In front of me in disbelief, I saw Miles
Davis and Jimi Hendrix
Walking further along the Salvador Dali
painting with inspiration
Where ended the irony - They spoke with
their instruments
They spoke that they were accompanied
by their souls and not their decendência
Because times have modes, fashions,
trends and fetters
Things must be broken, as the handcuffs

I made a rhyme to infinity
Endless as the souls of those I met
During this rebel trip

357

ANNEX P TRANSCRIPTS (ANA TIJOUX- CD *LA BALA*)

DESCLASIFICADO (ANA TIJOUX)

Soy el último eslabón de la pirámide
Desclasificado soy el último eslabón
Que miraron de lado
El corazón anclado
Desparramado porque nunca seré acepta-
do
El tiempo, el límite
El ..que nadie mide, el que enseñaron que
nunca será libre
Educarse para mí no sea accesible
Por más que el comercial diga que todo
es posible
A veces una y a veces nada
En donde quepo en que casilla mi cara
marcada
Perdida la mirada, la distancia, la ventana
Que será lo que define ya de mi cama
Toque todas las puertas
La vida desfilaba en el borde de esta
vereda
Me siento silenciado
Yo estoy desclasificado

Oh soy el último eslabón de la pirámide
Pirámide, pirámide, pirámide ..
Subir peldaños toma tiempo toma años
Los últimos de la fila luego serán los
primeros

Desclasificado soy el último peón que
cambiaron de lado
El sujeto problema objeto del dilema
El que no cabe en este esquema
Sigo pateando piedras, el que sueña a su
manera
Si me preguntan soy de cemento y tierra
Cual es mi clase quien dicta las bases

ANNEX P 1 TRANSCRIPTS AND TRANSLATIONS (ANA TI-JOUX- CD *LA BALA*)

DECLASSIFIED (ANA TIJOUX)

I am the last link of the pyramid
Declassified I am the last link
They looked aside
Heart anchored
Dispersed, because I will never be
accepted
The time, the limit
The one measures, the one they taught
will never be free
Be polite to me, do not be Accessedible
As much as the advertisement says that
everything is possible
Sometimes one and sometimes nothing
Where do I fit in that box, my face
marked
The lost look, the distance, the window
This will define my bed
Touch every door
Life paraded on the edges of the sidewalk
I feel muted
I am disqualified

Oh I am the last link of the pyramid
Pyramid, Pyramid, Pyramid ...
Climbing stairs takes time, it takes years
The last in line will soon be the first

Declassified I am the last pawn that
changed sides
The problematic- subject, dilemma object
The one that does not fit in this scheme
I go on kicking stones, a dreamer in his
own way
If they ask me, I am made of cement and
dust

Corrido en el disfarce ya que mi envase
no clase
Todo me delata mi pelo mi facha
Cual es la justicia cuando siempre se te
tacha
Me siento silenciado
Yo soy el desclassificado

Oh soy el último eslabón de la pirámide
Pirámide, pirámide, pirámide
Oh soy el último eslabón de la pirámide
Pirámide, pirámide, pirámide

Espere espere ya necesito
Ofrecerme al limbo quizás fracase (x3)
Pirámide, pirámide, pirámide ...
Si soy el último eslabón de la pirámide

My class is who dictates the rules
Confused, maladjusted, my package has
no rating
Everything betrays me, my hair, my band
What is justice when you always need it
I feel muted
I am Declassified

Oh I am the last link of the pyramid
Pyramid Pyramid Pyramid
Oh I am the last link of the pyramid
Pyramid Pyramid Pyramid

Wait, wait, I already need
To offer myself to limbo, if I fail (x3)
Pyramid, Pyramid, Pyramid
And I am the last link of the pyramid

ANNEX Q TRANSCRIPTS – (ANA TIJOUX- CD *LA BALA*)

LA BALA (ANA TIJOUX)

La pistola lo miraba fijamente bajo
El manto brillo cromo de su veneno
Un disparo repentino
Penetró cada partícula del aire
Luego se cayó

Se derramó la primera gota ya por la cien
(x3)
Por la cien

La muerte lo miró de forma desafiante
Con la sangre entre los dientes
Y una oscuridad reinante
La bala entre tanto suspendida fija

ANNEX Q 1 TRANSLATIONS – (ANA TIJOUX- CD *LA BALA*)

THE BULLET (ANA TIJOUX)

The gun was staring at him
The chrome cloak of its poison
A sudden shot
Penetrated every particle of the air
Then he fell.

The first drop was spilled for one hundred
(x3)
For one hundred

Death looked at him in a challenging way
With blood between the teeth
And a reigning darkness
The bullet, in this interval, suspended fixed

Bailaba una asesinato girando sobre sí misma
Se perdió de vista la vida con su pista
Mientras un joven padece ante el deseo de
conquista suelo
De rodilla su beso cambia lentamente
Del rojo al hielo

Angelitos de papel se han perdido por babel
¿Quién devolverá esta piel?
La madre le suplica al coronel
La muerte es un carrusel
Fúnebre en su vaivén
Un juicio final cruel
El ángel le suplica al coronel

Su mirada quedo congelada por el súbito
Sonido pulsante que lo valió
Hombre desplomado desangrado sin aliento
quedo pálida la vida le falló

Se derramó la primera gota ya por la
Cien (x3) Por la cien
Aquel cuerpo sin vida era su hijo
Maria estupefacta
Cayó al piso
Su rostro deformado se convirtió en un grito
Quedo solo un zumbido que significa(ase-
sino)
La hora del deceso marcaba por um beso
del adiós
De la madre perdida en desconsuelo
Hizo llover al cielo
Lágrimas del desierto y hasta la muerte
Se quedo callada por respeto

Angelitos de papel se han perdido por Babel
Quien devolverá esta piel?
La madre le suplica al coronel
La muerte es un carrusel
Fúnebre en su vaivén
Un juicio fina cruel
El ángel le suplica al coronel

Tiros suenan
Muertes llevan
Polvos queman
Prakapampam(x4)

Danced a murder, turning on itself
Lost sight of life and its track
As a young man suffers on the desire to
conquer the soil
On his knees its kiss slowly changes
From red to ice

Paper angels were lost by Babel
Who will return this skin?
The mother begged the Colonel
Death is a carousel
Funereal in its coming and going
A cruel judgment
The angel pleads to the Colonel

His gaze remained frozen by the sudden
pulsating noise that killed him
fallen man, bleeding, breathless
Blanched, life failed him

The first drop was spilled for one hundred
(x3)
for one hundred
That lifeless body was her son
Maria was shocked
Fell to the floor
Her deformed face became a scream
Just a buzz that means (killer)
The time is marked by a farewell kiss
Of a mother lost in disconsolate
Like rain for the sky
Desert tears and even death
Remained silent in respect

Paper angels were lost by Babel
Who will return this skin?
The mother begged the Colonel
Death is a carousel
Funereal in its coming and going
A cruel judgment
The angel pleads to the Colonel

Shots sounds
They bring death
Powder, Burning
Prakapampam (x4)

ANNEX R
TRANSCRIPTS
(ANA TIJOUX- CD *LA BALA*)

SI TE PREGUNTAN
(ANA TIJOUX)

Yeah
La Aldea
Ana Tijoux
Cuba y Chille, siéntelo!
Yo, yo, esta es otra historia
en la memoria de otra esquina del planeta

Otra victoria sin gloria, escoria que cual
espina penetra
Otro sonido de metra que se siente
De otro jodido rincón que no visitó el
presidente
Otros delincuentes tomando por asalto tu
mente
Armados con los problemas de su gente
Otros que como tú cargan errores, sienten
Sobrevivientes, vividores, solo eso nos hace
diferentes
A lo más bajo vente
Donde se vive al día, tú dime un día
en que no hay un fajo que cuentes, vente!
Donde vive esta mujer que
Te lo hace por dinero para que su hijo se
alimente

Donde no vas pues dices que es peligroso el
ghetto
La droga ahoga, pero no caen los que los
introdujeron
Las pandillas se matan, la policía maltrata
Mientras la mafia real come con cubiertos
de plata
Es nuestra realidad, no sabemos de lujo
Todo viene y se va, nadie controla el flujo
Mucha necesidad dentro de poco espacio
Vamos a más velocidad pues vivimos
despacio
Vicios o socio no hay ley

ANNEX R 1
TRANSLATIONS –
(ANA TIJOUX- CD *LA BALA*)

IF THEY ASK YOU
(ANA TIJOUX)

Yes
The village
Ana Tijoux
Cuba and Chile, feel them
This is another story
In memory of another corner of the planett
Another victory without glory, slag that
penetrates as a thorn
Another sound of machine gun that is felt
From another fucked up corner that the
president did not visit
Other offenders assaulting your mind
Armed with the problems of their people
Others lthat ike you carry mistakes, feel
Survivors, alive,only that makes them
different
To the lowest, come
Where you live one day, tell me one day
Where there is no beef to be told, go!
Where lives this woman that
Does it to you for money, to feed her child

Where you will not go, because you say
that the ghetto is dangerous
The drug drowns , but those who intro-
duced it do not fall
The gangs kill themselves, the police
mistreats
While the real mafia eats with silverware
It is our reality, we know no luxury
Everything comes and goes, no one con-
trols the flow
Too much need in a short space
We go faster, because we live slowly
Vices or partners, there is no law

Negocios, socio, no hay break
Aleluya vivimos en la calle
Nuestra casa es más grande que la tuya

Yo sé, que el amor... se fue
Cuando el dinero se pudrió de la fe
Que detrás de todo siempre hay interés
Pero a pesar de todo me mantengo de pie
Firme! Que me mantengo! Todo el tiempo!
Si te preguntan, di que somos de la calle!
Cuba, Chile y América
Cuba, Chile y América Latina
Santiago, la Habana, las capitales unidas
Centro, sur cordillera o planicie valle
Que vaya caminando ya hacia la isla
Desde el Malecón se abrirán las alamedas
Se prenderán las velas y la luz
Con sus estelas Centinelas sobre suelas,
Secuelas sobre las huellas
Revueltas las escuelas, la cautela no da
sueltas
Ella es la calle, ella es la madre
Ella es la abuela de todos los pilares
La que no te deja, ni menos te abandona
La que no te suelta si la vida te desploma
Ella es la base que hace taza y es tu casa
Es pedazo de cemento, es tu esquina, y es
tu plaza
La que no te falla, la que no te calla
Si tu lloras en su falda, ella te abraza en su
muralla
La que todo mira, todo observa y a la deriva
Esquiva de forma agresiva, la salida más
viva
Explosiva de vida, sin normativas viva
Creativa y activa, de la calle más combativa
Que vio nacer en su manto, que vio caer a
tantos, tantos
Que ningún canto alcanzaría para cuantos
Firme y fuerte por todos los ausentes
Firme y fuerte por todos los presentes

Yo sé, que el amor... se fue
Cuando el dinero se pudrio de la fe
Que detrás de todo siempre hay interés
Pero a pesar de todo me mantengo de pie

Business partners, no breack
Hallelujah, we live on the street
Our house is bigger than yours

I know that the love is gone
When money rotted faith
That behind it all there is always interest
But still I remain standing
Firm! I keep! All the time!
If they ask, say we are from the street!
Cuba, Chile and America
Cuba, Chile and Latin America
Santiago, Havana, as united capitals
Center, south, range, valley
Go walking to the island already
From Malecón will open fairways
The candles will be lit and the light
With its Sentinels on soles
It is the street, she is the mother
Revolt schools, caution is not loose
It is the street, she is the mother
She is the grandmother of all pillars
The one does not leave you or abandon you
The one that does not let go, if life falls apart
It is the foundation that makes coffee and
home
It is piece of cement, is its corner, and it is
your place
That does not fail, does not mute you
If you cry in her lap, she embraces you in its
walls
To every gaze, all eyes and in driftage
Dodges aggressively, the most vivid escape
Explosive of life, living without norms
Creative and active, the most combative of
the street
Has seen many being born in her cloak, she
saw the fall of many, many
That no corner would be enough for that
many
Firm and strong for all missing
Firm and strong for all present

I know that love... is gone
When money rotted faith
That behind it all there is always interest
But still I'm standing

Song of the Displaced

Firme! Que me mantengo! Todo el tiempo!
Si te preguntan, di que somos de la calle!

Yeah, vengo de un lugar oscuro, sobrado de
sombras
Donde la ley es no respetar la ley que
pongan
Donde la injusticia oficial pisado se compra
Y verdad que gira inspira la mentira que nos
ronda
Mantén tu fe fuerte, no dejes
Que la fechorías espirituales te afecten
Ni hagan efecto en tu alma, la infecten
Friend sin frenar, inclina tu frente
La vista pesa, la gente aprisa, va por la pista
Y la humanidad solo en la plata piensa
Y en la street la triste tristeza
Sigue free, fría, y frívola nos besa
Lava te que, la lava te quema
Nada te queda, nada te queda
Acaba esa sed que acaba tu sed
Escaba tu ser y clava tus pies donde puedas
La sangre corre, errores no hay quien borre
Forre esa y con responsabilidad
Y no respire hondo porque puede caer como
las torres
Y no resistirá ver que tu ser no se deshonre
El fin esta, canta y un gallo
La calle es un ring donde
King del King queremos ser tu caballo
Sacan la mano a la velocidad del rayo
Y más caro que un Roll Roice del año te
salen los fallos
Ana Tijoux hermana di tu
Si en Chile pagan en dólares y cobran en
club
Como el pana mapocho lucho para que
escuchen mi voz
En un lugar donde corrupto ahorita ya es
hasta dios

Yo sé, que el amor... se fue
Cuando el dinero se pudrió de la fe
Que detrás de todo siempre hay interés
Pero a pesar de todo me mantengo de pie
Firme! Que me mantengo! Todo el tiempo!
Si te preguntan, di que somos de la calle!

Firm! I keep! All the time!
If they ask, say we are from the street!

Yes, I come from a dark place, where the
shadows are abundant
Where the law is not respected
Where injustice is purchased
And the truth that turns inspires the lie that
haunts us
Keep your faith strong, do not allow
Spiritual crimes to affect you
Have no effect on your soul, infecting you
Friend without stopping, lift your face
The sight weighs, people rush, take the track
And humanity only thinks about cash
And on the street the sad sadness
Remain free, cold, frivolous and kisses us
Lava wants you, the lava that burns you
Theres nothing left, nothing left for you
Quench this thirst that ends your thirst
Escapes yourself, spiking its nails where it can
Blood flows, no one can erase mistakes
Prevent yourself and with responsibly
And do not take a deep breath because it can
fall like the towers
And will not bear to see no dishonor of
yourself
And the end is there, sings like a rooster
The street is a ring where
King of Kings, we want to be your horse
Theyremove their hand with lightning speed
And more expensive than a Rolls Royce of the
year, are your flaws
Tell your sister Ana Tijoux
In Chile they pay in dollars and charge at the
club
Like the friend Mapocho, I fight for them to
listen to my voice
In a place where corrupts will be up to God
soon enough.

I know that love.. is gone
When money rotted faith
That behind it all there is always interest
But still I'm standing
Firm! I keep! All the time!
If they ask, say we are from the street!

ANNEX S
TRANSCRIPTS
(ANA TIJOUX- CD *LA BALA*)

ANNEX S 1
TRANSLATIONS
(ANA TIJOUX- CD *LA BALA*)

SHOCK (*ANA TIJOUX*)

SHOCK (*ANA TIJOUX*)

Venenosos tus monólogos
Tus discursos incoloros
No ves que non estamos solos
Millones de polo a polo
Al son de um solo coro
Marcharemos com el trono
Com la convicción que
Basta de robo!

Poisonous are your monologues
Your speeches are colorless
Don't you see that we are not alone
Millions from pole to pole
At the sound of one choir
We will march with the tone
With the conviction that
Enough theft!

Tu estado de control
Tu trono podrido de oro
Tu politica y tu riqueza
Y tu tesoro no!
La hora sono! La hora sono!
No permitiremos mas, mas
Tu dotrina del shock!
La hora sono, la hora sono
Dotrina del shock 2x

Your state of control
Your rotten golden throne
Your politics and your wealth
And your treasure, no!
The time came! The time came!
We will not allow no more, no more.
Your doctrine of "shock"
The time came, came!
Doctrine of "shock" 2x

No hay países solo corporaciones
Quien tiene más, más más acciones
Trozos gordos, poderosos
Decisiones por muy pocos.
Constituición pinochetista
Derecho opus dei, libro fascista
Golpista disfrazado de un indulto elitista
Cae la gota, cae la bolsaL
A torna se torna la maquina rota
La calle no calle, la calle se raya
La calle no calla debate que estala.
Todo lo quitan, todo lo venden
Todo se lucra, la vida, la muerte
Todo es negocio como tu todos
Semilla, Pascuala, métodos y coro

There are no countries, only corporations
Who has more, more and more shares
large pieces, powerful
Decisions by very few
Constitution of Pinochet
"Opus dei" rights, fascist book
Coup leader disguised as an elitist reprieve
Falls the drop, drops the stocks
The decision is made, the machine, broken
The street does not shut, the street scratches itself
The street does not shut, the debate explodes
They take everything, they sell everything
Everything is profit, life and death
Everything is business, like you, all
Seed, Pascuala, methods and leather

Golpe a golpe, beso a beso
Con las ganas y el aliento
Con cenizas, con el fuego

Blow by blow, kiss by kiss
With desire and encouragement
With ash, with fire

Del presente con recuerdo
Con certeza y con desgarro
Con el objetivo claro
Con memoria y con la historia
El futuro es ahora!
Todo este tubo de ensayo,
Todo este laboratorio que a diario,
Todo este fallo, todo este económico
modelo condenado de dinosaurio.
Todo se criminaliza, todo se justifica en
la noticia,
Todo se quita, todo se pisa, todo se ficha
y clasifica.
Pero... tu política y tu táctica,
Tu típica risa y ética.
Tu comunicado manipulado
¿cuantos fueron los callados?
Pacos, guanacos y lumas,
Pacos, guanacos y tunas,
Pacos, guanacos no suman.
Cuantos fueron los que se robaron las
fortunas?

Venenosos tus monólogos
Tus discursos incoloros
No ves que non estamos solos
Millones de polo a polo
Al son de um solo coro
Marcharemos com el trono
Com la convicción que
Basta de robo!

From the present, with memories
With certainty and with fret
With the clear objective
With memory and history
The future is now
All this is a test tube,
All this is a laboratory for the everyday,
All this failure, All this is a damned eco-
nomic model from the dinosaur era.
Everything is criminalized, Everything is
justified on the news,
Everything is removed, Everything is
stepped on, Everything is indexed and
classified,
But... Your politics and your tactics,
Your general laughter and ethic.
Your manipulated press release,
How many did you silence?
Pacos, guanacos and lumas,
Pacos, guanacos and lumas,
Pacos, guanacos don't add up.
How many made off with the fortune?

Poisonous are your monologues
Your speeches are colorless
Don't you see that we are not alone
Millions from pole to pole
At the sound of one choir
We will march with the tone
With the conviction that
Enough theft!

ANNEX T TRANSCRIPTS – (ANA TIJOUX- CD *LA BALA*)

ANNEX T 1 TRANSLATIONS – (ANA TIJOUX- CD *LA BALA*)

SACAR LA VOZ (ANA TIJOUX)

RELEASE THE VOICE (ANA TIJOUX)

Respirar para sacar la voz
Despegar tan lejos como un águila veloz
Respirar un futuro esplendor, cobra más
sentido si lo creamos los dos.
Liberarse de todo el pudor, tomar de las
riendas, no rendirse al opresor.
Caminar erguido, sin temor, respirar y
sacar la voz.
Uhh, uhh, uhhh (x2).

Breathe to release the voice
Take off as far as a swift eagle
Breathing a splendorous future makes more
sense if we both create it
Get rid of all the shame and take the reins,
not surrendering to the oppressive
Walk erected without fear breathe and
release the voice
Uhh, uhh, uhhh (2x)

Tengo los bolsillos vacíos, los labios
partidos, la piel con escamas, cada vez que
miro hacia el vacío.
Las suelas gastadas, las manos atadas, la
puerta de entrada siempre tuvo el cartel,
que dijo que estaba cerrada.
Una espina clavada, una herida infectada,
entramada, una rabia colmada, en el todo
y en la nada.
El paso torpe, al borde, sin acorde, cada
vez que pierdo el norte, tengo la pérdida
del soporte.
El tiempo que clava, me traba la daga, me
mata, filuda la flama, sin calma, que de las
manos se me escapa.
Pero, tengo mi rincón florido, sacar la
voz, no estoy sola, estoy conmigo.
Liberarse de todo el pudor, tomar de las
riendas, no rendirse al opresor. Caminar
erguido, sin temor, respirar y sacar la voz.
Uhh, uhh, uhhh (x4).

I have empty pockets, chapped lips, skin
with scales, every time I look into the void
The sole of my shoe worn, hands tied, the
gateway always had a sign that said it was
closed
A spine spiked, an inflamed wound, resistant anger at the height of everything and
nothing
A unsteadily step on the edge without
chord, every time I lose the north I have
lost support
The time plunges, the knife locked in
me, kills me, the flame without calm that
escapes from my hands
But I have my flowery corner, release the
voice, I am not alone, I am me
Get rid of all the shame and take the reins,
not surrender to the oppressive
Walk erected without fear, breathe and
release the voice
Uhh, uhh, uhhh (4x)

Tengo el amor olvidado, cansado, ag-
otado, botado. Al piso cayeron todos los
fragmentos, que estaban quebrados.
El mirar encorvado, el puño cerrado,
no tengo nada, pero nada, suma en este

I have forgotten love, tired, exhausted.
Fell to the ground all the pieces that were
broken
The curved look, the clenched fist, I have

charco.
La mandíbula marcada, palabra prepara-
da, cada letra afilada, está en la cresta de
la oleada. Sin pena ni gloria, escribiré esta
historia, el tema no es caerse, Levantarse
es la victoria.
Venir de vuelta, abrir la puerta, estar
resuelto, estar alerta.
Sacar la voz que estaba muerta, y hacerla
orquesta
Caminar, seguro, libre, sin temor, respirar
y sacar la voz.
Liberarse de todo el pudor, tomar de las
riendas, no rendirse al opresor. Caminar
erguido, sin temor, respirar y sacar la voz.
Uhh, uhh, uhhh (x4).

El tiempo clava la daga
Haga lo que haga uno
Estraga oportuno
Tú no cobras lo que el tiempo paga.
Estraga saga tras saga
Raspa con su amarga espátula
Huérfano se hace de brújulas
Y lúcidamente en celo
Blanca el arma, blanco el pelo
Su blanca cara de crápula
'Ésta' dice un espinela
La que Violeta cantaba
La de la sílaba octava del pateador
Vieja escuela.
Y lo que duela, que duela
Si es que tiene que doler
La flama sin calma que arder tenga
Que siga ardendo
Que siga fosforeciendo

En un cordel, a colgar la copla, que el
viento mece,
Que pocas veces merece.
Cada pena, suelta voz, cada tos
Pensando en sacar la voz.
Uhh, uhh, uhhh (x2)

nothing more, but nothing adds anything
to this puddle
Scarred jaw , prepared word, each letter is
sharp, on the crest of the wave. Without
pain or glory, I will write this story, Falling is not failing, but rising is victory
Return again, open the door, be determined, be alert
Raise the voice that was dead and turn it
into orchestra
Get rid of all the shame and take the
reins, do not surrender to the oppressive
Walk raised without fear breathe and
release the voice
Uhh, uhh, uhhh (4x)

Time plunges the dagger
Whatever you do
Spoil an adjustment
You do not charge what time pays
Spoils, saga after saga
Scrapes with its bitter spatula
Orphaned is made of compasses
And lucidly in fervor
White weapon, white hair
His scoundrel white face
'This one' said a spinel
The Violet sang
The eighth syllable of the "kicker"
Old School
And what hurts, let it hurt
If it has to hurt
The flame without calm
That has to burn
Let it continue burning
Continue phosphorescing
Is it has to phosphoresce.

On a rope hung the song that scaled the
wind
That rarely deserves
Each pen, release the voice, every cough
Thinking of releasing the voice
Uhh, uhh, uhhh (x2)

ANNEX U
TRANSCRIPTS –

PROCURA DA POESIA
(CARLOS DRUMMOND
DE ANDRADE)

Não faças versos sobre acontecimentos.
Não há criação nem morte perante a
poesia.
Diante dela, a vida é um sol estático,
não aquece nem ilumina.
As afinidades, os aniversários, os incidentes pessoais não contam.
Não faças poesia com o corpo,
esse excelente, completo e confortável
corpo, tão infenso à efusão lírica.

Tua gota de bile, tua careta de gozo ou
dor no escuro
são indiferentes.
Não me reveles teus sentimentos,
que se prevalecem de equívoco e tentam a
longa viagem.
O que pensas e sentes, isso ainda não é
poesia.

Não cantes tua cidade, deixa-a em paz.
O canto não é o movimento das máquinas
nem o segredo das casas.
Não é música ouvida de passagem, rumor
do mar nas ruas junto à linha de espuma.

O canto não é a natureza
nem os homens em sociedade.
Para ele, chuva e noite, fadiga e esperança
nada significam.
A poesia (não tires poesia das coisas)
elide sujeito e objeto.

Não dramatizes, não invoques,
não indagues. Não percas tempo em mentir.
Não te aborreças.
Teu iate de marfim, teu sapato de diamante,
vossas mazurcas e abusões, vossos esquele-

ANNEX U 1
TRANSLATIONS –

SEARCH FOR POETRY
(CARLOS DRUMMOND
DE ANDRADE)

Do not make verses about events.
No creation or death before poetry.
Before her, life is a static sun,
no heat or lights.
Affinities, birthdays, personal incidents do
not count.
Do not do poetry with the body,
this excellent, complete and comfortable
body, so averse to lyrical effusion.

Your drop of bile, your grimace of joy or
pain in the dark
They are indifferent.
Do not betray your feelings,
that prevail misunderstanding and try the
long journey.
What do you think and feel, it is not
poetry.

Do not sing your city, let alone.
Singing is not the movement of the machines or the secret house.
There is music heard in passing sound of
the sea in the streets next to the foam line.

Singing is not nature
or men in society.
For him, rain and night, fatigue and hope
mean nothing.
Poetry (no tires poetry of things)
elide subject and object.

No dramatizes not invoques,
not indagues. Do not waste your time to lie.
Do not be aborreças.
Your ivory yacht, your diamond shoe,
mazurkas and abusões your, your family

Song of the Displaced

tos de família
desaparecem na curva do tempo, é algo
imprestável.
Não recomponhas
tua sepultada e merencória infância.
Não osciles entre o espelho e a
memória em dissipação.
Que se dissipou, não era poesia.
Que se partiu, cristal não era.

Penetra surdamente no reino das palavras.
Lá estão os poemas que esperam ser
escritos.
Estão paralisados, mas não há desespero,
há calma e frescura na superfície intata.
Ei-los sós e mudos, em estado de dicionário.

Convive com teus poemas, antes de
escrevê-los.
Tem paciência, se obscuros. Calma, se te
provocam.
Espera que cada um se realize e consume
com seu poder de palavra
e seu poder de silêncio.
Não forces o poema a desprender-se do
limbo.
Não colhas no chão o poema que se
perdeu.
Não adules o poema. Aceita-o
como ele aceitará sua forma definitiva e
concentrada
no espaço.

Chega mais perto e contempla as palavras.
Cada uma
tem mil faces secretas sob a face neutra
e te pergunta, sem interesse pela resposta,
pobre ou terrível que lhe deres:
Trouxeste a chave?

Repara:
ermas de melodia e conceito
elas se refugiaram na noite, as palavras.
Ainda úmidas e impregnadas de sono,
rolam num rio difícil e se transformam
em desprezo.

skeletons
disappear in the time curve is something
snotty.
Do not fix
your buried and melancholy childhood.
There osciles between the mirror and
dissipation in memory.
That cleared, was not poetry.
What is left, Crystal was not.

Penetrates dully in the realm of words.
There are poems waiting to be written.
Are paralyzed, but no despair,
there are quiet and freshness in the intact
surface.
Here they are alone and silent in dictionary state.

Coexists with your poems before writing
them.
Have patience, is unclear. Calm if they
cause you.
Expects each to perform and consume
with your word power
and its quiet power.
No forces the poem to loosen up the limb.
No colhas the ground that the poem was
lost.
No adules the poem. Accept it
as it accepts its final and concentrated
form
in space.

Come closer and includes the words.
Each one
It has a thousand secret faces under the
neutral face
and asks you, without interest for the answer,
poor or terrible give him,
Did you bring the key?

Notice:
melody and barren concept
they took refuge in the night, the words.
Still damp and impregnated with sleep,
roll a difficult river and turn into con-
tempt.

APPENDICES

APPENDIX TO
INTERVIEW WITH PRODUCER CAIO
ABUMANSSUR BERALDO (MC YOKA)

INTERVIEW CONDUCTED BY EMAIL, ON 26/09/2013

Biographical data

01) What is your full name?
A: Caio Abumanssur Beraldo.

02) What is your age?
A: 33 years.

03) Where were you born?
A: Maringa - Paraná.

04) What does the name MC Yoka mean?
A: It is a childhood nickname ...There was a time in my childhood where we spoke the words to the contrary, then it caught.

05) How did your story with rap *start?*
A: In my generation, rap was the musical style that influenced the people who had a more urban life, who lived on the streets, absorbing the culture, customs and experience the street has. So, since 12 years, I listened and I searched for rap, then when I moved to England and had more access to culture, I started to buy records, began to Dj and hence became a rap producer, at a particular time, I was attracting others from the medium (MCs) and so I entered the movement with a certain participation greater than just a listener of the genre.

On immigration and living abroad

06) When have you decided to leave Brazil?
A: I left Brazil for the first time in September 1999.

07) How many countries have you lived in?
A: A total of five: Brazil, United States, Portugal, England and Spain.

08) How is the life of an immigrant?
A: Well, it's hard to define the life of an immigrant, considering the phases and mutations that life will naturally have and also the social level of immigration .... It can vary greatly.But some things are fact. The imigration starts from a demand for work and better living conditions. Overall, the immigrant reaches the back door of a city, the immigrant executes the work that is in demand, usually lower level activities, that local people dispense due to the social level they occupy. Anyway ... there are many difficulties as an immigrant. We see a friendly atmosphere on the banks, but in order to get to the core it takes time depending on the degree of inclusion, determination and ambition of the immigrant. I am talking about immigration in general, that is, here in São Paulo, Rio de Janeiro, Barcelona, London .... anyway, I think these are general factors, both for those who came to a city to be motorcycle courier, or to be an engineer, these factors will influence their lives. Already talking about being an illegal immigrant in a country other than his own, the issues are all these and a lot more. I lived for 12 years in another country, much to the margins of society, but not in a marginalized way, as in Europe.Where I lived most of my exile, the social conditions allow for the immigrants, even if illegal, to enter more in society than a shantytown in Brazil .But the daily life of an immigrant in these circumstances is different from an ordinary citizen. They do not have access to free education, career incen-

tives, study, personal projects, in some places without possibility of using the health care system, they do not have access to social security, but they pay taxes from their salary also and are more vulnerable to labor issues, which are common.In other words, they end up hostage in a given situation, to be pending with the state in order to legalize the status of citizen of that place. They do not vote, you do not appear in statistics, not in the local census ...The point is, they end up being on the margin of error of equality, hahahahahaha.That's funny, because when I came back to Brazil in 2011, I had to go back to being a "citizen", taking my ID number, voter registration, having to pay my income tax ....And I had no habit of doing these things, somehow lived more free out there. I confess that I have put it on the scale. The conviviality in Europe gives you a social life, even illegally, quite decent compared to Brazilian standards, but when you start to notice and understand the system that this country creates for local citizens, the support the government provides for a person to prepare professionally or artistically, build their family, you notice that you are far behind and depending on your level of education that will revolt you.Is that... sometimes it's better not to know things, right?

09) Today you live in Brazil?Why and when you chose to come back?

A: Today I am in São Paulo for two years.I came back here directly from Barcelona.Since 2008, Europe is facing a very severe economic crisis and such social inclusion was becoming increasingly difficult to idealize, as jobs that were once for immigrants, are now being offered to the local people. But I in a way I had already planned it.I n 2007, I started university in Spain, worked many years to study there.Ever since I graduated, I began to feel the need to use my profession, but the labor market is very difficult, hence came the possibility of moving to São Paulo, where she knew peopl the middle of the song, and well .. .The chi am.

10) How long have you been an immigrant?

A: I've lived outside of Brazil for 12 years, and now I have been in Sao Paulo for two years I no longer consider the immigrant status as something irreversible. For me it is not a fixed condition.I consider myself a very understanding person to general and social issues, a hybrid citizen, like those mutts, that never had a vaccine and he never got sick, you know? hahahahaha ...And I love this current stage of my immigration status, I went from immigrant to master.Living outside makes you able to predict economic, educational, social events in general of a country like Brazil. It makes you observant and sensitive to issues and general conviviality, because we are living here today, already lived in Europe a long time ago.

11) For you, what is globalization?It can be experienced by everyone?

A: Look, I confess I do not quite understand the meaning of the word globalization, really. I am ashamed, I think somehow I have lived many years as part of a system and therefore I was and am unable to analyze it or define it.If the meaning of the globalization is to bring up living standards, industrialization, culture, traditions, granting power to everyone in an equal way, I sincerely hope that globalization is not experienced by all.The social changes that have happened in Europe kill many other issues that we still have. I live here in Brazil and I think it still has a huge weight against everything we desire in a way to have in our country, socially speaking.I would be unable to say where it is better to live. I just add treasure what we have here and in Europe we can not have more. It is irreversible. So, honestly, I do not know :-(

12) When (and how) did the idea for "Pássaro Imigrante" came?

A: When I lived in London between 2001-2006, we had a group called Project Illegal, I produced and the MC was animmigrant from Bahia, graduated in literature, who knew many books and of our literature. He was older than me, I was 18 at the time, and he influenced me a lot to open up my head to see the social judgments that existed. In other worlds, ifyou are out of your country, because it gives you social conditions. Over time it begins to be more iterating than your refuge. It also provides you with a very good condition... We'll buy a lot of records, especially Brazilian music, I met a lot of Brazilian sic Multiple while I lived in London. One day we found a vinyl of a Brazilian artist, Claudia, the album name was "Emigrant Bird" - 1978 (inversely proportional to my bird, haha) and of course, the name really caught our attention, we enjoyed this record for a long time and until today I am a big fan of this work.When I lived in Spain. After my course of Audio Engineering, I felt the need to assert myself as a producer since I had released stuff on the internet, but did not see much value in a job that was not physical, because we are always tucked in bookstores, buying and rediscovering old music, forgotten that I have always wanted to also make a vinyl record that one day would also rediscovered, so ...At this point, I had already lived in four other countries, knew enough people in the middle and also had a very mature opinion on the subject and decided to dedicate the album to this course, that was when I decided to gather people I met on this journey and honor the rap tradition.

13) Who are (and which are) partners that appear on your record? What the performances have in common?

A: Partners are Partnership of Sound (London), Link Chain (SP), Stodgy (Rio / Barcelona), Mamelo Sound System in (São Paulo) and Pulcro (Barcelona)... About the similarities of the performances, I do not know if it has much in common actually. Undoubtedly they were all influenced by my initiative, and maybe I introduced some energy together in the project, but the only song that decided the subject was *"Pássaro Imigrante"*, because I wanted to approach it and Stodgy loved the theme as it is a Mark of Rio de Janeiro who lives in Barcelona and live with the dilemmas that I quoted before, so pa ra it fit like a glove.What is there in a way largely of performances is the sense of walking in the counter direction of the majority, this is what we do when *raps,* questions things that people are too lazy to speak or not to Interam that They are part of their daily lives.I think that's the common factor, so if y ou are outside the majority, feel exiled from living, ideas, general customs and questions that you do not cease to be an immigrant Bird, or "Alien", how would you define best Albert Camus.

Opinion

14) Why are lyrics never revealed when it comes to rap-immigrant?Not only on your disk, but others too, there are hardly any inserts or transcribed music on the web ... This behavior sets actually some kind of resistance?

A: I doubt it's some kind of resistance, I find it simply that rap actually is something self-taught, done without school, without planning and without much commercial perspective, that is, in most projects there are different people looking after all production process of a disk, sales, distribution, inserts, design... Rap has long been a production of one or two people.I think it's more that than anything else.

15) You can survive of rap nowadays?(Do You live of your music or pursuing other activity?)

A: Look, I particularly think that if a person does not do everything for something and have their focus on what they want, they can get through anything.Of course, the case of the arts is necessary to have a certain talent but this autodidact "approach" brings some vices that hinder an individual's time to market their product, or to sell art, they also have to know what is working and WORK ...Many artists are not prepared to work and because of that they do not survive from their art.Unless your talent is indisputable and impossible to ignore, there some cases. Nowadays I live of art, yes, but in different directions.I make music foradvertising, films, videos, plays, working as technical sound with bands and theater shows and I have a record label through which I sign other artists to launch their records by my label. All this gives me the possibility of sharing power to keep doing my art, my music and make some money from this work.

16) Can we, nowadays, talk about a current Immigration of rap?

A: I think so, that rap is also migrating to other musical aspects, which I think can bring interesting things ...There is also the issue of musical style to be coming out of Rio-SP axis towards other cities and capitals of the country which is excellent .... being attentive to migratory effects, I am in favor of all.

17) What are your plans and dreams for the future?

R: I want children, a house and then making records and finding many others.

18) What do you think of this "wave" of protests that has been happening in Brazil?

A: I think it's great, everything!Of course some are in the midst of the demonstrations just to have a beer on the street, but the general plan is super valid, there are remains of Dictatorship Military falling.Even the violent events are related to this, and in the end, the thugs who are there breaking things and causing vandalism, are just barely children raised in our "Beloved Homeland Brazil."I always thought that parents are always the most responsible for the acts of their children, then the state should be more tolerant of the whole situation, because they created EVERYTHING!

APPENDIX B- INTERVIEW WITH (MC BETO) INTERVIEW CONDUCTED BY EMAIL, ON 10/15/2013

Biographical data

01) What is your full name?
A: Roberto Araujo Ishikawa

02) What is your age?
A: 41 years.

03) Where were you born?
A: In Brazil, São Paulo.

04) How did your story with the rap *begin?*
A: I like to dance Hip-Hop and a DJ friend gave me a tape of Racionais MCS. As their reality was not very different from what I had spent in my life, I decided to write my own lyrics. This began in Brazil and took a turn when I formed the Tensais MCS in Japan. I met Fábio Mesquita, who was nicknamed Kyu, or Q, in English, and made our first presentation in a house called Fuzzy Hon Atsugi. He had invited a Japanese who worked with me and they had a band called Hotch Potch Workshop which subsequently joined us to do a collaboration. The chemistry was so good that we united as Tensais MCS and from there we won a hearing produced by Sony Music Entertainment, Embassy of Brazil in Tokyo and the Club of Brazil. This was the beginning of everything.

05) What is your level of education?
A: Fifth grade, incomplete.

On immigration and living abroad

06) When have you decided to leave Brazil?
A: At 15, but it was not feasible, then I left at 17.

07) How is the life of an immigrant?
A: Basically full of difficulties, be they cultural, legislative, discriminatory or lack of guidance, since we're all illiterate in katakana, hiragana and kanji.

08) How is the life of a immigrant?
A: Globalization is in you, then it can be experienced by everyone. There are international agreements that favor groups of countries and harm others, those are the roots that create a balance in foreign trade and the doha round with all its obstacles, is already a great start.

09) In Japan, do you live of music?
A: No No, I never lived of music.I have paid some bills, but not lived of music.

10) When and how did the idea of Tensais MCS came?
A: The name arose from the tensai word meaning genius. And as we are abroad we "Brazilarated" the word for the plural. This is the history of the group explained above.

11) Who are (and which are) the members of the group?
A: The members are: MC Beto, Brazilian, leader; Pay-ment, Japanese musician and deputy leader; MCQ, Brazilian, rapper; SAT-SKILL, Japanese, rapper; Roza, Brazilian, singer and Rose, Brazilian, singer. I currently live in Tokyo,Q is in Brazil and the rest are still living in the province of Kanagawa Ken, near Tokyo.

12) Regarding the group formation, there have been changes since its inception? Why?

A: No changes, we are the same members, although we are momentarily inactive.

13) What is the target audience of Tensais MCS?

A: In the beginning was the nipobrazilian community, currently anyone without discrimination.

14) Where were you most often present?

A: Lately, Tokyo, Osaka, Gunma and Japanese schools.

Opinion

15) Why are the lyrics never revealed when it comes to rap-immigrant? Not only on your disk, but others too, there are hardly any inserts or transcribed music on the web ... This behavior sets actually some kind of resistance?

A: Rap has long letters and often complex and in the case of lirycs with multiple languagesthe situation is even worse.We have professionals available to translate but issues like accuracy,the record company and financial issues limit the range of the inserts.Obviously in the Hip Hop world there are groups who, for their own reasons, do not disclose their letters, but this was not the case.

16) You can survive of rap nowadays?(You live of your music or exercise other activities)?

A: It depends if it is a Criolo Doido, a Emicida (Brazilian Artists), may be so. Not because of sales of CDS, but the participation in shows, festivals, programs, etc. Here in Japan, the doors to multicultural artists are very rare and the music market is somewhat monopolized. Surviving of rap here is hard. I myself have an electrician job or any job that is available to support my family.

17) Can we, today, talk about a current migration of rap?

A: Maybe. The problem is: what kind of rap? Commercial or Hip-hop movement? Hip-Hop without social nature is growing. I find this disturbing. But overall, I think yes, it is possible, after all rap is a new musical genre and musical essences roam worldwide.

18) What do you think of this "wave" of protests that has been happening in Brazil?

A: It is legit at some points and hypocritical in many others. It has no concrete definitions and full of loopholes for the Vandals, opposition intruders, disguised criminals protesters and opportunists who take advantage of the protest. I see nothing organized or projects, or claims and alternatives shown clearly. It may even be that the giant awoke, but he still does not know what to do. That's my opinion.

www.ingramcontent.com/pod-product-compliance
Lightning Source LLC
Chambersburg PA
CBHW020251290326
41930CB00039B/546